CASSELL LANGUAGE GUIDES

FRENCH

A handbook of grammar, current usage and word power

*Revised paperback edition
with exercises*

Valerie Worth-Stylianou

CASSELL

Other titles in the Cassell Language Guides series are:

GERMAN Christian Eckhard-Black and Ruth Whittle
SPANISH Angeles Pérez, Rafael Sala, Manuel Santamarina
ITALIAN Noemi Messora

Cassell
Wellington House, 125 Strand
London WC2R 0BB, England

PO Box 605
Herndon, VA 20172
USA

Hardback edition first published 1992
This paperback edition with exercises first published 1993
Reprinted 1995, 1996

British Library Cataloguing in Publication Data
A catalogue entry for this book is available from
the British Library.

ISBN 0-304-32667-4

Typeset by Litho Link Ltd, Welshpool, Powys, Wales
Printed and bound in Great Britain by
Biddles Ltd, Guildford and King's Lynn

Contents

Contents

Contents

Contents

Contents

Acknowledgements

My thanks are due to a number of French and English friends and colleagues who generously shared their insights with me while I was writing this book. In particular, Josianne Parry offered detailed comments on a draft of the whole manuscript, and Steve Cook, my editor, and Sandra Margolies, of house editorial, were unstinting of time, enthusiasm and constructive advice. My husband has, as ever, been invaluable: he was an erudite thesaurus when my sense of English usage foundered, and an expert photographer for the photos to accompany the text.

All errors of fact and judgement remain my own.

V. W.-S.
1992

Introduction

Cassell is launching this completely new series of Language Guides to meet the needs of English-speaking learners and users of French. We are assuming that you, the reader, have some grasp of the basics of French, and want to improve your command of the spoken and written language. You may be studying French as part of your education, or it may be that in your professional capacity you have dealings with French-speaking colleagues or customers, or you may simply enjoy using your French when on holiday abroad. We believe that the unique three-part structure of our series is equipped to meet your needs.

Part 1 provides a concise reference grammar. We include all the main areas treated in full-length reference grammars, with a particular focus on those areas which cause problems to the English-speaking learner. Explanations are followed by examples from contemporary usage, and we make a point of indicating differences of usage between formal and informal French. The index to the book enables you to locate sections on specific points easily.

Part 2 demonstrates how to use the contemporary language in specific contexts. There are thirteen sections on key functions of language, such as giving advice, expressing agreement, making apologies. These sections aim to make you aware of the importance of the sociolinguistic context, i.e. that we adapt the way we express ourselves according to the situation we are in and the person to whom we are speaking. If you were asking for advice in English, you would be likely to express yourself differently when talking to a friend as opposed to an official whom you had never met before. Of course, similar nuances exist in French, and for the foreign speaker it is important to develop sensitivity to the right expression for a particular context. So the 'register' or degree of formality of expression is indicated. The last four sections of Part 2 look at the language required for specific tasks: telephoning, writing letters, essays and reports. Generous illustrations are given, again with attention to the context in which you are speaking or writing.

Part 3 concentrates on building up your word power in French. It offers a convenient bank of important idioms based on verbs, nouns, adjectives and adverbs. Other sections focus on particularly rich areas of vocabulary (synonyms, slang, *faux amis*, *franglais*, proverbs), or deal with key thematic areas relevant to various groups of readers (e.g. travel, finance, literature). Part 3 can be used for reference, if you come across a particular expression and want to track down its meaning, or as a basis from which to build up your own active vocabulary.

Since the series is aimed at English-speaking learners of French, one essential feature is the bilingual nature of the Language Guide. All examples, from short phrases to whole letters, are translated into English, so you can see at a glance what is being illustrated. Finally, all our examples are drawn from authentic contemporary situations. This is the 'real' French that is spoken and written in France and other French-speaking countries. To remind you of this, we include a number of illustrations which show French in action.

We hope you enjoy using this book, and *'Bonne chance et bonne continuation!'*

Note to revised and extended edition

This revised edition of *Cassell Language Guides: French* contains a new section, Part 4, which gives exercises for you to practise the main points covered in Part 1, the concise reference grammar. You could either work through all the exercises systematically to achieve a complete revision of grammatical usage, or just concentrate on those that relate to areas you find problematic. Each section of Part 4 corresponds to one or more of the sections of Part 1, and the cross-reference is given at the start of the section. I suggest you read through the relevant section or sections in Part 1 before doing the exercises.

In keeping with the bilingual and authentic focus of the rest of the book, Part 4 uses two types of exercise. Those labelled **A** require translation of individual sentences from English to French, and are designed to test a basic grasp of the grammatical point. Those labelled **B** require you to complete gaps or rewrite parts of authentic French texts, taken from a range of sources. As far as possible, I have indicated the author and title for books, and the title for magazines and periodicals used. At the end of the book you will find a key with suggested answers for the exercises, but remember that these provide only *one* correct, idiomatic version. In some cases there may be another slightly different but correct answer.

VALERIE WORTH-STYLIANOU
September 1993

Note to reader

If you want to find out more about French pronunciation in general, or to check the pronunciation of a given word in one of our examples, we suggest you consult *Cassell's French / English–English / French Dictionary*, which offers a key to pronunciation and gives the transcription of words according to the symbols of the International Phonetic Association.

English grammatical terms are kept to a minimum, but for further information consult Cassell's *English Usage*, edited by Tim Storrie and James Matson, which contains a grammatical survey of parts of speech and the rules of syntax.

The material presented in all three parts provides you with illustrations of key aspects of grammar, current usage and word power. If you would like to find out more about a particular topic, the list of books under 'Suggestions for further reading' (p.520) will be useful.

Examples in this book feature European French and do not take account of particularities of Canadian French.

Abbreviations and symbols used

f.	feminine
m.	masculine
pl.	plural
sg.	singular
subj.	subjunctive
coll.	colloquial
< >	indicates the register of language, e.g. < formal >
X—X	indicates an incorrect usage, not to be followed
★	indicates an important note
!!	indicates vulgar or slang words or usage

For our children, Anastasia Joanna and
Christopher John Stylianou

PART 1

A concise reference grammar

ARTICLES

There are three types of article in French:

- the definite article (*le, la, les*) the
- the indefinite article (*un* (*e*), *des*) a / an, any / some
- the partitive article (*du, de la, des*) some / any

Usually, every noun in French will be preceded either by one of these articles or by a demonstrative, possessive or interrogative adjective (see sections 22 and 23). There are some occasions on which the article is regularly omitted, and these are listed in section 2.

1 Forms of the article

(a) Definite article

le for masculine singular nouns beginning with a consonant or aspirate 'h':

> *le chat* the cat *le hibou* the owl

la for feminine singular nouns beginning with a consonant or aspirate 'h':

> *la pomme* the apple *la haie* the hedge

l' for masculine or feminine singular nouns beginning with a vowel or mute 'h':

> *l'oiseau* the bird *l'oreille* the ear *l'hiver* the winter

les for all plural nouns:

> *les enfants* the children *les mères* the mothers

The terms 'mute h' and 'aspirate h' are confusing for English speakers, since the 'h' is never sounded in modern French. Whereas a mute 'h' allows a preceding vowel to be elided – *l'homme* – an aspirate 'h' behaves like a consonant and does not permit elision or liaison: *le héros, la haine, les hérons*.

The most common nouns beginning with an aspirate 'h' are:

la hache axe	*le hâle* tan	*le hameau* hamlet
la haie hedge	*le hall* entrance hall	*le hamster* hamster
la haine hatred	*les halles* (f.) market	*la hanche* hip

3

le hangar hangar, shed	*le hautbois* oboe	*la Hongrie* Hungary
la harangue harangue	*la hauteur* height	*la honte* shame
le hareng herring	*le héraut* herald	*le hors d'oeuvre* starter
le haricot bean	*le héros* hero	*la houille* pit-coal
la harpe harp	*le hibou* owl	*la houle* swell
le hasard chance	*la hiérarchie* hierarchy	*la housse* loose cover
la hâte haste	*le hockey* hockey	*le / la Huguenot* (e)
la hausse increase	*la Hollande* Holland	Huguenot
le haut top	*le homard* lobster	*la hutte* cabin

(b) Indefinite article

un before a masculine singular noun:
un lapin a rabbit

une before a feminine singular noun:
une semaine a week

des before any plural noun:
des jeux any / some games
des poupées any / some dolls

Note that the indefinite article has the same form as the partitive article in the plural.

(c) Partitive article

du before a masculine singular noun beginning with a consonant or an aspirate 'h' (see list above):
du sucre some / any sugar
du homard some / any lobster

de la before a feminine singular noun beginning with a consonant or an aspirate 'h' (see list above):
de la confiture some / any jam
de la haine some / any hatred

de l' before a masculine or feminine singular noun beginning with a vowel or a mute 'h':
de l'or some / any gold
de l'encre some / any ink
de l'herbe some / any grass

des before any plural noun:
des bus some / any buses
des voitures some / any cars

(d) Prepositions *à* or *de* + definite article

These prepositions and the definite article contract to form a single word in the case of the articles *le / les*:

à:
au before a masculine singular noun beginning with a consonant or an aspirate 'h':
> *au garage* at / to the garage
> *au hasard* at random

à la before a feminine singular noun beginning with a consonant or an aspirate 'h':
> *à la ville* at / to the town
> *à la hauteur* at / to the height

à l' before a masculine or feminine singular noun beginning with a vowel or a mute 'h':
> *à l'oncle* to the uncle
> *à l'aube* at dawn
> *à l'hippodrome* at / to the racecourse

aux before any plural noun:
> *aux élèves* to the pupils
> *aux boutiques* at / to the shops

de:
du before a masculine singular noun beginning with a consonant or an aspirate 'h':
> *du ministère* of / from the ministry
> *du haut* off / from the top

de la before a feminine singular noun beginning with a consonant or an aspirate 'h':
> *de la guerre* of / from the war
> *de la hiérarchie* of / from the hierarchy

de l' before a masculine or feminine singular noun beginning with a vowel or a mute 'h':
> *de l'angle* of / from the corner
> *de l'origine* of / from the beginning
> *de l'hôtel* of / from the hotel

des before any plural nouns:
> *des villages* of / from the villages
> *des femmes* of / from the women

Omission of the article   *ex* 152

Even advanced students of French are quite frequently unsure when an article should be included or omitted. The general principle is that the article should always be included unless there is a specific rule of grammar or usage which justifies its omission.

★ N.B. If you have two or three items in a sentence in French you must repeat the article before each item (whereas English will often use the article in front of the first item only):

> *La chaleur et le travail les avaient fatigués.*
> The heat and work had tired them.

> *Elle apporta le pain et le fromage.*
> She brought the bread and cheese.

The most common instances in which the article is regularly omitted are:

(i) After a <u>negative</u>, the partitive or indefinite articles (*du, de la, des, un, une*) are replaced by *de* (cf. English 'any' after a negative):

> *Il n'avait pas de pain ni de confiture.*
> He didn't have / hadn't got any bread or jam.

> *Nous n'avons plus de pêches.*
> We don't have / haven't got any more peaches.

> *Pas de problème!* No problem!

For the rhetorical structure 'Never ... a' + noun, French uses *Jamais* + noun:

> *Jamais enfant n'aurait osé se plaindre.*
> Never would a child have dared to complain.

However, the <u>definite article</u> (*le, la, les*) stands unchanged after all forms of the <u>negative:</u>

> *Je n'ai pas vu les chevaux.*
> I didn't see the horses.

> *Jamais les soldats ne parlèrent aux habitants.*
> Never did the soldiers speak to the residents.

The singular forms of the indefinite article (<u>*un, une*</u>) may exceptionally be used after a negative if the speaker wants to stress 'not a single . . .':

> *Je n'ai pas un sou.* I haven't got a (single) penny.

(ii) In formal written (or spoken) French, the plural form of the partitive or indefinite article (*des*) is replaced by *de* when an adjective precedes the noun:

> *Il échangea des souvenirs de la guerre avec de vieux amis.*
> He exchanged reminiscences of the war with old friends.

> *Il faudra nous apprêter à d'énormes sacrifices.*
> We must prepare ourselves for enormous sacrifices.

In spoken and informal written French, this rule is now frequently ignored:

> *Nous avons vu des jolies maisons hier.* < coll. >   *cf: Nous avons vu de jolies maisons hier.*
> We saw some pretty houses yesterday.

However, in formal French it is preferable to observe the rule.

The rule never applies to *des jeunes gens* (which, through usage, is treated like a compound noun):

> *Le maire a voulu aider des jeunes gens.*
> The mayor wanted to help some young people.

The rule does not affect the singular forms of the partitive or indefinite articles (*du, de la, un, une*):

> *Un jeune garçon me parla.*
> A young boy spoke to me.

> *Tu veux du bon lait?*
> Do you want some good milk?

(iii) When a noun or a nominal phrase is used in apposition, the article is usually omitted. This structure occurs in formal or literary rather than colloquial style:

cf: Ma mère, qui était une fille unique...

> *Ma mère, fille unique, voulait voyager.* < formal / literary >
> My mother, an only child, wanted to travel.

> *Nous nous arrêtâmes à la première maison, bâtiment désaffecté et délabré.* < literary >
> We stopped at the first house, an uninhabited and run-down building.

However, when the noun in apposition is qualified in some detail, the article may well be included:

> *Il connaissait fort bien Monsieur Charlot, un professeur réputé pour sa pédagogie expérimentale.*
> He was well acquainted with Mr Charlot, a teacher known for his experimental pedagogic approach.

7

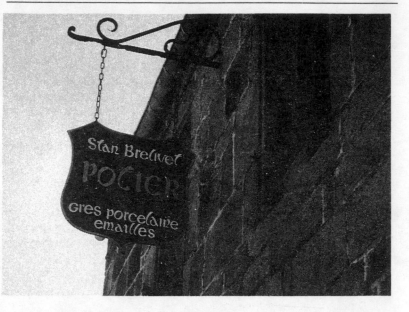

(iv) The article is omitted when giving someone's profession or status, especially following verbs such as *devenir, élire, être, (se) faire, (se) nommer*:

> *Ma soeur va devenir actrice.*
> My sister is going to become an actress.

> *Vous êtes employé ou patron?*
> Are you an employee or the boss?

> *Il est resté célibataire.*
> He's remained a bachelor.

But when the description of the profession or status is qualified, the article is often present:

> *Il a été nommé le chef de la région qui s'étend de la Loire à la Garonne.*
> He's been appointed (the) head of the region which stretches from the Loire to the Garonne.

(v) With lists of nouns, especially in more formal style, it is common to omit the article before all items:

> *Robes, chandails et jupes, elle ramena tous ces articles d' Italie.*
> Dresses, sweaters and skirts, she brought all these items back from Italy.

Note that if you do wish to include an article before one item, the article must be repeated before all the items in the list:

> *Il consulta le professeur, l'avocat et le prêtre.*
> He consulted the teacher, the lawyer and the priest.

★ **(vi)** The adjective *certain* cannot be preceded by the definite article. The indefinite article may precede *certain* with a singular noun, but in the plural the indefinite article is omitted before *certains* + noun:

> *J'ai demandé conseil à une certaine personne.*
> I asked advice from a certain person.
> *J'ai demandé conseil à certaines personnes.*
> I asked advice from certain people.

(vii) Similarly, the indefinite article is omitted before *divers* or *différents* + plural noun:

> *On rencontre diverses opinions.*
> One meets various opinions.
> *Différents auteurs ont abordé ce problème.*
> Different authors have tackled this problem.

However, both *différents* and *divers* + plural noun may be preceded by the definite article:

> *Les diverses personnes à qui j'ai parlé ont donné la même réponse.*
> The various people I spoke to gave the same reply.
> *Les différents groupes ont obtenu des résultats identiques.*
> The different groups obtained identical results.

(viii) In exclamations of the type 'What a . . .', the indefinite article is always omitted:

> *Quelle histoire!* What a fuss!

(ix) There are a number of established expressions based on *avoir* + noun which do not include an article, e.g.

> *avoir faim* to be hungry
> *avoir tort* to be wrong

See the list in section 126 p 273 ff.

However, if the noun in any of these expressions is qualified, the article must be introduced:

> *J'ai une soif incroyable.*
> I'm incredibly thirsty. (literally: I have an incredible thirst.)

9

(x) In many proverbial expressions, the article is traditionally omitted.

> *Si jeunesse savait, si vieillesse pouvait.*
> If youth had the wisdom of old age, or old age the physical
> strength of youth. (literally: If youth knew how, if old age were
> physically able.)

(See also sections 136-141.) pp 361-364

③ Uses of the definite article

As the grammatical term 'definite article' suggests, this article is used to refer to a noun which has a precise or definite identity. Effectively this means:

● either that the noun in question has been mentioned previously, or that it already has a specific identity in the mind of the speaker (and possibly the listener / reader)

● or that the noun will be defined by the adjectival phrase or relative clause which follows (*la maison sur la colline / la maison que j'ai achetée*).

These basic roles of the definite article are common to French and English. There are also some circumstances in which the definite article is not needed in English but must be included in French. The most important of these are:

(i) When a noun is used generically, to denote a category or type:

> *Le pétrole est un élément majeur dans l'économie occidentale.*
> Crude oil is a major factor in the Western economy.

> *Ma voisine ne supportait pas les petits enfants.*
> My neighbour couldn't stand little children.

(ii) By extension of (i) above, abstract nouns should be preceded by the definite article, when denoting a generic quality:

> *La vitesse est moins importante que la sécurité.*
> Speed is less important than safety.

(Of course, there may be occasions where the sense requires that an abstract noun should be preceded by an indefinite or partitive article.)

However, when an unqualified abstract noun follows a preposition
– i.e. forming an adverbial phrase – the definite article is omitted:

> *Il lui répondit sans aigreur.*
> He answered him / her without bitterness.
> (i.e. He did not answer bitterly.)

> *Ils y allèrent par pitié.*
> They went out of pity.

(iii) The definite article must be included before countries and
languages:

> *La France a découvert le Canada au seizième siècle.*
> France discovered Canada in the sixteenth century.

> *Est-ce que tu connais le russe ou le polonais?*
> Do you know Russian or Polish?

However, the definite article is omitted with *de* + country (unless
the country is qualified):

> *Il est revenu d'Espagne.*
> He's come back from Spain.

> *Les vins de France se vendent bien en Angleterre.*
> French wines (literally: the wines of France) sell well in England.

With languages, the definite article is omitted with *parler* +
language:

> *Elle parle italien.*
> She speaks Italian.

(iv) Saints' days are preceded by the feminine singular form of the
definite article (a contraction of *la fête de . . .*):

> *Je serai chez moi pour la Toussaint.*
> I'll be at home for All Saints' Day (early November public holiday).

(v) With references to periods of time (*jour, semaine, année,* etc.)
qualified by an adjective, the definite article must be included:

> *Si je ne peux pas le voir la semaine prochaine, ce sera le week-end
> suivant.*
> If I can't see him next week, it will be the following weekend.

(vi) The definite article is used before days of the week to express
'on Mondays', etc. – i.e. for actions regularly happening on that day:

> *Je ne travaille pas le mercredi.*
> I don't work on Wednesdays (i.e. all Wednesdays).

But:

> *Mercredi, je vais chez le dentiste.*
> On Wednesday (i.e. this particular Wednesday), I'm going to the
> dentist.

(vii) The definite article is normally used in French for references
to parts of the body, where English would use the possessive
adjective:

> *Elle se lava les cheveux.* She washed her hair.
>
> *Ouvrez la bouche!* Open your mouth!

However, the possessive adjective replaces the definite article if the
noun is qualified by an adjective:

> *C'est son long nez pointu qui fait reconnaître Cyrano de Bergerac.*
> Cyrano de Bergerac can be recognized by his long, pointed nose.

(viii) The definite article is used in French to express the relationship
between price and quantity, whereas English uses the indefinite
article:

> *Les figues sont 20 francs le kilo.* Figs are 20 francs a kilo.

(ix) When a proper name is preceded by an adjective, the definite
article must be used, except in exclamations:

> *Le pauvre Henri n'a jamais gagné.* Poor Henry's never won.
>
> (but: *Pauvre Henri!* Poor Henry!)

(x) Similarly, the definite article is used before proper names which
are preceded by a noun of title, rank or professional status:

> *L'ambassadeur a invité le comte de Beauvois, l'amiral de Fontenay
> et le docteur Michel.*
> The ambassador has invited Count de Beauvois, Admiral de
> Fontenay and Doctor Michel.

(xi) In commands or exclamations addressed to groups of children
or subordinates, the definite article should precede the noun
referring to the group:

> *Dépêchez-vous, les enfants!* Hurry up, children!
>
> *Arrêtez, les soldats!* Halt, men!

Note that in colloquial French, the same structure may be used
referring to adults to evoke a sense of group identity or complicity:

> *Allez, les gars!* <coll.> Come on, lads!

4 Uses of the indefinite article

As in English, in French the indefinite article refers to a noun which
has not been specifically identified. Note that the plural form 'some'
is frequently omitted in English, but must always be included in
French (except if the rules above for 'omission of the article' apply):

> *J'ai acheté des pêches et des poires.*
> I bought peaches and pears.

The indefinite article must also be included before a noun followed
by *de* + a singular abstract noun which is qualified:

> *Elle a une mère d'une tolérance exceptionnelle.*
> Her mother is exceptionally tolerant.
> (literally: She has a mother of exceptional tolerance.)
>
> *Il est d'une patience admirable.*
> He has admirable patience.
> (literally: He is of an admirable patience.)

5 Uses of the partitive article

The partitive article in French, as in English, expresses the notion
'some'. See section 4 on the necessity of including *des* even if 'some'
is omitted in English.

As a point of formal style, it is useful to remember that the partitive
article may sound awkward before an abstract singular noun, and is
often better replaced by *un certain / une certaine*:

> *Elle a montré une certaine générosité à leur égard.*
> She showed (some) generosity towards them.

6 Uses of the preposition *de* + article

★ Students of French are often uncertain whether to use only the
preposition *de* or the forms of *de* + definite article (*du, de la,
des*). Some of the confusion stems from the fact that these forms
are identical to the partitive article – but in fact represent a
contraction of *de* + definite article (see section 1d). There are three
major structures which require consideration:

(a) *de* + noun, used adjectivally

A first noun may be qualified by *de* + second noun. If the second noun denotes a general category, no article is used:

Tu auras besoin d'un agent de location.
You'll need a letting agent.

C'est un vin de qualité.
It's a quality wine.

However, if the second noun in such a structure refers to a person or thing which has been or will be defined, the forms *du / de la / des* must be used:

Tu auras besoin d'un agent de la location saisonnière.
You'll need an agent who specializes in holiday lets.

C'est un vin de la qualité voulue.
It's a wine of the required quality.

(b) Expressions of quantity + *de*

After adverbs of quantity + *de* no article is normally required. The most common of these adverbs are:

assez enough	*(un) peu* (a) few / (a) little
autant as much / as many	*plus* more
beaucoup a lot of / many	*tant* as much / as many
combien how much / how many	*trop* too much / too many
moins less	

The same rule also applies after nouns expressing quantity, such as *un kilo de, un litre de, un manque de, une surabondance de*:

Vous avez mis trop de sucre et pas assez de lait.
You've put in too much sugar and not enough milk.

Cette année il y a eu une surabondance de cerises et un manque d'abricots.
This year there has been an exceptional crop of cherries, but a lack of apricots.

However, if you wish to translate an expression of quantity + 'of the . . .', the expression of quantity is followed by *du / de la / des* + noun:

Il a mangé trop des pommes qui n'étaient pas mûres.
He ate too many of the unripe apples.

J'ai gardé trois kilos des haricots de notre jardin.
I've kept three kilos of the beans from our garden.

(c) Adjectives + *de*

There are a number of common adjectives which are followed by
de + noun: e.g. *chargé de, couvert de, plein de*. No article is required
before the noun when it denotes an unspecific object or category:

Le toit est couvert de tuiles.
The roof is covered with tiles.

La cave est pleine de toiles d'araignées.
The cellar is full of spiders' webs.

However, if the noun refers to an object or category which has been
or will be defined, the adjective should be followed by *du / de la /
des:*

Je suis chargé des cadeaux que ma mère t'envoie.
I'm loaded down with the presents my mother's sending you.

Il est coupable du crime.
He's guilty of the crime (i.e. of 'the crime' defined previously).

NOUNS

The form of the noun is relatively simple in French, since the case system, inherited from Latin, met its demise in the Middle Ages. The main problem for the foreign learner is knowing the gender of each noun (see sections 9–16).

In modern French, the form of a noun can be modified in two ways:

● to mark a reference to male or female (only applies to some nouns which denote people or animals), e.g.:

un ami a male friend
une amie a female friend

● to mark singular and plural (applies to almost all nouns, except those already ending in *-s / -x / -z* in the singular), e.g.:

une maison a house
des maisons (some) houses

For the masculine / feminine and singular / plural forms of adjectives used as nouns (i.e. substantively), see the sections on feminine and plural forms of adjectives (17b, c and d).

7 Masculine and feminine forms

Nouns referring to inanimate objects or abstract concepts have only one gender in French.

Many nouns referring to animals have only one gender in French but sometimes distinct masculine and feminine forms exist (see section 9b).

Nouns which refer to a person and can apply to either sex may or may not have distinct masculine and feminine forms. A particular problem occurs with nouns referring to previously or traditionally male-dominated professions (see section 9a). Otherwise, the basic rules are as follows:

(i) Nouns ending in *-e* apply to both male and female:

un élève a male pupil
une élève a female pupil

(ii) In most other cases, an -e is added to the masculine singular form of the noun to give the feminine singular:

> *un candidat* a male candidate
> *une candidate* a female candidate

(iii) For phonetic reasons, the whole final syllable of the masculine noun is changed to give the feminine form in the following:

- masculine in -er → feminine in -ère

  > *un fermier* a farmer (male)
  > *une fermière* a farmer (female) / farmer's wife

- masculine in -f → feminine in -ve

  > *un veuf* a widower
  > *une veuve* a widow

- masculine in -x → feminine in -se

  > *un époux* a spouse / husband
  > *une épouse* a spouse / wife

(iv) The change of the final syllable requires the consonant to be doubled in the following endings:

- masculine in -el   feminine in -elle
- masculine in -et   feminine in -ette
- masculine in -en   feminine in -enne
- masculine in -on   feminine in -onne

  > *un gardien de musée* a male museum-keeper
  > *une gardienne de musée* a female museum-keeper

(v) Nouns where the masculine ends in -eur form the feminine in one of two ways:

- most nouns in -eur deriving from verbs make the feminine in -euse:

  > *un chanteur* a male singer
  > *une chanteuse* a female singer

- most nouns ending in -deur/-teur (including some in -teur derived from verbs) make the feminine in -drice/-trice:

  > *un inspecteur* a male inspector
  > *une inspectrice* a female inspector

17

(vi) The following feminine forms are the most common exceptions to the rules above:

un compagnon	une compagne	companion, partner
un comte	une comtesse	count / countess
un dieu	une déesse	god / goddess
un duc	une duchesse	duke / duchess
un empereur	une impératrice	emperor / empress
un enchanteur	une enchanteresse	sorcerer
un favori	une favorite	favourite
un héros	une héroïne	hero / heroine
un hôte	une hôtesse	host / hostess
un jumeau	une jumelle	twin
un paysan	une paysanne	peasant
un pécheur	une pécheresse	sinner
un prince	une princesse	prince / princess
un traître	une traîtresse	traitor
un vengeur	une vengeresse	avenger

8 Singular and plural forms

(a) Formation of the plural

As in English, so in French the plural form of a noun is regularly made by adding an *-s* to the singular form:

un chat a cat   des chats (some) cats
une pierre a stone   des pierres (some) stones

There are some common categories which provide exceptions to this rule:

(i) Nouns ending in *-s / -x / -z* in the singular do not change in the plural:

un os a bone   des os (some) bones

(ii) Most nouns ending in *-al* in the singular form the plural in *-aux*:

un cheval a horse   des chevaux (some) horses

COMMON EXCEPTIONS:

un bal	des bals	ball, dance
le carnaval	les carnavals	carnival
un festival	des festivals	festival
un récital	des récitals	recital

(iii) Some nouns ending in *-ail* in the singular form the plural in *-ails*, but others form the plural in *-aux*. Among the latter, the most common are:

un bail	*des baux*	lease
un corail	*des coraux*	coral
un émail	*des émaux*	enamel
un soupirail	*des soupiraux*	air-hole
un travail	*des travaux*	work (plural usually refers to building or road works)
un vitrail	*des vitraux*	stained-glass window

(iv) Nouns ending in *-au / -eau / -eu* in the singular form the plural in *-aux / -eaux / -eux:*

un bateau a boat   *des bateaux* (some) boats

COMMON EXCEPTIONS

un bleu	*des bleus*	bruise
	(*des bleus* also overalls)	
un landau	*des landaus*	pram
un pneu	*des pneus*	tyre

(v) Some nouns ending in *-ou* in the singular form the plural in *-ous*, but others form the plural in *-oux*. Among the latter, the most common are:

un bijou	*des bijoux*	jewel
un caillou	*des cailloux*	pebble
un chou	*des choux*	cabbage
un genou	*des genoux*	knee
un hibou	*des hiboux*	owl
un joujou	*des joujoux*	toy
un pou	*des poux*	louse / lice

(vi) Common irregular plurals include:

un ciel	*des cieux*	heaven
	(but: *des ciels* skies)	
un oeil	*des yeux*	eye

(vii) Family names usually only occur in the singular form, even if preceded by a plural article:

Les Dupont et les Pinet ne pourront pas venir.
The Duponts and the Pinets will be unable to come.

However, in the case of historically famous families (especially

19

ruling dynasties), an *-s* is added to make the plural, signifying 'the family through the generations':

> *Les Bourbons ont joué un rôle primordial dans l'histoire de la France.*
> The Bourbons have played a vital role in French history.

(viii) The rules for forming the plural of compound nouns (i.e. nouns formed of two elements joined by a hyphen) have been simplified by the proposed spelling reforms of 1990.

• If the compound noun consists of verb + verb, it is invariable (i.e. the plural form is the same as the singular):

| *un garde-manger* | *des garde-manger* | larder |

• If the compound noun consists of noun + noun, or noun + adjective, both parts of the compound are put into the plural:

| *un chou-fleur* | *des choux-fleurs* | cauliflower |
| *un rouge-gorge* | *des rouges-gorges* | robin |

• If the compound noun consists of verb + noun, or preposition + noun, the noun is put into the plural:

| *un garde-robe* | *des garde-robes* | wardrobe |
| *un après-midi* | *des après-midis* | afternoon |

The only exceptions to this last rule concern compounds with proper names, or compounds where an article precedes a noun. In both cases the compound is invariable:

| *un prie-Dieu* | *des prie-Dieu* | praying stool |
| *un trompe-l'oeil* | *des trompe-l'oeil* | trompe l'oeil effect |

(ix) The rules for forming the plural of foreign words assimilated into French have also been simplified by the proposed spelling reforms of 1990. In brief, foreign loan-words are to be treated the same as French words, i.e.:

• If the singular form ends in *-s / -x / -z*, the plural is the same as the singular form:

> *un boss, des boss*   *un kibboutz, des kibboutz*

• In other cases, the plural is made by adding *-s* to the singular form:

> *un match, des matchs*
> *un maximum, des maximums* (sorry, Latinists!)

Note that for some words of Italian, Greek or Latin origin, where French already uses the foreign plural as a French singular, the

French plural is made by the addition of -s:

un media, des medias   *un graffiti, des graffitis*

(Those who are shocked might like to reflect that as long ago as the sixteenth century, champions of the development of the French language such as Du Bellay and Ronsard advocated a policy of 'naturalizing' foreign borrowings to suit the rules of French!)

(b) Nouns commonly used only in the plural

In theory, all nouns which occur in the plural can also be used in the singular, but in practice a number of nouns in French are met only in the plural form. This plural may sometimes correspond in meaning to a singular in English. The most common nouns occurring only in the plural are:

les abats (m.)	offal
les affres (f.)	dread, agony < literary >
les aguets (m.)	look-out / watch
les alentours (m.)	surrounding area
les archives (f.)	archives
les arrhes (m.)	deposit
*les cheveux** (m.)	hair
les ciseaux (m.)	scissors (*un ciseau* chisel)
les confins (m.)	confines
les débris (m.)	debris / rubbish
*les déchets** (m.)	waste / rubbish
les décombres (f.)	rubble / debris
les dépens (m.)	expenses
les échecs (m.)	chess (*un échec* failure)
les entrailles (f.)	entrails
les environs (m.)	surrounding area
les fiançailles (f.)	engagement
les frais (m.)	expenses
les funérailles (f.)	funeral ceremony
*les graffitis** (m.)	graffiti
les matériaux (m.)	materials
les manchettes (f.)	newspaper headlines
les moeurs (f.)	customs / manners
les obsèques (f.)	funeral
les pleurs (m.)	tears <literary>
les pourparlers (m.)	discussions, negotiations
les prémices (f.)	beginning < literary >
les représailles (f.)	reprisals
*les spaghettis** (m.)	spaghetti
les ténèbres (f.)	darkness / shadows < literary>
les vivres (m.)	provisions / rations

(* singular can occur, but is very rare)

21

GENDER

9 Gender and sex

French has two genders, masculine and feminine, and every noun belongs to one gender or the other. Even advanced non-native speakers make mistakes of gender, and whatever stage you have reached in learning French, you will have encountered the stumbling block: 'Is *x* masculine or feminine in French?' The problem arises because while some genders are 'natural' (e.g. *un homme, une femme*), the vast majority, especially for inanimate objects and abstract qualities, are purely grammatical. Grammatical gender most frequently depends on the Latin origin of a French word, though even here some words have changed gender over the course of centuries. In short, in the case of inanimate or abstract nouns the foreign speaker has to learn the gender of each noun (just as French infants do – but they seem to find the process easier!).

There are two types of rule which can help:
- gender according to meaning (see section 10)
- gender according to the ending of the noun (see section 11)

You will find that it pays to make a point of learning the gender of any new noun you meet. Those who have a strong visual memory may prefer to list masculine and feminine nouns in different columns on a page. Others find it useful to learn a noun in a short phrase, with an adjective or demonstrative pronoun to reinforce the gender (e.g. *ce grand garage, cette petite fleur*).

There are few instances in which the gender of a noun causes uncertainty among French native speakers (see section 15), but references to professions and to animals produce some quandaries.

(a) Gender of professional occupations

Sometimes, there exist distinct masculine and feminine forms:

un assistant social a male social worker
une assistante sociale a female social worker

un inspecteur a male inspector
une inspectrice a female inspector

In other instances, especially for nouns ending in -*iste*, the noun does not change, but can be used with an article of either gender:

> *un touriste, une touriste* a tourist
> *un bibliothécaire, une bibliothécaire* a librarian

However, problems loom with many traditionally or previously male-dominated professions. It is common for the masculine form to be used to refer to either a man or a woman: *un médecin* can be a male or female doctor. If you wish to make it clear that you are talking about a woman doctor, add *une femme* before the profession: *une femme médecin.* Compare also:

> *une femme écrivain* a woman writer
> *une femme pilote* a woman pilot

For government office, the female equivalent to *Monsieur le ministre* is *Madame le ministre.*

The French language may well change further to reflect social and professional developments. One example: strictly, *le professeur* is masculine, and a woman professor / teacher will probably be formally addressed as *Madame le professeur.* However, students and teachers alike use both *le prof / le professeur* and *la prof / la professeur* in everyday speech.

(b) Gender of animals

Many nouns referring to animals exist either only in the masculine or (far less commonly) only in the feminine form. So whatever the sex of the animal in question, there will be one form of the noun, the gender of which is purely grammatical.

> *un écureuil* (male or female) squirrel
> *une souris* (male or female) mouse

If you need to specify the sex of a particular squirrel, mouse, etc., this is done by adding the adjectives *mâle* or *femelle* – without changing the gender of the noun:

> *un écureuil mâle* a male squirrel
> *un écureuil femelle* a female squirrel
>
> *une souris mâle* a male mouse
> *une souris femelle* a female mouse

Sometimes, there exist distinct male and female nouns for an animal:

> *le taureau* bull   *la vache* cow

However, in some such instances the masculine noun or form may be used to designate any cat, dog, etc. – unless, like its owners, you are concerned to be accurate about the animal's sex:

> *Voici un joli chat.*
> That's a pretty cat. (could be male or female)
>
> *Notre chatte est malade.*
> Our (she-) cat's ill. (concerned owners speaking)

10 Rules of gender according to meaning

(a) People

Apart from the examples looked at above, words designating a man or woman are masculine or feminine respectively e.g. *le père, la mère.*

However, the following nouns are always feminine, even when they refer to a man:

> *la connaissance* acquaintance   *la sentinelle* sentry
> *la dupe* dupe   *la vedette* star
> *la personne* person   *la victime* victim
> *la recrue* recruit

(b) Things

The following general rules apply, and two or three examples are given for each category. However, note the common exceptions given in brackets.

Trees and shrubs are masculine

> *le chêne* oak, *le sapin* pine
> (EXCEPTIONS: *une aubépine* hawthorn, *la bruyère* heather, *la ronce* bramble, *la vigne* vine)

Fruits and vegetables are masculine if they do not end in -e

> *le citron* lemon, *le haricot* bean

Fruits and vegetables are feminine if they end in -e

> *la fraise* strawberry, *la carotte* carrot
> (EXCEPTIONS: *le concombre* cucumber, *le pamplemousse* grapefruit)

Metals and minerals are masculine

> *le fer* iron, *le sel* salt
> (EXCEPTIONS: *la chaux* chalk, *la pierre* stone, *la roche* rock,
> *une émeraude* emerald, *la perle* pearl)

Languages are masculine

> *la français* French, *le grec* Greek

**Days of the week, months, seasons, points of the compass
are masculine**

> *le lundi* Monday, *le printemps* spring, *le sud* south

Countries are feminine if they end in -e

> *la Chine* China, *la Hollande* Holland
> (EXCEPTIONS: *le Cambodge* Cambodia, *le Mexique* Mexico,
> *le Mozambique, le Zaïre, le Zimbabwe*)

Countries are masculine if they do not end in -e

> *le Canada, le Luxembourg*

11 Rules of gender according to ending of noun

If you can master the following principles, you will be well on the
way to removing the guesswork from French genders.

(a) Masculine endings

Nouns with the following endings are always masculine (two or
three examples are given for each):

-ail / -eil / -euil	*le chandail* sweater, *le conseil* advice, *le seuil* doorstep
-at	*le chocolat* chocolate, *un état* state
-c / -d	*le bec* beak, *le pied* foot
-ès / -et	*le procès* trial, *le secret* secret
-ing	(mainly *franglais*, see section 134): *le shopping, le camping*
-isme	*le christianisme, le tourisme*
-oir	*le couloir* corridor, *le soir* evening
-ou	*le genou* knee, *le trou* hole

There are other endings which usually indicate that the noun is
masculine. These may be conveniently divided into two groups.

25

(i) Endings in -e

By far the most important category is words in *-age*:

> *le paysage* countryside, *un orage* storm
> (SIX COMMON EXCEPTIONS: *la cage* cage, *une image* image / picture,
> *la nage* swimming, *la page* page of a book, *la plage* beach,
> *la rage* rage / rabies)

The following endings are also predominantly masculine:

-ède	*le remède* remedy, *un intermède* interval
	(EXCEPTION: *la pinède* pine-forest)
-ège	*le collège, le siège*
-ème	*le poème, le problème*
	(EXCEPTION: *la crème*)
-gone	*le polygone, un hexagone*
-graphe	*le paragraphe, le télégraphe*
-ide	*le suicide, le parricide*
-phone	*le magnétophone* tape-recorder, *le téléphone*

(ii) Endings other than those in -e

(Exceptions to these rules – i.e. nouns with these endings but which are feminine – are listed in section 13.)

-ai / -oi	*le balai* broom, *le roi* king
-eau	*le bateau* boat, *le rideau* curtain
-er / -ier	*le reporter, le cahier* exercise book
-i	*un abri* shelter, *le cri* cry
-ment	*le gouvernement, le monument*

(b) Feminine endings

Again, it is helpful to divide these into two groups:

(i) Endings other than those in -e

-aison	*la maison* house, *la saison* season
-sion / -tion	*la confusion, la civilisation*
	(EXCEPTION: *le bastion*)

(ii) Endings in -e

The following are **always** feminine:

-ace	*la glace* ice / ice-cream, *la surface*
-aie	*la haie* hedge, *la roseraie* rose garden
-ance	*une ambulance, la confiance* confidence

-anse	*une anse* handle, *la danse* dance
-euse	*une ouvreuse* usherette, *une tondeuse* lawn-mower
-tude	*une attitude, la solitude*

It is fair to say that the majority of other endings in *-e* (apart, of course, from those listed above as masculine) are more likely to be feminine than masculine, but there are several hundred common exceptions. So familiarize yourself with the list in section 12, 'Common masculine nouns ending in *-e*'.

(c) The ending *-eur*

The ending *-eur* generally shows that a noun is masculine if it refers to

- a male (or male-dominated) profession

  le facteur postman, *le pêcheur* fisherman

- a physical (often mechanical) object

  le moteur motor, *un ordinateur* computer
  (EXCEPTIONS: *la fleur* flower, *la liqueur* liqueur, *la sueur* sweat, *la vapeur* steam)

The ending *-eur* generally shows that a noun is feminine if it refers to

- an abstract quality or emotion

  la douceur softness / kindness, *la peur* fear
  (EXCEPTIONS: *le bonheur* happiness, *le malheur* unhappiness, *un honneur* honour, *le déshonneur* dishonour, *le labeur* labour / toil)

(d) Endings in *-é*

Nouns ending in *-é* are usually feminine if the ending is

-té	*la bonté* goodness, *la vérité* truth
	(EXCEPTIONS: *un arrêté* decree, *le comité* committee, *le comté* county, *le côté* side, *un été* summer, *le pâté*, *le traité* treaty)
-tié	*une amitié* friendship, *la pitié* pity

In all other cases, the ending *-é* usually indicates that the noun is masculine:

  le blé corn, *le marché* market
  (EXCEPTIONS: *la clé* key, *la psyché*)

12 Common masculine nouns ending in *-e*

One of the most common sources of error among foreign speakers is to assume that all nouns ending in *-e* are feminine. Listed here are the most common nouns ending in *-e* which are masculine. I give the basic meaning of each word; look in a good dictionary for less common meanings. (In several instances the same word exists in the feminine gender also, but with a different meaning; see section 16.)

(This list does not include those masculine nouns ending in *-age /
-ède / -ège / -ème*, etc., given above as standard masculine endings.)

un abîme abyss
un acte act
un angle angle
un anniversaire birthday /
   anniversary
un antre cave
un appendice appendix
un arbre tree
un arbuste shrub / bush
un article article
un asile asylum
un atome atom
un axe axe

le baptême baptism
le bénéfice profit / benefit
le beurre butter
le blâme blame

le câble cable
le cadavre corpse
le cadre frame / setting
le capitaine captain
le caprice whim
le caractère character
le Carême Lent
le carosse carriage
le casque helmet
le centre centre
le cercle circle
le change exchange
le chapitre chapter
le charme charm

le chèque cheque
le chiffre number / figure
le cierge candle
le cigare cigar
le cimetière cemetery
le cirque circus
le code code
le coffre safe
le comble summit
le commentaire commentary
le commerce trade
le compte account
le conte story
le contraste contrast
le contrôle control / test
le costume suit / costume
le coude elbow
le couple couple
le couvercle cover
le crâne skull
le cratère crater
le crépuscule twilight
le crime crime
le critère criterion
le cube cube
le culte cult / worship
le cycle cycle

les décombres (pl.) debris
le déluge flood
le désastre disaster
le dialecte dialect
le dictionnaire dictionary

le *dilemme* dilemma
le *diocèse* diocese
le *diplôme* diploma
le *disque* record
le *divorce* divorce
le *domaine* area
le *domicile* dwelling
le *doute* doubt

un *édifice* building
un *éloge* praise
un *empire* empire
un *épisode* episode
un *équilibre* balance
un *espace* space
un *estuaire* estuary
un *exemplaire* copy / model
un *exemple* example
un *exercice* exercise

le *fleuve* river
le *foie* liver
le *frigidaire* refrigerator

le *génie* genius / spirit
le *genre* genre / kind
le *geste* gesture
le *gîte* (simple) country house
le *globe* globe
le *golfe* gulf
le *gouffre* chasm
le *groupe* group

un *hélicoptère* helicopter
un *horaire* timetable

un *immeuble* block of flats
un *incendie* fire
un *indice* clue
un *intervalle* space / interval
un *itinéraire* itinerary

le *jeûne* fast

le *kiosque* kiosk

le *laboratoire* laboratory
le *labyrinthe* maze
le *légume* vegetable
le *linge* washing / linen

le *livre* book
le *lustre* chandelier
le *luxe* luxury
le *lycée* senior school

le *magazine* magazine
le *malaise* nausea
le *manche* handle (broom, etc.)
le *masque* mask
le *massacre* massacre
le *mélange* mixture
le *membre* member / limb
le *mensonge* lie
le *mérite* merit
le *mètre* metre
le *meurtre* murder
le *ministère* ministry
le *miracle* miracle
le *missile* missile
le *mode* method / way
le *modèle* model
le *moine* monk
le *monastère* monastery
le *monde* world
le *moule* mould
le *murmure* murmur
le *muscle* muscle
le *musée* museum
le *mystère* mystery

le *navire* ship
le *nombre* number

un *obstacle* obstacle
un *office* duty / office
un *ongle* nail
un *orchestre* orchestra
un *ordre* order

le *pacte* pact
le *pamplemousse* grapefruit
le *parachute* parachute
le *paradoxe* paradox
le *parapluie* umbrella
le *pare-brise* windscreen
le *parterre* flowerbed
le *participe* participle
le *patrimoine* heritage

29

le peigne comb
le peuple nation / people
le phare lighthouse
le phénomène phenomenon
le pique-nique picnic
le poêle stove
le poivre pepper
le portefeuille wallet
le poste job / position / radio or
   TV set
le précepte precept
le presbytère presbytery
le prestige prestige
le principe principle
le pupitre desk

le refuge den / refuge
le régime diet / regime
le registre register
le règne reign
le renne reindeer
le reproche reproach
le reste remainder
le rêve dream
le réverbère streetlight
le rhume cold
le risque risk
le rite ritual
le rôle role
le royaume kingdom
le rythme rhythm

le sable sand
le sacrifice sacrifice
le salaire salary
le satellite satellite
le scandale scandal
le scrupule scruple
le sexe sex
le siècle century
le signe sign
le silence silence
le site site
le solde balance of money
le songe daydream

le sosie dummy / double
le souffle breath
le spectacle show
le squelette skeleton
le stade stadium
le store blind
le style style
le sucre sugar
le supplice torture
le suspense suspense
le symbole symbol
le symptôme symptom
le synonyme synonym

le temple temple / church
le terme term
le texte text
le théâtre theatre
le timbre stamp
le titre title
le tome volume
le tonnerre thunder
le triomphe triumph
le trône throne
le trouble disturbance
le tumulte tumult
le type type / man < slang >

le vase vase
le véhicule vehicle
le ventre stomach / womb
le verbe verb
le verre glass
le vertige dizziness
le vestibule hall
le vestige trace
le vice fault / vice
le vignoble vineyard
le violoncelle cello
le vocabulaire vocabulary
le voile veil
le volume volume
le vote vote

le zèle zeal

13 Common feminine nouns not ending in -e

It is a mistake to assume that all feminine nouns end in -e. This list gives the most common ones which do not.

(This list does not refer to groups of feminine nouns in -sion / -tion / -aison / -eur / -té / -tié, which are dealt with in section 11.)

la boisson drink	la loi law
la chair flesh	la main hand
la clé key	la mer sea
la cour courtyard	la merci mercy
la cuiller spoon	les moeurs (pl.) customs
la dent tooth	la moisson harvest
la dot dowry	la mort death
l'eau water	la noix walnut
la façon way	une oasis oasis
la faim hunger	la paroi partition / wall
la fin end	la part share
la foi faith	la peau skin
la fois time	la religion religion
la fourmi ant	la tour tower
la jument mare	la toux cough
la leçon lesson	la villa villa
la légion legion	la voix voice

14 Gender of compound nouns

The rules for the gender of compound nouns can be summarized broadly as follows:

(a) Compound noun = verb + noun, preposition + noun: **masculine**

> le gratte-ciel skyscraper
> le porte-clés key-ring
> un en-cas stand-by
> (EXCEPTIONS: la garde-robe wardrobe, la passe-rose hollyhock)

(b) Compound noun = noun + noun: **gender of principal noun**

(The principal noun is the one that is most essential to the object / concept, usually the first noun of the compound.)

> le centre-ville town centre (still considered a neologism by purists)
> la station-service petrol station

31

(c) Compound noun = noun + preposition + noun: **gender of first noun**

> *le fer à cheval* horseshoe   *la main-d'oeuvre* workforce
> (EXCEPTION: *le tête-à-tête*)

(d) Compound noun = adjective + noun, noun + adjective, adverb + noun, prefix + noun: **gender of the noun**

> *le bas-bleu* blue-stocking   *le coffre-fort* safe
> *une arrière-boutique* back of the shop   *la demi-finale* semi-final
> (EXCEPTIONS: *le Peau-Rouge* redskin, *le rouge-gorge* robin,
> *le terre-plein* central reservation)

15 Nouns taking two genders

There are a small number of nouns taking either gender, with no distinction in the meaning. The most common is *un / une après-midi*.

More importantly, there are some common nouns whose meaning or usage may change according to gender:

chose
The simple noun is feminine; compounds are masculine.

> *la chose* the thing
> *autre chose* (m.) something else
> *grand-chose* (m.) much (used mainly in the negative, e.g.: *Je n'ai pas grand-chose.* I haven't got much.)
> *peu de chose* (m.) not much
> *quelque chose* (m.) something (e.g. *un petit quelque chose* a little something)

gens
Usually *gens* is treated as masculine plural for the sake of the agreement of adjectives / past participles:

> *Les gens que j'ai vus étaient contents.*
> The people I saw were happy.

However, if there is an adjective immediately before *gens*, this adjective will be feminine plural, but other adjectives / past participles later in the sentence will still be masculine:

> *Les vieilles gens sont partis.*
> The old people have left.

(It is preferable to avoid such awkward instances by substituting *personnes* for *gens*.)

To say 'all people', use the masculine, *tous les gens*, unless there is another adjective (i.e. feminine) before *gens*:

> *Tous les gens sont ici.*
> All the people are here.

oeuvre

L'oeuvre (m. sg.) is now used only in the sense of the complete works of a writer or artist:

> *L'oeuvre de Vigny est impressionnant.* < literary >
> The complete works of Vigny are impressive.

To refer to one work, use the feminine singular *une oeuvre*; to refer to several works, use the feminine plural *des oeuvres*:

> *Il y a une oeuvre de David que j'admire beaucoup.*
> There is one work by David which I particularly admire.

> *Quelles sont les oeuvres les plus importantes de cet auteur?*
> Which are the most important works by this author?

orgue

The word for organ is usually masculine in both singular and plural:

> *Il y a un orgue de Barbarie.*
> There's a street organ.

When the reference is to a large (church) organ, the feminine plural is common:

> *Elle va jouer des grandes orgues de Notre-Dame.*
> She will play the organ at Notre Dame.

pâque

In the feminine singular, *la pâque (juive)* (Jewish) Passover.

In the feminine plural, *les Pâques* Easter
(e.g. *joyeuses Pâques* Happy Easter).

In the masculine singular, without an article, *Pâques* is used as an ellipsis of *le jour de Pâques*:

personne

Personne is feminine when it means 'person / people':

> *Je connais une personne qui s'y intéressera.*
> I know a person who will be interested in it.

When *personne* is negative, meaning 'nobody', it is masculine singular:

> *Personne n'est venu.* No one came.

16 Words identical in form but different in gender and meaning

The words listed below are the most common examples of those which look and sound alike, but where the meaning differs according to the gender. In some instances the two words derive from the same root, but in others the similarity is fortuitous.

le critique critic	*la critique* criticism / review
le garde guardsman / keeper	*la garde* guard duty
le guide guidebook / male guide	*la guide* female guide
le livre book	*la livre* pound sterling
le manche handle (broom, etc.)	*la manche* sleeve / Channel
le manoeuvre labourer	*la manoeuvre* manoeuvre
le mémoire short thesis	*la mémoire* memory
le merci thanks	*la merci* mercy
le mode method / way	*la mode* fashion
le moule mould	*la moule* mussel
le page pageboy	*la page* page (book)
le pendule pendulum	*la pendule* clock
le poêle stove	*la poêle* frying pan
le poste job / position / radio or TV set	*la poste* postal service
le solde balance (of account)	*la solde* pay
les soldes (m.) sales	
le somme short sleep	*la somme* sum / amount
le tour turn / trick / lathe	*la tour* tower
le vapeur steamship	*la vapeur* steam
le vase vase	*la vase* silt / mud
le voile veil	*la voile* sail

ADJECTIVES

In French, adjectives are variable: they agree with the noun(s) or pronoun(s) they qualify according to gender and number. The main problems for the student of French concern irregular forms of adjectives, and the position of the adjective in relation to the noun.

17 Forms of the adjective

(a) Some irregular masculine singular forms before a vowel

Normally the masculine singular form of the adjective is the same in all circumstances. However, in the case of a few common adjectives which regularly or often precede the noun, there are two forms: the standard form, and the form to be used before a noun beginning with a vowel or a mute 'h' (see section 1a):

STANDARD MASCULINE SINGULAR FORM		MASCULINE SINGULAR FORM BEFORE VOWEL		
beau	(un beau jour)	bel	(un bel oiseau)	beautiful
fou	(un fou projet)	fol	(un fol homme)	mad
mou	(un bruit mou)	mol	(un mol oreiller)	soft
nouveau	(un nouveau cas)	nouvel	(un nouvel élève)	new
vieux	(un vieux livre)	vieil	(un vieil ornement)	old

Note that the feminine singular forms of these adjectives are also irregular (see below).

(b) Feminine singular form

If the masculine singular form of the adjective already ends in -e, the feminine singular form is identical:

> Paul est triste. Paul is sad.
> Marie est triste. Marie is sad.

Otherwise, the feminine singular is regularly formed by adding -e to the masculine singular:

> Mon oncle est content. My uncle is pleased.
> Ma tante est contente. My aunt is pleased.

35

For phonetic reasons, if the masculine singular form of the adjective has any of the endings listed below in the first column, the feminine singular form ends as shown in the second column.

MASCULINE SINGULAR	FEMININE SINGULAR	EXAMPLE
-c	-che	blanc, blanche
-eil	-eille	vermeil, vermeille
-el	-elle	personnel, personnelle
-en	-enne	ancien, ancienne
-er	-ère	léger, légère
-et	-ette	muet, muette
-f	-ve	neuf, neuve
-g	-gue	long, longue
-on	-onne	bon, bonne
-x	-se	heureux, heureuse

There are some common exceptions to the above rules (or instances where the feminine form requires the addition of an accent):

MASCULINE SINGULAR	FEMININE SINGULAR	MEANING
bref	brève	brief
complet	complète	complete
concret	concrète	concrete
discret	discrète	discreet
doux	douce	sweet
faux	fausse	false
grec	grecque	Greek
inquiet	inquiète	worried
public	publique	public
roux	rousse	red-haired
sec	sèche	dry
secret	secrète	secret
turc	turque	Turkish
vieux	vieille	old

The other most important irregular feminine forms of adjectives are:

MASCULINE SINGULAR	FEMININE SINGULAR	MEANING
bas	basse	low
beau	belle	beautiful
bénin	bénigne	benign
épais	épaisse	thick
exprès	expresse	deliberate / rapid
favori	favorite	favourite
fou	folle	mad
frais	fraîche	fresh
gentil	gentille	kind

MASCULINE SINGULAR	FEMININE SINGULAR	MEANING
gras	*grasse*	fatty / greasy
gros	*grosse*	big / fat
hébreu	*hébraïque*	Hebrew
las	*lasse*	weary
malin	*maligne*	mischievous / cunning
mou	*molle*	soft
nouveau	*nouvelle*	new
nul	*nulle*	no / none
sot	*sotte*	foolish
vieillot	*vieillotte*	out-dated

(c) Masculine plural forms

If the masculine singular form of the adjective ends in -s / -x, the masculine plural form is the same:

> *un prix bas, des prix bas*
> *un homme heureux, des hommes heureux*

Otherwise, the masculine plural form is regularly made by adding -s to the masculine singular form of the adjective:

> *un garçon intelligent, des garçons intelligents*
> *un pays riche, des pays riches*

★ If the masculine singular form of the adjective ends in -au / -al / -eu, the masculine plural form ends in -aux / -eux:

> *un beau tableau, de beaux tableaux*
> *un problème national, des problèmes nationaux*
> *un nom hébreu, des noms hébreux*

There are a few common exceptions, where the masculine singular form ends in *-al*, and the masculine plural ends in *-als*:

bancal, bancals rickety
fatal, fatals
final, finals (*finaux* can occur)
glacial, glacials (*glaciaux* can ocur)
idéal, idéals (*idéaux* can occur)
naval, navals

(d) Feminine plural form

The feminine plural form of an adjective is made by adding *-s* to the feminine singular form:

une rose rouge, des roses rouges
une femme heureuse, des femmes heureuses

The only adjectives which prove an exception to this rule are those which are invariable (see section 18c).

(e) Forms of compound adjectives

When a compound adjective is formed from two adjectives or an adjective + participle, both parts usually agree with the noun which the compound adjective qualifies:

des spécialités aigres-douces sweet-and-sour specialities

If the adjective in the first part of such a compound ends in *-i / -o*, only the second part agrees:

une forme gréco-italienne a Greco-Italian form

When the compound adjective is formed from an adjective employed adverbially + adjective, only the second part of the compound agrees:

des personnes haut-placées highly placed people

For the rules concerning compound adjectives of colour, see section 18c(i).

18 Agreement of the adjective

In French, adjectives agree with the noun or pronoun they qualify in gender and number, irrespective of whether the adjective occurs with the noun, or after a verb such as *devenir, être, se révéler*:

Il y a de grands nuages blancs.
There are big white clouds.

La maison est petite mais charmante.
The house is small but delightful.

(a) Adjectives qualifying two or more nouns

An adjective qualifying two or more nouns (in a list or joined by *et*) takes the plural form. If there are both masculine and feminine nouns, the adjective takes the masculine plural form:

Ma mère et ma grand-mère sont très heureuses.
My mother and grandmother are very pleased.

La fenêtre, la porte et les verroux sont neufs.
The window, the door and the bolts are new.

Note that in an example such as the last one, it is stylistically preferable to put the masculine noun next to the masculine plural adjective.

When an adjective qualifies two nouns joined by *ou*, the adjective is normally plural if it refers to both nouns:

Je cherche une maison ou un appartement pas chers.
I'm looking for a cheap house or flat. (i.e. both cheap)

Je cherche un appartment ou une maison pas chère.
I'm looking for a flat or a cheap house. (i.e. only the house need be cheap)

When an adjective qualifies two nouns joined by *ainsi que, aussi bien que, autant que, comme, de même que, tel que*, etc., the agreement is usually made in the singular, with the first noun:

Ma fille, comme votre fils, a été déçue par la visite.
My daughter, like your son, was disappointed by the visit.

Le premier avion, aussi bien que le suivant, a été abattu.
The first plane, like the next one, was shot down.

(b) Problematic instances of agreement

(i) *Demi* and *nu* do not agree if they precede the noun they qualify and are joined to it by a hyphen. If they follow the noun, they agree regularly:

> *une demi-heure*   *une heure et demie*
> *nu-tête*   *les pieds nus*

(ii) *Attendu, y compris, excepté, ci-inclus, ci-joint, passé* and *vu* are treated as adverbs and are therefore invariable if they precede the noun they refer to. If they follow the noun, they agree regularly:

> *Vous trouverez ci-joint ma lettre.*
> You will find my letter herewith / enclosed.

> *La lettre est ci-jointe.*
> The letter is herewith / enclosed.

> *Toute la famille viendra, y compris mes deux grand-mères.*
> *Toute la famille viendra, mes deux grand-mères y comprises.*
> The whole family will come, including both my grandmothers.

(iii) *Plein* is usually invariable when it precedes the noun it refers to, but if it follows the noun the agreement is made regularly:

> *J'en ai plein les mains.* <coll.>
> I've got my hands full.

> *Il avait les mains pleines de bonbons.*
> He had his hands full of sweets.

In the colloquial idiom *plein de* + noun (lots of / masses of), *plein* is always invariable:

> *Tu as plein d'idées.* <coll.>
> You've got masses of ideas.

(iv) In a number of compounds with feminine nouns, *grand* remains invariable:

> *grand-chose* (m.) much, something
> *la grand-mère* grandmother
> *la grand-messe* High Mass
> *la grand-tante* great aunt

> *avoir grand-faim* to be very hungry
> *avoir grand-soif* to be very thirsty
> *avoir grand-peur* to be very afraid
> *à grand-peine* with great difficulty

When qualifying any other nouns, *grand* agrees regularly. Note that even when *grand* is used adverbially to qualify another adjective, the agreement with the noun is still made:

> *J'ai laissé la porte grande ouverte.*
> I've left the door wide open.

(v) When *tout* is used as an adjective, qualifying a noun, the usual rules of agreement apply:

> *Tous les enfants sont partis.* All the children have left.

> *Toute la classe était absente.* The whole class was absent.

When *tout* is used adverbially, qualifying another adjective (meaning 'quite / completely'), it is normally invariable. However, for reasons of euphony, when the other adjective is feminine and begins with a consonant or an aspirate 'h' (see section 1a), the forms *toute* and *toutes* should be used:

> *Les enfants étaient tout étonnés.*
> The children were quite astonished.

> *L'assistante était toute honteuse de ne pas pouvoir me répondre.*
> The assistant was quite ashamed of not being able to give me an answer.

> *Les couleurs sont toutes vivantes.*
> The colours are very lively.

(vi) With the expression *avoir l'air* + adjective, the agreement tends to be made with the subject of the expression, rather than with the noun *air* (although it is not incorrect to make the agreement with *air*):

> *Ma soeur a l'air fatiguée.* My sister looks tired.

(vii) Adjectives qualifying the pronoun *on* are masculine singular if the reference is to 'one'. If (especially in colloquial usage) *on* refers to a specific person / group of people, qualifying adjectives should be put in the feminine or plural if appropriate:

> *On est malheureux loin de chez soi.*
> One is unhappy away from home.

> *Dans les collèges de jeunes filles, on doit être très disciplinées.*
> In girls' schools you / pupils have to be very well behaved.
> (*on* refers to a feminine plural group)

(viii) For the agreement of adjectives qualifying *gens*, see section 15.

(c) Invariable adjectives

There are a small number of adjectives which are invariable: that is to say, only one form is used, irrespective of the gender or number of the noun or pronoun referred to.

(i) Some adjectives of colour are also nouns, and are invariable. The most important are:

cerise cherry   *crème* cream
lilas lilac   *marron* brown
orange orange   *saumon* salmon pink

une jupe marron a brown skirt
des robes orange orange dresses

But note that *écarlate, mauve, pourpre, rose*, although originally nouns, have been assimilated as adjectives and do agree with the noun qualified:

des guirlandes roses et mauves pink and mauve garlands

When any colour adjective is qualified by another adjective, e.g. *clair, foncé, vif*, both adjectives are invariable (because the structure is a contraction of [*d'un*] *bleu foncé*):

une tapisserie gris clair a pale grey wallpaper

(ii) When *possible* is used to qualify a superlative adjective it is adverbial and therefore never agrees:

Il raconte des histoires des plus drôles possible.
He tells the funniest stories you could imagine.

(iii) *Soi-disant* ('so-called') is always invariable:

une soi-disant princesse a so-called princess

The archaic adjective *feu* ('the late / deceased') usually precedes the article / possessive adjective + noun, and it is invariable:

feu la comtesse the late / deceased countess

(iv) Some adjectives are used adverbially in certain set phrases, in which they are always invariable. The most common of these are:

bas   *jeter bas* to throw down
       parler bas to speak in a low voice

bon   *sentir bon* to smell good
       tenir bon to hold fast

cher	*coûter cher* to cost a lot / be expensive
	payer cher to pay a lot / pay dear
clair	*voir clair* to see clearly
court	*couper court* to cut short
droit	*aller tout droit* to go straight ahead
dur	*travailler dur* to work hard
faux	*chanter faux* to sing out of tune
	sonner faux to sound false / wrong
fort	*parler fort* to speak loudly / speak up
gros	*gagner gros* to earn a lot
	perdre gros to lose a lot
haut	*dire tout haut* to say aloud
juste	*deviner juste* to guess right
	tirer juste to shoot straight
mauvais	*sentir mauvais* to smell bad
net	*parler net* to speak plainly / straight
	refuser net to refuse point-blank
sec	*boire sec* to drink heavily

Position of adjectives

Whereas in English adjectives qualifying a noun are always placed before it (a red hat, a small cat, etc.), in French the general rule is that adjectives follow the noun they qualify. However, there are some notable exceptions: certain adjectives always precede the noun, and in some contexts the position of other adjectives may be open to the speaker's discretion.

(a) Adjectives which follow the noun

This category includes most types of adjective not listed under (b) below.

(i) In particular, adjectives used in a literal or concrete sense normally follow the noun. This applies especially to the literal use of adjectives of colour and nationality, to present and past participles used adjectivally, and to adjectives derived from proper names (e.g. political or artistic groups):

> *Le représentant américain portait un chapeau marron.*
> The American representative wore a brown hat.

> *J'ai remarqué un visage souriant parmi la foule des députés*
> *socialistes.*
> I saw a smiling face among the crowd of socialist M.P.s.

(ii) If adjectives are qualified by an adverb, they normally follow the noun:

> *C'est un film extrêmement intéressant.*
> It's an extremely interesting film.

However, adjectives which normally precede the noun (see (b) below) may still do so if qualified by a monosyllabic adverb such as *bien, plus, moins, si,* or by *assez* or *aussi*:

> *C'est une si jolie chaumière.*
> It's such a pretty thatched cottage.

(iii) The adjective almost always follows the noun if it is qualified by *à* + infinitive or *trop ... pour* + infinitive:

> *Voici un problème difficile à résoudre.*
> Here is a problem which is difficult to solve.

> *C'est une voiture trop vieille pour faire de longs voyages.*
> It's a car which is too old to do long journeys.

(b) Adjectives which precede the noun

(i) Possessive and demonstrative adjectives always precede the noun they qualify (see sections 22 and 23):

> *ce livre bleu* this blue book
> *mon frère aîné* my elder brother

(ii) The indefinite adjectives *autre, certain, chaque, plusieurs, quelque, tel* and *tout* precede the noun they qualify:

> *Un autre homme m'a raconté toute l'histoire.*
> Another man told me the whole story.

(iii) Numerals or cardinal numbers (see section 142) precede the noun:

> *Les deux frères Leroux étaient les premiers propriétaires de ce*
> *restaurant.*
> The two Leroux brothers were the first owners of this restaurant.

(iv) A number of common, short adjectives regularly precede the noun they qualify: *beau, bon, bref, grand, gros, haut, jeune, joli, mauvais, meilleur, moindre, petit, sot, vaste, vieux, vilain*:

> *Elle veut une jolie petite maison située dans un beau village.*
> She wants a pretty little house in an attractive village.

(v) Adjectives of colour may precede the noun they qualify if used metaphorically:

> *une noire journée* a black (i.e. unfortunate) day

(vi) In current French usage, especially journalistic style, there is a tendency for adjectives which normally follow a noun to precede it for emphasis:

> *C'est une importante affaire qui amène le Président à Bourges.*
> It's an important matter which brings the President to Bourges.

This device obviously loses its impact if overdone, and should be imitated sparingly.

(c) Adjectives whose meaning changes according to position

There are a number of common adjectives whose meaning changes according to whether they are placed before or after the noun they qualify:

ancien	*une ancienne église* a former church
	une église ancienne an old / ancient church
brave	*un brave garçon* a good / fine lad
	un garçon brave a brave lad
certain	*un certain échec* a certain / particular failure
	un échec certain a certain / definite failure
cher	*un cher ami* a dear / beloved friend
	un magasin cher a dear / expensive shop
court	*un court entretien* a short / brief interview
	un nez court a short nose
dernier	*le dernier jour du règne de Louis XIV* the last day of Louis XIV's reign (i.e. last in fixed sequence)
	la semaine dernière last week (i.e. previous to this week: used for specific periods of time)
différent	(in plural only) *différentes idées* various ideas
	(in singular or plural) *une idée différente* a different / another idea
divers (pl.)	*diverses opinions* various opinions
	des opinions diverses differing opinions

45

grand	*un grand artiste* a great artist
	un artiste grand a tall artist
même	*la même personne* the same person
	la personne même the very person
nouveau	*un nouveau projet* a new / different plan
	un projet nouveau a novel / newly created plan
pauvre	*une pauvre famille* a poor family (expressing sympathy)
	une famille pauvre a poor / impoverished family
prochain	*la prochaine date* the next date (i.e. in a sequence)
	une date prochaine a date not far off
	la semaine prochaine next week (i.e. after this week)
propre	*ma propre voiture* my own car
	une voiture propre a clean car
sale	*un sale coup* <coll.> a dirty / nasty blow
	une rue sale a dirty road (not clean)
seul	*le seul tableau* the only / single picture
	le tableau seul the picture alone / only the picture
vrai	*une vraie histoire* a real story
	une histoire vraie a true / authentic story

(d) Position of two or more adjectives qualifying a noun

• When one noun is qualified by two adjectives, both of which normally precede the noun, the order is:

ordinal numerals / indefinite adjectives
+ *nouveau / jeune / vieux / vrai*
+ *bon / beau / gros / haut / joli / mauvais / méchant / sot / vilain*
+ *grand / petit*

> *un joli petit bébé* a pretty little baby
> *chaque jeune arbre* each young tree

Two adjectives preceding the noun may be linked by *et*, indicating that the two characteristics are distinct:

> *un beau et vieux portrait* a fine, old portrait

If either of the adjectives is qualified by an adverb, it should follow the noun:

> *un mauvais quartier très vaste* a bad, very large district

• When one noun is qualified by two adjectives both of which usually follow the noun, the adjectives should be joined by *et*:

> *un homme courageux et intelligent* a brave and intelligent man

However, if both the adjectives define the status of the noun, *et* is omitted:

> *le représentant socialiste italien* the Italian Socialist representative

• When one noun is qualified by two adjectives, one of which normally precedes and the other follows the noun, the order of the adjectives is unchanged:

> *une vieille ferme provençale* an old Provencal farm

20   Negation of adjectives

For adjectives occurring after the noun they qualify, there may exist an antonym, or negative form:

> *les cheveux courts / longs* short / long hair
>
> *une réponse admissible / inadmissible*
> an acceptable / unacceptable reply
>
> *une personne contente / mécontente* a happy / unhappy person

If such a form does not exist, the adjective can be negated by *peu*, especially in formal usage:

> *une proposition peu rentable* <formal> an unprofitable proposal
>
> *un employé peu disposé à s'adapter* <formal> an employee
> unwilling to adapt

In less formal usage, it would be more common to negate the verb:

> *Cette proposition n'est pas rentable.* This proposal isn't profitable.

21   Comparative and superlative forms of adjectives

(a) Comparisons of equality or inequality

To say that something is 'as (adjective) . . . as', the regular form of the adjective is used in the construction *aussi* (adjective) . . . *que*. The adjective agrees in the normal manner with the noun qualified:

> *Elle est aussi charmante que sa soeur.*
> She is as charming as her sister.

To say that something is 'not as (adjective) . . . as', the regular form of the adjective is used in the construction *pas si* (adjective) . . . *que*:

> *Ce livre-ci n'est pas si cher que celui-là.*
> This book is not as expensive as that one.

(b) Comparative forms: 'more' or 'less' + adjective

In French the comparative form of adjectives requires *plus / moins* before the regular form:

> *Cette rue est plus longue que l'autre.*
> This road is longer than the other.

> *Ce village est moins propre que le nôtre.*
> This village is less clean / not as clean as ours.

If the comparison uses 'so much more / less (adjective) ... than', use *tellement plus / moins* (adjective) ... *que*:

> *Ce nouveau bâtiment est tellement plus joli que l'ancien.*
> This new building is so much prettier than the old one.

> *Mon jardin est tellement moins bien organisé que le tien.*
> My garden is so much less well organized than yours.

Several adjectives have irregular comparatives.

(i) The comparative form of the adjective *bon* is irregular: *meilleur*:

> *Ce vin est meilleur que celui de l'année dernière.*
> This wine is better than last year's.

(ii) The adjective *mauvais* has the regular comparative form *plus mauvais*, and also an irregular form *pire*. The form *plus mauvais* prevails in speech (or may frequently be replaced by *moins bon*):

> *Ce disque est plus mauvais / moins bon que le dernier.*
> This record is worse than the last.

Pire is largely restricted to literary or formal written style, or to the phrase *C'est pire*:

> *Le comportement du nouvel élève était encore pire.* <literary>
> The new pupil's behaviour was even worse.

> *Vous avez entendu la dernière nouvelle? C'est pire.*
> Have you heard the latest news? It's worse.

(iii) *Petit* has the regular comparative form *plus petit*, which is always used for references to physical size:

> *Antoine est plus petit que Jacques.*
> Antoine is smaller than Jacques.

There is also the irregular comparative form, *moindre*, which is rare, occurring only in literary style:

> *Ce détail est d'un moindre intérêt.* <literary>
> This detail is of less interest.

48

(c) Superlative forms

The superlative form of adjectives is made by introducing the definite article (*le / la / les*) – or if appropriate the possessive adjective – before the comparative form of the adjective:

> *C'est mon plus beau tableau.*
> It's my finest picture.
>
> *Ce sont les garçons les plus travailleurs de la classe.*
> They are the most hard-working boys in the class.

Note that, in examples such as the last one, the superlative + 'in' is rendered in French by the superlative + *de*.

When the comparative form of an adjective is irregular, the superlative is also based on this irregular form.

(i) The adjective *bon* has as its superlative form *le meilleur*:

> *C'est le meilleur choix.* It's the best choice.

(ii) The adjectives *mauvais* and *petit* each have two superlative forms.

Le plus mauvais is used more frequently than *le pire*:

> *C'est le plus mauvais acteur que j'aie* (subj.) *vu.*
> He's the worst actor I've seen.

Le plus petit is used to refer to physical size, while *le moindre* is common (even in speech) with abstract nouns:

> *C'est la plus petite salle.* It's the smallest room.
>
> *Vous pouvez me consulter si vous avez la moindre difficulté.*
> You can consult me if you have the least difficulty.

22 Demonstrative adjectives

A demonstrative adjective stands before a noun, in place of an article, and has the meaning 'this / that / these / those'. The French demonstrative adjective agrees in gender and number with the noun it qualifies, as shown in the examples below. Note that the plural form is the same for both genders.

● Masculine singular noun beginning with a consonant or aspirate 'h':

> *ce* this / that   *ce chien* this / that dog
>   *ce héros* this / that hero

- Masculine singular noun beginning with a vowel or mute 'h':

    cet this / that   *cet enfant* this / that child
                                cet hiver this / that winter

- Feminine singular (all forms):

    cette this / that   *cette fleur* this / that flower
                                cette haie this / that hedge

- Plural (both genders):

    ces these / those   *ces rideaux* these / those curtains
                                ces cartes these / those cards

★ Note that, contrary to English usage, in French the appropriate form of the demonstrative adjective must be repeated before every noun when there are two or more items:

> *Ces chaises, ces fauteuils et cette table iront dans la salle de séjour.*
> These chairs and armchairs and this table will go in the living room.

As the above examples show, the French demonstrative adjective does not convey the distinction between 'this' and 'that'. Where the distinction is important, *-ci* (this / these) or *-là* (that / those) must be added to the end of the noun being qualified:

> *Est-ce que vous préférez ce manteau-ci ou ce blouson-là?*
> Do you prefer this coat or that jacket?

> *Ces figues-ci sont trop mûres, mais ces bananes-là sont bonnes.*
> These figs are over-ripe, but those bananas are good.

23 Possessive adjectives

A possessive adjective stands before a noun, in place of an article, and means 'my / your / his / her / its / our / their'.

(a) Forms of the possessive adjective

★ N.B. The possessive adjective always agrees in number and gender with the noun qualified (**not** with the person possessing the object):

MASCULINE SINGULAR	FEMININE SINGULAR	PLURAL	
mon	*ma*	*mes*	my
ton	*ta*	*tes*	your
son	*sa*	*ses*	his / her / its
notre	*notre*	*nos*	our
votre	*votre*	*vos*	your
leur	*leur*	*leurs*	their

★ For a feminine singular noun beginning with a vowel or a mute 'h', the forms *mon / ton / son* are used (in place of *ma / ta / sa*):

> *Ton idée n'est pas mauvaise.* Your idea isn't bad.
>
> *Son héroïne est intéressante.* His / her heroine is interesting.

In colloquial French, the possessive pronoun may be emphasized by putting the following forms after the noun:

> *mon / ma / mes . . . à moi* my
> *ton / ta / tes . . . à toi* your
> *son / sa / ses . . . à lui* his / its
> *son / sa / ses . . . à elle* her / its
> *notre / nos . . . à nous* our
> *votre / vos . . . à vous* your
> *leur / leurs . . . à eux* their (all m. or m. and f. owners)
> *leur / leurs . . . à elles* their (all f. owners)
>
> *C'est ta voiture à toi?* <coll.> Is that your car?
>
> *Ce n'est pas leur maison à eux.* <coll.>
> It's not their (own) house.

This emphatic form is particularly common with *son / sa / ses . . . à lui / à elle*, since the possessive adjective alone does not differentiate between 'his' and 'her':

> *C'est son bateau?*
> Is it his / her boat? (no distinction made between 'his / her')
>
> *C'est son bateau à lui?* Is it his boat?
>
> *C'est son bateau à elle?* Is it her boat?

(b) Uses of the possessive adjective

Note that the possessive adjective is usually repeated before each noun qualified:

> *Mon frère aîné, mon cousin et mes soeurs vont venir.*
> My elder brother, (my) cousin and (my) sisters are going to come.

French uses the possessive adjective, whereas English does not, before some forms of address. This can be either a sign of affection or familiarity, or a sign of respect (especially in the army or the church):

> *Vous avez faim, mes enfants?* Are you hungry, children?
>
> *Ça te fait mal, ma puce?* < to a child >
> Does that hurt, darling? (literally: my flea!)

51

Oui, mon colonel! <military> Yes, sir!

Bonjour, mon père. <to priest> Good morning, Father.

There are two contexts in which English commonly uses the possessive adjective, but French does not.

(i) Where English uses the possessive adjective before parts of the body, French is more likely to use the definite article before the part of the body, together with a reflexive verb, or a construction with an indirect object pronoun:

Je dois me laver les cheveux. I must wash my hair.

Il s'est cassé la jambe. He's broken his leg.

Les doigts de pied lui font mal. His toes hurt.

(ii) Where English uses the possessive adjective 'its' or 'their' referring to objects, in formal style French may prefer the pronoun *en* rather than the possessive adjectives *son / sa / ses* or *leur / leurs*:

Mon collègue connaît le dossier. Il en a mesuré l'importance. <formal>
My colleague knows the file. He is aware of its importance.

Le physicien travaille avec ces appareils. Il en apprécie les avantages.
The physicist works with these pieces of apparatus. He appreciates their advantages.

ADVERBS

Adverbs are used to qualify verbs, adjectives or other adverbs. They are always invariable in French. The only points which require attention are their form (in most cases very regular) and their position in the sentence.

For some important idiomatic uses of adverbs in French, see section 129.

For some cases where adjectives are used adverbially in French, see section 18b and c.

24 Forms of the adverb

(a) Formation of adverbs of manner ending in *-ment*

Most adverbs of manner (describing the way in which you do something, e.g. kindly, quickly) are formed from the corresponding adjective.

(i) When an adjective ends in a vowel in the masculine singular form, the adverb is formed by adding *-ment*:

triste	*tristement*	sadly
aisé	*aisément*	comfortably
vrai	*vraiment*	truly
cru	*crument*	crudely

★ Note that the proposed spelling reforms of 1990 eliminate the circumflex accent which used to be added to some adverbs in *-ument* (as the last example above).

EXCEPTIONS: There are a small number of adverbs formed from masculine singular adjectives ending in a vowel which end in *-ément*:

aveugle	*aveuglément*	blindly
commode	*commodément*	conveniently
énorme	*énormément*	enormously
immense	*immensément*	immensely
impuni	*impunément*	with impunity
incommode	*incommodément*	inconveniently
intense	*intensément*	intensely
uniforme	*uniformément*	uniformly

(ii) When the masculine singular adjective ends in a consonant (other than *-ant/-ent*), the adverb is formed from the feminine singular adjective + *-ment* :

certain(e)	*certainement*	certainly
complet/-ète	*complètement*	completely, fully
heureux/-se	*heureusement*	happily

EXCEPTIONS: A small number of adverbs formed from feminine singular adjectives end in *-ément*:

commun(e)	*communément*	commonly
confus(e)	*confusément*	confusedly
diffus(e)	*diffusément*	diffusely
exprès/-esse	*expressément*	deliberately
importun(e)	*importunément*	importunately
opportun(e)	*opportunément*	opportunely
obscur(e)	*obscurément*	obscurely
précis(e)	*précisément*	precisely
profond(e)	*profondément*	deep, deeply
profus(e)	*profusément*	profusely

(iii) When the masculine singular adjective ends in *-ant/-ent*, the adverb is formed by replacing the last syllable of the adjective by *-amment/-emment* :

courant	*couramment*	commonly
conscient	*consciemment*	consciously

EXCEPTIONS: Three adjectives ending in *-ent* form their adverbs from the feminine singular form:

lent(e)	*lentement*	slowly
présent(e)	*présentement*	presently
véhément(e)	*véhémentement*	vehemently

(iv) Other irregular forms include:

bref/brève	*brièvement*	briefly
gentil(le)	*gentiment*	kindly
mauvais(e)	*mal*	badly
traître/traîtresse	*traîtreusement*	treacherously

★ Note that *bien* (well) is the adverb usually corresponding to the adjective *bon(ne)* (good). The adverb *bonnement* is only used in the expression *tout bonnement* (quite simply):

Elle danse bien. She dances well.

J'ai tout bonnement posé la question.
I quite simply asked the question.

(b) Adverbs of time, place, quantity, affirmation, negation and interrogation

For these adverbs there are usually no comparable adjectives, and the adverbs must be learned in their own right, e.g.

hier yesterday   *ici* here
beaucoup a lot / much   *volontiers* willingly
jamais never   *comment* how?

25 Position of adverbs

(a) Adverbs qualifying verbs

(i) An adverb qualifying a verb in one of the simple tenses, i.e. the present, future, imperfect, past historic, or present conditional, should follow the verb:

Ils s'arrêtèrent brièvement.
They stopped briefly.

Ils arriveront inévitablement en retard.
They will inevitably arrive late.

(ii) Adverbs of place and other longer adverbs qualifying a verb in one of the compound tenses, i.e. the perfect, pluperfect, future perfect, or conditional perfect, follow the past participle:

Nous sommes restés ailleurs.
We stayed elsewhere.

Mon frère l'aurait écrit lisiblement.
My brother would have written it legibly.

(iii) Other, shorter adverbs usually come immediately before the past participle in compound tenses:

Je n'aurais jamais bien compris.
I should never have understood properly.

L'avait-elle déjà oublié?
Had she already forgotten it?
(but: *L'avait-elle oublié déjà?* is also acceptable)

★ In all these cases, the adverb must not separate the subject and verb / auxiliary verb:

> *Nous avons demandé l'addition aussitôt.*
> We immediately asked for the bill.
> X *Nous aussitôt avons demandé l'addition.* X

Adverbs such as *apparemment, assurément, heureusement, malheureusement, naturellement, peut-être, probablement* may occur either in the regular position in relation to the verb, or (for emphasis) at the beginning of the sentence + *que*:

> *Il ne m'a rien dit, naturellement.*
> He said nothing to me, naturally.
>
> *Naturellement qu'il ne m'a rien dit.*
> Naturally, he said nothing to me.

(b) Adverbs qualifying adjectives, other adverbs or adverbial phrases

Adverbs usually immediately precede the adjectives, other adverbs or adverbial phrases which they qualify:

> *Vous êtes parfaitement conscient de ce que vous faites?*
> Are you perfectly well aware of what you are doing?
>
> *La voiture démarra très lentement.*
> The car started up very slowly.
>
> *Il faut revoir les chiffres, surtout à court terme.*
> We must review the figures, especially in the short term.

(c) Adverbs introducing or qualifying a whole sentence

An adverb usually stands at the beginning of a sentence if it introduces or qualifies the whole sentence. This position adds emphasis to the adverb:

> *Malheureusement, je n'avais pas vérifié son adresse.*
> Unfortunately, I hadn't checked his / her address.
>
> *Surtout, il faut se garder de réagir trop vite.*
> Above all, we must take care not to react too hastily.

Similarly, an adverb which provides a link with the previous statement will normally occur at the beginning of the sentence:

Le nouveau curé était très apprécié. Pourtant, il y avait des détracteurs.
The new priest was very well thought of. However, there were those who criticized him.

26 Adverbial phrases of manner used to replace adverbs

When an adverb is three or more syllables in length, it can be a cumbersome item in a sentence. There is therefore a tendency in good style to avoid excessive use of long adverbs, replacing them by adverbial phrases.

To express the manner in which an action is performed, for example, you can use *d'une façon* + adjective or *d'une manière* + adjective:

Elle réussit d'une façon inévitable.
She inevitably succeeded.

Il le refusa d'une manière peu polie.
He refused rudely.

With verbs of speech, adverbs may be replaced by *d'un ton* + adjective or *d'une voix* + adjective:

Le capitaine lui parla d'un ton irrité.
The captain spoke to him irritably.

D'une voix douce, elle lui expliqua la vérité.
She gently explained the truth to him.

With reference to people's facial expressions, adverbs may be replaced by *d'un air* + adjective:

Ils le regardèrent d'un air furieux.
They looked at him furiously.

In more formal style, an adjective may qualify the subject, replacing an adverb:

Ma soeur, prudente, ne voulait pas avancer. <formal>
My sister prudently refused to go any further.

27 Comparative and superlative forms of adverbs

(a) Comparisons of equality and inequality

Note the following structures which are used to express comparisons of equality or inequality:

Vous ne buvez pas autant que lui. (*autant* qualifies verb)
You don't drink as much as him.

Il faudra le récompenser davantage. (*davantage* qualifies verb)
He'll have to be rewarded more / given a greater reward.

Cette voiture roule aussi rapidement que l'autre. (*aussi* qualifies adverb in positive statement)
This car goes as fast as the other.

Il ne m'écrit pas si / aussi souvent que vous. (*si* or *aussi* qualifies adverb in negative statement)
He doesn't write to me as often as you do.

★ *Plus j'étudie ce livre, plus j'admire l'auteur.* (*Plus* ... introduces each clause; note that 'the' [more] is not translated in French.)
The more I study this book, the more I admire the author.

(b) Comparative forms

The comparative form of the adverb is made by putting *plus* before the regular form:

Ce mot s'emploie plus couramment.
This word is more commonly used.

There are several common irregular comparative forms:

beaucoup much	*plus* more
bien well	*mieux* better
peu little	*moins* less

The adverb *mal* has the regular comparative form *plus mal*:

Mon oncle va plus mal.
My uncle is feeling / getting worse.

There is also an irregular comparative form, *pis*, which is now only used in such expressions as:

de mal en pis from bad to worse
Tant pis! Never mind!

(c) Superlative forms

The superlative form of the adverb is made by putting *le* before the comparative form. This applies to regular and irregular comparative forms.

★ Since adverbs are invariable, *le* is used irrespective of the gender / sex and number of the subject of the verb:

Ma nièce a tout mangé le plus vite possible.
My niece ate everything as quickly as possible.

Les magasins vendaient ces articles le plus cher possible.
The shops sold these items at the highest price they could.

PRONOUNS

Pronouns stand in place of a noun. One of their main functions is to allow the speaker to avoid repeating a noun which has already been used. Pronouns usually occur as the subject, object or indirect object of a verb, or after a preposition. There are a number of categories of pronouns. This section treats personal, demonstrative, possessive, relative and indefinite pronouns. Negative and interrogative pronouns are illustrated in sections 56c and 62(iii) respectively.

28 Personal pronouns: conjunctive forms

There are two kinds of personal pronoun in French: conjunctive and disjunctive. Conjunctive pronouns are the subject, object or indirect object of the verb, and stand immediately before the verb (except in positive commands – see c(iii) below). Disjunctive pronouns are (as the name suggests) separated from the verb, and usually occur either after a preposition, or to emphasize a personal pronoun.

(a) Forms of conjunctive pronouns

Conjunctive pronouns can act as the subject, direct object or indirect object of a verb:

Il va arriver. (Il = subject of verb)
He is going to arrive.

Je vous verrai ce soir. (vous = direct object of verb)
I shall see you tonight.

Elle doit leur parler. (leur = indirect object of verb, i.e. to them)
She must speak to them.

The form of the subject pronoun is different from that of the object pronoun in all persons except *nous* and *vous*. The forms of the direct and indirect object pronouns differ only in the third person singular and plural:

SUBJECT		DIRECT OBJECT		INDIRECT OBJECT	
je	I	me	me	me	to me
tu	you	te	you	te	to you
il	he / it	le	him / it	lui	to him / to it
elle	she / it	la	her / it	lui	to her / to it
nous	we	nous	us	nous	to us
vous	you	vous	you	vous	to you
ils	they (m.)	les	them	leur	to them
elles	they (f.)	les	them	leur	to them

The forms *me / te / le / la* are elided to give *m' / t' / l'* before a verb beginning with a vowel or a mute 'h':

> *Il m'a parlé.*
> He spoke to me.
>
> *Ma mère l'apprécie.*
> My mother appreciates him / her / it.

★ Remember that the indirect object pronoun *leur* (to them) never ends in -*s*. The form *leurs* is the plural of the possessive adjective: *leurs vélos* their bikes (see section 23).

(b) Particular uses of third-person subject and object conjunctive pronouns

(i) When referring to objects or abstract nouns, English uses the pronoun 'it', but French uses *il* or *elle* (or the appropriate object or indirect object pronouns), according to the gender of the noun:

> *Où est le colis? Il est sur la table.*
> Where's the parcel? It's on the table.
>
> *J'ai besoin de la voiture. Je la prendrai jusqu'à demain.*
> I need the car. I'll take it until tomorrow.

However, if 'it' is the subject of *être* + article + noun, use the demonstrative pronoun *ce* (see section 30a):

> *Je travaille à Aix-en-Provence. C'est une belle ville.*
> I work at Aix-en-Provence. It's a beautiful town.

In colloquial speech, it is common to use *ça* ('it') as the subject of verbs other than *être* to refer to concrete objects:

> *Il y a un ascenseur mais ça tombe en panne tout le temps.* <coll.>
> There's a lift but it's always breaking down.

(ii) The subject pronoun *on* literally means 'one', but is frequently used in colloquial French with the meaning we / you:

> *Tu es sûr qu'on peut se garer ici?* <coll.>
> Are you sure you / we can park here?

> *Qu'est-ce qu'on va manger ce soir?* <coll.>
> What are we going to eat this evening?

For the agreement of adjectives and past participles qualifying *on*, see section 18b(vii).

There are two sets of direct and indirect object pronouns corresponding to *on*. When the subject of the verb is *on*, the reflexive pronoun *se* is used for the direct or indirect object:

> *On ne peut pas s'entendre avec cette musique.* (*se* = direct object)
> One can't hear oneself / You can't hear yourself with that music.

> *On se demande ce qu'il faut faire.* (*se* = indirect object)
> One wonders what's to be done. / You ask yourself what should be done.

To translate 'one' as direct or indirect object, when the subject of the verb is not *on*, use *vous*:

> *Si la police vous voit, c'est grave.*
> If the police see one / you, it's serious.

> *Ce genre de personne vous demande toujours des services.*
> (*vous* = indirect object)
> That sort of person always asks one / you for help.

(c) Order and position of conjunctive pronouns

(i) Conjunctive subject pronouns always precede the verb, except in the case of inversion, e.g. interrogative sentences (see section 54):

> *Nous connaissons ton père.*
> We know your father.

> *Connaissez-vous mon père?*
> Do you know my father?

(ii) Conjunctive object pronouns always immediately precede the verb, except in positive commands. In compound tenses, the object pronouns immediately precede the auxiliary verb (not the past participle). The order of pronouns before the verb is fixed:

1	2	3	4	5	VERB
me	le	lui	y	en	
te	la	leur			
nous	les				
vous					

Il ne nous en a pas acheté. He hasn't bought us any.

Ils vous les enverront. They will send them to you.

In the rare instances where two of the pronouns *me / te / nous / vous* would occur together, only the direct object occurs in the conjunctive form, the indirect object being rendered by *à* + disjunctive pronoun (see section 29):

Je m'intéresse à toi. I'm interested in you.

When object pronouns occur with a conjugated verb + infinitive, their usual position is immediately before the infinitive:

Je peux te les rendre. I can return them to you.

However, with *faire / laisser* + infinitive, object pronouns are placed before the first verb:

Je l'ai fait réparer au garage. I got it mended at the garage.

Je dois vous laisser partir. I must let you leave.

(iii) When object pronouns occur with a positive command, the pronouns are placed after the verb. Pronouns are joined to the verb and each other by hyphens (except in the case of the elided forms *m' / t' / l'*). The order of two or more pronouns is:

1	2	3	4
direct object	indirect object	y	en

The regular forms of the conjunctive pronouns are used, except that if *me* or *te* would be the last pronoun, it is replaced by the forms *moi* or *toi* (for ease of pronunciation):

Donnez-le-moi. Give it to me.

Servez-vous-en. Help yourselves to it.

(d) Particular uses of the pronouns *le / la / les*

(i) The direct object pronouns *le / la / les* are introduced in French when the object of the sentence is placed before the subject. This can be a literary construction used for emphasis, but is also very common in colloquial French. English would rarely imitate this construction, relying instead on intonation for emphasis.

> *Les belles matinées ensoleillées, mon grand-père les savourait.*
> <literary>
> My grandfather savoured (the) fine, sunny mornings.
>
> *Ta soeur, je la connais déjà.* <coll.>
> I already know your sister.

(ii) The direct object pronoun *le* can refer to a previous statement or idea (often the previous sentence or clause). This may correspond to the use of 'so' in English:

> *Il est catholique, du moins je le crois.*
> (*le* = *qu'il est catholique*)
> He is Catholic, at least I think so.
>
> *Elle a payé la facture sans me le dire.*
> (*le* = *qu'elle l'a payée*)
> She paid the bill without telling me.

This use of *le* is particularly common before verbs of saying, knowing, understanding, etc.:

> *Il est malade. – Oui, je le sais.*
> He's ill. – Yes, I know.

(iii) *Le* is also introduced before verbs such as *devenir, être, paraître* to refer to an adjective, or to a noun of status or profession used in the previous clause or statement. Note that *le* is used, whether the adjective or noun in question is masculine or feminine, singular or plural:

> *Vous êtes contents? – Oui, nous le sommes.*
> Are you pleased? – Yes, we are.
>
> *Yves était président du club, mais il ne l'est plus.*
> Yves was president of the club, but he isn't any longer.

(iv) However, where English introduces 'it' in the construction 'to think / find it + adjective ... / that ...', French does not use a pronoun:

> *Je trouve difficile de la croire coupable.*
> I find it hard to believe her guilty.
>
> *Il a trouvé nécessaire que vous soyez* (subj.) *prévenu.* <formal>
> He thought it necessary that you should be warned.

(e) Use of the pronoun y

Y is a pronoun which only refers to inanimate concrete nouns (i.e. things, places) or abstract nouns. It is never used to refer to people. *Y* replaces the preposition *à* + inanimate concrete / abstract noun. *Y* is used whatever the gender or number of the noun replaced.

> *Tu vas à Paris? – Oui, j'y vais demain.*
> (*y* replaces *à Paris*)
> Are you going to Paris? – Yes, I'm going there tomorrow.

> *J'ai entendu le téléphone, mais je n'ai pas eu le temps d'y répondre.*
> (*y répondre = répondre au téléphone*)
> I heard the phone but I didn't have time to answer it.

Since *y* has the general meaning of 'there', it can also replace *ici / là*, or prepositions other than *à* which indicate position / direction towards:

> *La lettre doit être sur la table. – Non, elle n'y est plus.*
> (*y = sur la table*)
> The letter should be on the table. – No, it's not there now.

> *Il courait vers la voiture, il y courait de toutes ses jambes, et puis il est tombé.*
> (*y = vers la voiture*)
> He was running towards the car, he was running as fast as he could, and then he fell.

As in the last example, English may not always include 'there', but if the sense implies it, *y* should always be included in French.

There are a number of important idioms in French which include *y*. Among the most common in which it is not clear what noun *y* has replaced are:

> *il y a* there is / are
> *Ça y est!* There you are! / There we are!
> *Vas-y! / Allez-y!* Go ahead! / Go on!
> *J'y suis pour quelque chose.* I'm involved / responsible.
> *Je n'y suis pour rien.* It's nothing to do with me.
> *Je n'y peux rien.* There's nothing I can do (about it).

(f) Use of the pronoun en

Like *y*, *en* is a pronoun which refers to inanimate concrete nouns (i.e. things, places) or abstract nouns. It is only used to refer to people in constructions (ii) and (iii) below.

(i) *En* replaces the preposition *de* + inanimate concrete / abstract noun. *En* is used whatever the gender or number of the noun replaced.

> *Vous êtes passé par Marseille? – Oui, j'en suis parti ce matin.*
> *(en = de Marseille)*
> Did you go through Marseilles? – Yes, I left from there this morning.

> *J'ai besoin des outils. – Tu en auras besoin demain aussi?*
> *(en = des outils)*
> I need the tools. – Will you need them tomorrow as well?

(ii) *En* is also used to replace the partitive article (*du / de la / des*) + noun. This may correspond to the way English uses 'some' to avoid repeating a noun:

> *J'ai trouvé des champignons. – Nous en avons trouvé aussi.*
> *(en = des champignons)*
> I've found some mushrooms. – We've found some as well.

> *Il y avait des Américains au colloque. – Oui, j'en ai vu au restaurant hier soir.*
> *(en = des Américains)*
> There were some Americans at the conference. – Yes, I saw some (of them) at the restaurant yesterday evening.

★ **(iii)** In a sentence which states the number or quantity of *x*, *en* must be inserted if the noun (*x*) is not repeated. Note that English will not usually bother to include 'of it / of them':

> *Vous voulez combien d'oranges? – J'en prendrai six.*
> How many oranges do you want? – I'll have six.

> *Vous voulez tout le fromage? – Non, j'en prendrai la moitié.*
> Do you want the whole cheese? – No, I'll have half.

> *Il y a des touristes déjà? – Oui, il y en a une trentaine à l'Hôtel Beauvais.*
> Are there tourists already? – Yes, there are about thirty at the Hotel Beauvais.

(iv) *En* can mean 'as a result of this' / 'from this'. This use of *en* is common with verbs of deduction or conclusion in French, although English may not express 'from this':

> *Nous avons fait le bilan de la situation. Il en ressort qu'il faudra freiner nos dépenses.*

We've weighed up the situation. It emerges that we shall need to limit our outgoings.

(v) *En*, like *y*, is used in a number of idioms where it is not clear what noun *en* replaces. Among the most common of these are:

s'en aller to go away
Va-t'en! / Allez-vous-en! Go away!
Ne t'en fais pas! / Ne vous en faites pas! Don't worry!
Je n'en reviens pas. I can't get over it. / I'm amazed.

29 Personal pronouns: disjunctive forms

★ The distinction between conjunctive and disjunctive pronouns is one which frequently troubles English learners of French. Remember that the conjunctive pronouns **must** be used in the cases outlined above (i.e. broadly, where there is a verb before which they can stand – or, in the case of positive commands, a verb after which they can stand). Disjunctive pronouns can be used only when a conjunctive pronoun is impossible – see below.

(a) Forms of the disjunctive pronoun

There is one form of the disjunctive pronoun corresponding to each subject pronoun (in several cases the disjunctive and subject pronouns are identical):

SUBJECT PRONOUN	DISJUNCTIVE PRONOUN
je	*moi*
tu	*toi*
il	*lui*
elle	*elle*
on	*soi*
nous	*nous*
vous	*vous*
ils	*eux*
elles	*elles*

The disjunctive pronoun *soi* (corresponding to the subject pronoun *on*) also corresponds to the indefinite subject pronouns *chacun, tout le monde, personne*.

67

(b) Uses of the disjunctive pronoun

The main circumstances in which disjunctive pronouns are used are outlined here.

(i) To emphasize the subject of the verb (i.e. noun or conjunctive subject pronoun):

Moi, j'aime bien voyager, mais mon frère, lui, préfère rester à la maison.
Personally I like travelling, but my brother prefers to stay at home.

The disjunctive subject pronoun may occur for emphasis:
- immediately before the subject (see above example)
- immediately after the subject if the subject is a noun (see above example)
- at the end of the clause if the subject is a pronoun:

Tu y vas souvent, toi? Do you go there often?

The use of the disjunctive pronoun before the subject is very common in colloquial speech, even when no strong emphasis is intended.

The third-person disjunctive forms – *lui / elle / eux / elles* – may stand before the verb in place of the conjunctive subject pronoun, for emphasis. But in the first and second persons, the conjunctive pronoun must also be included:

Eux sont partis. They've left.

Vous, vous restez? Are you staying?

(ii) The disjunctive pronoun must be used after a preposition, and after *comme* or *que* in a comparison:

Je suis parti avant eux.
I left before them.

Comme toi, je n'aurais pas pu le faire sans elle.
Like you, I couldn't have done it without her.

Charles est plus grand que lui.
Charles is bigger than him.

When a pronoun is required to replace the prepositions *à / de* + noun, the conjunctive pronouns *lui / leur / y / en* should be used if possible (see above, section 28). However, the construction *de* + animate noun (i.e. person) is replaced by *de* + disjunctive pronoun:

Tu dois te méfier de Pierre / de lui.
You should beware of Pierre / of him.

The construction *à* + animate noun (i.e. person) is replaced by *à* + disjunctive pronoun after a reflexive verb, and after the following common verbal expressions:

avoir affaire à to deal with
en appeler à to make an appeal to
être à to belong to
faire appel à to call on
penser à to think of
renoncer à to give up
songer à to think / daydream of

Vous pouvez faire appel à eux pour la musique.
You can call on them for the music.

On ne peut pas se fier à toi.
We can't trust you. / You can't be trusted.

(iii) The disjunctive pronoun is used when either two pronouns or a noun and a pronoun are the subject of a verb:

Lui et elle sont partis.
He and she have left.

Lui et ma soeur se connaissent déjà.
He and my sister know each other already.

(iv) The disjunctive pronoun is joined to *même(s)* by a hyphen to give the forms 'myself / yourself', etc.:

Ils l'ont fait eux-mêmes.
They did it themselves.

(v) When a pronoun is required after the verb *être*, the disjunctive form is used:

C'est lui qui t'a envoyé?
Was it him who sent you?

(vi) Disjunctive pronouns are used in exclamations or short answers without a main verb:

Lui, s'occuper du chien! Jamais!
Him take care of the dog! Never!

Qui se chargera des provisions? – Moi.
Who'll take care of the food? – Me.

30 Demonstrative pronouns

Demonstrative pronouns are pronouns meaning 'this (one)' / 'that (one)', 'these (ones)' / 'those (ones)'. Demonstrative pronouns can act as the subject or object of verbs, or stand after prepositions (in place of a noun).

There are three groups of demonstrative pronouns in French:

- *ce*
- *ceci / cela / ça*
- *celui / celle / ceux / celles*

(a) Uses of the pronoun *ce*

(i) The pronoun *ce* (it) can act as the subject of *être*, or of *devoir / pouvoir* + *être*:

> *C'est mon frère.*
> It's my brother.

> *Ce doit être lui qui arrive.*
> It must be him arriving.

> *Ce pouvait être le bruit d'une moto.*
> It could have been the noise of a motorbike.

Note that in the last two examples (*devoir / pouvoir* + *être*), *ce* would commonly be replaced by *ça* in colloquial French.

For the distinction between *c'est / il est* to translate 'it is', see (b) below.

(ii) *Ce* can be inserted before *être* to emphasize the subject of a sentence, even though English does not include 'it' in such cases. This use of *ce* to refer back to a noun or pronoun, or to an infinitive used as a noun is optional:

> *Sa défaite, c'était inévitable.*
> His defeat was inevitable.

> *Quitter un bon ami, c'est toujours pénible.*
> Leaving a good friend is always painful.

Interestingly, these examples could occur in either literary or colloquial style. In the literary register, the insertion of *ce* is used sparingly, for careful emphasis. In speech, the insertion of *ce* is frequent and thus carries little weight.

The insertion of *ce* to refer back to the subject is almost always necessary when a relative or subordinate clause provides the subject of *être*:

> *Tout ce que je peux vous dire, c'est que la décision sera annoncée bientôt.*
> All I can tell you is that the decision will be announced soon.

> *Qu'il refuse* (subj.) *de nous aider, ce n'est pas ce qui me choque.*
> That he should refuse to help us is not what shocks me.

(b) The distinction between *c'est* and *il est*

★ The distinction between *c'est* and *il est* to translate 'it is' causes many problems, not least because there is often a discrepancy between what is perceived as good written style and informal spoken usage. In general, colloquial French opts for *c'est* at the expense of *il est*, whereas written French maintains the distinction.

(i) If 'it' is the subject of a verb other than *être*, and refers to a noun previously mentioned, use *il / elle* (see section 28b(i)).

If 'it' refers to a noun previously mentioned and is the subject of *être* + adjective, use *il* or *elle*:

> *Voici notre jardin. Il n'est pas très grand.*
> This is our garden. It's not very big.

> *Voici la photo. Elle n'est pas très bonne.*
> Here's the photo. It's not very good.

(In colloquial French *ce* might replace *il / elle* in either of the above examples, in which case the adjectives would be in the masculine singular.)

(ii) If 'it' is the subject of *être* and is indefinite – i.e does not refer to a specific noun or pronoun previously mentioned – *ce* or *il* must be used. The choice depends on the part of speech which follows *être*, and may be broadly summarized as follows:

● 'It is' + **noun** (preceded by article / numeral / possessive, demonstrative, indefinite or interrogative adjective) = *ce* + *être*:

> *Ce sont les nouveaux locaux.* It's / They're the new premises.

> *C'est mon premier poste.* It's my first job.

- 'It is' + **pronoun** = *ce* + *être*:

  C'est moi! It's me!

- 'It is' + **adverb** (of time / place) = *ce* + *être*:

  C'est maintenant qu'il faut l'acheter.
  It's now that you need to buy it.

- 'It is' + **preposition** = *ce* + *être*:

  C'est / Ce fut en 1900 qu'on créa cette machine.
  It was in 1900 that this machine was designed.

  C'est avec regret que je vous écris.
  It is with regret that I write to you.

- 'It is' + **conjunction** = *ce* + *être*:

  C'est parce que vous travaillez à la mairie que je vous demande service.
  It's because you work at the Town Hall that I'm asking you a favour.

- 'It is' + **adjective** = *ce* + *être* if the adjective is the last word in the sentence, or is followed by *à* + infinitive (i.e. 'it' refers back to an earlier item):

  Il fait froid, c'est vrai.
  It's cold, it's true.

  Je ne sais pas ce qu'il décidera. C'est difficile à prévoir.
  I don't know what he'll decide. It's hard to foresee.

But: 'it is' + **adjective** = *il* + *être* if the adjective is followed by a subordinate clause / *de* + infinitive (i.e. 'it' refers forward to an item to follow):

  Il est vrai que je n'ai pas terminé tout le travail.
  It is true that I have not finished all the work.

  Il est difficile d'oublier ses mots.
  It is difficult to forget his / her words.

However, in colloquial French, *c'est* might replace *il est* in either of these examples – perhaps because speakers have not always planned in advance the syntactic conclusion to their phrase!

- 'It is' + **expression of time** = *il est* :

  Il est midi et demi.
  It's half past twelve.

- When 'it is' = 'there is', use *il est*:

Il était une fois un roi et une reine. <literary>
There were once a king and a queen.

Note that this structure is now largely archaic.

(c) Uses of *ceci / cela* and *ça*

(i) *Ceci* and *cela* (or the colloquial form *ça*) mean 'this' and 'that'. They can be used to refer to a statement or idea, or to an object which has not been specifically named.

Because *ceci* and *cela / ça* are non-specific, they only occur in the one (masculine singular) form, whatever the statement, object or idea referred to:

Il a promis d'arriver avant midi, mais cela m'étonnerait.
Il a promis d'arriver avant midi, mais ça m'étonnerait. <coll.>
(cela / ça = qu'il arrive avant midi)
He promised to arrive before midday, but that / it would
surprise me.

Si tu veux porter ceci, je prendrai la valise.
If you can carry this, I'll take the case.

Ne fais pas cela, c'est dangereux.
Ne fais pas ça, c'est dangereux. <coll.>
Don't do that, it's dangerous.

Although broadly *ceci* = 'this' (i.e. object nearby, or reference forward) and *cela* = 'that' (i.e. object further away, or reference back), the distinction is not strictly observed in speech, where *cela / ça* predominates.

(ii) *Cela / ça* translates the indefinite use of 'it' (i.e. not referring back to a specific noun) when 'it' is the subject of a verb other than *être*:

Nous ne lui écrirons plus. Cela ne servira à rien.
We shan't write to him / her any more. It won't achieve
anything.

Quand tu essaies de danser, ça me fait rire. <coll.>
When you try to dance it makes me laugh.

(d) Uses of *celui / celle / ceux / celles*

(i) The demonstrative pronouns *celui* (m. sg.), *celle* (f. sg.), *ceux* (m. pl.) and *celles* (f. pl.) are used to refer to a specific noun or nouns already mentioned. The form of the demonstrative pronoun corresponds to the number and gender of the noun referred to. *Celui, celle*, etc., are commonly followed by a relative pronoun (e.g. *celui qui / que / dont . . .*), meaning 'the one who / whom / whose . . .'

> *J'ai vu tes deux voisines. Celle qui est la plus jeune travaille à l'hôpital.*
> I've seen your two neighbours. The one who is younger works at the hospital.

> *Parmi tous les projets, ceux que nous avons retenus sont les deux suivants.*
> Of all the projects, those which we have accepted are the following two.

Celui, celle, etc., are also commonly followed by *de*, meaning 'that of . . .' / 'those of . . .' This can render the sense of ''s' in English:

> *C'est ton appareil? – Non, c'est celui de mon frère.*
> Is it your camera? – No, it's my brother's.

> *J'aime les romans du dix-neuvième siècle, surtout ceux de Zola.*
> I like nineteenth-century novels, especially those of Zola / especially Zola's.

(ii) The forms *celui qui, celle qui*, etc. can be used as indefinite pronouns meaning 'he who . . .' / 'whoever . . .' / 'she who . . . ', etc.:

> *Celui qui vous a dit cela ne connaît pas les règles.*
> The person who / Whoever told you that does not know the rules.

> *Ceux qui n'ont pas reconfirmé leurs billets doivent se présenter au guichet.*
> Those who have not reconfirmed their tickets should go to the counter.

(iii) The endings *-ci* and *-là* can be added to the forms *celui, celle*, etc. to mean 'this one' and 'that one':

> *Voici les deux photos. Celle-ci est plus floue que celle-là.*
> Here are the two photos. This one is less sharp than that one.

Celui-ci and *celui-là* (etc.) also have the meaning 'the latter' and 'the former':

> *L'agent interpella Christine et Anne. Celle-ci ne dit rien, mais celle-là reconnut son erreur.*
> The police officer questioned Christine and Anne. The latter (Anne) said nothing, but the former (Christine) admitted her mistake.

This structure is mainly confined to written French, but in this context is used more frequently than 'the former / the latter' in English.

31 Possessive pronouns

Possessive pronouns in French correspond to the English forms 'mine, yours, his', etc. – i.e. they replace a possessive adjective + noun (see section 23).

(a) Forms of the possessive pronoun

The possessive pronoun agrees in number and gender with the noun it refers to (i.e. it does **not** agree with the possessor). The possessive pronoun is preceded by the definite article.

MASCULINE SINGULAR	FEMININE SINGULAR	MASCULINE PLURAL	FEMININE PLURAL	MEANING
le mien	la mienne	les miens	les miennes	mine
le tien	la tienne	les tiens	les tiennes	yours
le sien	la sienne	les siens	les siennes	his / hers / one's
le nôtre	la nôtre	les nôtres	les nôtres	ours
le vôtre	la vôtre	les vôtres	les vôtres	yours
le leur	la leur	les leurs	les leurs	theirs

(b) Uses of the possessive pronoun

The possessive pronoun can follow the verb *être*:

> *A qui sont ces papiers? – Ce sont les miens.*
> Whose are these papers? – They're mine.

(Note that possession can also be expressed by *à* + disjunctive pronoun: *les papiers sont à moi*.)

A possessive pronoun can also be the subject or object of a verb, or occur after a preposition:

> *Les petits magasins ont eu une année difficile. Le nôtre n'a pas fait de bénéfices.*
> Small shops have had a hard year. Ours hasn't made any profit.

> *Nous avons envie d'une véranda. Est-ce que je pourrais passer voir la tienne?*
> We'd like a conservatory. Could I drop in and look at yours?

Note the following idiomatic uses of the possessive pronouns:

> *les miens / les tiens,* etc. my family / your family, etc.
> *être des nôtres / vôtres / leurs* to be one of us / you / them
>
> *J'espère que vous serez des nôtres.*
> I hope you'll join us / be with us.

32 Relative pronouns

Relative pronouns establish a connection between a noun or clause and the following clause. In English the relative pronouns are 'who, whom, whose, which'. Of these, 'who, whom, which' are often replaced by 'that' in less formal usage, or may even be omitted altogether. It is important to note that in French the relative pronoun can **never** be omitted in this way:

> *Le cheval que j'ai vu était noir.*
> The horse I saw was black.
> The horse that / which I saw was black.

(a) Use of the forms *qui* and *que*

Qui translates 'who / which / that' when it refers to a noun / pronoun already used and which is the **subject** of the verb which follows:

> *L'étudiant qui arrive ce soir doit repasser des examens.*
> (*qui* refers to *l'étudiant* and is the subject of the following verb, *arrive*)
> The student who is arriving this evening has to retake some exams.

Note that when the following verb is *être*, 'who / which / that' must always be translated by *qui*:

> *Voici le tableau qui a été exposé.*
> Here's the painting which has been put on display.

Que translates 'who(m) / which / that' when it refers to a noun / pronoun already used and which is the **object** of the verb which follows:

> *Le journal que je préfère ne paraît pas le dimanche.*
> (*que* refers to *le journal* and is the object of the following verb, *préfère*)
> The newspaper (which / that) I prefer does not come out on Sundays.

As a rule of thumb for translating from English to French, use *qui* for 'who / which / that' if there is **not** another noun / pronoun before the following verb. Use *que* if there is another noun / pronoun (i.e. the subject). The only exception to this rule occurs in literary style when the subject may follow the verb in a relative clause – see section 55b(ii).

★ When you have noun + *que* + verb in a compound tense (i.e. perfect, pluperfect, past anterior, future perfect, conditional perfect), remember that the past participle will agree with the preceding direct object (see section 38b):

> *Les vélos que j'ai achetés ont disparu.*
> The bikes (which) I bought have disappeared.

(b) Use of the form *dont*

The relative pronoun *dont* refers to a noun or pronoun already used and translates 'whose / of whom / of which'. 'Whose' cannot be omitted in English, but in informal usage 'of whom / of which' can be omitted, with the preposition 'of' occurring at the end of the clause. In French *dont* can **never** be omitted:

> *L'homme dont je parlais a déménagé.*
> The man of whom I was speaking has moved.
> The man I was speaking of has moved.

★ The main problem for English speakers is the word order after *dont*. This must always be *dont* + subject + verb + object:

> *La femme dont j'ai trouvé les gants m'a remercié.*
> The lady whose gloves I found thanked me.
>
> *Voici le garçon dont tu connais le père.*
> There's the boy whose father you know.

The past participle **never** agrees with *dont*.

(c) The forms *ce qui, ce que, ce dont*

(i) Whereas the forms *qui / que* translate 'who / whom / which / that' referring to a specific noun or pronoun already used, *ce qui / ce que* translate 'which' when this refers to the whole previous clause. In such cases 'which' effectively means 'the fact of which'.

Ce qui refers to the previous clause and is the subject of the following verb:

> *Il a oublié d'apporter la clé, ce qui était ennuyeux.*
> He forgot to bring the key, which (the fact of which) was annoying.

Ce que refers to the previous clause and is the object of the following verb:

> *Elle s'est absentée en raison d'une grippe, ce que je comprends bien.*
> She stayed away because of flu, which (the fact of which) I quite understand.

Note that the past participle of the following verb does not agree with *ce que*.

(ii) The forms *ce qui* and *ce que* also translate 'what' in indirect or reported questions, i.e. after 'I asked what / I knew what', etc.

Ce qui translates 'what' in an indirect question if 'what' is the subject of the following verb:

> *Tu sais ce qui fait ce bruit?*
> Do you know what is making that noise?

★ Note that with the verbs *arriver, avoir lieu, se passer, se produire* (to happen), 'what' in an indirect question will always be *ce qui*:

> *J'ai demandé à ma collègue ce qui s'était passé.*
> I asked my colleague what had happened.

Ce que translates 'what' in an indirect question if 'what' is the object of the following verb:

> *Il m'a demandé ce que mes enfants faisaient pendant les vacances.*
> He asked me what my children were doing during the holidays.

(iii) *Ce qui* and *ce que* translate 'what' when 'what' introduces a clause functioning as subject or object of another clause. As in (i) and (ii) above, *ce qui* is the subject of its verb, *ce que* the object:

> *Ce qui est étrange c'est qu'il ne m'a pas téléphoné.*
> What is strange is that he has not phoned me.

> *Ce que vous cherchez ne se vend pas à ce prix.*
> What are you looking for is not sold at that price.

(iv) The form *ce dont* literally translates 'that of which'. It is the equivalent of the English 'what' (in indirect questions, or as subject of another clause) when the verb in the same clause requires a construction with the preposition *de* (e.g. *parler de, avoir besoin de*):

> *Ce dont vous parlez ne les intéresse pas.*
> (literally: That of which you are speaking does not interest them.)
> They are not interested in what you are talking about.

Le médecin espère découvrir ce dont il a besoin.
The doctor hopes to discover what he needs.

Ce dont belongs to a more formal register of French. In informal spoken French, the above examples would be likely to be phrased differently:

Ils ne s'intéressent pas à ça.
Le médecin espère découvrir ce qu'il lui faut.

(d) The forms *lequel, laquelle,* etc.

(i) The forms *lequel* (m. sg.), *laquelle* (f. sg.), *lesquels* (m. pl.) and *lesquelles* (f.pl.) mean 'who / whom / which / that' and agree in number and gender with the noun replaced. These forms can be used in place of *qui / que*, but the construction is mainly confined to formal written style. Its main advantage is to resolve any ambiguity (by the indication of number and gender) as to which of two or more nouns is being referred to:

Je me suis renseigné auprès d'un avocat et d'une assistante sociale,
laquelle m'a conseillé de m'adresser à la mairie. <formal>
I asked the advice of a lawyer and a social worker; the latter
advised me to approach the Town Hall.
(*Laquelle* can clearly only refer to the feminine noun *une assistante sociale.*)

(ii) In both informal and formal French, the forms *lequel, laquelle,* etc. translate 'which' after a preposition:

Je ne peux pas retrouver le sac dans lequel j'ai mis les clés.
I can't find the bag I put the keys in.

Est-ce que vous savez les raisons pour lesquelles il a annulé sa
réservation?
Do you know the reasons for which / why he cancelled his
reservation?

When using the prepositions *à / de* + *lequel,* etc., note the contraction of all forms except the feminine singular:

MASCULINE SINGULAR	*auquel*	*duquel*
FEMININE SINGULAR	*à laquelle*	*de laquelle*
MASCULINE PLURAL	*auxquels*	*desquels*
FEMININE PLURAL	*auxquelles*	*desquelles*

Les pays auxquels ces produits sont destinés sont européens.
The countries for which these products are intended / which these
products are intended for are European.

79

The forms *duquel,* etc. are usually replaced by *dont* unless preceded by a compound preposition:

> *Le visage dont il se souvenait était celui de la photo.*
> *Le visage duquel il se souvenait était celui de la photo.* <literary>
> The face which he remembered was that of / in the photo.

When the relative pronoun 'which' is preceded by a compound preposition (*à côté de, en raison de,* etc. – see section 51), *dont* **cannot** be used. You must use the compound preposition + *duquel / de laquelle,* etc.:

> *La réunion à propos de laquelle je voudrais te parler aura lieu le 13 janvier.*
> The meeting I'd like to speak to you about will take place on 13 January.
>
> *Le village près duquel ils s'arrêtèrent s'appelait Aubray.*
> The village near which they stopped was called Aubray.

(iii) *Lequel, laquelle,* etc. can also be used to translate 'who / whom' after a preposition, but this construction is usually only found in formal written French. In spoken French it is more common to use preposition + *qui*:

> *La personne à laquelle les nouveaux venus devaient s'adresser se trouvait assise derrière un grand bureau.* <formal>
> The person to whom newcomers were meant to report was sitting behind a big desk.
>
> *La femme pour qui j'ai commandé le hi-fi n'est pas revenue.* <less formal>
> The woman for whom I ordered the hi-fi / the woman I ordered the hi-fi for hasn't come back.

(e) Use of *où* in place of preposition + relative pronoun

(i) In relative clauses referring to position or place, *où* may replace the structure *dans lequel / auquel / à laquelle,* etc. (when *dans* or *à* refer to a fixed position, not a direction):

> *Voici la rue où (dans laquelle) j'habite.*
> This is the road where / in which I live.
>
> *C'est l'endroit où (auquel) il s'est arrêté.*
> This is the place where / at which he stopped.

(ii) In relative clauses referring to a noun which states a period of time, English uses 'when', but French must use *où* or *que*. Generally, *où* is more common in informal usage, or if the noun is preceded by the definite article (*le moment où*). *Que* tends to be used if the noun is preceded by the indefinite article (*un jour que*):

> *L'année où il n'a pas plu pendant trois mois, les cerisiers sont morts.*
> The year when it did not rain for three months, the cherry trees died.

> *Une nuit que j'avais mal dormi, je me suis levé à l'aube.*
> One night when I had slept badly I got up at dawn.

33 Indefinite pronouns

The most important indefinite pronouns in French are listed below, with comments on any difficulties they present to the English speaker.

d'autres (m. pl.) others
D'autres can be used of people or things, and always takes a plural verb.

> *Certains clients se disent très contents, mais d'autres se plaignent.*
> Some customers say that they are very happy, but others are complaining.

autrui (m.) someone else
Autrui is now confined to literary usage and normally occurs as the direct object or after a preposition. (It is very rarely the subject.)

> *C'était une femme qui agissait toujours pour le compte d'autrui.*
> <literary>
> She was a woman who always acted for the good of someone else.

autre chose (m.) something else
Autre chose implies 'something else, not this', whereas *quelque chose d'autre* can imply 'something else in addition'.

> *Il veut changer de métier pour faire autre chose.*
> He wants to change his profession and do something else.

81

chacun everyone

The masculine form *chacun* is used, unless the context specifically applies to women, in which case use *chacune* (each woman). *Chacun(e)* takes a singular verb.

> *Chacun a contribué selon ses moyens.*
> Everyone contributed according to his / their means.

grand-chose (m.) much / a lot

Grand-chose is only used after a negative, as the direct object, or after a preposition.

> *Ils n'ont pas gagné grand-chose aujourd'hui.*
> They haven't earned much today.

plusieurs (m. pl.) some / several

Plusieurs can be used of people or things. It can stand as the subject or object of the verb, but if it is the object, either the pronoun *en* (of them) should be included before the verb or *plusieurs* should be qualified by *de / parmi* + noun.

> *Cette question a dérouté plusieurs de mes élèves.*
> This question tripped up several / some of my students.

> *Quant aux restaurants chinois, j'en connais plusieurs.*
> As for Chinese restaurants, I know several.

quelque chose (m. sg.) something

Quelque chose can stand as subject or object of the verb or after a preposition.

> *Quelque chose l'a effrayé.*
> Something has frightened him.

★ To translate 'something' + adjective, use *quelque chose de* + masculine singular adjective.

> *J'ai entendu quelque chose d'intéressant à la radio.*
> I heard something interesting on the radio.

quelqu'un (m. sg.) someone

Quelqu'un can stand as the subject or object of a verb, or after a preposition.

> *Quelqu'un vous demande au téléphone.*
> Someone's asking for you on the phone.

★ To translate 'someone' + adjective, use *quelqu'un de* + masculine singular adjective.

Nous cherchons quelqu'un d'exceptionnel pour ce travail.
We are looking for someone exceptional for this work.

quelques-uns (m. pl.) / **quelques-unes** (f. pl.) some / a few
The forms *quelques-uns / -unes* can stand as subject or object of a
verb or after a preposition. If they are the object, either the pronoun
en (of them) should be included before the verb or *quelques-uns /
-unes* should be qualified by *de / parmi* + noun.

*Beaucoup d'entreprises ont visité la foire. Quelques-unes ont
demandé des brochures.*
Lots of firms visited the trade-fair. Some asked for brochures.

*Il y a trois cents personnes qui travaillent ici, mais je n'en connais
que quelques-unes / je ne connais que quelques-unes parmi elles.*
There are 300 people who work here, but I know only a few of
them.

quiconque (m. sg.) whoever / anyone who
Quiconque can stand as the subject of the following verb, meaning
'whoever / anyone who'. Alternatively, it can stand as the direct or
indirect object of the preceding verb and also act as the subject of
the next verb, meaning 'anyone who'.

*Quiconque veut investir mille livres jouira d'un grand bénéfice d'ici
deux ans.* <formal>
Whoever decides to invest a thousand pounds will see a good
profit in two years' time.

*Ce magasin offre un cadeau à quiconque promet d'acheter un
lave-vaisselle.* <formal>
This shop is offering a gift to anyone who promises to buy a
dishwasher.

The use of *quiconque* is associated with a fairly formal register.
More colloquial French is likely to use *tous ceux qui...*, or to
rephrase the statement using the pronouns *on / tu / vous*, e.g.:

*Ce magasin vous offre un cadeau si vous promettez d'acheter un
lave-vaisselle.*

l'un ... l'autre / les uns ... les autres

(1) each other / one another
These forms can be used to stress a reflexive pronoun meaning
'each other / one another'. In this case the indefinite pronouns
usually occur after the verb.

Ils s'entraidaient très souvent les uns les autres.
They very frequently helped each other.

Note the word order in the French translation of preposition +
'each other': *l'un / les uns* + preposition + *l'autre / les autres.*

Ils se sont séparés l'un de l'autre.
They separated from each other.

(2) the one . . . the other / some . . . others

These forms are used to distinguish between two people or things,
or two groups of people or things.

*La banque a deux guichets automatiques, l'un devant la
cathédrale, l'autre derrière le marché.*
The bank has two cashpoints, one in front of the cathedral, the
other behind the market.

*Les voyageurs étaient gênés par la grève: les uns ont attendu, les
autres sont partis à pied.*
Those travelling were affected by the strike: some waited, others
set off on foot.

VERBS

In French, the form of the verb changes according to the subject, voice, tense and mood. The Appendix provides tables for the conjugation of the classes of regular and the most common irregular verbs.

34 Agreement of subject and verb

Three points require further clarification: impersonal verbs, and the agreement of verbs with composite and collective subjects.

(a) Impersonal verbs

Impersonal verbs have as their subject the neuter pronoun *il* (it / there). An impersonal verb can therefore only be used in the third person singular form, or as an infinitive or participle. It is important to distinguish between verbs which are used only in the impersonal form, and those which may be used in this form or with other subjects.

The following verbs are used only impersonally:

s'agir	*il s'agit de* (+ noun) it is a question of
y avoir	*il y a* there is / are
falloir	*il faut* it is necessary
neiger	*il neige* it is snowing

Other verbs occur in their common, literal meaning only with an impersonal subject, e.g.:

geler	*il gèle* it is freezing
pleuvoir	*il pleut* it is raining

As in English, some French verbs admit either a personal or an impersonal subject. Common cases include:

arriver	*Il va arriver un accident.*
	There's going to be an accident.
	Un accident va arriver.
	An accident's going to happen.

85

exister	*Il existe plusieurs solutions.*
	There are several solutions.
	Plusieurs solutions existent.
	Several solutions exist.
se passer	*Il s'est passé quelque chose de remarquable.*
	Quelque chose de remarquable s'est passé.
	Something remarkable has happened.
se trouver	*Il se trouvait dans le parc une vieille statue.*
	There was an old statue in the park.
	Une vieille statue se trouvait dans le parc.
	An old statue was / stood in the park.

(b) Agreement of verbs with composite subjects

A composite subject consists of two or more nouns or pronouns.

When a verb has as its subject two or more nouns in a list or joined by *et*, the verb is put in the third person plural:

La fidélité, la générosité et la tolérance sont des qualités importantes.
Fidelity, generosity and tolerance are important qualities.

When a verb has as its subject two nouns joined by *ou*, the verb is put in the third person plural if *ou* expresses the idea of conjunction (i.e. 'both . . . and . . .'):

La neige ou le verglas rendent cette route très dangereuse.
Snow or ice (i.e. both snow and ice) make this road very dangerous.

But if the two nouns joined by *ou* are in opposition, the verb is put in the third person singular (i.e. 'either . . . or . . .'):

Le ministre ou son député va assister à la cérémonie.
The minister or his deputy (i.e. either the minister or his deputy) will attend the ceremony.

When the subject of a verb is a first or second person pronoun plus another pronoun / noun, the verb agrees with the first person (if there are both first and second persons) or with the second person (if there are second and third persons). It is usual to include the pronoun *nous* or *vous* after the composite subject, before the verb:

Suzanne et moi, nous allons au théâtre ce soir.
Suzanne and I are going to the theatre this evening.

Votre frère et vous, vous pourriez ouvrir un magasin diététique.
You and your brother could open a health-food shop.

(c) Agreement of verbs with collective subject

A collective subject is a noun occurring in the singular which refers to a plural group of people or objects e.g. the police (all those employed in the police force).

Usually in French a singular collective noun requires the third person singular of the verb (whereas English may use a plural verb):

La foule s'est dispersée. The crowd has / have scattered.

Tout le monde a applaudi. Everyone applauded.

When a singular collective noun is followed by *de / des* + plural noun, the verb may occur in either the singular or plural. There is a greater tendency to use the plural when the plural noun is qualified:

Un groupe de manifestants a été arrêté.
A group of protesters has / have been arrested.

La sélection des fromages français qui sont proposés dans ce magasin viennent surtout de Normandie.
The selection of French cheeses which are sold in this shop come mainly from Normandy.

The plural form of the verb must be used after the following collective subjects:

force + plural noun = many a <literary>
une infinité de + plural noun = a good many
nombre de + plural noun = many <formal>
un assez grand nombre de + plural noun = a substantial number of
le plus grand nombre / le plus grand nombre de + plural noun
   = the majority
la plupart / la plupart de + plural noun = the majority
quantité de + plural noun = many <formal>

La plupart des conférenciers viennent de l'étranger.
Most of the speakers / lecturers are from abroad.

35 Active and passive voices

All verbs have an active voice in French (i.e. the subject performs the action):

Pascal a planté les tomates. Pascal planted the tomatoes.

All transitive verbs (i.e. those which take a direct object) can also be used in the passive voice. Here, the action is done to the subject:

> *Les tomates ont été plantées par Pascal.*
> The tomatoes were planted by Pascal.

(a) Forming the active and passive voices

The table of conjugations of regular and irregular verbs in the Appendix gives the tenses and moods in which the active voice can be used. The passive voice can be used in exactly the same tenses and moods. The passive is formed from the appropriate tense and mood of *être* + past participle. In the passive, the past participle always agrees with the subject:

> *Mes filles seront surprises par ton arrivée.*
> My daughters will be surprised by your arrival.
>
> *Ma soeur a été sélectionnée par le jury.*
> My sister has been / was selected by the panel.
>
> *Il faut que ce dossier soit révisé.*
> This dossier must be revised.

★ Note that the translation of the English passive form 'was / were -ed' causes particular problems. The same form is used in English for both the imperfect and the simple past, whereas in French care must be taken to distinguish between the imperfect and the past historic or perfect (see section 38):

> *La voiture a été / fut réparée.*
> The car was repaired. (perfect or past historic refer to the action of the repair being completed)
>
> *La voiture était réparée.*
> The car was repaired. (imperfect gives a description of the state of the car)

(b) Forms which may replace the passive

There are some cases either where the passive cannot be used in French, or where a different construction is preferred on stylistic grounds. It is fair to say that the passive often sounds more awkward in French than in English.

Since only transitive verbs have a passive voice in French, it follows that the indirect object of an active verb cannot simply become the subject of a passive verb. Thus some English passive forms cannot be translated directly into French:

> *L'employé a demandé à mon mari de le rappeler demain.*
> The employee asked my husband to ring back tomorrow.

Because the verb *demander* takes an indirect object (*à mon mari*), 'My husband was asked by the employee to ring back tomorrow' cannot be translated literally (using a passive) into French.

The most common alternative forms corresponding to the English use of the passive are:

(i) The use of the indefinite subject *on*, when it is not important to specify who performed the action:

> *On m'a informé que je dois comparaître devant le juge d'instruction la semaine prochaine.*
> I've been told that I have to appear before the judge conducting the trial next week.

(ii) The use of a reflexive form where one exists – there may well be no equivalent reflexive form in English:

> *Est-ce que ces champignons se mangent?*
> Can these mushrooms be eaten?
> (literally: Do these mushrooms eat themselves?)

> *Le problème va se résoudre.*
> The problem's going to be resolved.

(iii) The use of the structures *se faire / se laisser* + infinitive, implying that the subject undergoes or suffers the action in question:

> *Attention! Tu vas te faire renverser par une voiture!*
> Careful! You'll be / get yourself knocked over by a car!

> *Ses réserves se laissent entendre dans la lettre.*
> His / Her reservations can be felt in the letter.

(iv) The use of an impersonal structure. This is particularly common in the case of verbs taking an indirect object in French. This structure belongs to a more formal register:

> *Il est permis aux élèves de s'absenter des cours le mercredi après-midi.* <formal>
> Pupils may choose not to attend classes on Wednesday afternoons.

89

36 Tenses: the indicative model

The choice of tenses allows the speaker to distinguish references to the past, present and future, and even to make further distinctions within these three categories, especially the past. In many cases, the tense used in English and French will be the same, but there are important cases where the languages differ. It is helpful to remember at the outset that English usually has three forms within any one tense: the basic form, the continuous form, and the emphatic form with 'do' (used in negative and interrogative structures). The following are all forms of the present tense.

> I walk a lot.
> I'm walking a lot these days.
> I don't walk a lot. Do you walk a lot?

French provides only one form for each tense. Where it is important to stress the continuous aspect, another structure such as *être en train de* (to be in the process of) must be introduced:

> *Je ne peux pas répondre au téléphone, je suis en train de me laver les cheveux.*
> I can't answer the phone, I'm washing my hair.

The sections 37–40 below, which outline the forms and uses of tenses, refer exclusively to the indicative mood, which has the fullest system of tenses. The tenses of the subjunctive and conditional moods are treated in sections 44 and 45 respectively.

37 Present indicative

(a) Form

The conjugation of regular and irregular verbs in the present tense is given in the Appendix. Note particularly the groups of verbs such as *appeler*, *jeter* and *acheter*, which although regular -*er* verbs are subject to stem changes for reasons of pronunciation.

(b) Uses of the present indicative

The uses of the present in English and French are broadly the same. As in English, the present tense in French can be used to refer to the future, especially in conjunction with a temporal adverb or adverbial phrase:

> *Demain c'est l'anniversaire de ma grand-mère.*
> Tomorrow is my grandmother's birthday.

> *Le P.-D. G. prend sa retraite en juillet.*
> The Managing Director is retiring in July.

French makes more frequent use than English of the 'historic present', i.e. the use of the present tense to narrate an incident which has already occurred. This device can occur in both literary and popular style, and usually makes the account more vivid:

> *Les employés travaillaient dans la grange. Sans le moindre bruit, Martin s'approche de l'escalier, et puis il appelle Justine, qui l'attend, un couteau à la main.* <literary>
> The employees were working in the barn. Martin made no noise as he approached the stairs. Then he called Justine, who was waiting for him, holding a knife.

> *Devine ce qui m'est arrivé tout à l'heure. Je gare ma voiture là-bas, je suis en train de prendre un billet à l'horodateur quand un type commence à fouiller dans le coffre!* <coll.>
> Guess what just happened to me. I parked the car over there, and I was just getting my ticket from the automatic machine, when a bloke started fishing around in the boot!

For the use of the present tense in constructions with *depuis*, see section 49.

38   Perfect and imperfect indicative and past historic

(a) Form of the perfect tense

The perfect tense is formed from the present tense of *avoir* or *être* (the auxiliary verb) + past participle. Most verbs use the auxiliary *avoir*, but there are two groups which require the auxiliary *être*:

- all reflexive verbs
- a group of 14 common intransitive verbs (mainly denoting movement). These 14 verbs are:

aller	*entrer*	*naître*	*rester*	*sortir*
arriver	*monter*	*partir*	*retourner*	*venir*
descendre	*mourir*	*rentrer*	*tomber*	

Intransitive compounds of these verbs (e.g. *devenir, remonter*) also form the perfect with the auxiliary *être* (except for *convenir*, 'to suit', which uses *avoir*).

★ Note that when *descendre, monter, rentrer* and *sortir* are used transitively (i.e with a direct object) they form the perfect with *avoir*:

> *Il est descendu.* (intransitive)
> He came down.

> *Il a descendu l'escalier.* (transitive: *l'escalier* is the direct object)
> He came down the stairs.

> *Vous êtes rentré déjà?* (intransitive)
> Have you returned / Are you back already?

> *Vous avez rentré les vélos?* (transitive: *les vélos* is the direct object)
> Have you brought in the bikes?

A small number of other verbs can be conjugated with either *avoir* or *être*. In particular, *apparaître* (to appear) can be used with either auxiliary without any change in the meaning. In the case of the following common verbs, *avoir* is used when recording an action, *être* when recording a change of state:

atterrir to land	*échapper* to escape
changer to change	*grandir* to grow bigger
déménager to move house	*passer* to pass
disparaître to disappear	*vieillir* to grow old

> *J'ai passé devant la porte du magasin.* (emphasizes the action)
> I went past the door of the shop.

> *Le facteur est déjà passé.* (emphasizes the completed state of affairs)
> The postman's already gone past.

(b) Agreement of the past participle in compound tenses

The agreement of the past participle is one of the main problems presented by compound tenses (i.e. the perfect, pluperfect, future perfect, conditional perfect and past anterior) for both foreign learners and Francophones. Since the changes frequently do not affect the pronunciation of the past participle, it is in the written language that particular care is needed. There are two types of agreement:

(i) Verbs conjugated with *avoir* and reflexive verbs (although conjugated with *être*) only agree if there is a preceding direct object (P.D.O.) – i.e. if the direct object of the verb (noun or pronoun) occurs before the verb. If the P.D.O. is feminine singular, an *-e* will be added to the past participle; if it is masculine plural, an *-s* will be added (except where the past participle already ends in *-s*); if it is feminine plural *-es* will be added. In most cases, the P.D.O. will be a direct object pronoun:

> *Où sont les clés? Je les ai mises sur la table.* (P.D.O. *les* = *les clés*)
> Where are the keys? I put them on the table.

Note that no agreement is made with the pronouns *en* and *y* (see section 28e and f).

Sometimes the P.D.O. can be a noun occurring in an interrogative or relative structure:

> *Quelle brochure avez-vous demandée?* (P.D.O. *Quelle brochure*)
> What brochure did you ask for?
>
> *Les produits que j'ai testés me semblaient bons.*
> (P.D.O. *Les produits que*)
> The products I tested seemed fine.

In the case of reflexive verbs, the reflexive object pronoun is commonly a P.D.O.:

> *La petite fille s'est habillée tout seule.* (P.D.O. *se*)
> The little girl got dressed on her own.

However, occasionally the reflexive object pronoun may in fact be the indirect object, the direct object being a noun occurring after the verb. In this case, since there is no P.D.O., there is no agreement of the past participle:

> *Elle s'est cassé la jambe.*
> (indirect object *se*; direct object *la jambe*)
> She broke her leg.

(ii) Non-reflexive verbs conjugated with *être* always make an agreement (of gender and number) between the subject and the past participle:

> *Les ingénieurs sont arrivés ce matin.*
> The engineers arrived this morning.
>
> *Ma secrétaire est partie.*
> My secretary has left.

(c) Form of the imperfect tense

The imperfect tense is formed from the stem of the *nous* form of the present tense + the endings *-ais, -ais, -ait, -ions, -iez, -aient*. Thus *nous voulons* gives the imperfect form *je voulais*.

There is only one exception to this rule, the imperfect of *être*, which is *j'étais, tu étais*, etc.

(d) Form of the past historic

The past historic is formed from the stem of the verb + the endings according to the conjugation:

- regular *-er* verbs have the endings
  -ai, -as, -a, -âmes, -âtes, -èrent
- regular *-ir* and *-dre* verbs have the endings
  -is, -is, -it, -îmes, -îtes, -irent
- some irregular verbs (see Appendix) have the endings
  -us, -us, -ut, -ûmes, -ûtes, -urent
- the verbs *tenir* and *venir* have an irregular conjugation in the past historic (see Appendix).

(e) Uses of the perfect and past historic

The perfect and past historic tenses are both used to refer to a completed action in the past. The main distinction in modern French is that the perfect can occur in any context, whereas the past historic has effectively disappeared from the spoken language. Thus the past historic is only found in formal written narratives, e.g. novels, formal newspaper reports (*Le Monde*), and sometimes radio news bulletins (which are read aloud from a written text). The perfect must be used in place of the past historic in conversation, and in informal correspondence:

> *Mon frère a reçu une lettre, et il a contacté son avocat tout de suite.* <spoken>
> My brother received a letter, and he contacted his lawyer straight away.

> *Monsieur Lebrun reçut une lettre et tout de suite il contacta son avocat.* <formal written narration>
> Mr Lebrun received a letter and straight away he contacted his lawyer.

In written French, it is important to be consistent in the choice of narrative tense. Most novelists still use the past historic as their narrative tense (although cf. Camus, *L'Etranger*, which is narrated in the perfect). An author who begins narrating his story in the past historic will conventionally only use the perfect for recording conversations, or on the rare occasions where it is necessary to convey the sense of the English perfect ('has / have done'):

Cet homme quitta mon appartement et se mit en route pour Le Havre. Je ne l'ai jamais revu depuis.
That man left my flat and set off for Le Havre. I have never seen him since.

(f) Uses of the imperfect

The French imperfect corresponds to the English form 'was / were doing'. It is used, like the English form, to describe a continuous state in the past:

Le soleil brillait et la mer était très calme.
The sun was shining and the sea was very calm.

It is also used to record an action which 'was happening' at the same time as another action, or when another action intervened:

Nous prenions un café alors qu'on a frappé à la porte.
We were having a coffee when someone knocked at the door.

Since the imperfect conveys this idea of simultaneity, it is used after conjunctions such as *comme*, or *pendant que* (even where English uses the simple past):

Comme il fermait le robinet il remarqua une fuite d'eau.
As he turned off / was turning off the tap, he noticed water dripping.

A second use of the imperfect is to record repeated or habitual actions in the past. This corresponds to the English form 'used to' (or 'would'):

Quand je faisais mes études, je me couchais assez tard.
When I was studying, I used to / would go to bed quite late.

For the use of the imperfect in constructions with *depuis*, see section 49.

★ (g) The contrast between the imperfect and the perfect / past historic

The rules given above outline the main differences between the imperfect and the perfect / past historic. English speakers of

French, however, may find particular difficulty in deciding which tense to use to translate 'was / were' – since English does not distinguish between the preterite (i.e. simple past) and imperfect of the verb 'to be'. When 'was' implies a change of state (i.e. the verb 'to be' might be replaced by 'to become'), the perfect or past historic will generally be required:

A cette époque nous étions pauvres. (imperfect conveys a continuous state)
At this time we were poor.

J'ai été / Je fus bouleversé en recevant la nouvelle. (perfect or past historic conveys sudden change of state)
I was overwhelmed / stunned when I received the news.

Even more unexpected to the English speaker is the use of the perfect / past historic to translate 'was / were not' where the reference is to a single action (which did not happen):

Je frappai à la porte mais il n'y eut aucune réponse.
I knocked on the door, but there was no reply.

When translating the English structure 'it was . . . who / that . . .', you must use the past historic, not the imperfect, for 'it was' if the verb in the following clause is also in the past historic. This is a logical sequence of tenses:

Ce fut le soldat qui parla le premier.
It was the soldier who spoke first.

Note that in literary style, it is also possible to replace the past historic in the first clause of the above example with the present tense:

C'est le soldat qui parla le premier. <literary>

A number of French verbs are commonly found only in the imperfect, not the perfect or past historic, although in English the preterite may be used. This particularly applies to verbs such as *connaître, croire, savoir, vouloir.* The perfect / preterite should be used only to mark a sudden change in knowledge / thought / wishes:

Je croyais que ton collègue voulait savoir les résultats.
I thought your colleague wanted to know the results.

Au moment où tu es entré, j'ai cru que c'était un cambrioleur.
As you came in, I thought for a moment that it was a burglar.

39 Pluperfect indicative and past anterior

(a) Form of the pluperfect

The pluperfect tense is formed by using the imperfect of the auxiliary verb (*avoir* or *être*) + past participle. For the use of the auxiliary, and rules for agreement of the past participle, see section 38a and b.

(b) Form of the past anterior

The past anterior is formed by using the past historic of the auxiliary verb (*avoir* or *être*) + past participle. For the use of the auxiliary, and rules for agreement of the past participle, see section 38a and b.

(c) Use of the pluperfect and past anterior

Both the pluperfect and the past anterior correspond in meaning to the English pluperfect, 'I had done / I had been doing'. That is to say that they refer to an action which happened at a point in the past earlier than that referred to by the previous or subsequent verb in the past historic or perfect:

> *Il s'était déjà installé quand je suis arrivé.*
> He had already settled in when I arrived.

> *Aussitôt qu'il fut parti, elle nous téléphona.*
> <formal written narration>
> As soon as he had left, she telephoned us.

In some cases, English may use the preterite in place of the pluperfect, but French always uses the pluperfect / past anterior to denote the appropriate time sequence:

> *Lundi j'ai retrouvé le dossier que vous aviez préparé l'année dernière.*
> On Monday I came across the file which you prepared / had prepared last year.

In spoken French, only the pluperfect, not the past anterior, is used. Because the past anterior uses the past historic to form the auxiliary, it is associated with formal written French. It should be

97

used in formal written French in place of the pluperfect if the following three circumstances **all** apply:

- you would otherwise use the pluperfect, referring to a single completed action in the past (not a repeated habitual action)
- the main narrative tense of the passage is the past historic (not the perfect)
- the clause which requires the past anterior is introduced by one of the following time conjunctions: *aussitôt que / dès que* (as soon as), *après que* (after), *à peine que* (hardly), *quand / lorsque* (when):

> *Dès qu'il eut annoncé sa décision de vendre la maison, des agents immobiliers s'empressèrent de le contacter.*
> <formal written narration>
> As soon as he had announced his decision to sell the house, estate agents rushed to make contact with him.

> *A peine se fut-elle couchée que le bruit recommença.*
> <formal written narration>
> Scarcely had she gone to bed when the noise started again.

In some areas of France, the use of the past anterior in a time clause is replaced in spoken language by a 'double compound' tense. However, this is not universally accepted, and is better avoided by the foreign speaker:

> X ~~Quand il a eu fini le travail, il est rentré chez lui.~~ X <regional>
> When he had finished the work, he went home.

> *Quand il avait fini le travail, il est rentré chez lui.*
> <standard French>

40 Future and future perfect

(a) Forms of the future and future perfect

The future tense of regular verbs is formed from the infinitive (dropping the final -*e* in the case of the -*dre* conjugation) + the endings -*ai*, -*as*, -*a*, -*ons*, -*ez*, -*ont*. For the future stem of irregular verbs, see the Appendix.

The future perfect of all verbs is formed from the future of the auxiliary verb (*avoir* or *être*) + past participle. For the use of the auxiliary and the rules for the agreement of the past participle, see section 38a and b.

(b) Use of the future and future perfect tenses

The use of the future and future perfect tenses is broadly similar to the use of the future ('I shall / You will do') and future perfect ('I shall have done / You will have done') in English.

In addition, the future / future perfect must be used in French in a time clause which is dependent upon a main clause in the future tense. This 'logical' or 'disguised' future replaces the use of the present or perfect in English:

Quand vous viendrez à Paris, on pourra visiter le Musée d'Orsay.
When you come to Paris (literally: when you will come), we'll be able to visit the Musée d'Orsay.

Tu pourras sortir quand tu auras fini tes devoirs.
You'll be able to go out when you have finished (literally: when you will have finished) your homework.

★ Note that this use of the disguised or logical future does **not** apply after *avant que* and *jusqu'à ce que* (both of which require the subjunctive – see section 44c), or after *si* (see section 46a).

One particular use of the future in French is as a formal but polite alternative to the imperative. This is associated with giving a person advice or instructions:

Quand vous arriverez au premier carrefour, vous tournerez à gauche, et ensuite vous prendrez la deuxième rue à droite.
When you get to the crossroads, turn left and take the second road on the right.

The future can also be used to express a hypothesis of which you are confident (cf. the use of the conditional for unconfirmed information – see section 45b(iii)). This can be used to translate the English 'must be' in a supposition:

Quelqu'un veut me parler. Ce sera mon frère.
Someone wants to talk to me. It must be my brother.

41   Non-finite forms of the verb

A finite form of the verb is one which has a subject and is conjugated, e.g. *je viens, tu viens*. Non-finite forms of the verb do not have a subject pronoun, and cannot be conjugated. In French there are two non-finite forms of all verbs: the infinitive and the participle, both of which are used in the present and the perfect form.

(a) The infinitive

The present infinitive is the form of the verb which is given in standard dictionaries or reference works, since it indicates (for regular verbs) the conjugation to which the verb belongs (see Appendix). The basic meaning of the present infinitive is 'to do':

donner to give   *choisir* to choose   *vendre* to sell

The perfect infinitive is formed from the present infinitive of the auxiliary (*avoir* or *être*) + past participle. In the case of reflexive verbs, the reflexive pronoun stands before the auxiliary (*être*). The basic meaning of the perfect infinitive is 'to have done':

avoir mangé to have eaten
être parti to have left
s'être levé to have got up

The infinitive may be used either in its own right, or dependent upon a previous conjugated verb.

(i) The infinitive stands in its own right in the following circumstances:

- Used as a verbal noun: as subject, complement or object of a conjugated verb. This form is often the equivalent of the English verbal noun form '-ing'. Note that the infinitive is not preceded by a preposition when used as a verbal noun:

    Passer toute la journée à travailler sur des microfilms est fatigant.
    To spend / Spending the whole day working on microfilms is tiring.

    Je n'aime pas danser. I don't like dancing.

- Preceded by *à* to form a clause which is not grammatically dependent on the next conjugated verb:

    A vous entendre parler, on dirait que l'élection est déjà perdue.
    To hear you speak, one would think the election is already lost.

- After certain interrogative adverbs, e.g.:

    Pourquoi appeler la police?
    Why call the police?

    Comment régler cette dispute?
    How can this dispute be resolved?

- To express an exclamation (surprise, indignation, etc.):

    Revendre la maison! Jamais! Sell off the house! Never!

● In place of the imperative in formal, written commands (especially public notices):

>   *Ne jeter aucun objet par la fenêtre.* <public notice>
>   Do not throw objects out of the window.

● After a number of conjunctions, such as *pour, de peur de,* etc.:

>   *Il faut composer l'indicatif pour téléphoner de Paris en province.*
>   You must dial the code in order to / to phone the provinces from Paris.

>   *Elle n'a rien dit de peur de me gêner.*
>   She said nothing for fear of upsetting me.

(ii) The main use of the perfect infinitive is in the structure *après avoir / après être* + past participle ('after doing / after having done').

★ Note that in French it is **not** possible to use the present infinitive in place of the perfect infinitive in this structure:

>   *Après avoir lu l'article, j'ai écrit une lettre au* Figaro.
>   After reading the article I wrote a letter to the *Figaro*.

>   *Après s'être regardés tendrement, ils s'embrassèrent.*
>   After looking at each other tenderly, they embraced.

(iii) The infinitive is the verb form which must follow any conjugated verb in the same clause. The infinitive may follow the verb directly, or be preceded by one of the prepositions *à / de / par* (see section 52):

>   *J'espère arriver demain.*
>   I hope to arrive tomorrow.

>   *Vous avez décidé d'écrire à la Chambre de commerce?*
>   Have you decided to write to the Chamber of Commerce?

>   *Ils ont réussi à réparer le mur.*
>   They've managed to repair the wall.

Note particularly the construction *faire / laisser* + infinitive (no preposition), meaning 'to get or have something done / let something happen':

>   *Il a fait venir le contremaître.*
>   He got the foreman to come / sent for the foreman.

>   *Le veilleur de nuit a laissé entrer les étudiants.*
>   The night porter let the students in.

(b) The present participle

The present participle is formed from the *nous* form of the present indicative, with the *-ons* ending replaced by *-ant*:

choisir	*choisissant*	choosing
donner	*donnant*	giving
se plaindre	*se plaignant*	complaining

The present participle may be used as an adjective, qualifying a noun, or after a verb such as *être*. In this case, the present participle behaves like an adjective, agreeing with the noun referred to:

La femme souriante est ma belle-soeur.
The smiling woman is my sister-in-law.

Cette histoire semble très amusante.
This story seems very funny.

In the following instances, where the present participle has a verbal function, it is invariable:

(i) The present participle can stand in apposition to a noun, translating the English form '-ing':

Les recrues, arrivant trop tard pour prendre le train, ont dû passer la nuit à Saumur.
The recruits, arriving too late to catch the train, had to spend the night at Saumur.

(ii) The present participle can introduce an adverb or adverbial phrase which elaborates upon the way in which the action of the main verb was performed:

Je me mis à le poursuivre, courant à toute vitesse.
I set off in pursuit of him, running as fast as I could.

(iii) The present participle may be preceded by the preposition *en*, giving the meaning 'while doing' or 'by doing':

En regardant le tableau, il a observé que le peintre ne l'avait pas signé.
While looking at the painting he noticed that the artist hadn't signed it.

Nous avons pu acheter la maison en empruntant de l'argent à mon oncle.
We've been able to buy the house by borrowing money from my uncle.

(iv) The present participle may be preceded by *tout en*, conveying the notion of the simultaneity of this action and the main verb:

> *Le conseiller matrimonial posa une question, tout en notant la dernière réponse de son client.*
> The marriage guidance counsellor asked a question, while at the same time noting down the last reply of his client.

Tout en + present participle can also be used to convey an idea of concession:

> *Tout en admirant votre travail, je suis obligé de dire que sur un plan financier il ne me semble guère rentable.*
> Much though I admire your work, I am forced to say that financially speaking it scarcely seems profitable.

(c) The past participle

The past participle is formed by changing the infinitive ending as follows:

-er becomes *-é*:	*noté*	noted
-ir becomes *-i*:	*rougi*	blushed / turned red
-dre becomes *-du*:	*rendu*	returned

The past participles of irregular verbs need to be learned separately.

The past participle can be used in a number of ways. For the use of the past participle after the auxiliary verbs *avoir* or *être* to form compound tenses, see sections 38–40. This use of the past participle produces a finite verb form.

When the past participle is used on its own, without an auxiliary verb, it is a non-finite verb form. Frequently, the past participle is used in the same way as an adjective, agreeing in number and gender with the noun qualified:

> *C'est du temps perdu.*
> It's a waste of time. (literally: wasted time)

> *Les solutions proposées par mon collègue pourraient être mises en place dès le mois de mai.*
> The solutions proposed by my colleague could be introduced from May.

One particular use of the past participle is in an absolute clause: i.e. the past participle qualifies a noun or pronoun which is syntactically distinct from the main clause. This construction is characteristic of literary French:

> *Les discussions terminées, les deux familles rentrèrent chez eux.*
> <literary>
> The discussion having finished, the two families returned home.

> *Lui parti, nous pouvions nous entretenir sans gêne.* <literary>
> When he had left / After his departure, we were able to talk freely.

42 Moods of the verb

The mood of the verb is a grammatical category which broadly reflects the speaker's attitude towards what is said: whether this is a fact, a dubious assertion, a hypothesis, a command. In practice, the choice of mood in modern French is determined both by the meaning of what is said and by certain grammatical constraints. Although some grammars would consider the infinitive and participles as moods, most agree that French has only four moods: the indicative, the subjunctive, the conditional and the imperative. Of these, the indicative, the subjunctive and the conditional can occur in different tenses.

43 Indicative mood

The indicative is the basic mood, used to express most statements and questions. It is helpful to consider the indicative as the mood which will always be used unless there is a reason for selecting the subjunctive, conditional or imperative. The indicative is used in the full range of tenses, expressing references to the past, present and future: see sections 36–40.

44 Subjunctive mood

The subjunctive mood is often associated with doubt or uncertainty, whereas the indicative suggests factual certainty. However, in modern French, the speaker only rarely has a free choice between indicative and subjunctive. In most cases, grammatical rules, or conventions of usage, determine whether the indicative or subjunctive should be used. In the explanations below of the most important uses of the subjunctive, it is clear that some instances are obviously related to notions of doubt and uncertainty, whereas in others the use of the subjunctive has lost any real 'modal' significance.

It needs to be said at the outset that there is a popular misconception among English students of French that the subjunctive has either 'disappeared' from modern French, or that it should at least always be avoided at all costs. In fact, the present subjunctive, and to a lesser extent the perfect subjunctive, are alive and well, and are used in everyday conversation by most native speakers who have even a minimum education. What is true is that the imperfect and pluperfect subjunctives are extremely rare in spoken French, and increasingly avoided in all but the most literary written French. Also, while most speakers of French will normally use the subjunctive in the majority of the instances listed below, there are some cases where, as indicated, the use of the subjunctive is not respected except in a more formal sociolinguistic context.

(a) Tenses of the subjunctive

The subjunctive has four tenses in French: present, perfect, imperfect and pluperfect. Note that the subjunctive has no future tense.

(i) Present subjunctive

This is made from the *nous* form of the present indicative: the ending *-ons* is removed, and the endings *-e, -es, -e, -ions, -iez, -ent* are added.

As illustrated by the sample conjugations in the Appendix, in the case of *-er* verbs the *je, tu, il* and *ils* forms are identical in the present indicative and subjunctive.

Irregular verbs may have an irregular present subjunctive: see the Appendix.

The present tense is the normal form of the subjunctive in spoken and informal written French, unless explicit reference to the past is required. Even when the main verb of the sentence is in the perfect or imperfect, it is common for the present subjunctive to be used:

J'ai dû attendre jusqu'à ce qu'il soit de retour.
I had to wait until he returned.

Je ne voulais pas qu'il découvre le secret.
I didn't want him to discover the secret.

(ii) Perfect subjunctive

This is formed from the present subjunctive of the auxiliary verb (*avoir* or *être* – see Appendix) + past participle. In spoken or informal written French, this tense of the subjunctive is used in place of the present to distinguish a statement referring to the past from one referring to the present:

Bien qu'elle soit malade, elle a assisté à la réunion. (present subjunctive)
Although she is ill, she attended the meeting.

Bien qu'elle ait été malade, elle a assisté à la réunion. (perfect subjunctive)
Although she has been ill, she attended the meeting.

Je crains qu'il ne lui arrive un accident. (present subjunctive)
I'm worried he might have an accident.

Je crains qu'il ne lui soit arrivé un accident. (perfect subjunctive)
I'm worried he might have had an accident.

(iii) Imperfect subjunctive

Although this tense is called the imperfect subjunctive (by analogy with its Latin equivalent), it is in fact formed from the past historic of the indicative. It is largely because the past historic is no longer used in speech or informal written French that the imperfect subjunctive has disappeared from these same contexts. There is no question of contrasting the meaning of the imperfect and perfect subjunctives in the way one would contrast the perfect and imperfect indicatives (see section 38g).

The imperfect subjunctive is formed from the stem of the past historic + the endings *-sse, -sses, -̂t, -ssions, -ssiez, -ssent.*

Even in literary French, only the form of the third person singular of the imperfect subjunctive is regularly used, and this only when the verb of the main clause is in the imperfect, past historic or pluperfect (or, sometimes, the conditional):

Il refusa de croire que son fils fût coupable. <literary>
He refused to believe that his son was guilty.

The first person singular of the imperfect subjunctive may be tolerated for monosyllabic verb forms (e.g. *eusse / fusse*):

Pour instruit que je fusse, je n'avais jamais appris l'hébreu.
<literary>
Educated though I was, I had never learned Hebrew.

For all the other persons, the imperfect subjunctive should be avoided. Although grammatically 'correct', a phrase such as the following will produce laughter or at least an ironic smile even in educated French circles:

X ~~Le professeur aurait préféré que nous nous concentrassions sur l'oeuvre de Proust.~~ X

The professor would have preferred us to concentrate on the work of Proust.

It would be normal to substitute the present (or perfect subjunctive) in such a case, even though this produces an odd sequence of tenses:

Le professeur aurait préféré que nous nous concentrions sur l'oeuvre de Proust.

(iv) Pluperfect subjunctive

This tense is formed from the imperfect subjunctive of the auxiliary (*avoir* or *être*) + past participle. It conveys the same meaning as the pluperfect tense of the indicative. However, like the imperfect subjunctive, its use is now confined to literary French, and effectively to the first and third persons singular:

La guerre éclata avant que le roi n'eût remplacé son ancien commandant. <literary>
War broke out before the king had replaced his former commander.

(b) Constructions requiring the subjunctive: main clauses

The subjunctive is only rarely used in a main clause, as outlined below.

(i) With the following verbs, expressing a command or a wish:

être
Soit un rectangle. <formal scientific hypothesis>
Let us take a rectangle.

pouvoir

> *Puissiez-vous ne jamais connaître un tel malheur!* <literary>
> May you never know such unhappiness!

savoir

> *Je ne sache pas que vous ayez* (subj.) *l'autorité d'agir de la sorte.*
> <formal / literary>
> I am not aware that you are authorized to act in such a manner.

venir

> *Vienne la nuit, la fête commencera.* <literary>
> Come nightfall, the festivities will start.

vivre

> *Vive la reine!* Long live the queen!

(ii) With a few fixed expressions, of which the most common are:

> *advienne que pourra* come what may
> *ainsi soit-il* so be it / amen
> *coûte que coûte* at all costs
> *n'en déplaise à . . .* with due respect to . . .
> *Dieu soit loué!* Thank goodness! / Thank heavens!

(iii) The imperfect and pluperfect subjunctives may replace the present or perfect conditionals in certain circumstances. This structure is confined to literary style (see section 46d(ii)).

(iv) In very formal French, orders relating to a third party may be expressed by *Que* + subjunctive:

> *Le roi dit: 'Qu'il ne revienne jamais à la cour!'* <formal>
> The king said: 'Let him never come back to the court!'

(c) Constructions requiring the subjunctive: subordinate clauses

The subjunctive occurs most commonly in subordinate clauses. The main contexts which require the subjunctive are outlined in (i) – (xiii) below.

(i) After the following types of conjunction:

concessives

> *bien que / quoique* although
>
> X *malgré que* X although (This conjunction is confined to colloquial

usage and is not accepted by purists.)
non que / non pas que not that

expressions of condition

à condition que on the condition that
à moins que . . . ne unless
de peur que . . . ne / de crainte que . . . ne lest / for fear that
pour peu que if only / if ever   *sans que* without
pourvu que provided that   *à supposer que* supposing

purpose

afin que / pour que in order that
de façon que / de manière que / de sorte que so that
(but: *de façon que / de manière que / de sorte que* + indicative =
with the result that)

temporal

avant que . . . (ne) before (the expletive *ne* is common in formal or
literary style; see section 56d)
jusqu'à ce que until

Some speakers use a subjunctive after *après que*, by analogy with
avant que, but this is not generally accepted.

(ii) After verbs of 'wishing that', particularly:

désirer que to wish
préférer que to prefer
souhaiter que to wish
vouloir que to want
vouloir mieux que to prefer

L'hôtel voulait que nous versions des arrhes.
The hotel wanted us to pay a deposit.

Note, however, that if the same subject governs the verb 'to wish'
and the following verb, French – like English – will use an infinitive
construction:

Le syndicat aurait préféré terminer les discussions demain.
The union would have preferred to finish the discussions
tomorrow.

N.B. *espérer que* (to hope that) takes the indicative, unless used in
the negative or interrogative (when it is followed by the
subjunctive).

(iii) After verbs or adjectives of emotion introducing a subordinate clause, e.g.:

> *se réjouir que* to be delighted that
> *regretter que* to regret / be sorry that
> *être étonné que* to be astonished that
> *être déçu que* to be disappointed that

> *Nous sommes ravis que vous puissiez nous rendre visite.*
> We're delighted that you can visit us.

> *Il s'étonnait que personne ne nous ait avertis.*
> He was astonished that no one had warned us.

Comprendre que takes the subjunctive when it implies 'to understand the reason why' (i.e. empathizing):

> *Je comprends tout à fait que vous n'ayez pas voulu aborder le sujet.*
> I quite understand why you didn't want to raise the subject.

But when *comprendre que* means 'to think / to be given to understand that', it is followed by the indicative:

> *Il est parti? Mais j'avais compris qu'il nous attendait.*
> Has he left? I'd thought / been given to understand that he was waiting for us.

(iv) After verbs of fearing: *craindre que / avoir peur que*, etc. Note that the verb which follows *que* is preceded by an expletive *ne* (see section 56d):

> *J'ai peur que vous ne perdiez votre temps.*
> I'm afraid you are / may be wasting your time.

However, if the same subject governs the verb 'to fear' and the following verb, an infinitive construction is used in place of the subjunctive:

> *Elle avait peur de se faire mal.*
> She was afraid of hurting herself.

(v) After verbs giving orders, prohibitions, etc., e.g.:

> *demander que* to ask   *insister pour que* to insist
> *exiger que* to demand   *ordonner que* to order
> *permettre que* to allow / *ne pas permettre que* to forbid

> *Le juge a ordonné que le procès soit arrêté.*
> The judge ordered the trial to be stopped.

(vi) After verbs conveying an idea of purpose or expectation, e.g.:

attendre que to wait until
s'attendre à ce que to expect that
tenir à ce que to be anxious / to insist that
veiller à ce que to take care that <formal>

Nos clients s'attendent à ce que nous fassions plusieurs sondages.
Our clients are expecting us to carry out several opinion polls.

(vii) After verbs of saying or thinking used in the negative or interrogative:

Vous ne croyez pas qu'il y ait eu une erreur?
You don't think there has been a mistake?

Penses-tu que cela puisse se faire?
Do you think this can be done?

However, in informal speech the indicative – especially the future tense – may replace the subjunctive when the speaker is certain about the statement:

Le météo n'a pas dit qu'il neigera demain. <coll.>
The weather forecast hasn't said it will snow tomorrow.

Verbs which in themselves imply doubt are usually followed by the subjunctive. But if such verbs are used in the negative, they are commonly followed by the indicative (a double negative effectively being a strong affirmation):

Le jockey a nié que son cheval ait été dopé.
The jockey denied that his horse had been doped.

Je ne doute pas que vous aurez envie de prendre un jour de congé.
I've no doubt (I'm sure) that you'd like to take a day's holiday.

(viii) After expressions of possibility or uncertainty, e.g.:

il se peut que it's possible / it may be that
il est possible que it's possible that
il est peu probable que it's unlikely that
il n'est pas sûr que it's not certain that

Il est peu probable que nous puissions vous livrer le matériel avant la semaine prochaine.
It's unlikely that we'll be able to deliver the materials to you before next week.

However, expressions of probability are followed by the indicative:

Il est très probable que vous obtiendrez votre mutation.
It's very likely that you'll be granted a change of posting.

With the verbs *sembler* and *paraître*, the subjunctive is normally used after the impersonal structures *il semble que / il paraît que*. However, the indicative usually replaces the subjunctive if a personal pronoun is included in the structure (*il me semble que / il te paraît que*, etc.):

Il semble que le crime ait été commis vers trois heures.
It seems that the crime was committed at about three o'clock.

Il nous semble que ce contrat est le plus favorable.
It seems to us (we think) that this contract is the most favourable.

(ix) After impersonal expressions relating to the necessity or acceptability of something, e.g.:

il convient que it is fitting that <formal>
il faut que it's necessary that / ... must
il importe que it is important that <formal>
il est essentiel / nécessaire que it's essential / necessary that
il est inadmissible que it's unacceptable that
il est normal que it's normal / natural that
il est regrettable que it's unfortunate that

Il n'est pas normal qu'on vous demande de travailler deux samedis de suite.
It's not right for you to be asked to work two Saturdays running.

(x) In a relative clause whose antecedent includes a superlative adjective, or one of the adjectives *seul / unique / premier / dernier*:

C'est le plus beau château qui ait jamais été construit.
It's the most beautiful castle that was ever built.

Est-ce que c'est le seul exemplaire de ce livre qu'on puisse consulter en Europe?
Is it the only copy of this book which is available in Europe?

Note, however, that the phrases *la première / dernière / seule fois que* are followed by the indicative:

La première fois que j'ai rencontré Hélène, nous faisions du ski tous les deux.
The first time I met Hélène, we were both skiing.

There is a trend in the evolution of the contemporary language for the subjunctive to be replaced by the indicative if the speaker wants to stress the truth of a superlative claim. This is particularly characteristic of the language of marketing:

> *Le nouveau modèle 408 est la seule voiture qui peut atteindre cette vitesse.* <marketing>
> The new model 408 is the only car which is capable of reaching this speed.

(xi) The subjunctive commonly occurs in a relative clause whose antecedent is a negative (*personne / rien*) or an indefinite pronoun (*quelque chose / quelqu'un*), or a noun introduced by the indefinite article (*un / une ...*). The use of the subjunctive is particularly appropriate when the rest of the sentence suggests the speaker does not know whether such a person or thing exists:

> *Nous aimerions trouver une maison qui ait une piscine, un grand jardin et au moins dix pièces.* (subjunctive implies speaker does not know whether such a property can be found)
> We'd like to find a house which had / has a swimming-pool, a large garden and at least ten rooms.

> *Voici la photo d'une chaumière que nous avons beaucoup admirée en Bretagne.* (indicative used here because speaker knows such a cottage exists)
> Here's the photo of a cottage in Brittany which we found very attractive.

> *Notre entreprise cherche un interprète qui sache traduire du portugais en bulgare.* (subjunctive implies speaker does not know whether such an interpreter exists)
> Our firm is looking for an interpreter who can translate from Portuguese into Bulgarian.

> *Notre entreprise cherche un interprète qui sait traduire en allemand.* (indicative implies such an interpreter does exist)
> Our firm is looking for an interpreter who can translate into German.

(xii) The subjunctive is always used in clauses introduced by the following indefinite pronouns and adjectives:

> *qui que* = whoever (subject of following verb)
> *qui que ce soit que* = who(m)ever (object of following verb)
> *quoi que* = whatever
> *quelque(s)* + noun *que* (+ verb other than *être*) = whatever
> *quel (le)(s) que soit / soient* + noun = whatever

quelque / aussi / si + adjective / adverb = however
où que = wherever

Quel que soit le problème, et quoi que vous décidiez de faire,
n'oubliez pas de consulter votre chef de section.
Whatever the problem may be, and whatever you may decide to
do, don't forget to consult with the head of your department.

Quelque / aussi / si fatiguée qu'elle fût, elle ne manqua jamais de
me faire bon accueil.
However tired she was, she never failed to make me feel welcome.

(xiii) When *que* at the start of a sentence introduces a clause of the
type 'The fact that . . .', the verb is commonly in the subjunctive.
This construction is usually confined to more formal French:

Que certains des tableaux attribués à cet artiste soient des
imitations, c'est un fait généralement reconnu. <formal>
The fact that certain paintings attributed to this artist are
imitations is generally recognized.

However, it is sometimes possible for the indicative to replace the
subjunctive in such a structure if the speaker wishes to stress the
accuracy of the information:

Que l'armée ennemie n'a jamais pu franchir le fleuve, c'est ce qui
explique notre victoire. <formal>
The fact that the enemy army was never able to cross the river
explains our victory.

45 Conditional mood

There is some debate between grammarians about whether the
conditional in French should be classed as a tense or a mood. In
fact the conditional verb forms can convey information about both
time (future, or 'future in the past') and the attitude of the speaker
(making a hypothetical statement).

(a) Forms of the conditional

(i) Present conditional
The present conditional is formed from the future stem + imperfect
endings:

je donnerais, tu donnerais, etc.
I would / should give, you would give, etc.

(ii) Conditional perfect

The conditional perfect is formed from the present conditional of
the auxiliary verb (*j'aurais / je serais*) + past participle:

> *J'aurais donné* I would have given.
> *Tu serais parti.* You would have left.

★ Note, for recognition purposes, that in literary French *eût* or *fût*
(i.e. the imperfect subjunctive) may replace *aurait* or *serait* as the
auxiliary verb. This structure is almost always confined to the third
person singular:

> *Il eût aimé lui parler.* <literary> (= *Il aurait aimé lui parler.*)
> He would have liked to speak to him / her.
>
> *Il se fût vengé.* <literary> (= *Il se serait vengé.*)
> He would have taken revenge.

(b) Uses of the conditional

The main uses of the conditional are:

(i) To express a hypothesis, most commonly in the form: 'If *x*
happened, I would do . . . / If *x* had happened, I would have done . . .'

> *Si je gagnais 100.000 francs, je m'achèterais une nouvelle voiture.*
> If I won 100,000 francs, I would / should / I'd buy a new car.
>
> *Si j'avais su ton adresse, je serais venu te voir.*
> If I had known your address, I would have / should have / I'd have
> come to see you.

(ii) In indirect speech or thought after *si* (to ask / know whether
something would happen / would have happened):

> *Il m'a demandé si je viendrais.*
> He asked me if / whether I would come.
>
> *Nous ne savons pas si elle aurait préféré passer l'année dernière à
> Cannes.*
> We don't know if / whether she would have preferred to spend
> last year in Cannes.

Note that this is one of the only cases in which it is correct in
French to use the conditional after *si*. A quick way to check whether
an English sentence fits this category is to ask: can 'if' be replaced
by 'whether'?

He asked if I would change my job. (He asked whether I would
change my job.)
Il m'a demandé si je changerais d'emploi.

(iii) In a main clause, to imply that the information is as yet
unconfirmed. This form is rarely used in general speech, being most
commonly associated with newspaper or other media reports.
There is no directly equivalent form in English:

Le Président des Etats-Unis serait malade. <news report>
The President of the United States is said / rumoured to be ill.

Un avion aurait été abattu ce soir. <news report>
A plane is reported to have been shot down.

(iv) In questions, giving a tentative supposition:

La voiture n'est plus là. Ta fille serait partie?
The car's gone. Might your daughter have left? / Perhaps your
daughter's left?

Est-ce qu'ils auraient dépensé tout l'argent déjà?
Is it possible they've already spent all the money?

(v) In exclamations to convey that something is unlikely (and
possibly to suggest some indignation at its being suggested):

Moi, je lui enverrais une carte postale!
Can you imagine me sending him a postcard! / I'd never send him a
postcard!

Lui, il aurait lu ce journal-là!
Can you imagine him having read that newspaper! / He'd never
have read that newspaper!

(c) Cases where the English forms 'would / should' are not translated by the conditional in French

There are two important cases where in English 'would / should'
may be used, but where French requires a different construction.

★ (i) 'Would' conveying the sense of 'used to' (i.e. a repeated action in
the past). Translate into French by the imperfect (see section 38f):

When we were travelling in France, we would stay at youth
hostels. (When we were travelling in France, we used to stay at
youth hostels.)

116

Quand nous voyagions en France, nous restions dans des auberges de jeunesse.

★ **(ii)** 'Should / should have' conveying the sense of 'ought to / ought to have' (i.e. obligation). Translate into French by the present conditional / conditional perfect of *devoir* + infinitive:

I should phone my mother tonight. (I ought to phone my mother tonight.)
Je devrais téléphoner à ma mère ce soir.

We should have turned right at the traffic lights. (We ought to have turned right at the traffic lights.)
Nous aurions dû tourner à droite aux feux rouges.

46 Moods in hypothetical clauses

(a) Choice of mood and tense after *si*

★ **(i)** English-speaking students of French commonly make two mistakes in their choice of mood and tense after *si*. Bear in mind that:

- the verb in the clause introduced by *si* cannot be in the future or conditional (except in the case of reported speech; see section 45b (ii)):

  X *Si je le verrai je te le dirais.* X
  X *Si je le verrais je te le dirais.* X

  Si je le voyais je te le dirais.
  If I saw him I'd tell you.

- the verb in the clause introduced by *si* should be in the indicative not the subjunctive:

  X *Si on ait le temps, on pourrait se promener jusqu'au château.* X
  Si on avait le temps on pourrait se promener jusqu'au château.
  If there was / were time, we could walk as far as the castle.

The subjunctive is associated with many constructions expressing uncertainty, but *si* is not one of them in modern French. For one rare case where in literary, rather archaic, style the pluperfect subjunctive may follow *si*, see below.

(ii) All true conditional sentences follow one of three patterns:

- If . . . happens (present), . . . stay at home! (imperative)
                              . . . people always stay at home. (present)
                              . . . we'll stay at home. (future)

French uses identical tenses to English:
Si + present, . . . imperative
            . . . present
            . . . future

> *S'il y a une grève, reste chez toi!*
> If there is a strike, stay at home!
>
> *S'il y a une grève, les Parisiens restent chez eux.*
> If there is a strike, people living in Paris stay at home.
>
> *S'il y a une grève, je resterai chez moi.*
> If there is a strike, I shall stay at home.

- If . . . happened (simple past), *x* would stay at home (present conditional).

★ Here, French uses the imperfect, not the simple past, after *si* (cf. in English 'if something were to happen').

Si + imperfect, . . . present conditional

> *S'il y avait une grève, est-ce que vous resteriez chez vous?*
> If there was / were a strike, would you stay at home?

- If . . . had happened (pluperfect), *x* would have stayed at home (conditional perfect).

French uses identical tenses to English:
Si + pluperfect, . . . conditional perfect

> *Si j'étais tombé malade, je serais resté chez moi.*
> If I had fallen ill, I would have stayed at home.

In literary, rather archaic, French, the pluperfect subjunctive may replace the pluperfect indicative after *si*, underlining the purely hypothetical nature of the statement:

> *Si l'homme eût développé des ailes, ses poumons auraient été plus puissants.* <literary, archaic>
> If man had developed wings, his lungs would have been stronger.

(b) *Si* + two hypothetical statements

★ When *si* is followed by two hypotheses, the first should be put in the indicative (present / imperfect / pluperfect – see above), and the

S46 Moods in hypothetical clauses

second should be introduced by *et que* + subjunctive:

> *Si ce parti gagne / gagnait l'élection et qu'il tienne ses*
> *promesses...*
> If this party wins / won the election and keeps / kept its
> promises...

This structure is common in written and more formal spoken French. In everyday speech the structure may be avoided:

> *Si ce parti gagne l'élection, et enfin s'il tient ses promesses...*

(c) *Si* + perfect / past historic in 'rhetorical' hypotheses

Where English says 'If I did *x*', French uses the imperfect in place of the English simple past tense (see a(ii) above). However, there is one literary / rhetorical structure in which *si* + perfect / past historic translates the English simple past. This is when the 'If I did *x*' clause refers not to a true hypothesis, but to something that has actually happened (i.e. the sentence is not really a hypothesis at all, but an emphatic statement).

> *Si ce poète est revenu / revint à Paris, c'est pour une seule raison.*
> <literary>
> If this poet came back to Paris, it was for only one reason. (= The
> fact that this poet came back to Paris is due to just one reason.)

(d) Ways of expressing hypotheses without using *si*

In both literary and colloquial speech, there are ways of expressing hypotheses without using a conditional sentence introduced by *si*.

(i) In literary style, the hypothetical clause can be introduced by the present subjunctive, with verb and subject inverted:

> *Survienne le moindre problème (et) ils abandonneront le projet*
> *tout de suite.* <literary>
> If the slightest problem occurs, they will immediately abandon the
> project.

(ii) In literary style, the hypothetical clause can be introduced by the imperfect / pluperfect subjunctive, with the verb and subject inverted. This implies an even greater degree of hypothesis than (i) above:

Dussé-je renoncer à tous mes biens, je ne voudrais jamais le revoir.
<literary>
Even had I to give up all my belongings, I would never wish to see
him again.

*Le gouvernement aurait dû nous avertir, ne fût-ce que parce que le
péril était si grave.* <literary>
The government should have warned us, if only because the
danger was so serious.

(iii) In colloquial usage, to emphasize the hypothetical nature of a
statement, the first clause can be introduced by *quand (même)* +
conditional and the second clause also put in the conditional:

Quand (même) tu me le dirais, je ne le croirais pas. <coll.>
Even if you told me so, I wouldn't believe it.

(iv) In colloquial usage, the first and second clauses may both
occur in the conditional, joined by *que*:

Vous chercheriez toute la soirée que vous ne le trouveriez pas.
<coll.>
If you hunted all evening you still wouldn't find it.

47 Imperative mood

The imperative mood is used for giving commands. Verbs have
imperative forms for the second persons, and for the first person
plural.

For non-reflexive verbs, the imperative is formed from the *tu, vous* or *nous* forms of the present indicative: the subject pronoun is omitted. Note that the imperative form for the second person singular of *-er* verbs drops the final *-s* of the present indicative form:

> *Regarde / Regardez ces chaussures!*
> Look at those shoes!

> *Choisis / Choisissez un numéro!*
> Choose a number!

> *Parlons de ce que nous devrions faire!*
> Let's talk about what we should do!

Reflexive verbs form the imperative in the same way as non-reflexive verbs, except that the reflexive object pronoun is included after the verb, joined to it by a hyphen. In the case of the second person singular, the disjunctive pronoun form *-toi* is used:

> *Réveille-toi! / Réveillez-vous!*
> Wake up!
> *Arrêtons-nous un instant!*
> Let's stop for a minute!

However, when the imperative of a reflexive verb is used in the negative, the reflexive object pronoun is placed before the verb:

> *Ne te fâche pas! / Ne vous fâchez pas!*
> Don't be cross!

Most irregular verbs form the imperative in the standard way, from the appropriate present indicative form. However, the imperative forms of *aller, avoir, être, savoir* and *vouloir* are irregular; see Appendix.

For constructions other than the imperative which may be used for commands and suggestions, see section 72.

PREPOSITIONS

48 Function of prepositions

Prepositions have very similar functions in French and English. Most commonly they stand before a noun or pronoun, and express position, direction, possession, etc:

François est parti pour Paris sans eux.
François has left for Paris without them.

C'est le fils de nos voisins.
He's the son of our neighbours.

In certain French structures, prepositions can also stand before verbs, adjectives, adverbs, or a clause:

Il a fini par céder.
He ended up by giving way.

Elle passe pour intelligente.
She's thought to be intelligent.

La loi entre en vigueur dès maintenant.
The law comes into force from now.

Je ne me souviens plus de ce qu'il m'a chargé de vous dire.
I can't remember what he told me to say to you.

In many cases, prepositions can be translated literally from English to French, but one of the main sources of error for a foreign speaker is the idiomatic use of prepositions. The list in section 49 summarizes the most important ways in which prepositions are used before nouns.

For adjectives or verbs that are followed by a preposition, it is best to learn the prepositional structure together with the adjective or verb (see section 52). Remember that in some cases an adjective or verb can be followed by various prepositions, the choice of preposition determining the meaning of the phrase:

J'ai commencé à apprendre l'espagnol.
I've started learning Spanish.

J'ai commencé par apprendre l'espagnol, puis je me suis mis au portugais.
I started by learning Spanish, then I took on Portuguese.

49 Simple prepositions before nouns

Simple prepositions consist of a single word (*à, dans, par,* etc.), as opposed to compound prepositions, which consist of preposition + noun + preposition (*à côté de, en dehors de,* etc.).

(a) Prepositions governing two or more nouns

When one preposition governs (i.e. stands before) two or more nouns, it should be repeated before each noun in the case of the prepositions *à, de, en.* (This rule is strictly observed in formal written French, but not always in informal speech.)

> *J'ai montré les photos à ma mère et à ma soeur.* <formal>
> I showed the photos to my mother and sister.

In the case of other prepositions governing two or more nouns, there is no need to repeat the prepositions if the nouns are similar in meaning.

> *Il est parti avec une valise et un sac à dos.*
> He went off with a case and rucksack.

However, the preposition should be repeated before each noun if the nouns have distinct or opposing meanings.

> *On se marie pour le pire et pour le meilleur.*
> Marriage is for better or worse.

As a general rule, it is more common (and usually a mark of good style) to repeat prepositions in formal written French.

123

(b) Main literal and idiomatic uses of simple prepositions before nouns

à at / to
(For the contracted forms of *à* + definite article, see section 1d.)

> *Je t'attendrai à l'arrêt de bus.* I'll wait for you at the bus stop.
>
> *Tu veux venir à la réception?*
> Do you want to come to the reception?

(i) *à* denotes position in phrases such as:

> *à la campagne* in the country
> *à droite / à gauche* on the right / left
> *au deuxième étage* on the second floor
> *à l'extérieur / à l'intérieur* on the outside / inside
> *au lit* in bed
> *au mur / au plafond* on the wall / ceiling

(ii) *à* denotes position with reference to parts of the body:

> *avoir mal à la tête* to have a headache
> *avoir mal à la jambe gauche* to have a pain in one's left leg
> *se blesser au pied droite* to hurt / injure one's right foot
> *Ça te fait mal au genou?* Does that hurt your knee?
> *Ce produit fait du bien aux yeux.* This product is good for your eyes.

(iii) *à* introduces a distinguishing physical feature (cf. English 'with'):

> *un immeuble à six étages* a six-storey building
> *un trèfle à quatre feuilles* a four-leaved clover
> *la maison à la grille rouge* the house with the red gate
> *l'homme aux cheveux noirs* the man with black hair

(iv) *à* indicates the purpose an object serves:

> *une boîte à lettres* a letterbox   *une tasse à café* a coffee cup

(v) *à* can be used either after a noun or in the structure *être à quelqu'un* to denote ownership:

> *Voici les documents à Jean.* Here are John's documents.
> (an emphatic or colloquial equivalent of *les documents de Jean*)
> *Le sac est à Philippe.* The bag's Philip's.
> *Il cherche une maison à lui.* He's looking for a house of his own.

(vi) *à* denotes the manner in which an action is performed (especially with verbs of speech and movement):

> *crier à tue-tête* to shout at the top of one's voice
> *lire à haute voix* to read out loud
> *marcher à grandes enjambées* to stride along
> *rentrer à pas de loup* to return on tiptoe / stealthily
> *s'habiller à la mode française* to dress in a French style

(vii) *à* denotes the means by which an action is performed (including references to non-mechanized forms of transport):

> *aller à pied* to walk
> *fait à la main* made by hand
> *enfoncer la porte à coups de pied* to kick the door down

après after

> *Il s'est installé à Paris après la guerre.*
> He moved to Paris after the war.
>
> *Je suis arrivé après les autres membres du groupe.*
> I arrived after the other members of the group.

Après conveys the idea 'next to / second to' in terms of a preference:

> *Après Toulouse, je préférerais habiter Bordeaux.*
> Next to / Second to Toulouse I'd rather live in Bordeaux.

avant before (of time)

> *Téléphone-moi si tu arrives avant neuf heures.*
> Give me a ring if you arrive before nine o'clock.
>
> *Il a occupé ce poste avant mon frère.*
> He held that position before my brother.

Avant conveys the idea 'more than' in terms of a preference:

> *J'aime les randonnées en montagne avant tout.*
> I like mountain hikes above all / more than anything.

avec with

(But cf. idiomatic uses of *à* and *chez* to translate some uses of 'with' in English.)

> *Ma mère viendra avec ma soeur.*
> My mother will come with my sister.

Il m'a regardé avec un certain mépris.
He looked at me with some scorn.

Avec ce petit dictionnaire tu risques de ne pas comprendre le texte.
With / If you're using that little dictionary, you're not likely to
understand the text.

chez at (the house of) / to (the house of)

Chez may be used before a noun or pronoun referring to a person or
group of people.

J'achèterai le sucre chez l'épicier.
I'll buy the sugar at the grocer's.

Ce soir nous sommes invités chez Anne et Thierry.
This evening we're going to Anne and Thierry's.

(i) *Chez* means 'in the case of / with' when it refers to a person's or
group of people's characteristics:

Chez Jean, l'énervement est un signe d'anxiété.
With John, being irritable is a sign of anxiety.

Il y a un certain optimisme chez les médecins généralistes.
There is a mood of some optimism among / in the case of G.P.s.

(ii) The use of *chez* meaning 'in the case of' extends to geographical
groups:

Chez nous on boit beaucoup de thé.
In our country we drink lots of tea.

(iii) *Chez* is used to translate 'in (the work of)' with reference to
writings or artistic work:

Chez Sartre, la notion de la liberté est remise en question.
In Sartre's work / writings, the concept of freedom is called into
question.

contre against

L'équipe hollandaise a remporté une victoire contre les Américains.
The Dutch team scored a win against the Americans.

(i) *Contre* is used to translate the English 'with' in 'to be angry with':

J'espère que vous n'êtes pas fâché contre moi?
I hope you're not angry with me?

(ii) *Contre* is used to translate the English 'for' in 'to exchange one thing for another':

> *J'ai échangé ma moto contre un vélo de course.*
> I exchanged my motorbike for a racing bike.

(iii) *Contre* is used to translate the English 'to' in records of scores, votes, etc.:

> *Le projet a été retenu, dix voix contre deux.*
> The proposal has been accepted by ten votes to two.

dans in / into

(But cf. idiomatic uses of *en* to translate 'in' and section 50 on prepositions expressing time and place.)

> *Dans le nord de l'Italie, on mange plus de riz.*
> In the north of Italy people eat more rice.

> *Je vais travailler dans le jardin.*
> I'm going to work in the garden.

> *Il est entré dans la boulangerie.*
> He's gone into the baker's.

> *Dans le cas des jeunes chômeurs, il faut une solution plus radicale.*
> In the case of young people who are unemployed, we need a more radical solution.

de from / of

(For the contracted forms of *de* + definite article, see section 1d.)

> *Ces oranges viennent d'Espagne.*
> These oranges come from Spain.

> *Du jour au lendemain la situation politique s'est transformée.*
> From one day to the next the political situation has been transformed.

> *Tu as vu la photo de notre équipe?*
> Have you seen the photo of our team?

> *Paris est la capitale de la France.*
> Paris is the capital of France.

(i) *De* can express the way in which something is done, especially with the following nouns:

> *d'un seul coup* with a single blow
> *d'une façon surprenante* in a surprising way

d'une manière aimable in a friendly way
d'un pas rapide walking fast / at a fast pace
d'un ton irrité in an irritated tone / voice
d'une voix douce in a soft voice

(ii) *De* can be used to translate the English 'with' to express the means or cause (cf. also *par*):

accablé de terreur overcome with terror
chargé de fruits loaded with fruit
plein d'espoir full of / filled with hope

(iii) *De* expresses the substance something is made of (cf. also *en*), or what it contains:

un mur de briques a brick wall
une boule de cristal cristal ball
une femme de fer an iron lady (metaphor)
une assiette de charcuterie a plate of cold meats
une tasse de thé a cup of tea

(iv) *De* is used to translate '(more / less) than' when *plus* or *moins* is followed by a number or quantity:

Il y a plus de 500 délégués.
There are more than 500 delegates.

Il nous reste moins d'un litre de lait.
We have less than a litre of milk left.

(v) *De* is used after adjectives expressing measurements:

un trou large de deux mètres a hole two metres wide

(vi) *De* is used after the verb *être* when prices, numbers and quantities are given:

Le prix de la pension complète est de 950 francs.
Full board costs 950 francs.

Le nombre des manifestants était de 6000.
The number of protesters was 6000. / There were 6000 protesters.

La consommation moyenne est de deux litres d'eau par jour.
On average two litres of water are drunk a day.

(vii) *De* is used after a superlative adjective to translate the English 'in / of':

C'est le plus beau pays du monde.
It's the most beautiful country in the world.

C'est le modèle le plus économique de toutes les petites voitures.
It's the most economical of all the small cars.

depuis　from / since

Je n'ai pas revisité Paris depuis 1968.
I haven't been back to Paris since 1968.

Depuis son enfance il rêvait de devenir pilote.
From his childhood, he dreamed of becoming a pilot.

(i) *Depuis* is used to translate 'for' with reference to an action which has / had been continuing for a certain period of time.

★ Note that French requires different tenses from English in this structure. The English form 'I have been doing ... for ...' is rendered by the present tense in French + *depuis*. The English form 'I had been doing ... for ...' is rendered by the imperfect tense in French + *depuis*.

Nous travaillons avec cette compagnie depuis l'année dernière.
We have been working with that company since last year.

Le gouvernement menait des négociations avec ses partenaires depuis trois mois.
The government had been negotiating with its partners for three months.

(ii) The structure *depuis ... jusqu'à* translates 'from ... to' in reference to place or time:

Il y aura des embouteillages depuis les Alpes jusqu'à la côte d'Azur.
There will be traffic jams from the Alps to the Cote d'Azur.

Ils s'étaient absentés depuis le matin jusqu'au soir.
They had stayed away from morning to evening.

derrière　behind

Notre agence se trouve derrière l'Hôtel de Ville.
Our branch is located behind the Town Hall.

dès　from / from the time of

Pour la braderie nous ouvrirons dès huit heures.
For the annual sales we shall be open from eight o'clock.

Dès notre première rencontre nous nous sommes très bien entendus.
From the time of our first meeting we got on very well together.

Dès can also be used to translate 'from' + place name, when the implication is 'from this place onwards':

Dès la région nantaise la production viticole devient importante.
From the region of Nantes onwards, wine production becomes significant.

devant in front of

J'ai garé ma voiture devant la tienne.
I've parked my car in front of yours.

en in

(Cf. certain uses of *dans* given above.)

Note that *en* is almost always followed by a noun without an article (except in a few set phrases, e.g. *en l'an 2000* 'in the year 2000').

(i) *En* is used to translate 'in' before the year, the names of months, or the seasons of summer, autumn and winter (but 'in the spring' is *au printemps*):

Le projet de loi fut voté en 1989.
The bill was passed in 1989.

Il faut visiter la Provence en automne, en octobre par exemple.
Provence should be visited in the autumn, in October for example.

(ii) *En* is used to translate 'in' or 'to' in references to a feminine country (but use *au* for a masculine country):

Vous allez en Espagne cet été?
Are you going to Spain this summer?

Nous avons des succursales en Italie.
We have branches in Italy.

(iii) *En* is used to translate 'in' meaning the time needed to do something:

Le garage pourra tout faire en deux heures.
The garage will be able to do everything in two hours. (i.e. will take two hours)

(iv) *En* is used to translate 'as / like' after such verbs as:

se comporter en adulte to behave like an adult
se déguiser en cowboy to dress up as a cowboy
traiter quelqu'un en ami to treat someone as a friend

(v) *En* is used to translate 'into' after verbs denoting 'changing into', 'dividing into':

Ce bureau sera réaménagé en salle de conférence.
This office will be turned into a seminar room.

Mon grand-père répartit ses terres en cinq lotissements.
My grandfather divided his lands up into five building plots.

(vi) *En* can be used to translate the idea 'made of' (but cf. also this use of *de*) or 'in' for colours:

une bouteille en plastique a plastic bottle
une chope en étain a pewter mug
être habillé en noir et blanc to be dressed in black and white

(vii) *En* is used to translate 'by' in references to most mechanized forms of transport:

Vous allez faire le voyage en avion ou en voiture?
Are you going to travel by plane or by car?

entre between

Le courrier arrive entre huit et neuf heures.
The post arrives between eight and nine o'clock.

Nous habitons entre Bergerac et Castillon-la-Bataille.
We live between Bergerac and Castillon-la-Bataille.

(i) *Entre* is used to translate 'between / from' with verbs of selecting or choosing:

J'ai dû faire le choix entre les deux modèles.
I had to make a choice between the two models.

(ii) *Entre* is used to translate 'among' (cf. also *parmi*):

Nous en parlons souvent entre amis.
We often speak of it among friends.

(iii) *D'entre* is used instead of *entre* to translate 'of / among' before a disjunctive pronoun:

Nous avons consulté plusieurs d'entre eux.
We consulted several of them.

envers towards

Envers is used to translate 'towards' in the sense of attitudes or emotions towards people (i.e. not literal movement towards, for which see *à* and *vers*):

> *Le juge se montra sévère envers les malfaiteurs.*
> The judge was harsh towards the offenders.

hormis except <confined to archaic literary usage>

(Cf., more commonly, *sauf*.)

> *Il les accusa tous hormis ses avocats.* <archaic and literary>
> He accused everyone except his lawyers.

hors outside / except

Hors is normally only used as a simple preposition in the following set phrases:

> *hors commerce* not on sale to the public
> *hors jeu* offside
> *hors la loi* outlawed
> *hors série* out of production

malgré despite / in spite of

> *Malgré la grève, l'usine a produit une centaine de voitures cette semaine.*
> Despite the strike, the factory has produced about a hundred cars this week.

outre besides / beyond <literary>

> *Outre deux tomes des* Essais *de Montaigne, il possédait les* Confessions *de Rousseau.* <literary>
> Besides two volumes of Montaigne's *Essays*, he owned Rousseau's *Confessions*.

Outre also occurs in less literary registers in the following set phrases:

> *outre-Atlantique* across the Atlantic (i.e. in America)
> *outre-cela* besides that
> *outre-Manche* across the Channel (i.e. in Britain)
> *outre-mer* overseas
> *outre-Rhin* on the other side of the Rhine (i.e. in Germany)
> *outre-tombe* beyond the grave

par by / through

> *L'enfant a été retrouvé par la police.*
> The child was found by the police.

> *Le budget sera voté par le Conseil Municipal.*
> The budget will be approved by the Town Council.

> *Pour venir chez toi, est-ce qu'il faut passer par Caen?*
> Do we have to go through Caen to get to you?

(i) *Par* is used to translate 'out of' before an abstract noun:

> *Il a joué le rôle du grand mécène par vanité.*
> He played the part of the big patron out of vanity.

> *Par pitié, il leur a payé le prix du voyage.*
> Out of pity, he paid for their journey.

(ii) *Par* is used to translate the English 'a' when expressing the frequency of something:

> *Je travaille trois jours par semaine.*
> I work three days a week.

> *Il y a une réunion officielle deux fois par an.*
> There is an official meeting twice a year.

(iii) Among the most common other idiomatic uses of *par* are:

> *par conséquent* as a result
> *par contre* but on the other hand
> *par écrit* in writing
> *par exemple* for example
> *par la fenêtre* out of the window
> *par hasard* by chance
> *par ici* this way
> *par intervalles* at intervals / intermittently
> *par terre* on the ground

parmi among

> *Le château était caché parmi les arbres.*
> The castle was hidden among the trees.

> *Il faut citer Flaubert parmi les plus grands écrivains du dix-neuvième siècle.*
> One must include Flaubert among the greatest writers of the nineteenth century.

(i) *Parmi* can be used to translate 'of' when you are speaking of 'some of a group':

> *Parmi mes amis, la plupart s'intéressent à l'art contemporain.*
> The majority of my friends are interested in modern art.

(ii) *Parmi* can be used + plural disjunctive pronoun to translate 'of us / you / them':

> *Il y en avait beaucoup parmi eux qui avaient travaillé aux Etats-Unis.*
> There were many of them who had worked in the United States.

pendant during

> *Pendant les vacances nous avons repeint la maison.*
> During the holidays we redecorated the house.

Pendant is used to translate 'for', especially with reference to duration of past time:

> *Il était hospitalisé pendant quinze jours.*
> He was kept in hospital for a fortnight.

pour for

> *Il y a une lettre pour vous.*
> There's a letter for you.

> *Les chips sont pour l'apéritif ce soir.*
> The crisps are for the drinks party tonight.

(i) *Pour* can mean 'for the sake of':

> *Il a tout sacrifié pour ses principes politiques.*
> He sacrificed everything for his political principles.

(ii) *Pour* can mean 'in favour of':

> *Vous êtes pour l'union monétaire?*
> Are you in favour of monetary union?

(iii) *Pour* can be used to translate 'as' in the sense 'to use as':

> *Pour toute lumière il ne nous restait que deux bougies.*
> We had only two candles left as our sole source of light.

(iv) In expressions of time, *pour* can normally only be used to translate 'for' with reference to the future:

Je vais prendre un appartement à Rome pour trois mois.
I shall rent a flat in Rome for three months.

sans without

Il est parti sans son parapluie.
He left without his umbrella.

★ Note that when 'without' is followed by 'a / any' in English, no article is required after *sans* in French:

Vous ne pouvez pas voir la directrice sans rendez-vous.
You cannot see the headmistress without an appointment.

C'est une ville sans divertissements.
It's a town without any leisure activities.

Sans can also be used to translate 'but for':

Je me serais perdu sans la carte.
I would have got lost but for the map.

sauf except

Tout le monde est présent sauf Sylvie.
Everyone is here except Sylvie.

Sauf is used in a few formal phrases to mean 'save':

Les comptes sont bons, sauf erreur de ma part. <formal>
The accounts are in order, save for any error on my part.

selon according to

Selon le porte-parole du gouvernement, la décision sera annoncée demain.
According to the government spokesperson, the decision will be announced tomorrow.

C'est un produit bien adapté au marché européen selon lui.
It's a product which is well suited to the European market according to him / in his opinion.

sous under

Les enfants se sont arrêtés sous mon balcon.
The children stopped under my balcony.

Sous Mitterrand, le Parti Socialiste est arrivé au pouvoir.
Under Mitterrand the Socialist Party has come to power.

(i) *Sous* is used in formal French to express 'within' + time:

> *Nous espérons obtenir son accord sous peu.* <formal>
> We hope to obtain his / her agreement within a short time.

(ii) *Sous* is used to translate 'in / from' with reference to perspective or viewpoint:

> *Il faut envisager le problème sous un autre angle.*
> We need to look at the problem from another angle.

> *L'avocat a représenté leur demande sous un jour favorable.*
> The lawyer presented their request in a favourable light.

(iii) *Sous* is also used in the following common idioms where English uses a different preposition:

> *sous forme de* in the form / shape of
> *sous main* at hand
> *sous prétexte de* under the pretext of
> *sous le règne de* in the reign of

sur on / upon

> *Les clés sont sur la table.*
> The keys are on the table.

> *Votre jugement est basé sur quels critères?*
> What criteria is your judgement based upon?

(i) *Sur* is used to translate 'in / out of' for fractions or statistics:

> *Un mariage sur trois va aboutir au divorce.*
> One marriage in three will end in divorce.
> *Le professeur lui a donné treize sur vingt pour sa dissertation.*
> The teacher gave him / her thirteen out of twenty for his / her essay.

(ii) *Sur* is used in the construction noun + *sur* + same noun, to mean 'after / upon':

> *Ce pays a reçu coup sur coup.*
> This country has received blow after / upon blow.

(iii) *Sur* is used in the following common idioms where English uses a different preposition:

> *sur le champ* at the time / on the spot
> *sur les (deux) heures* towards (two) o'clock

sur le moment   at the time

sur un ton (+ adjective)   in a (adjective) voice

vers towards

(See also *envers*, 'towards', of emotions, sentiments.)

L'agent se dirigea vers les Champs Elysées.
The policeman headed towards the Champs Elysées.

Vers la fin de sa vie, il se rapprocha de l'église.
Towards the end of his life, he grew close to the church again.

Vers is used to translate 'at about' with reference to times:

Le concert va commencer vers huit heures.
The concert will start at about eight o'clock.

50   Prepositions in expressions of time and place

The list of simple prepositions above includes many of the rules for the use of prepositions in expressions of time and place. However, as these are areas which cause particular problems, the most important points are summarized below.

(a) Expressions of time

(i) To translate the English preposition 'in', French uses *dans* or *en*, or sometimes *au bout de* or *d'ici*.

Dans refers to the time in the future, 'from now', at which the action will be performed:

Je commencerai à vider la chambre dans une semaine.
I'll start to clear out the room in a week. (i.e. in a week from now)

En refers to the length of time taken to complete an action:

Nous avons fait le trajet en une heure.
We did the journey in an hour. (i.e. it took an hour)

Au bout de is used in formal written style for the narration of actions in the past. It translates 'in (*x* minutes / hours)' meaning '*x* minutes / hours later':

Jacques quitta son amie. Au bout d'une heure il revint,
accompagné de la concierge. <formal>
Jacques left his girlfriend. In an hour (i.e. an hour later) he came back, together with the caretaker.

D'ici is used to refer to a point in the future and means 'in . . . from now':

> *D'ici quinze jours notre bureau aura déménagé.*
> In two weeks our office will have moved. (i.e. in two weeks from now)

(ii) To translate the English preposition 'for', French uses *pour*, *pendant*, or *depuis*.

Pour is normally only used with reference to a period of time in the future (relative to the speaker) and conveys an idea of purpose:

> *Je vais m'inscrire à la faculté pour l'année prochaine.*
> I shall register at the university for next year.

Pendant is used to express the duration of an action, and must be used to translate 'for' when it refers to an action in the past:

> *Le boulanger a fermé son magasin pendant trois semaines.*
> The baker closed his shop for three weeks.

Depuis is used to refer to an action which 'has been -ing / had been -ing' for a certain period of time. See section 49b for the correct tenses in French.

> *J'enseigne dans ce lycée depuis trois ans.*
> I've been teaching in this school for three years.
>
> *Madame Pineaux ne sortait plus depuis quelques semaines.*
> For a few weeks Madame Pineaux had no longer been going out.

(iii) 'From' can be translated by *de*, *dès*, *depuis* or *à partir de*.

De is commonly used in conjunction with *à* (from ... to):

>*Ils ont travaillé du matin au soir.*
>They worked from morning to evening.

Dès conveys the idea 'right from ...':

>*Dès sa nomination, elle se renseigna sur la ville.*
>From the time of her appointment (i.e. as soon as she was appointed), she found out about the town.

Depuis conveys the idea 'from ... onwards':

>*Depuis sa maladie, ma grand-mère n'aimait pas habiter toute seule.*
>From the time of her illness (onwards) my grandmother did not like living alone.

A partir de also conveys the idea 'from ... on', but usually refers only to the future, and emphasizes the time at which the new situation starts:

>*A partir de demain vous serez responsable de la section du marketing.*
>From tomorrow you will be responsible for the marketing section.

(b) Expressions of geographical place

The translation of 'in' or 'to' with geographical place names depends on whether the place is a continent or country, a province, a county or *département*, or a town.

(i) For countries and continents of feminine gender (the majority) and for masculine ones beginning with a vowel use *en*:

>*Mon fiancé habite en Espagne.*
>My fiancé lives in Spain.

>*Est-ce que vous accepterez de voyager en Afrique?*
>Will you be willing to travel to Africa?

>*Est-ce qu'il faut un visa pour aller en Israël?*
>Does one need a visa to go to Israel?

For countries of masculine gender beginning with a consonant use *au* (or *aux* for a plural noun):

>*Ils ont acheté un appartement au Portugal.*
>They have bought a flat in Portugal.

>*Nous serons obligés de retourner aux Etats-Unis.*
>We shall have to return to the United States.

(ii) For French provinces which are feminine use *en*:

Il y a beaucoup de petits ports de pêche en Bretagne.
There are many small fishing ports in Brittany.

For French provinces which are masculine use *dans le*:

Dans le Poitou il se trouve de belles églises médiévales.
In the Poitou area there are many fine medieval churches.

(iii) For French *départements* (administrative areas) and English counties, the usual preposition is *dans* + definite article:

La police s'inquiète du nombre d'incendies dans le Var cet été.
The police are worried by the number of outbreaks of fire in the Var this summer.

Nous habitons dans le Kent depuis dix ans.
We've been living in Kent for ten years.

However, for French *départements* whose name is made up of two nouns joined by *et*, and for the English county of Cornwall, the preposition *en* is used (without any article):

Le nouveau Disneyland a été créé en Seine-et-Marne.
The new Disneyland has been set up in Seine-et-Marne.

Tu vas passer tes vacances en Cornouailles?
Are you going to spend your holiday in Cornwall?

(iv) With French or foreign town names, the preposition *à* is used (or *à* combined with the article in the case of towns whose names begin with an article):

Tu devras aller à Bordeaux demain.
You'll have to go to Bordeaux tomorrow.

Notre siège social se trouve au Havre.
Our registered office is at Le Havre.

51 Compound prepositions before nouns

Compound prepositions (sometimes called prepositional phrases) consist of two or more words, the last of which is normally the preposition *de* or (less commonly) *à*. The most common compound prepositions are illustrated below, in alphabetical order of the main word in the structure.

d'après according to

> *D'après mon collègue, l'information est fausse.*
> According to my colleague the news is wrong.

au bord de by / alongside

> *Il aime passer ses vacances au bord de la mer.*
> He likes spending his holidays by the sea.

auprès de near / in comparison with

> *Elle préfère une table auprès de la fenêtre.*
> She prefers a table near / by the window.

> *Auprès du nouveau technicien, l'ancien manquait de formation.*
> Compared with the new technician, the old one hadn't been well trained.

autour de around

> *Ils veulent faire une promenade autour du centre-ville.*
> They want to go for a walk around the town centre.

à cause de because of

> *Je suis arrivé en retard à cause d'un accident.*
> I arrived late because of an accident.

à côté de beside / in comparison with

> *Vous habitez à côté de l'église?*
> Do you live beside the church?

> *A côté des Américains, les Européens consomment peu de Coca-Cola.*
> In comparison with Americans, Europeans are not great drinkers of Coca-Cola.

en dehors de outside / except for

> *Est-ce que vous voyez Michel en dehors du travail?*
> Do you see Michael outside work?

> *Nous fréquentons peu les gens du village en dehors de quelques vieux amis.*
> We have little contact with people from the village except a few old friends.

141

au delà de beyond / over and above

> *Vous arriverez au delà des Alpes en deux heures.*
> You'll get beyond the Alps in two hours.
>
> *Au delà des billets qu'on vous a offerts, vous avez le droit à trois places à demi-tarif.*
> Over and above the tickets you've been given, you're entitled to three half-price seats.

au-dessous de below

> *Au-dessous de mon balcon il y a l'entrée de la pharmacie.*
> The entrance to the chemist's is below my balcony.

au-dessus de above

> *Le moustique passait au-dessus de sa tête.*
> The mosquito flew above his head.

à l'exception de with the exception of / except for

> *La secrétaire a reçu toutes les réponses à l'exception de celle de notre association de Cherbourg.*
> The secretary has received all the replies except for the one from our Cherbourg association.

face à faced with / given

> *Face à ce problème, comment voulez-vous que je réagisse?*
> How do you expect me to react faced with / given this problem?

en face de opposite

> *Le parking se trouve en face de la gare.*
> The car park is opposite the station.

faute de for lack of

> *Faute de personnel, nous sommes obligés de fermer le mardi.*
> We have to shut on Tuesdays because of lack of staff.

en fonction de in relation to / according to

> *Le salaire sera décidé en fonction de votre expérience professionnelle.*
> The salary will be fixed in relation to your professional experience.

grâce à thanks to

> *Grâce à votre générosité, nous avons remboursé l'emprunt sur la maison.*
> Thanks to your generosity we have paid off the loan on the house.

à l'insu de unknown to

> *A l'insu de ses parents elle s'était acheté une voiture.*
> Unknown to her parents she had bought a car.

jusqu'à up to / as far as

> *Notre jardin s'étend jusqu'à la rivière.*
> Our garden stretches as far as the river.

au lieu de instead of

> *Je prendrai un poulet au lieu du rôti de boeuf.*
> I'll buy a chicken instead of the joint of beef.

le long de / au long de along / throughout

> *Nous avons remarqué de jolies villas le long de la route.*
> We noticed some pretty villas along the road.

> *Il n'a cessé d'interrompre tout au long de la réunion.*
> He kept interrupting all through the meeting.

lors de during / at the time of <literary>

> *Lors de la Révolution, cette prison fut détruite.* <literary>
> During / At the time of the Revolution this prison was destroyed.

à partir de as from

> *Voici mon numéro de téléphone à partir de demain.*
> Here's my phone number as from tomorrow.

près de near

> *L'arrêt de bus se trouve près de la mairie.*
> The bus stop is near the Town Hall.

à propos de in connection with / on the subject of

> *Il me téléphonera à propos du contrat.*
> He'll telephone me in connection with the contract.

quant à as for

> *Quant aux résultats, téléphonez-moi demain.*
> As for the results, phone me tomorrow.

à raison de at the rate of

> *Les ouvriers sont payés à raison de 100 francs par pièce.*
> The workers are paid at the rate of 100 francs an item.

en raison de because of

> *L'expérience a été abandonnée en raison du mauvais temps.*
> The experiment was cancelled because of the bad weather.

par rapport à in comparison with

> *Par rapport à l'année dernière, nous avons augmenté notre part du marché.*
> In comparison with last year, we've increased our share of the market.

au sujet de about

> *Le directeur veut vous parler au sujet des examens.*
> The headmaster wants to speak to you about the exams.

à travers across / through

> *A travers les siècles notre ville a beaucoup évolué.*
> Our town has greatly developed through / over the centuries.

52 Prepositions governing verbs

(a) The use of *en* + present participle

In all cases except one, prepositions can only be followed by the infinitive form of the verb. The exception is *en* + present participle (by / on doing):

> *En entrant dans la pièce j'ai observé que quelques tableaux avaient été volés.*
> On entering the room I noticed that several pictures had been stolen.

> *L'avocat a gagné le procès en démontrant que l'inculpé avait été ailleurs au moment du crime.*
> The lawyer won the case by proving that the accused had been elsewhere at the time of the crime.

(b) The use of *à* + infinitive

Following the verb *être*, *à* can be used before the infinitive to mean
'to be -ed / for . . .':

> *C'est la lettre à mettre à la poste?*
> Is this the letter to be posted / for posting?
>
> *Est-ce que cette maison est à vendre?*
> Is this house for sale?

In notices, it is common to find a simplified form of this structure,
i.e. *à* + infinitive / noun + *à* + infinitive:

> *A louer.* <notice> For hire.
>
> *Bail à céder.* <notice> Lease to be let / available.

(c) The use of *après / pour / sans* + infinitive

(i) *après* + perfect infinitive = after doing

★ N.B. the present infinitive cannot be used in this construction.

> *Après avoir déposé ses bagages à la gare, Denise se dirigea vers le
> syndicat d'initiative.*
> After leaving her bags at the station, Denise headed for the tourist
> office.
>
> *Après s'être assurés que personne ne les regardait, ils ouvrirent le
> coffre de la voiture.*
> After checking that no one was watching them, they opened the
> boot of the car.

(ii) *pour* + present infinitive = in order to

Il a téléphoné pour dire qu'il arriverait vers cinq heures.
He phoned in order to say / to say he would arrive at about five
o'clock.

However, with verbs of movement, it is not normally necessary to
use *pour* to translate 'in order to'. The construction verb of
movement + infinitive suffices:

Elle est partie chercher sa belle-mère.
She's left to / in order to fetch her mother-in-law.

(iii) *sans* + present infinitive = without (doing)

Monsieur Corentin a annulé sans nous prévenir.
Mr Corentin cancelled without giving us any warning.

(d) Compound prepositions + infinitive

There are a small number of compound prepositions which can be
followed by the infinitive, such as *avant de*:

Il faut remplir la fiche avant de passer au guichet.
You must fill in the form before going up to the counter.

The most common compound prepositions + infinitive are:

afin de	in order to
avant de	before
de crainte de	for fear of
faute de	for lack of
jusqu'à	to the point of
au lieu de	instead of
à moins de	unless
de peur de	for fear of
près de	on the point of / near to
quant à	as for

(e) Verbs + preposition governing an infinitive

Some verbs are followed by a second verb in the infinitive with no
intervening preposition:

Je veux changer ce pullover.
I want to change this pullover.

In other instances a preposition (most commonly *à* or *de*, but
occasionally *par*) is required before the second verb in the
infinitive:

146

Il a décidé de partir.
He's decided to leave.

Qui a réussi à faire cet exercice?
Who's managed to do this exercise?

In almost all cases, only one structure (i.e. no preposition, or *à*, or *de*, or *par*) is possible, according to the verb which precedes the infinitive. There are a small number of verbs which may admit two or more constructions, with the meaning changing according to the structure used:

Je suis venu vous dire bonjour.
I've come to say hello.

Je viens de lui dire bonjour.
I've just said hello to him.

The most common verbs which fall into each category are listed in (i)–(iv) below.

(i) Verbs + infinitive (no preposition)
This category includes the 'modal' verbs (*devoir, pouvoir, savoir, vouloir*); verbs of perception (*entendre, voir,* etc.); and verbs of movement (*aller, venir,* etc.).

adorer	to love to
aimer	to like to (the construction *aimer à* + infinitive is still possible in literary style, but is becoming archaic)
aimer mieux	to prefer to
aller	to go / to be going to
apercevoir	to notice (-ing)
compter	to intend / plan to
croire	to believe / think (that) (e.g. *Je crois l'avoir vu.* I believe / think I've seen it.)
désirer	to wish to
détester	to hate to
devoir	to have to
écouter	to listen to (-ing)
entendre	to hear (-ing)
espérer	to hope to
faillir	nearly to (do) (e.g. *J'ai failli tomber.* I nearly fell.)
faire	to have / get something done (e.g. *J'ai fait réparer la voiture.* I've had the car repaired.)
falloir	to be necessary to

(Continued on next page)

Verbs + infinitive (no preposition) continued

s'imaginer	to imagine (-ing)
laisser	to let / allow something to be done / to have something done
oser	to dare to
paraître	to seem / appear to
penser	to intend / plan to
pouvoir	to be able to
préférer	to prefer to
regarder	to look at / watch (-ing)
savoir	to know how to
sentir	to feel (-ing)
souhaiter	to wish to
valoir mieux	to be better to
venir	to come to
voir	to see (-ing)
vouloir	to want to

(ii) Verbs + *à* + infinitive

aider (quelqu'un) à	to help (someone) to
amener (quelqu'un) à	to persuade (someone) to
s'amuser à	to have fun (-ing)
appeler (quelqu'un) à	to call upon (someone) to
apprendre à	to learn how to
apprendre (à quelqu'un) à	to teach (someone) to
s'apprêter à	to get ready / prepare to
arriver à	to manage to / succeed in (-ing)
aspirer à	to aspire to
s'attendre à	to expect to
autoriser (quelqu'un) à	to allow (someone) to
avoir (quelque chose) à (faire)	to have something to do
chercher à	to try to
commencer à	to begin to
condamner (quelqu'un) à	to condemn (someone) to (-ing)
consentir à	to agree to
continuer à	to continue to
contribuer à	to contribute to
décider (quelqu'un) à	to persuade (someone) to
se décider à	to make up one's mind to
demander à	to ask (permission) to
encourager (quelqu'un) à	to encourage (someone) to
enseigner (à quelqu'un) à	to teach (someone) how to
s'habituer à	to get used to
hésiter à	to hesitate to
inviter (quelqu'un) à	to invite (someone) to
laisser (à quelqu'un) à	to leave it up to someone to

se mettre à	to begin to
obliger (quelqu'un) à	to force someone to
parvenir à	to succeed in (-ing)
passer (le temps) à	to spend time (-ing)
pencher à	to be inclined to
persister à	to persist in (-ing)
se plaire à	to take pleasure in (-ing)
renoncer à	to give up (-ing)
résister à	to resist (-ing)
réussir à	to succeed in (-ing)
songer à	to think of (-ing) / plan to
suffire à	to be enough to
tarder à	to delay (-ing)
	(commonly used in negative: *ne pas tarder à* not to delay)
tenir à	to insist on (-ing) / be anxious to
venir à	to happen to
viser à	to aim to

(iii) Verbs + *de* + infinitive

Far more verbs are followed by *de* + infinitive than by any other preposition.

It is helpful to make a subgroup of verbs, mainly of asking or telling someone to do something, which are followed by *à* + person + *de* + infinitive:

> *Le client a demandé à la vendeuse de rembourser le prix de l'article.*
> The customer asked the shop assistant to give a refund on the price of the item.

conseiller à quelqu'un de	to advise someone to
défendre à quelqu'un de	to forbid someone to
demander à quelqu'un de	to ask someone to
dire à quelqu'un de	to tell someone to
écrire à quelqu'un de	to write to someone to
interdire à quelqu'un de	to forbid someone to
jurer à quelqu'un de	to swear to someone to
offrir à quelqu'un de	to offer someone to
ordonner à quelqu'un de	to order someone to
pardonner à quelqu'un de	to forgive someone for (-ing)
permettre à quelqu'un de	to allow someone to
persuader à quelqu'un de	to persuade someone to (but *persuader quelqu'un de* is also common)
promettre à quelqu'un de	to promise someone to
proposer à quelqu'un de	to suggest to someone to
suggérer à quelqu'un de	to suggest to someone to

Other common verbs followed by *de* + infinitive are:

accuser (quelqu'un) de	to accuse (someone) of (-ing)
affecter de	to pretend to
s'agir de	to be a question of (-ing)
avertir (quelqu'un) de	to warn someone of (-ing)
avoir peur / crainte de	to be afraid of (-ing)
brûler de	to long to
cesser de	to stop (-ing)
charger (quelqu'un) de	to get / instruct (someone) to
choisir de	to choose to
convenir de	to agree to
craindre de	to fear (-ing)
décider de	to decide to
empêcher (quelqu'un) de	to prevent (someone) from (-ing)
entreprendre de	to undertake to
essayer de	to try to
éviter de	to avoid (-ing)
faire semblant de	to pretend to
féliciter (quelqu'un) de	to congratulate someone on (-ing)
finir de	to finish (-ing)
manquer de	to fail / omit to
ne pas manquer de	to make sure of (-ing)
mériter de	to deserve to
négliger de	to neglect / fail to
omettre de	to omit to
oublier de	to forget to
prendre garde de	to take care not to
prier (quelqu'un) de	to beg someone to
refuser de	to refuse to
regretter de	to regret (-ing) / be sorry for (-ing)
remercier (quelqu'un) de	to thank (someone) for
risquer de	to risk (-ing)
rougir de	to blush / to be ashamed of (-ing)
soupçonner (quelqu'un) de	to suspect (someone) of (-ing)
se souvenir de	to remember to
supplier (quelqu'un) de	to beg someone to
tâcher de	to try to
tenter de	to try to
venir de	to have just (done)

(iv) Verbs + *par* + infinitive
There are a small number of verbs which require this construction:

commencer par	to begin / start by (-ing)
continuer par	to carry on / continue by (-ing)
finir par	to end up by (-ing)

SENTENCE STRUCTURE

The parts of speech analysed in the preceding sections are the 'building bricks' which must be combined to form sentences. These final sections of Part 1 outline some of the major rules and principles of sentence structure in French.

53 Simple and complex sentences

A simple sentence usually consists of a single clause:

Le taxi vous attend, Madame Joliffe.
The taxi is waiting for you, Madame Joliffe.

A more elaborate form of the simple sentence includes several main clauses, joined together by co-ordinating conjunctions (*et, mais, alors, puis,* etc.). Although the clauses form a single sentence, the word order and construction of each individual clause is not affected by the co-ordination:

Je voulais vous téléphoner, mais j'ai perdu votre numéro.
I wanted to phone you, but I've lost your number.

Complex sentences consist of one or more main clauses and one or more subordinate clauses. A subordinate clause may be introduced by a subordinating conjunction, or by a relative pronoun:

L'acteur qui jouait le rôle d'Hamlet s'est foulé la cheville pendant que nous répétions le dernier acte.
The actor who was playing Hamlet strained his ankle while we were rehearsing the last act.

Vous avez vu l'homme qui a volé mon sac?
Did you see the man who stole my handbag?

Some subordinating conjunctions may affect the tense or mood of the following verb, or the word order of the following clause (see below). In particular, note the subordinating conjunctions which require the use of the subjunctive (see section 44c). Relative pronouns may also affect the order of the following clause (see section 55b (ii)).

54 Declarative and interrogative sentences

A declarative sentence makes a statement. The word order in declarative sentences is standard, i.e. most simply, subject – verb – object:

> *Nous avons passé un bon séjour.*
> We had a pleasant stay.

An interrogative sentence asks a question. A declarative sentence may be turned into a question in three basic ways in French:

(i) The word order of the declarative sentence may be retained, but with the voice raised at the end of the sentence to mark a question. This form of interrogation is particularly common in colloquial speech:

> *Tu as déjà invité Raymond pour demain?* <coll.>
> Have you already invited Raymond for tomorrow?

(ii) The declarative sentence may be prefaced by *est-ce que*. This form is more common in spoken than written French (in the latter it may seem clumsy):

> *Est-ce que vous avez vu ce film?* <spoken>
> Have you seen that film?

(iii) Inversion of the subject and verb of the declarative sentence may be used. This form is more characteristic of formal spoken or written French, and may sound stilted in normal conversation. In particular, even in written French and certainly in conversation, it is rare to use inversion with the subject *je* and a verb in the present tense (but *puis-je* and *suis-je* are honourable exceptions).

When the subject of a verb is a pronoun, the inversion is straightforward:

> *Savez-vous si le train sera à l'heure?*
> Do you know if the train will be on time?

With verbs ending in a vowel, -*t*- must be introduced between the inverted verb and the subject pronouns *il / elle / on*. This is for reasons of pronunciation:

> *A-t-il répondu?* Has he answered?

Apprécie-t-on jamais les richesses de la vie? <formal>
Does one ever appreciate the treasures of life?

When the subject of a verb is a noun, simple inversion cannot be used. Instead, the noun stands at the start of the phrase, followed by the verb + the pronoun corresponding to the subject (i.e. complex inversion):

L'étudiant savait-il qu'il est défendu de fumer dans les salles de classe?
Did the student know that it is forbidden to smoke in the classrooms?

Questions introduced by interrogative adverbs, pronouns or adjectives (*comment? qui? quel?*) can also be formed in the three ways outlined above. This is illustrated in detail in section 62 (iii).

55 Other uses of inversion

Inversion of the subject and verb also occurs in a number of other contexts, in some cases being obligatory, in others a mark of good formal style. Inversion can be simple or complex. Simple inversion means that the subject and verb are inverted, whether the subject is a noun or pronoun. Complex inversion means that the subject and verb are inverted if the subject is a pronoun, but that if the subject is a noun, the corresponding pronoun must be supplied to make the inversion (cf. the rule for interrogation using inversion, section 54 (iii)).

(a) Cases where inversion is obligatory

(i) Simple inversion occurs when a verb such as 'he said' / 'she thought' is given after some direct speech or thought. Note that the inversion is necessary even if only one or two words of the direct speech or thought have occurred:

'Pourquoi', demanda-t-il, 'n'êtes-vous pas resté chez Madame Bertrand?'
'Why', he asked, 'didn't you stay with Madame Bertrand?'

'J'aimerais vous parler', dit Francine.
'I'd like to speak to you', said Francine.

(ii) Similarly, if the form 'it appears / seems' occurs part of the way through a sentence, simple inversion is required:

> *Il y a, paraît-il, un conflit.* There is, it appears, a conflict.
>
> *Lucille avait menti, semblait-il, lors du procès.*
> Lucille had lied, it seemed, during the trial.

(iii) Complex inversion is necessary when any of the following adverbs or adverbial phrases are the first item in the clause or sentence. However, if they occur later in the clause or sentence, the word order is unchanged.

> *aussi* and so
> *du moins* at least
> *à peine* scarcely
> *peut-être* perhaps
> *sans doute* probably / doubtless
> *toujours* nonetheless
>
> *Sans doute aimeriez-vous voir la maison?*
> *Vous aimeriez sans doute voir la maison?*
> Doubtless you'd like to see the house?

With *peut-être* and *à peine*, inversion may be replaced by *que* + standard declarative word order. This second construction is common in informal speech or writing:

> *Peut-être qu'il a oublié notre rendez-vous.* <informal>
> Perhaps he's forgotten our meeting.
>
> *A peine que j'ai reçu la nouvelle, mon frère m'a téléphoné.*
> <informal>
> I'd scarcely received the news when my brother phoned.

(b) Cases where inversion is optional

(i) The following adverbs and adverbial phrases are commonly followed by complex inversion when they are the first item in the clause or sentence. However, the inversion is not obligatory:

> *ainsi* thus
> *(et) encore* even so
> *rarement* rarely
> *en vain / vainement* in vain
>
> *Ainsi la vedette a-t-elle annoncé sa retraite.*
> *Ainsi, la vedette a annoncé sa retraite.*
> And so / Thus the star has announced her retirement.

(ii) After the relative pronouns *que / ce que / dont / ce dont / où*, simple inversion may occur when the subject is a noun (not a pronoun). This use of inversion tends to occur in formal style when the subject is substantially longer than the verb:

> *Je citai l'exemple du village où habitait mon grand-père maternel.* <formal>
> I gave the example of the village where my maternal grandfather was living.

(iii) Similarly, simple inversion may be used in the second half of a comparison (after *que*), especially when the subject is longer than the verb:

> *Ce produit est plus toxique que ne l'a dit le ministère de la Santé.* <formal>
> This product is more toxic than the Ministry of Health has said.

(iv) In formal or literary style, simple inversion of subject and verb may be used at the start of the sentence to throw the subject into relief. Equivalent emphasis in English may be achieved by the use of the subject 'there'.

> *Restent trois points à discuter.* <formal>
> There remain three points to be discussed.

56 Negation

(a) Negation of parts of speech other than verbs

When the word to be negated is a part of speech **other than** a verb (i.e. noun, pronoun, adjective, etc.) the negation is made by the use of *non, non pas* or *pas* before the word. *Non* or *non pas* (more emphatic) are characteristic of correct formal French, but *pas* is common in colloquial French:

> *L'ambassadeur cherche une résidence secondaire, non / non pas un appartement.* <formal>
> The ambassador is looking for a country residence, not a flat.

> *J'avais commandé une salade verte, pas des frites.* <coll.>
> I'd ordered a green salad, not chips.

(b) Negation of the verb: *ne . . . pas*

When negation applies to the verb, the main difference between English and French is that English uses the single word 'not', whereas the French negative is composed of two parts, *ne . . . pas,* placed on either side of the verb. In compound tenses, *ne* occurs before and *pas* after the auxiliary. If there are object pronouns before the verb, the *ne* will stand before the first object pronoun (see section 28c).

> *Non, je ne les achèterai pas.*
> No, I won't buy them.

> *Le P.-D.G. n'y est pas allé lui-même.*
> The Managing Director did not go there himself.

Note that in informal spoken French, it is very common for the *ne* to be dropped and only the *pas* retained. This trait may be imitated in writing to give the impression of colloquial speech:

> *Tu sais pas ce qui m'est arrivé?* <coll.>
> Don't you know what happened to me?

Conversely, in formal or literary French *pas* may be omitted (but *ne* retained) with the verbs *cesser / oser / pouvoir / savoir* (especially in the conditional) + infinitive:

> *Le directeur d'orchestre n'a pu terminer le morceau.*
> The conductor was unable to finish the piece.

When negation applies to a verb in the infinitive, it is usual for *ne pas* to be grouped together before the infinitive:

> *Il vaudrait mieux ne pas partir trop tard.*
> It would be better not to leave too late.

(c) Negation of the verb: other forms

Other forms of negation applying to a verb also consist of *ne* + a second negative particle, both of which are used in writing and formal speech:

> *ne . . . aucun (e)* + noun = no / none
> *ne . . . guère* scarcely <formal>
> *ne . . . jamais* never
> *ne . . . ni . . . ni* neither . . . nor
> *ne . . . nul (le)* + noun = no / none <formal>
> *ne . . . nulle part* nowhere
> *ne . . . nullement* in no way / not at all <formal>

>   ne ... personne no one
>   ne ... plus no longer
>   ne ... point not at all <literary>
>   ne ... que only
>   ne ... rien nothing

However, in informal speech the *ne* may be omitted from any of the above forms.

The word order with most of the above negative forms is identical to that with *ne ... pas*. The exceptions are:

(i) In compound tenses, the particles *aucun / ni ... ni / nul / nulle part / personne* follow the past participle:

>   *La police n'a pu trouver aucune trace de sang.*
>   The police could not find any traces of blood.
>
>   *Vous n'avez vu personne depuis deux heures?*
>   You haven't seen anyone since two o'clock?

(ii) The particle *que* is positioned immediately before the word it qualifies in the sentence:

>   *Je ne les ai invités que pour te faire plaisir.*
>   The only reason I invited them was to please you.
>
>   *Elle n'y est restée que deux minutes.*
>   She stayed there for only two minutes.

(iii) The particles *aucun* (+ noun) / *nul* (+ noun) / *personne* / *rien* can act as the subject of a verb, in which case they precede *ne* + verb:

>   *Aucun objet n'a été retrouvé.*
>   No item has been found.
>
>   *Rien ne justifie cette décision.*
>   Nothing justifies that decision.

(iv) The particles *jamais / nulle part* can precede *ne* + verb for emphasis:

>   *Jamais l'usine n'a connu de grève.*
>   Never has the factory known a strike.
>
>   *Nulle part ailleurs on ne trouverait une qualité pareille.*
>   Nowhere else would you find such quality.

157

(v) When the negative form *ne . . . personne* applies to a verb in the infinitive, the particle *personne* must follow the infinitive:

> *Il m'a demandé de n'informer personne de son départ.*
> He asked me not to tell anyone of his departure.

(d) Uses of the expletive *ne*

There are a number of occasions in French when what is apparently a positive declarative statement requires the inclusion of *ne* before the verb, at least in formal written style. In such cases, where *ne* is used without *pas* or any other negative particle, and without making the meaning of the clause negative, this is called the expletive (or pleonastic) *ne* – terms which imply that the *ne* is superfluous in that it does not contribute to the sense. It is therefore not surprising that the expletive *ne* is often omitted in informal and especially spoken French. However, in correct written French, it should be included. Note that if any of these constructions is used to express a true negative, *ne . . . pas* is required in the standard way.

An expletive *ne* is commonly required in the circumstances outlined in (i) – (vi) below.

(i) After the following subordinating conjunctions:

> *avant que* before
> *à moins que* unless
> *de peur que / de crainte que* lest / for fear that
>
> *Pourriez-vous contacter Pierre, à moins qu'il ne soit* (subj.) *en vacances?* <formal>
> Could you contact Pierre, unless he's on holiday?

(ii) After verbs and expressions of fearing, e.g. *avoir peur que*, *craindre que*:

> *Je crains que vous ne soyez* (subj.) *déçu.* <formal>
> I'm afraid that you may be disappointed.

(iii) After several other expressions, particularly:

> *empêcher que* to prevent
> *éviter que* to avoid
> *peu s'en falloir que* very nearly (to do)
> *prendre garde que* to take care (lest / not to)

Prenez garde que vous ne tombiez (subj.) *dans l'escalier!* <formal>
Take care that you don't fall down the stairs!

Nous avons évité que la situation ne se reproduise (subj.).<formal>
We have avoided a recurrence of the situation.

(iv) After *douter* used in the negative or interrogative, and after *ne pas nier que* + subjunctive:

Il ne doutait pas qu'elle ne préférât (subj.) *son rival.*
<formal / literary>
He did not doubt that she preferred his rival.

Vous ne niez pas que ce ne soit (subj.) *un échec?* <formal>
You don't deny that it is a failure?

(v) After *depuis que / il y a ... que / voici ... que / voilà ... que* + perfect or pluperfect, referring to the period of time (or point in time) when something last happened:

Beaucoup de choses ont changé depuis que je ne l'ai vu. <formal>
Many things have changed since I last saw him.

Voici six semaines qu'on ne s'est pas parlé en fait. <formal>
It's been six weeks since we last talked.

(vi) In the second half of a comparison (i.e. after *que*), which is implicitly negative:

Cette actrice danse mieux qu'elle ne chante. <formal>
This actress is better at dancing than singing. (i.e. she does not sing as well as she dances)

Nous avons plus de candidats que je ne l'aurais cru. <formal>
We have more candidates than I would have thought. (i.e. I did not think we would have so many candidates)

159

Contemporary functional language

COURTESY OR
LES FORMULES DE POLITESSE

Speaking good idiomatic French requires not only a sound grasp of grammar and vocabulary, but also a sensitivity to the different registers appropriate to situations. How speakers suit the form of expression to the social context has given rise to the branch of study known as sociolinguistics. You will notice in Part 2 of this book a particular emphasis on differing styles and registers. As an introduction, here are some guidelines on courtesy in common situations, i.e. *les formules de politesse.*

57 Greetings

(a) Saying hello

When greeting a stranger or an adult you know only slightly, remember to include the polite title:

Bonjour, Monsieur / Madame / Mademoiselle.

When a young woman ceases to be *Mademoiselle* and becomes *Madame* depends technically on her marital status, but, if you do not know this, on whether she looks under or over about 20 to 25 years old. If in doubt, err on the side of caution by using *Madame.*

For informal or closer acquaintances, it is common to say the name after the greeting:

Bonsoir, Monsieur Dufour.
Bonjour, Annabel.

Salut is a familiar greeting, equivalent to 'Hi!', much used among young people:

Salut, Carine! Hi, Carine!

An initial greeting is usually accompanied by a (firm) handshake (*serrer la main à quelqu'un*) if you do not know the person well, or between men. For family and closer friends, particularly two women or a woman and a man, it is usual to *faire la bise* – to kiss on both cheeks. The number of *bises* given varies from region to region, two being the minimum, four the maximum: follow local custom! Note that the French expect to shake hands or *faire la bise* not just on a first introduction, but on subsequent meetings. For example, if you work in an office, you usually shake hands with your colleagues every morning and possibly again to say goodbye in the evening.

(b) Saying goodbye

You will be familiar with the ubiquitous:

Au revoir! A bientôt!

However, there are a number of other ways of taking your leave, depending on what the other person is going on to do:

A la prochaine!
Hope to see you again at some time. (i.e. not in the immediate future)

Bon appétit!
Have a good meal! (they are going out to eat)

Bonne chance!
Good luck!

Bon courage!
Good luck! (when they are facing something difficult – an exam, a long hike, etc.)

Bon voyage!
Have a good journey! (for any mode of transport)

Bonne route!
Drive safely! (for car journeys)

Bonnes vacances!
Have a good holiday!

Bonne fin de séjour!
Enjoy the rest of your stay!

Bonne continuation!
All the best for the future! (e.g. to a student who has started learning English, and will be carrying on)

58 Titles and modes of address

(a) Titles

All (adult) strangers should be addressed as *Monsieur / Madame / Mademoiselle*, preferably in the first sentence you say to them:

> *Pardon, Madame, vous pourriez m'indiquer la gare routière?*
> Excuse me, could you show me the way to the bus station, please?

People in particular professional positions – priest, mayor, M.P. – should be addressed as:

> *Monsieur le curé*   *Madame le maire*
> *Monsieur le député*

When addressing someone you have already met, you may have to choose between surname and first name. While the younger generation tend to use first names as freely as the English / Americans, with older people be cautious about dropping courtesy titles unless you are invited to do so. Because of the complexity of the choice between *tu* and *vous* (see below), some older people may be reluctant to rush onto first-name terms.

To make a polite reference in the third person to someone, use:

> *le monsieur* the gentleman / the man
> *la dame* the lady
> *la jeune femme* the lady / young lady (approximately 18–40!)
> *la jeune fille* the young lady (approximately 13–20)

Note that *la fille* is not a polite way to refer to a girl (roughly translatable as 'chick'). But groups of young people may be described as *les gars* (the lads) and *les filles* (the girls).

(b) *Tu* or *vous?*

Even for the French, the choice between *tutoiement* – calling someone *tu* – and *vouvoiement* – calling someone *vous* – can be delicate. For the English speaker, used to the all-purpose 'you', it is both intriguing and baffling. The point is that there are not always hard-and-fast rules: practice varies according to generation, social context, individual background – and, ultimately, personality. While someone you address by their title and surname will almost always be *vous*, it does not follow automatically that the use of first names implies *tu*.

Books can and have been written on the subject. I offer just a few outlines below, but, remember, if in any doubt it is far better to use *vous* – and leave it up to your interlocutor to suggest:

> *On pourrait se tutoyer.*
> We could call each other *'tu'*.
>
> *Vous pouvez me dire 'tu'.*
> You can use *'tu'* to me.

And should anyone presume to call you *tu*, implying unacceptable familiarity (e.g. man chatting up an unwilling lady), you could use one of the following as a polite put-down:

> *Je n'aime pas qu'on me dise 'tu'.*
> I don't like being called *'tu'*.
>
> *Je préfère que vous continuiez de me vouvoyer.*
> I'd rather you kept calling me *'vous'*.

When should you always use *tu*, or always use *vous*?

- *Tu* is always used to speak to animals or young children (i.e. pre-adolescent).

- In the vast majority of families, relatives call each other *tu*. However, in some very *bourgeois* households, children may be expected to use *vous* to parents and older relatives, and there are still some couples in such households who use *vous* to each other (except perhaps at moments of intimacy!). Note that in-laws do not automatically qualify for *tutoiement*: it will depend on the particular family.

- Schoolchildren and students automatically call their peers *tu* – even if they have never met them before.

- *Vous* is of course always used to address two or more people – whatever the degree of acquaintance.

- Adult strangers should always be addressed as *vous* initially. If friendship blossoms later, you may slip into a *tutoiement*.

This leaves the tricky area not covered by the above indications, where you have a choice between *tu* and *vous*. Broadly, the following factors influence the choice:

(i) Age

This is probably the biggest single factor. It is very common to *tutoyer* friends or colleagues of roughly your own age, especially if you belong to the generation which grew up during or after 1968. It is far less common to slip into *tu* with those of an older generation, and it should usually be the older person who initiates the *tutoiement.*

(ii) Sex

In a non-amorous context, two women or two men tend to move more quickly to *tu* than two people of opposite sexes.

(iii) Professional status

It is common for peers to use *tu* (e.g. teachers at the same school, or a group of salesmen), but with someone who is your superior (headteacher, personnel manager, etc.) both you and the other party will use *vous*. It is perhaps still true that *tutoiement* among peers comes more naturally in working-class environments, but many younger professionals who have been through university also use *tu* freely with their peers.

(iv) Personality and context

This is the indefinable element: if you feel you are establishing a good rapport with a new friend or colleague, the movement from *vous* to *tu* may cement it.

Finally (for reference rather than use!), in a heated argument – e.g. between motorists – complete strangers may use *tu* as a form of insult.

59 Introductions

As in English-speaking countries, if you have to introduce two people to each other, you should start by telling the woman the man's name, or the older person the younger person's name. In a formal context, introductions will run as follows:

> *Madame Lafayette, permettez-moi de vous présenter Monsieur Magnien, mon ancien professeur d'anglais.*
> *Bonjour, Monsieur.*
> *Enchanté, Madame.*

> Mrs Lafayette, may I introduce you to Mr Magnien, my former English teacher?
> How do you do?
> How do you do?

In an informal situation, you can introduce two people more simply:

> *Isabelle, je crois que tu ne connais pas mon copain Jean?*
> *Non, en fait. Bonjour, Jean.*
> *Bonjour, Isabelle.*

> Isabelle, I don't think you've met my friend Jean?
> No I haven't. How do you do? / Hello!
> How do you do? / Hello!

60 Asking someone to repeat something

A familiar situation for the foreigner conversing with Francophones is the need to slow down the other person and ask him / her to repeat things. In a formal situation, use:

> *Pardon, est-ce que vous pourriez répéter votre question, s'il vous plaît?*
> Excuse me. Would you mind repeating your question please?

> *Pardon, je ne vous ai pas bien entendu.*
> I'm sorry, I didn't hear / understand what you said.

> *Pardon, est-ce que vous pourriez répéter cela un peu plus lentement?*
> I'm sorry. Would you mind repeating that a little more slowly?

In informal situations, use:

> *Comment? Qu'est-ce que tu as dit?*
> Sorry, what did you say?

> *Je n'ai pas bien compris.*
> I didn't quite get what you said.

> *Doucement!*
> Slow down a bit!

The brief (impolite) interjection, exactly equivalent to 'What?', is *Quoi?*

61 Gestures

Ultimately, you cannot speak authentic French unless you adopt some of the Gallic gestures – facial expressions, expansive gestures with the hands, shrugs of the shoulders.

The 'paralanguage' of gesture is closely allied to verbal communication: just observe French conversations in the street, and you will see what I mean!

Some gestures are international, others specific to one culture and language. Here are some common French ones, and the expressions which often accompany them.

Mon oeil!

"You're pulling my leg"
"A likely-tale!"

Il est bourré

"He's plastered"

Bof!

"I haven't got a clue"
"What do you expect me to do?"

faire un pied de nez

to cock a snook

T'es dingue?

"Are you mad?"
"Are you off your rocker?"

Je m'en fiche!

"Get lost!"
"I couldn't care less about that!"

INFORMATION AND ADVICE

To ask for information and advice, an interrogative (question) form is often required (see section 54).

When you are talking about information or advice, note the use of both singular and plural forms of the following:

un conseil a piece of advice
des conseils several pieces of advice

une information an item of information or news
des informations several items of information or news

une nouvelle a piece of news
des nouvelles several pieces of news

un renseignement an item of information
des renseignements several items of information

RENSEIGNEMENTS :

Le Musée des Beaux-Arts est ouvert tous les jours, sauf le mardi de 9h30 à 12h00 et de 14h00 à 18h30. En juillet et en août, le musée est ouvert tous les jours de 9h30 à 18h30. Du 7 mai au 30 septembre 1990, visites commentées pour les groupes, sur demande.

En juillet et en août, visites commentées pour tous les visiteurs à 10h00 et à 14h30. Adresse : Musée des Beaux-Arts, 40 place Saint Corentin, face à la Cathédrale. Tél. : 98.95.45.20 Tarif : Plein tarif 20 F, Demi tarif 10 F

---

62 Asking for information

(i) To stop someone (in the street) to ask for information, use:

S'il vous plaît, Monsieur / Madame / Mademoiselle . . .
Pardon, Monsieur / Madame / Mademoiselle . . .
Excuse me . . .

(Remember to include the formal title, otherwise you will sound impolite.)

(ii) To ask for information in a formal context (Tourist Office, reception desk, etc.), use one of the following:

Pourriez-vous me dire où se trouve la salle 304?
Could you tell me where to find room 304?

Pourriez-vous m'expliquer le système de carnets de bus?
Could you explain to me how to use the books of bus tickets?

Pourriez-vous m'indiquer l'Hôtel de Ville?
Could you show me / point out the Town Hall?

Nous avons besoin de plusieurs renseignements sur votre société.
We need some information about your company.

Nous aurions besoin d'un chauffeur.
We'd like to find a chauffeur.

Est-ce que vous savez comment téléphoner aux Etats-Unis?
Do you know how to phone the States?

C'est bien la résidence universitaire ici?
This is the university hall of residence, isn't it?

(iii) Other questions may require one of the following interrogative forms:

Comment pouvons-nous le contacter? <formal>
Nous pouvons le contacter comment? <coll.>
How can we get in touch with him?

Où peut-on acheter des timbres? <formal>
C'est où qu'on peut acheter des timbres? <coll.>
Where can I / we buy stamps?

Pourquoi le médecin ne vous a-t-il pas répondu? <formal>
Pourquoi le médecin ne vous a pas répondu? <coll.>
Why didn't the doctor give you an answer?

Quand faudrait-il rendre le livre? <formal>
Il faudrait rendre le livre quand? <coll.>
When should the book be returned?

Qu'avez-vous demandé? <formal>
Vous avez demandé quoi? <coll.>
What did you ask for?

Quel type / Quelle sorte de parfum désirez-vous? <formal>
Tu cherches quel type / quelle sorte de parfum? <coll.>
What sort of perfume are you looking for?

Lequel / Laquelle des deux préférez-vous? <formal>
Tu préfères lequel / laquelle des deux? <coll.>
Which of the two do you prefer?

A quelle heure la bibliothèque est-elle ouverte? <formal>
La bibliothèque est ouverte à quelle heure? <coll.>
What time is the library open?

Qui a envoyé le télex? <formal>
C'est qui qui a envoyé le télex? <coll.>
Who sent the telex?

63 Asking for advice

(i) More formal ways of requesting advice include:

Nous aimerions vous demander conseil.
We'd like to ask your advice.

Veuillez nous envoyer vos propositions à ce sujet.
<formal, for letters only>
We should be grateful to receive your proposals / suggestions on
this point.

Pourriez-vous nous suggérer comment procéder?
Could you advise us on how to proceed?

Pourriez-vous nous proposer une autre date?
Could you suggest another date to us?

*Pourriez-vous nous recommander / indiquer un bon hôtel dans le
même quartier?*
Could you recommend us a good hotel in the same area?

Est-ce que vous nous conseillez de lui confier la tâche?
Do you advise us to entrust the task to him?

Que devrais-je faire à votre avis?
In your opinion, what should I do?

(ii) In informal colloquial contexts, ways of asking advice include:

Tu peux me donner conseil?
Can you give me some advice?

J'ai besoin de ton avis.
I need your opinion.

Je dois lui téléphoner, ou il vaut mieux écrire?
Should I ring him, or would it be better to write?

Tu crois que c'est la personne qu'il me faut?
Do you think he / she's the right person for the job?

64 Giving information

To give information and advice, there exists a range of expressions
from the tentative suggestion to the affirmative statement. For the
use of the imperative to give orders, see section 47.

(i) To introduce the required information in a letter or in formal
speech:

> *En réponse à votre question, je me permets de citer notre
> brochure.*
> In reply to your question, allow me to cite our brochure.

> *Pour répondre à ce que vous me demandez, j'aimerais signaler que
> nous ouvrirons un nouveau magasin en janvier.*
> In reply to your question, I'd like to point out that we are opening
> a new shop in January.

(ii) In less formal contexts, information will often be introduced by
one of the following phrases (which may serve to suggest the
speaker's authority):

> *Alors, . . . / Eh bien, . . .*
> Well, . . .

> *Alors, écoutez, ce que je peux vous dire, c'est que . . .*
> Well, look, what I can say is that . . .

(iii) If your information takes the form of instructions, use one of
the following forms:

> *Prenez la deuxième rue à gauche après les feux.* (imperative)
> Take the second street on the left after the traffic lights.

> *Vous continuez tout droit jusqu'au carrefour.* (present tense)
> You have to carry straight on until you get to the crossroads.

> *Vous sonnerez et ma soeur vous fera entrer.* (future tense)
> If you ring the doorbell my sister will let you in.

65 Giving advice

(i) The following expressions range from the tentative to the emphatic:

Il serait prudent d'attendre sa réponse.
It would be advisable to wait for his answer.

Vous me permettriez d'ajouter une proposition? <formal>
Might I add a suggestion?

On pourrait envisager une réunion à Paris dans deux mois.
We might think along the lines of a meeting in Paris in two months' time.

Si vous n'y voyez pas d'inconvénient, ce que vous pourriez faire c'est la chose suivante.
If you don't have any objection, this is what you could do.

Je vous conseillerais de consulter mon collègue.
I'd advise you to speak to my colleague.

(Et) Si vous alliez la chercher à la gare?
How about going and fetching her from the station?

Pourquoi ne pas y aller à pied?
Why don't we walk there? / Why not walk there?

Vous avez pensé à lui demander de l'aide?
Have you thought of asking him for help?

Tu as songé à demander à l'Office du Tourisme?
Have you thought of asking at the Tourist Office?

Vous avez tout intérêt à suivre ce stage.
It would be very much in your interests to go on this course.

Tu sais, ce que tu pourrais faire, ce serait de lui écrire.
You know, if you wanted, you could try writing to him.

(ii) To stress that the advice is your own point of view, you can preface your remarks by:

Personnellement, je le ferais. Personally, I would do it.

Pour vous parler franchement, je ne lui ferais pas confiance.
Just between you and me, I wouldn't trust him.

A votre place / à ta place, j'accepterais sa demande.
If I were you, I'd accept his / her request.

A mon avis, tu ferais mieux de ne rien dire.
In my view, you'd do better to say nothing / you'd be better off saying nothing.

66 Dissuasion

The expressions in the previous section on giving information and advice can be used negatively to dissuade someone from a course of action. The following expressions are also useful:

Il est formellement déconseillé de présenter plus d'une seule lettre de candidature. <formal notice>
You are strongly advised not to send more than one application letter.

Veuillez ne pas toucher les fleurs. <formal notice>
Please refrain from touching the flowers.

Veillez à ne pas casser les objets exposés dans la vitrine! <formal notice>
Take care not to break the articles on display!

Vous auriez tort de lui en tenir rigueur. <formal>
You shouldn't hold it against him.

Je vous déconseille tous ces hôtels.
I can't recommend any of these hotels to you. / I must warn you all these hotels are bad.

Méfiez-vous des pickpockets!
Watch out for pickpockets! Beware pickpockets!

Je me demande si vous ne feriez pas mieux d'attendre quelques jours.
I wonder whether you shouldn't wait for a few days.

A votre / ta place, je ferais très attention de ne pas perdre mon temps.
If I were you, I'd be careful not to waste my time.

Moi, j'hésiterais à y retourner.
Personally, I wouldn't choose to go back there.

Attention, tu risques de payer une amende!
Careful, you might end up with a fine!

Tu auras des ennuis si ça continue. <coll.>
You'll be in trouble if it carries on.

AUTHORIZATION AND REQUESTS

Public notices frequently concern permission and prohibition – what you can and cannot do. In conversation, different structures will express the same concepts in more or less formal ways. Don't commit Gladstone's error of addressing Queen Victoria as though she were a public meeting! See section 47 for the use of imperative forms.

67 Seeking permission

(i) More formal ways of seeking permission include:

Me permettriez-vous de m'absenter cet après-midi?
Would you allow me to excuse myself from this afternoon's session?

Nous serait-il possible de revenir sur ce point?
Might we go back over that point?

Il est permis de fumer dans la cour?
Is smoking allowed in the courtyard?

Cela vous gênerait / dérangerait si je ne vous accompagnais pas?
Would you mind if I didn't come with you?

(ii) To seek permission in informal contexts:

Ça vous dérange si je ne reviens pas demain?
Do you mind if I don't come back tomorrow?

Nous avons le droit à deux plats?
Are we allowed / entitled to two courses?

Puis-je / Je peux vous poser une question?
Can I ask you something?

Je pourrais peut-être emprunter ta voiture?
Do you think I could borrow your car?

68 Granting permission

(i) Public notices express authorization concisely:

Un seul bagage à main est autorisé.
Only one piece of hand luggage is permitted.

Chiens acceptés. Dogs allowed.

To indicate that an establishment has been granted recognition by a formal body, you will see the adjectives *autorisé* or *agréé*:

Centre de formation autorisé Recognized training centre

Centre de sports nautiques agréé Official water sports centre

Fournisseur agréé du roi Suppliers by appointment to His Majesty

(ii) In other formal contexts, permission is conveyed as follows:

Nous ne voyons aucun inconvénient à ce que vous le remettiez (subj.) *à demain.*
We have no objection to your delaying it until tomorrow.

Nous acceptons volontiers que vous nous envoyiez (subj.) *la réponse par fax.*
We are quite agreeable to your sending your reply by fax.

Je vous dispense de ce devoir.
There is no need for you to do this exercise.

A la rigueur, vous pouvez me consulter demain.
If necessary, you can consult me tomorrow.

Vous êtes libres de visiter jusqu'à quatre heures.
You are free to look around until four o'clock.

Vous avez le droit à deux exemplaires gratuits.
You're entitled to two free copies.

Vous avez le droit de retirer jusqu'à 2000 francs.
You're entitled to withdraw up to 2000 francs.

(iii) To grant permission informally:

Bien sûr, tu peux prendre la clé.
Of course you can have the key.

Aucun problème si tu veux prendre un jour de congé demain.
That's fine if you want a day off tomorrow.

A la limite, tu peux te passer des formalités.
If need be, you can skip the formalities.

69 Prohibitions

In many contexts, prohibition can be expressed by using in the negative the structures for giving permission listed above. There also exist the following expressions specific to prohibition.

(i) Public notices express prohibition concisely:

Défense de marcher sur la pelouse.
Do not walk on the grass.

Stationnement interdit.
No parking.

Il est interdit d'afficher.
No posters allowed. / Stick no bills.

(ii) In other formal contexts, prohibition is expressed by:

Je vous interdis / défends d'en reparler.
I forbid you to bring up the subject again.

Je m'oppose formellement à ce que vous acceptiez (subj.) *le projet.*
I am most strongly opposed / I cannot possibly agree to your accepting the project.

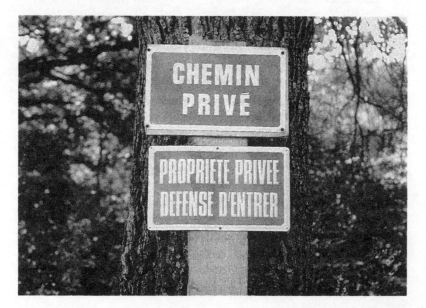

Je ne peux absolument pas autoriser votre absence.
I certainly cannot give permission for you to be absent. / I must refuse you permission to be absent.

Il ne faut pas se présenter au guichet sans pièce d'identité.
You cannot go up to the counter without some proof of identity.

(iii) To tell someone not to do something in informal contexts:

Je te défends de sortir ce soir. <e.g. parent to child>
You're not to go out tonight.

Tu ne dois pas trop travailler.
You mustn't work too hard.

Fais attention de ne pas le déranger.
Make sure you don't disturb him.

Tu ne peux pas payer. Il n'en est pas question!
You can't pay. It's out of the question!

70 Offering to do something

Offers, requests and orders can vary from the peremptory to the most discreetly worded. In sections 70–2 you will see that the use of a conditional as opposed to the present indicative (e.g. *je pourrais* in place of *je peux*) often provides a more polite form, appropriate in cases where you do not know the other party well.

See also some of the phrases in sections 64–5. We can distinguish broadly between expressions appropriate to formal correspondence and transactions, and those occurring in everyday contexts.

(i) In formal correspondence or transactions, the following forms may be used:

Nous sommes heureux de proposer à tous nos clients un rabais de 10 pour cent.
We are pleased to offer all our customers 10 per cent discount.

Aujourd'hui nous proposons des réductions au rayon de bricolage.
Today there are special offers in the D.I.Y. department.

Nous espérons que tous les actionnaires voudront accepter cette prime.
We trust that all our shareholders will accept this bonus.

La maison est prête à céder le bail.
The firm is willing to give up the lease.

(iii) In everyday contexts, offers may take the form of statements, questions or imperatives.

Je peux le contacter, si tu veux.
I can get in touch with him if you like.

On pourrait l'inviter vendredi prochain.
We could invite him / her for next Friday.

Je suis très heureux de le faire à ta place.
I'm perfectly happy to replace you / to do it for you.

J'irais volontiers à votre place.
I would be quite happy to replace you / to go in your place.

Je m'occuperai du courrier tant que vous serez en vacances.
I'll take care of the mail while you're on holiday.

Je me chargerai de leur expédier les nouveaux tarifs.
I'll be responsible for sending them the new prices.

Voulez-vous que je vienne (subj.) *demain?* <fairly formal>
Do you wish me to come tomorrow?

Vous voulez / Tu veux que je réserve (subj.) *deux places?*
<less formal>
Do you want me to book two seats?

Je te dépose à la gare? <coll.>
Shall I drop you at the station?

Si ça vous / te rend service, je pourrais garder Marie demain.
If it helps, I could look after Marie tomorrow.

Prévenez-moi si vous avez besoin de quelque chose. <formal>
Do let me know if there's anything you need.

N'hésitez pas à nous faire signe si vous repassez à Angers.
Please do let us know if you're ever back in Angers.

Tu me dis si tu as besoin de moi. <coll.>
Let me know if you need me.

Comptez sur moi pour la réunion de dimanche.
You can rely on me for Sunday's meeting.

Laissez-moi au moins payer les cafés.
Do let me at least pay for the coffees.

Ah, non, les glaces sont pour moi. Je t'invite. <coll.>
No, I'll pay for the ice-creams. They're my treat.

71 Making requests

Again, it is helpful to distinguish between expressions used in public notices or formal correspondence, as opposed to everyday ways of making requests. See also section 63.

(i) Requests made over public-address systems or in notices use certain formulae:

Les passagers du vol Air France 805 sont priés de se présenter à la porte numéro 4.
Passengers on Air France flight 805 are invited to proceed to gate 4.

Les passagers motorisés sont invités à rejoindre leurs véhicules.
Passengers with cars are asked to return to their vehicles.

Vous êtes invités à respecter la zone non-fumeur.
Please respect the no-smoking area.

La ligne est occupée. Veuillez rappeler plus tard.
The line is engaged. Please call back later.

(ii) In formal correspondence, other formulae occur (see also sections 106 and 111):

Veuillez avoir l'obligeance de nous envoyer vos coordonnées.
Please be kind enough to notify us of your address and telephone number.

Nous vous serions obligés de respecter ces délais.
We respectfully ask you to observe these deadlines.

Nous vous saurions gré de nous en envoyer un échantillon.
We should be grateful if you could send us a sample.

Je vous serais reconnaissant(e) de bien vouloir noter la nouvelle adresse.
I would ask you to note the new address.

(iii) In less formal circumstances, requests can be made more or less directly:

Nous aimerions visiter le Musée de l'Homme.
We'd like to visit the Museum of Mankind.

Je pourrais vous demander un service?
Could I / Might I ask a favour of you?

Pourriez-vous me prêter votre livre? Could you lend me your book?

Tu peux me prêter 200 francs? Can you lend me 200 francs?

Giving orders

Obviously, the imperative can be used to give orders (see section 47), but in many situations you may wish to avoid the instruction sounding too brusque, and alternative expressions may be more suitable. When using the imperative, remember that *donc* or *je vous en prie / je t'en prie* can be added afterwards for politeness or emphasis.

> *Entrez donc.* Do come in.
>
> *Servez-vous, je vous en prie.* Please do help yourself.
>
> *Fais comme chez toi, je t'en prie.* Please do make yourself at home.
>
> *Rappelez-moi demain.* Call me back tomorrow.
>
> *Voulez-vous me rappeler demain?* Would you call me back tomorrow?
>
> *Vous me rappelez demain?* Could you call me back tomorrow?

AIMS, RESPONSIBILITIES AND ABILITIES

Expressions concerning your aims, responsibilities and abilities rely on a range of verbs or verbal phrases and adjectives. With some key verbs, such as *devoir* or *pouvoir*, different shades of meaning can be conveyed by the distinction between the present indicative and the present conditional.

73 Aims and intentions

The future tense, or the use of *aller* + infinitive, can convey definite aims and intentions. Other verbs can convey more provisional future projects.

Nous assisterons à la réception demain.
We shall attend tomorrow's reception.

Ils vont rester trois nuits à Montpellier.
They're going to spend three nights at Montpellier.

J'espère consacrer deux semaines à ce numéro du magazine.
I hope to spend two weeks on this issue of the magazine.

Vous comptez passer au bureau demain?
Are you intending to call into the office tomorrow?

Nous envisageons de lancer ce produit en mars.
We're planning to launch this product in March.

Tu as l'intention de changer de travail?
Are you planning to look for a new job?

J'ai nullement l'intention de déménager cette année.
I have no intention at all of moving this year.

Nous cherchons à louer une villa dans le Midi.
We're hoping to / thinking of renting a villa in the South of France.

Ils ont prévu un rendez-vous pour deux heures. <formal>
They've organized a meeting for two o'clock.

Nous nous proposons le but suivant. <formal>
We are setting ourselves the following goal.

Nous nous proposons de nommer deux cadres supérieurs.
<formal>
We are intending to appoint two senior managers.

183

★ Note also when expressing intentions the different constructions using *décider*, and the appropriate prepositions in each case.

> *Nous avons décidé d'acheter une vieille ferme.*
> We've decided to buy an old farmhouse.

> *Ils se sont décidés à quitter Bruxelles.* (more emphatic)
> They've decided / definitely made up their minds to leave Brussels.

> *La compagnie est décidée à embaucher cinquante ouvriers.* (more emphatic)
> The company has made the decision / resolved to take on fifty workers.

74 Responsibilities and obligations

Remember that impersonal expressions of obligation when followed by *que* (*il faut que, il est nécessaire que*) require the subjunctive (see section 44c (ix)).

★ The forms *obliger* ('to oblige'), *être obligé*, or *obligatoire* ('obligatory') occur far more commonly in French than their counterparts in English.

(i) Public notices expressing obligation use set formulae:

> *Uniforme obligatoire.*
> Uniform compulsory.

> *Pièce d'identité obligatoire.*
> Proof of identity is required.

> *Aucun rendez-vous sans préavis.*
> Meetings by appointment only.

(ii) In other contexts, formal expressions of responsibility or obligation include:

> *J'ai le triste devoir de vous informer que nous ne pourrons pas renouveler votre contrat.*
> I regret to inform you that we cannot renew your contract.

> *Il revient à moi de clore cette séance.*
> It falls to me to bring this session to a close.

> *Il faudrait que vous nous envoyiez* (subj.) *des arrhes avant la fin du mois.*
> We require you to send us a deposit by the end of the month.

J'ai exigé qu'ils m'envoient (subj.) *une pièce de rechange.*
I have insisted that they should send me a spare part.

Il est obligatoire de réserver les places huit jours avant le spectacle.
Seats must be reserved a week before the performance.

Il est indispensable de nous contacter le plus tôt possible.
It is essential that you contact us at the first opportunity.

Il sera nécessaire que nous en reparlions (subj.).
We shall have to raise the matter again.

Il est de mon devoir de justifier notre réponse. <literary>
I think it my duty to offer an explanation of our reply.

Il m'incombe de nous représenter à ce colloque. <formal>
It falls to me to represent us at this conference.

(iii) Less formal expressions of obligation or responsibility include:

Vous devez appeler ma soeur.
You must phone my sister.

Vous devriez la prévenir.
You should warn her.

Il faut mettre ces chaussures à la poubelle.
These shoes have to be / must be thrown away.

Il nous faut aller à la mairie. / Il faut que nous allions (subj.) *à la mairie.*
We have to / need to go to the Town Hall.

Je suis obligé de travailler samedi.
I have to work on Saturday.

Ils m'ont obligé à partir plus tard.
They made me late getting away.

Je suis censé la remplacer la semaine suivante.
I'm meant to replace / stand in for her next week.

Il faut que tu sois (subj.) *là. C'est indispensable.*
You must be there. It's essential.

(iv) Adverbs or adverbial phrases can be added to emphasize the degree of obligation:

Tu dois absolument le voir.
You really / absolutely must see him.

Il faut surtout l'inviter.
It's essential to invite him.

185

En tout cas, lui, il est indispensable.
Whatever happens / Anyway, we can't manage without him.

Il faudra que tu viennes (subj.) *bon gré mal gré.*
You must come whether you like it or not.

Au pis-aller, il faudra trouver quelqu'un d'autre.
If it comes to the worst, we'll have to find someone else.

Vous ne devez y toucher en aucun cas.
You mustn't touch it whatever happens.

75 Abilities and competence

★ Note that French distinguishes between *pouvoir* – to be able to do something physically – and *savoir* – to know how to do something, e.g.:

Tu sais nager?
Can you swim? (Do you know how to swim?)

Tu peux nager plus vite?
Can you swim faster? (Are you physically capable of swimming faster?)

(i) Formal expressions of ability or competence include:

Nous cherchons une secrétaire qui sache (subj.) *parler russe.*
We are looking for a secretary who speaks Russian.

Je crois avoir l'aptitude nécessaire pour réussir.
I believe I have the necessary qualities to succeed.

Nous ne sommes pas encore en mesure de vous confirmer les prix.
We are not yet in a position to confirm the prices.

Etes-vous à même de diriger ce projet?
Do you think you are capable of running this project?

Ma mère est toujours sous le choc; elle n'est pas en état de vous recevoir.
My mother is still in a state of shock; she's not in a position to see you.

Il m'est impossible de garantir cette nouvelle.
I cannot / am unable to confirm the news.

Nous nous trouvons dans l'impossibilité d'accepter votre proposition. <formal correspondence>
We are regretfully unable to accept your proposal.

186

(ii) Less formal expressions of ability or competence include:

Tu es arrivé à le repérer?
Have you managed to track him down?

J'arrive à peine à le croire.
I can hardly believe it.

Je n'y peux rien.
I can't do anything about it. / There's nothing I can do.

PERSONAL TASTES

To express likes, dislikes and preferences, French has a range of verbs and adverbial phrases. In most cases, adverbs can be added which express a more precise shade of feeling. Remember that structures on the lines of 'to like / dislike / prefer someone to do something' require the subjunctive (see section 44c (ii) and (iii)).

76 Likes

(i) French has two main ways of expressing 'I like something': the verbs *aimer* (usage identical to 'like' in English) and *plaire* (used in the third person: *quelque chose me plaît*, literally 'something pleases me'):

> *J'aime la musique classique.*
> *La musique classique me plaît.*
> I like classical music.

> *J'aime les grands magasins de Bordeaux.*
> *Les grands magasins de Bordeaux me plaisent.*
> I like the department stores in Bordeaux.

For the construction 'I like' + verb, only *aimer* is commonly used:

> *Vous aimez aller au théâtre?* Do you like going to the theatre?

> *Ils aiment que nous passions* (subj.) *les voir le dimanche.*
> They like us to drop in on them on Sundays.

The conditional of *aimer* is used for polite requests or suggestions:

> *Nous aimerions acheter des oeufs de ferme.*
> We'd like to buy some free-range eggs.

> *Vous aimeriez reprendre la discussion demain?*
> Would you like to resume talks tomorrow?

(ii) To qualify the extent to which one likes something, the following adverbs can be used:

J'aime		I like this artist	
	beaucoup cet artiste.		a lot.
	énormément		tremendously
	surtout		particularly
	pas mal < coll. >	I quite like this artist.	

(iii) Other verbs / verbal phrases to express likes include:

Ils adorent la planche à voile.
They love windsurfing.

Ils raffolent du nouvel album. < coll. >
They're mad over the new album.

Ce qu'ils aiment le mieux, c'est de rester à l'hôtel.
What they most like is to stay at the hotel.

Ma fille a un faible pour ce chanteur. < coll. >
My daughter's keen on this singer.

La poterie artisanale fait toujours plaisir aux touristes.
Handmade pottery is always popular with the tourists.

Vous avez envie de manger au restaurant?
Do you feel like eating out?

Ça te dit de passer le week-end chez nous? < coll. >
Would you like to come to us for the weekend?

★ **(iv)** It is difficult to give a single translation of the English verb 'to enjoy'. Note the following possibilities:

Le concert vous a plu?
Did you enjoy the concert?

Nous avons apprécié / admiré son interprétation du rôle.
We enjoyed his interpretation of the role.

Cela / Ça m'a fait grand plaisir de faire votre connaissance.
I've very much enjoyed meeting you.

J'ai été très heureux / -euse d'en parler avec vous.
I've enjoyed talking it over with you.

Les enfants se sont bien amusés chez mes parents.
The children enjoyed themselves at my parents.

77 Dislikes

As well as the idioms listed below, the phrases used to express likes, given above in section 76, can be used in the negative to express dislikes. As indicated, expressions of dislike range from the formal to the markedly colloquial.

★ To express strong dislike, use *détester*, not *haïr*. The latter is given in many dictionaries, but is now almost totally confined to literary style.

> *Il déteste les réunions qui durent trop longtemps.*
> He hates meetings which last too long.

> *Elle déteste qu'on la fasse* (subj.) *attendre.*
> She hates being kept waiting.

> *Le ton de cette lettre me déplaît.* < formal >
> I do not like the tone of this letter.

> *Il m'est pénible de vous faire cette réflexion.* < formal >
> I do not like having to make this criticism of you.

> *Nous avons trouvé cette brochure affreuse.*
> We thought this brochure was terrible.

> *Il a pris ses nouveaux collègues en aversion.*
> He has taken a dislike to his new colleagues.

> *Elle a pris ses nouveaux collègues en grippe.* < coll. >
> She's taken a dislike to her new colleagues.

> *J'ai horreur des grands immeubles.* < coll. >
> I can't stand tall blocks of flats.

> *Je supporte très mal les longs voyages en car.*
> I'm no good at long coach journeys.

> *L'idée ne m'emballe pas.* < coll. >
> I'm not wild on the idea.

> *C'est pas terrible.* < coll. >
> It's not much good / not much cop.

> *Franchement, ça ne me dit rien.* < coll. >
> To be honest, it's not my scene / it doesn't appeal.

78 Preferences

★ (i) As well as the verb *préférer*, French commonly uses the expressions *aimer mieux* (personal preference) and *valoir mieux* (general suitability / preferability).

> *Tu préfères y aller tout de suite ou plus tard?*
> Would you prefer to go there straight away or later?

> *Ils préfèrent qu'on ne fasse* (subj.) *pas de bruit après dix heures.*
> They prefer us not to make any noise after ten o'clock.

> *Ils aiment mieux réserver à l'avance.*
> They prefer to make an advance booking.

190

J'aime mieux que vous me parliez (subj.) *directement.*
I'd prefer you to speak to me personally.

Il vaut mieux lui téléphoner.
It's better / preferable to phone him / her.

Il vaudrait mieux que vous reveniez (subj.) *demain.*
It would be better if you came back / could come back tomorrow.

(ii) Preferences can also be expressed by the following verbs or adverbs:

Le directeur a favorisé les élèves de terminale. < formal >
The headmaster has given preference to those in the Upper Sixth.

Le Conseil Municipal a privilégié les transports collectifs.
< formal >
The Town Council has given priority to public transport.

Je penche pour une solution plus simple.
I tend to favour a simpler solution.

Elle travaille le soir de préférence.
She prefers to work in the evening.

Je prendrais plutôt celui-là. I'd rather take that one.

Ils aiment autant l'un que l'autre. They like both equally.

79 Indifference

It is important to distinguish between polite expressions suggesting you are equally happy to do any of the things under discussion and statements of a total lack of interest.

(i) Polite expressions include:

C'est comme vous voulez. Ça m'est complètement égal.
It's up to you. I don't mind at all.

Je n'ai aucune préférence. < more formal >
I have no particular preference.

Oui, n'importe lequel. Yes, I don't mind either / whichever.

(ii) To express a lack of interest:

Ça ne me dit rien. < coll. >
It's not my scene. / It doesn't appeal.

Bof! < coll., accompanied by a Gallic shrug of the shoulders >
I couldn't care less.

DIFFERENT VIEWPOINTS

Agreement, disagreement and opinions can be expressed briefly and categorically, often by one or two words, but in other contexts it may be important to phrase your point of view tactfully. The expressions suggested below include the most important brief responses as well as more formal expressions. Of course, paralinguistic gestures and facial expressions can play an important role in conveying your precise feelings!

80 Agreement

(i) To convey immediate agreement in a conversation:

Oui, d'accord. Yes, that's all right / O.K.

Oui, tout à fait. Yes, exactly.

C'est vrai. That's right.

Bien entendu. Of course.

Évidemment. Obviously.

Effectivement. <more formal > Exactly.

C'est exact. < more formal > Precisely.

Certes. < more formal, and can suggest a concession > I'd agree.

(ii) To elaborate on the fact that you agree when talking informally:

★ Remember the very basic distinction between *avoir raison* (a person in the right) and *être juste* (something is right / accurate).

Je crois que tu as raison. I think you're right.

Oui, c'est juste, il est déjà parti. Yes, that's right, he's already left.

There are a number of expressions of agreement which include the words *d'accord* or *accord*:

Alors, tu es d'accord pour demain? < coll. >
It's O.K. by you for tomorrow then?

Nous sommes d'accord sur ce problème.
We're in agreement about this problem.

Ils sont tombés d'accord quand ils se sont parlé.
They agreed / came to an agreement when they met.

Il faut nous mettre d'accord sur la date.
We'll have to agree / come to an agreement on the date.

Mon père a donné son accord.
My father's agreed / said yes.

(iii) In more formal conversations or in writing, agreement can be expressed by:

Vous avez raison de dire que nous devrions nous méfier du sondage.
You're right to say we should not trust the opinion poll.

Je suis prêt à vous apporter / accorder mon soutien.
I'm willing to give / lend you my support.

Notre société est favorable à cette proposition.
Our company is agreeable to this proposal.

Ayant regardé le dossier, je trouve votre demande tout à fait acceptable.
Having looked at the file, I find your request quite acceptable.

Vous acceptez les grandes lignes du schéma?
Do you accept the outline of the scheme?

Nous adhérons aux conclusions apportées par nos recherches.
We stand by the conclusions drawn from our research.

81 Disagreement

The expressions listed under sections (ii) and (iii) above can be used in the negative to express disagreement. For the use of the subjunctive after verbs of thinking / saying used negatively, see section 44c (vii).

(i) To convey immediate disagreement in a conversation:

Non, pas du tout! No, not at all / that's wrong.

C'est faux. That's wrong.

C'est inexact. < formal > That's untrue.

Absolument pas. Certainly not. / There's no question of it.

Sûrement pas. < formal > Certainly not.

Tu n'y comprends rien. You just don't understand.

Tu n'as rien compris. You've got it all wrong.

(ii) To elaborate on the fact that you disagree in an informal conversation:

★ Remember the distinction between *avoir tort* (a person is wrong / incorrect) and *être faux* (something is wrong / incorrect):

> *Je suis sûr que vous avez tort.* I'm sure you're wrong.
>
> *Ce que vous avez dit hier est faux.*
> What you said yesterday is wrong.
>
> *Je ne suis pas de ton avis.* I don't agree with you.
>
> *Pour les enfants, ce n'est pas le cas.*
> It's not true as far as the children are concerned.
>
> *Tu raisonnes faux.*
> Your argument's wrong. / Your argument doesn't stand up.
>
> *Vous vous trompez là-dessus.*
> You're wrong on that score.

(iii) In more formal conversations and writing, disagreement can be expressed by:

> *Je regrette que je ne partage* (subj.) *pas votre avis.*
> I am afraid I don't agree with you.
>
> *Je suis désolé de vous contredire, mais c'est inexact.*
> I am sorry to have to contradict you, but that's untrue.
>
> *Il me semble que vous faites une erreur.*
> I rather think you're wrong.
>
> *Les faits sont en contradiction avec votre supposition.*
> The facts contradict what you're suggesting.
>
> *Je dois m'opposer formellement à cette solution.*
> I must express my strong opposition to this solution.
>
> *Nous rejetons catégoriquement cette assertion.*
> We categorically deny that statement.

82 Hedging your bets

There are times when you are asked to agree or disagree, but you would rather hedge your bets! The following expressions may be useful.

(i) Short responses:

C'est possible. Possibly. / It may be so.

Sans doute. (can express a degree of disapproval) Possibly.

Oui, plus ou moins. Yes, more or less.

A la limite, oui. If you really want. / I suppose so.

Oui, en principe. Yes, I suppose so. / Yes, probably.

Ah, tu crois / vous croyez? Do you think so?

(ii) To convey your unwillingness to commit yourself, in more formal contexts:

Si je ne me trompe pas, c'est possible.
If I'm not mistaken, it may be so.

Je n'y ai pas vraiment réfléchi.
I haven't really given it much thought.

Je préfère ne pas me prononcer.
I'd prefer not to commit myself.

Je n'aimerais pas m'engager sur cette question.
I'd prefer not to comment on that question.

83 Opinions

(i) To suggest that what follows is a personal opinion, you can preface remarks by:

A mon avis . . . / Pour moi . . . In my opinion . . .

Personnellement . . . Personally . . .

Pour ma part . . . As far as I'm concerned . . .

Selon leur porte-parole . . . According to their spokesperson . . .

D'après le journaliste . . . According to the journalist . . .

A en croire cet article . . . (implies some doubt)
According to this article . . . / If you can believe this article . . .

Au dire de Gide . . . < literary >
According to Gide . . . / In the words of Gide . . .

(ii) Verbal expressions to state a personal opinion include:

Je suis de l'avis qu'on devrait le consulter.
I believe that we should consult him.

Nous avions l'impression que cela ferait l'affaire.
We were under the impression / We believed that it was what was needed.

Elle pense / trouve que je n'aurais pas dû refuser le poste.
She thinks I shouldn't have refused the job.

Ils considèrent que ce serait trop compliqué. < formal >
They think it would be too complicated.

Je jugeais votre démarche périlleuse. < formal >
I considered your action to be dangerous.

Ils estiment que le premier témoin a menti. < formal >
They think the first witness lied.

(iii) To ask someone else for their opinion:

Quel est ton / votre avis?
What's your view / opinion?

Que pensez-vous du tunnel sous la Manche?
What do you think of the Channel tunnel?

J'aimerais savoir ce que vous pensez de notre nouveau président.
< formal >
I'd like to hear what you think of our new president.

Quelle est votre attitude en ce qui concerne ce projet? < formal >
What is your view on this project?

84 Expressing approval

For expressions used to seek approval, see section 67.

(i) At the simplest level, approval may be expressed by a single adjective or short phrase of exclamation:

Parfait! Perfect!

Super! / Chouette! / Formidable! < coll. > Great! / Fantastic!

Génial! < coll. > Brilliant!

Excellente idée! An excellent idea!

Volontiers! Sure! / Willingly!

(ii) To elaborate on approval in an informal context:

Tu as tout à fait raison de te plaindre.
You're quite right to complain.

Je comprends bien que tu aies (subj.) *envie de participer.*
I quite understand that you want to take part.

Je trouve que c'est une excellente idée.
I think it's an excellent idea.

J'applaudis ta décision.
You've made the right decision.

(iii) To elaborate on approval more formally:

Ma femme pense le plus grand bien de votre travail.
My wife thinks very highly of your work.

Mon mari a trouvé votre présentation admirable.
My husband was very impressed with your presentation.

Ils ont fini par approuver la création d'une nouvelle gare routière.
They finally approved the construction of a new bus station.

Nous vous félicitons d'avoir trouvé une maison si charmante!
How clever of you to find such a lovely house!

Le grand mérite de ce jeune architecte, c'est qu'il sait écouter ses clients.
That young architect's great strength is that he listens to his clients.

Le comité a accueilli vos propositions avec enthousiasme.
The committee greeted your proposals warmly.

Le Trésorier a porté un jugement favorable sur ce dossier.
The Treasurer approved this file.

85 Expressing disapproval

Disapproval can be expressed by using the expressions in sections (ii) and (iii) above in the negative, as well as by the expressions given below. Adverbs provide a useful way to nuance the degree of your disapproval.

★ Remember that constructions of 'regret that . . .' are followed by the subjunctive (see section 44c (iii)).

(i) To express disapproval by a short exclamation:

Ah non, ce n'est pas possible! Oh, no. You can't!

C'est moche! < coll. > It's horrible!

!! *C'est dégueulasse!* < slang > It's foul! / It makes you puke!

! *Quel culot!* < slang > What a bloody cheek!

C'est scandaleux! It's outrageous!

C'est honteux! < formal > It's a disgrace!

(ii) To elaborate on disapproval in an informal context:

Elle est contre l'avortement.
She's against / opposed to abortion.

Je suis complètement opposé à ce que tu y restes (subj.) *tout seul.*
I'm not going to hear of your staying there on your own.

J'en ai assez des personnes qui laissent tomber des papiers partout.
< coll. >
I'm fed up with people who drop litter everywhere.

Il m'en veut d'avoir vendu l'appartement.
He doesn't like the fact that I sold the flat.

C'est dommage que tu n'aies (subj.) *pas fait de progrès.*
It's a pity you didn't make any progress.

(iii) To elaborate on disapproval in a formal context:

Ils ne pouvaient admettre que je prenne (subj.) *la responsabilité.*
They couldn't accept my taking responsibility.

La direction est formellement opposée aux nouveaux tarifs.
The management is strongly opposed to the new prices.

Je dois protester contre cette injustice.
I must protest at this injustice.

Le syndicat s'est élevé contre les modifications.
The union protested at the changes.

Nous désapprouvons toute tentative de réaménagement des halles.
We disapprove of any attempt to rebuild / redesign the covered market.

Il est fort regrettable que vous ne nous ayez (subj.) *pas avertis plus tôt.*
It is most unfortunate that you did not advise / warn us earlier.

DEGREES OF CERTAINTY AND POSSIBILITY

86 Certainty

Affirmative expressions of certainty and probability take the indicative (see section 43). Compare this with the predominance of the subjunctive in sections 88 and 90, for possibility and doubt.

(i) To convey certainty by a single word or short phrase:

Il viendra demain? – Certainement.
Will he come tomorrow? – Definitely.

On les invitera? – Ah, oui, sûrement.
Will they be invited? – Yes, of course.

Ce candidat sera élu, c'est sûr.
This candidate is sure to be elected.

(ii) Fuller expressions of certainty rely mainly on adjectives or verbs. Among the useful expressions based on adjectives are, first, those with a personal subject:

Je suis sûr que vous réussirez.
I'm sure you'll succeed.

Vous êtes sûr d'avoir mis la lettre à la poste?
Are you sure you posted the letter?

Elle est convaincue que c'est la meilleure solution.
She's convinced it's the best solution.

Nous sommes persuadés de son innocence.
We're convinced of his innocence.

Ils sont persuadés qu'il y a eu une erreur.
They're convinced there's been a mistake.

Il ne changera pas d'avis. Il était absolument formel.
He won't change his mind. He was emphatic.

Expressions using the impersonal subjects *ce* or *il* to convey certainty include:

> *Il n'y aura pas de session d'été. C'est formel.*
> There won't be a summer session. That's final.

> *Il est certain que beaucoup d'enfants ont besoin d'aide.*
> It is certainly the case that many children need help.

> *Il est sûr maintenant que le Ministre va démissionner.*
> It is now certain that the Minister is going to resign.

> *Il est incontestable que ces appartements sont vétustes.* < formal >
> It is undeniable that these flats are badly run down.

(iii) Expressions of certainty based on verbs generally belong to a more formal register of speech, and include:

> *Le gouvernement a confirmé cette annonce.*
> The government has confirmed this announcement.

> *La responsable a confirmé qu'il y a eu dix blessés.*
> The woman in charge confirmed that ten people had been injured.

> *Vous pouvez certifier qu'il s'agit d'un employé de la maison?*
> Can you vouch for the fact that the person is employed here?

> *Je peux garantir votre sécurité.*
> I can guarantee your safety.

> *Nous avons garanti que la livraison serait faite demain.*
> We guaranteed that the delivery would be made tomorrow.

> *Je vous assure que j'ai déposé l'argent sur mon compte hier.*
> I assure you that I put the money in my account yesterday.

> *Ils ont attesté qu'aucune expérience n'a eu lieu sur des animaux.*
> They testified / affirmed that no experiments on animals had taken place.

★ (iv) The word *doute* can be used in several expressions to make a categorical affirmation – but remember that *sans doute* means 'probably'.

> *Il n'y a aucun doute qu'elle l'emportera la prochaine fois.*
> Of course she'll win next time.

> *Il ne fait aucun doute qu'il a bien mérité son succès.*
> There's no doubt that his success is well deserved.

> *Sans aucun doute ils le payeront plus cher en Suisse.*
> There's no doubt they'll pay more for it in Switzerland.

(v) Two expressions with *certitude* convey a similar degree of affirmation:

> *J'ai la certitude qu'il m'a déjà posé la même question.*
> I'm absolutely sure he's already asked me the same question.

> *Elle sait avec certitude qu'elle sera envoyée au Japon.*
> She knows that she'll definitely be sent to Japan.

87 Probability

For the use of the conditional tense to suggest that a statement is probably true, but not guaranteed, see section 45b (iii).

(i) To convey that something is probable in a word or short phrase:

> *Tu assisteras au mariage? – Sans doute.*
> You'll go to the wedding? – Most probably. / Probably.

> *Ils sont partis au bord de la mer? – Vraisemblablement.*
> Have they gone away to the sea? – Probably. / It's quite likely.

> *C'est ta mère qui a téléphoné? – Probablement.*
> Was it your mother who rang? – Probably.

> *Il fait du théâtre maintenant? – Paraît-il.*
> He's doing some acting now, is he? – So it seems.

> *Vous allez poser le carrelage vous-même? – En principe.*
> Are you going to lay the tiles yourself? – That's the idea.

(ii) The combination of the verb *pouvoir* with the adverb *bien* provides the basis for a number of expressions of probability:

> *Je peux bien prendre le train.*
> I may well take the train.

> *Ils pourraient bien téléphoner ce soir.*
> They're likely to phone this evening.

> *Il se peut bien que j'aie* (subj.) *besoin de ton garage.*
> I may well need your garage.

(iii) Other structures expressing probability include:

Il est très / fort probable qu'elle jouera le rôle de la reine.
It's very / highly likely that she'll play the role of the queen.

Il y a de fortes chances que j'obtiendrai une bourse.
There's a very good chance that I'll get / obtain a grant.

Ils sont censés arriver par le train de six heures.
They're meant to be arriving on the six o'clock train.

Ils devraient vous rembourser tout de suite.
They should reimburse you immediately.

88 Possibility

Most constructions expressing 'the possibility that . . .' or 'doubt that . . .' are followed by the subjunctive (see section 44c (vii and viii)). Compare this with the predominance of the indicative in expressions of certainty (section 86) and probability (section 87).

(a) Brief responses to indicate that something is possible include:

Il est malade? – C'est possible.
Is he ill? – Possibly. / Maybe.

Tu auras besoin de la voiture? – Ça se peut.
Will you need the car? – Possibly. / I might.

Tu pourrais le remplacer? – Oui, éventuellement.
Could you replace him? – Possibly.

(b) More elaborate expressions of possibility often use the verb *pouvoir* :

Ils ont pu perdre leur chemin. They may have lost their way.

Il se peut que la voiture soit tombée (subj.) *en panne.*
It's possible the car's broken down.

A la limite, on pourrait croire qu'il l'a fait exprès.
You might almost think he did it deliberately.

★ **(c)** The adverb *peut-être* expresses possibility. It needs care on two counts.

- It never governs the subjunctive: even *peut-être que* is followed by the indicative.

- If *peut-être* is the first item in the clause, you must either invert the verb and subject which follow, or use *peut-être que* with normal word order. If *peut-être* comes later in the clause, there is no need for *que* or inversion.

Peut-être faudrait-il lui écrire. <formal>
Perhaps we should write to him.

Peut-être qu'il a oublié l'heure. <less formal>
Perhaps he's forgotten the time.

Je vais peut-être mettre une petite annonce dans le journal.
I might put an advert in the paper.

(d) Possibility can also be expressed by a range of idiomatic phrases:

Il est possible que je sois (subj.) *en mesure de vous aider.*
It may be that I'm in a position to help you.

Nous vous soutiendrons dans la mesure du possible.
We shall support you as far as we can.

Elle a fait tout son possible pour que tu sois (subj.) *nommé.*
She did all that she could to have you appointed.

Ce que vous proposez, c'est très faisable.
What you're suggesting is quite possible / do-able.

Tu crois que c'est un projet réalisable?
Do you think the plan could work / is feasible?

C'est un successeur éventuel, à mon avis.
He's a possible successor in my opinion.

89 Impossibility

The expressions used to denote possibility listed in section 88 can be used in the negative to suggest impossibility.

(i) Other adjectival expressions for suggesting impossibility include:

La date nous est impossible.
The date's impossible for us. / We can't make the date.

Mon fils a toujours tenté l'impossible.
My son's always tried to do the impossible.

J'aimerais faire le tour du monde, mais c'est un rêve irréalisable.
I'd like to travel round the world, but it's an impossible dream.

L'accord était voué à l'échec. <formal>
The agreement was impossible / bound to fail.

(ii) Other structures to express impossibility:

> *Il est impossible qu'elle soit* (subj.) *exclue de l'équipe.*
> She can't possibly be excluded from the team.

> *Votre démarche a rendu impossible tout compromis.*
> Your action has made any compromise impossible.

> *Il est hors de question que vous le fassiez* (subj.) *à sa place.*
> <formal>
> It's out of the question for you to do it instead of him / her.

> *Il est exclu de penser qu'elle revende* (subj.) *le mobilier.* <formal>
> There is no question of her selling off the furniture.

 90 Doubt

(i) French possesses the verb *douter*, the cognate of the English verb 'to doubt'. The constructions in which it is used can perplex English speakers. Note especially that *se douter de quelque chose* means 'to suspect that something is the case' (i.e. the opposite of doubt).

> *On peut douter de l'authenticité de la signature.*
> There is reason to doubt whether the signature is authentic.

> *Je doute qu'il ait eu* (subj.) *le temps de tout faire.*
> I doubt if / that he had time to do everything.

> *Il est parti? Je m'en doutais.*
> Has he left? I thought as much.

> *Je me doutais de ses intentions.*
> I suspected those were his intentions.

(ii) Other verbal constructions to express doubt:

> *J'ai hésité à vous réveiller.*
> I wasn't sure whether I should wake you up.

> *Je me suis méfié de ce qu'il a dit.*
> I wasn't sure whether to trust what he said.

> *On peut avoir des doutes sur ses capacités.*
> There's reason to doubt his abilities.

> *Rien n'indique qu'il ait décidé* (subj.) *de revenir.*
> There's nothing to suggest he's decided to come back.

(iii) Adverbial and adjectival constructions to express doubt:

Il ne sera pas forcément d'accord.
He won't necessarily be in agreement.

Je serais difficilement convaincu.
It would be difficult to persuade me.

Il est fort peu probable que le magasin soit (subj.) *ouvert dimanche.*
It's very unlikely that the shop's open on Sunday.

Il est douteux qu'elle se représente (subj.) *aux prochaines élections.*
<formal>
It is doubtful whether / unlikely that she will stand again at the next election.

L'issue est incertaine.
The outcome is undecided / unsure.

Le verdict était contestable.
The verdict was debatable / open to question.

C'est une procédure tout à fait aléatoire.
It's a completely random procedure. / The procedure leaves everything to chance.

COMPLAINTS AND EXPLANATIONS

91 **Making complaints**

(i) To make polite or tentative complaints:

> *Je suis désolée, mais j'ai demandé la pointure 37 et la chaussure que vous m'avez donnée, c'est du 36.*
> I'm sorry, but I asked for a size 37, and the shoe you've given me is size 36.

> *Je crois qu'il y a une erreur dans l'addition.*
> I think there's a mistake in the bill.

> *Je crains qu'on ne se soit mal compris* (subj.) / *qu'il n'y ait eu* (subj.) *un malentendu.*
> I'm afraid there's been a misunderstanding.

> *Est-ce que je pourrais vous demander de vérifier la somme?*
> Could I ask you to check the amount?

> *Est-ce que vous voulez rectifier la facture?*
> Would you correct the bill / invoice?

(ii) To make more forceful or official complaints:

> *Nous aimerions parler au propriétaire tout de suite.*
> We'd like to speak to the owner straightaway.

> *Je dois me plaindre de la condition de la chambre.*
> I must complain about the state of the bedroom.

> *Je dois vous signaler que cet escalier est très dangereux.*
> I must point out to you that this staircase is very dangerous.

> *Mon mari ne peut plus supporter ce bruit.*
> My husband can't stand that noise any longer.

> *La direction ne peut plus ignorer votre manque d'assiduité.*
> The management can no longer overlook your irregular time-keeping.

> *Si vous ne retirez pas votre accusation, je serai obligé de porter plainte.* <formal>
> If you do not withdraw your accusation, I shall be forced to make an official complaint.

Je vais déposer une plainte contre l'administration du collège.
<formal>
I'm going to lodge an official complaint against the college
administration.

**(iii) There are various adjectives to suggest that something is
unacceptable, which can be used to strengthen complaints:**

Nous trouvons cette démarche inadmissible.
We find this course of action quite unacceptable.

Je juge son attitude inacceptable.
I consider his attitude unacceptable.

Ces enfants sont franchement insupportables. <coll.>
These children are absolutely impossible.

C'est un manque de politesse inexcusable.
It shows an unforgivable lack of manners.

Je trouve cette remarque impardonnable.
I consider that remark unforgivable.

Votre question est déplacée.
Your question is impertinent / inappropriate.

92 Making apologies

In French, as in most languages, there are set formulae for making
your apologies, and accepting those of someone else.

★ Constructions expressing 'I am sorry that / I regret that ...' are
followed by a subjunctive (see section 44c (iii)).

(i) Apologizing to friends / close colleagues:
At the simplest level, you may use one of these exclamations:

Oh, pardon! Sorry!

Je m'excuse! My apologies! / I'm sorry!

Je suis désolé! I'm really sorry!

Slightly more elaborate ways of apologizing and admitting responsibility include:

C'est ma faute. Excuse-moi. It's my fault. Sorry.

Je m'en veux beaucoup. I'm really cross with myself for it.

J'espère que tu ne m'en veux pas / ne m'en voudras pas?
I hope you're not too upset with me.

Je suis désolé de t'avoir dérangé.
I'm really sorry to have disturbed you.

If you want to apologize but also suggest you are not entirely to blame, use *Je suis désolé*, and one of the following:

Je ne l'ai pas fait exprès.
I didn't do it on purpose / deliberately.

Je ne pouvais pas faire autrement.
I had to. / There was nothing else I could do.

J'essayais simplement de vous aider.
I was only trying to help you.

Je n'avais pas le choix. I didn't have any choice.

(ii) More formal apologies in conversation:

To apologize briefly:

Oh, pardonnez-moi! (e.g. if you tread on someone's toes)
Oh, I'm sorry!

Excusez-moi! (when you've done something wrong)
I'm sorry. / My apologies.

C'est moi le coupable. It's my fault. / I'm to blame.

To elaborate on your apologies:

Nous sommes désolés que les produits ne soient (subj.) *pas arrivés.*
We're very sorry that the products haven't arrived.

Je me sens très coupable de ne pas vous avoir prévenu.
I feel very bad that I didn't warn you. / It's my fault, I really should have warned you.

Je crains de vous avoir blessé. I'm afraid I've upset you.

J'espère que vous ne m'en tiendrez pas rigueur?
I hope you won't hold it against me?

Le directeur regrette infiniment que notre photographe ne soit (subj.) *pas ici aujourd'hui.* <formal>
The manager is extremely sorry that our photographer isn't here today.

Le maire-adjoint vous prie d'accepter ses excuses. Il est retenu ailleurs.
The deputy mayor sends his apologies. He had another engagement.

Je ne peux que renouveler nos excuses pour ce fâcheux incident.
<formal>
I can only reiterate our apologies for this unfortunate incident.

(iii) To apologize in formal correspondence:

Veuillez nous excuser de vous répondre avec un certain retard.
Please forgive us for the delay in replying to you.

Je vous prie d'excuser notre erreur, que nous avons déjà rectifiée.
I apologize for our error, which we have already corrected.

Nous regrettons de devoir vous informer que notre magasin sera fermé pendant tout le mois d'août.
We regret to inform you that our store will be closed for the whole of August.

Nous regrettons que cette pièce de rechange ne soit (subj.) *pas actuellement disponible.*
We regret that this spare part is not currently available.

La compagnie tient à présenter ses excuses pour le bruit occasionné par les travaux.
The company apologizes for the noise caused by the building works.

93 Accepting apologies

(i) To accept apologies without reservation:

Ce n'est pas grave. It doesn't matter.

Je t'en prie. / Je vous en prie. Don't mention it. / Forget it.

Il n'y a pas de quoi. That's all right.

Ne t'en fais pas. / Ne vous en faites pas. Don't worry.

N'en parlons plus. Let's forget it.

(ii) To accept an apology, but stress that the fault must not happen again:

Ça va, pourvu que tu ne recommences (subj.) *pas!* (especially to children)
That's all right. Just don't do it again.

Je vous excuse, mais vous devriez faire mieux attention à l'avenir.
I forgive you, but you should take more care in future.

Espérons du moins que cela ne se reproduira pas. <formal>
Let us hope it doesn't happen again.

94 Asking for and offering explanations

★ Note that while the verb *expliquer* is used to translate 'to explain', the reflexive form *s'expliquer* often suggests 'to quarrel' (or, in colloquial usage, 'to have a fight') and *une explication* can suggest an acrimonious exchange of views.

> *Ils se sont expliqués hier.* They had a quarrel yesterday.
>
> *Elle a eu une explication avec ses parents.*
> She had a quarrel / a showdown with her parents.

(i) Asking someone for an explanation:

This may be a neutral request for information (as in the first two examples below), or a demand that the person addressed should justify himself / herself (as in the subsequent examples).

> *Est-ce que vous pourriez m'expliquer les modes d'emploi?*
> Could you explain the instructions / instruction book to me?
>
> *Tu peux m'expliquer ce qui se passe?*
> Can you explain to me what's happening?
>
> *Je vous demanderais de m'expliquer votre décision.*
> May I ask you to explain your decision?
>
> *J'espère du moins que vous pourrez expliquer votre absence.*
> I trust you can account for your absence.
>
> *Comment voulez-vous justifier ce retard?*
> How do you intend to justify this delay?

(ii) Offering an explanation:

(For an explanation which is also an apology, see section 92.)

> *Vous aimeriez que je vous explique* (subj.) *la structure de notre société?* <more formal>
> Would you like me to explain to you our company's structure?
>
> *Si tu veux, je peux te montrer comment l'appareil fonctionne.*
> If you like, I'll show you how the machine works.
>
> *Permettez que je vous explique* (subj.) *notre raisonnement.*
> Allow me to explain our reasoning to you.
>
> *Si vous permettez, j'essayerai d'éclairer la raison de ce malentendu.*
> May I try to explain the reason for this misunderstanding?
>
> *Il voulait me faire comprendre les obstacles.*
> He wanted to explain the obstacles to me.

Mon collègue pourra vous rendre compte de nos progrès.
My colleague will be able to tell you about our progress.

Je dois m'excuser de ma conduite hier.
I must apologize for my conduct yesterday.

Je ne veux pas y aller. Je vais prétexter un rendez-vous.
I don't want to go. I'll make the excuse that I've got a meeting.

95 Giving explanations

Other sections of this book also provide useful material on giving explanations. See particularly the sections on essay writing (119–21) and reports (122–3), and on giving advice and information (62–5).

Constructions for giving explanations rely heavily on prepositions / prepositional phrases, conjunctions, or verbs of explanation.

(i) Prepositions / prepositional phrases:

Il n'a pas pris la voiture à cause du brouillard.
He didn't take the car because of the fog.

La bibliothèque sera fermée le mardi en raison des congés annuels. <more formal>
The library will be closed on Tuesdays due to staff holidays.

Le stock est épuisé en vertu des demandes exceptionnelles. <more formal>
Supplies have been exhausted due to exceptional demand.

Par suite d'encombrements, nous ne pouvons pas répondre à votre appel. <formal notice / announcement>
Since all the lines are engaged, we cannot answer your call.

Etant donné le mauvais temps, la fête sera annulée.
In view of the bad weather, the fete will be cancelled.

★ *Etant donné* is invariable.

Vu les sacrifices que vous avez dû faire, on essayera de vous récompenser. <formal>
In view of the sacrifices you've had to make, we shall try to recompense you.

★ *Vu* is invariable in this structure.

Grâce à sa générosité, nous pourrons réparer l'église.
Thanks to his generosity, we shall be able to repair the church.

Les fouilles ont été achevées à l'aide d'une prestation municipale.
<formal>
The excavations were completed with the help of a grant from the
local council.

*Ils augmenteront leur chiffre d'affaires au moyen d'un
investissement considérable.* <formal>
They'll increase their turnover thanks to large-scale investment.

Devant les accusations, il a dû retirer sa candidature.
In view of the accusations, he had to withdraw from the election.

Malgré la pluie, on est sortis. We went out despite the rain.

Le concert a eu lieu en dépit des protestations des riverains.
<formal>
The concert took place, despite protests from local residents.

Faute de personnel, nous sommes obligés de fermer à midi.
Due to staff shortages, we have to shut / are shut at lunchtime.

(ii) **Conjunctions which indicate an explanation:**

Je ne peux pas venir parce que j'ai un dîner ce soir.
I can't come because I've got a dinner tonight.

*Il faudra augmenter les contrôles de sécurité puisqu'il y a un risque
d'attentat.* <formal>
Security checks will have to be increased since there is a risk of an
assassination attempt.

*Elle a reçu sa formation au Mexique, ce qui fait qu'elle parle bien
espagnol.*
She did her training in Mexico, which means / so she speaks good
Spanish.

*Nous avons perdu deux employés, si bien que le courrier a pris du
retard.*
We've lost two members of staff, so we're behind with the mail.

*On a besoin d'un étudiant en sciences naturelles. Voilà pourquoi
j'ai pensé à toi.*
They need someone studying biology. That's why I thought of you.

Cet auteur est très apprécié, car il traite un sujet d'actualité.
<formal>
This author is highly thought of because he writes about a topical
subject.

Je me chargerai des invitations, à condition que vous m'envoyiez
(subj.) *la liste des adresses.*
I'll take care of the invitations, provided you send me the address
list.

Nous sommes rentrés hier, bien qu'ils / quoiqu'ils aient voulu (subj.)
nous garder un jour de plus.
We came back yesterday, although they wanted us to stay a day
longer.

Je n'ai pas sonné de peur que / de crainte que vous ne soyez (subj.)
déjà couché.
I didn't ring the bell in case you were already in bed.

(iii) Verbal constructions used to give an explanation:

L'érosion résulte surtout des intempéries.
The erosion is mainly caused by adverse weather.

La querelle provenait d'un conflit de tempéraments. <formal>
The quarrel stemmed from a clash of temperaments.

Ce sujet de doléance remontait aux conditions de vie à l'époque.
<formal>
This grievance could be traced to living conditions at the time.

On peut attribuer son succès à son enthousiasme.
His / Her success can be attributed to his / her enthusiasm.

La crise s'explique par le manque d'investissement.
The crisis can be explained by the lack of investment.

INVITATIONS

For making informal suggestions and proposals, see section 65. For formal written or printed invitations, see section 113.

96 Giving an invitation

(i) When talking informally, to friends or close colleagues:

Tu as envie de venir boire un pot?
Would you like to come for a drink?

Tu viendras arroser la sortie de mon livre?
Will you come to the drinks party for the launch of my book?

Nous allons pendre la crémaillère demain. J'espère que vous pourrez venir tous les deux.
We're having a housewarming party tomorrow. I hope you can both come.

Je t'invite à venir fêter la nouvelle au restaurant.
Let me take you out to lunch / dinner to celebrate the news.

On va aller au théâtre. C'est moi qui t'invite.
We'll go to the theatre. It's my treat. / It's on me.

Vous êtes libres pour prendre l'apéritif chez nous?
Are you free to come and have a drink with us before lunch / dinner?

(ii) When issuing an invitation more formally:

J'espère que vous pourrez vous joindre à nous dimanche soir.
We hope you'll be free to join us on Sunday evening.

Cela nous ferait très plaisir de vous voir parmi nous.
We'd be delighted if you could join us.

Nous aimerions vous inviter au vernissage de l'exposition.
We'd like to invite you to the opening of the exhibition.

Nous serions très heureux de vous recevoir chez nous en septembre.
We'd be very happy to see you / have you to stay in September.

97 Accepting an invitation

(i) Brief or informal acceptance:

Oui, volontiers. Yes, with pleasure.
Ah, c'est gentil, merci. That's very kind of you, thank you.
J'en serai ravi. I'll be delighted.
Nous serons très heureux de venir. We'll be very happy to come.

(ii) More formal verbal acceptance:

C'est très gentil de votre part. / Vous êtes très aimables.
That's most kind of you.

J'accepte avec le plus grand plaisir.
I'm delighted to accept.

Cela nous fera très plaisir de nous joindre à vous.
We'll be very happy to join you.

Nous serons enchantés d'assister à la cérémonie.
We'll be delighted to attend the ceremony.

98 Declining an invitation

(i) Brief or informal refusal:

C'est dommage, je ne peux pas. What a pity. I can't.

Malheureusement, c'est impossible la semaine prochaine.
Unfortunately next week's out / we can't make next week.

Ah, j'aurais bien voulu, mais je suis déjà pris.
I'd have loved to, but I've already got something on.

Je suis désolé, on nous a déjà invités ce soir-là.
I'm really sorry, we've got another invitation that evening.

(ii) More formal refusal:

Je suis désolé, nous ne serons pas libres avant la fin de juillet.
I'm so sorry, but we aren't free until the end of July.

Je regrette beaucoup de ne pas être parmi vous.
I'm most sorry that I shan't be able to join you.

C'est très aimable de votre part, mais j'ai déjà accepté un autre rendez-vous.
It's very kind of you, but I already have a prior engagement.

Je me vois dans l'impossibilité d'accepter votre invitation. <formal / written>
I am afraid that I am unable to accept your invitation.

USING THE TELEPHONE

Speaking a foreign language on the phone is often daunting, but the task becomes easier if you know some of the standard responses you are likely to hear, and if you have worked out in advance what you want to say. If you are telephoning from a public call box in France, remember that the use of *la télécarte* (phone card) is widely replacing coinboxes.

If you have to give a telephone number, it is usual to split it up into groups of two digits, given together, e.g. 0865-515479 would be given as 08.65.51.54.79, i.e. *le zéro huit, soixante-cinq, cinquante et un, cinquante-quatre, soixante-dix-neuf.*

99 Answering the phone

(i) There are several standard ways of answering a call, but it is rare simply to give the number (as many people do in Britain).

> *Allô, Roger Thomas à l'appareil.*
> Hello, this is Roger Thomas.

> *L'Hôtel Montpensier, bonjour.*
> Hotel Montpensier, good morning / good afternoon.

> *La Société Framboise, j'écoute.*
> Framboise, good morning / good afternoon.

(ii) To check if you have the right number:

> *Je suis bien chez Madame Didier?*
> Is that Madame Didier / Madame Didier's number?

> *C'est bien le 42.78.20.19.?*
> Is that 42-782019?

The standard answer that it is the person you want sounds odd to an English speaker, because it is given in the third person:

> *Oui, c'est lui-même / elle-même.*
> Speaking.

217

(iii) If you have the wrong number, you will hear:

Ah, non, vous avez dû faire un faux numéro.
Ah, non, vous vous êtes trompé de numéro.
No, you must have the wrong number.

Quel numéro voulez-vous?
What number did you want?

Ah, non, il a changé de numéro. Vous devez raccrocher et
composer le 60.51.24.77.
No, he's no longer on this number. You'll have to try again and dial
60-512477.

100 Getting put through

(i) To ask for the person you want:

Je pourrais parler à Marie-Christine, s'il vous plaît?
Could I speak to Marie-Christine, please?

Je voudrais parler au directeur. < more formal >
I'd like to speak to the manager.

Le poste 43, s'il vous plaît.
Extension 43, please.

Pourriez-vous me passer Madame Monnier, s'il vous plaît?
Could you put me through to Madame Monnier, please?

SERVICES D'URGENCE

Police	**17**	ou pour votre localité la gendarmerie :	

Pompiers	**18**	ou pour votre localité :	

(ii) The person who answers or is putting you through may say:

C'est de la part de qui?
Who is it calling?

Je vous le passe. Ça sonne maintenant.
I'll put you through. It's ringing now.

Le poste est occupé. Vous patientez?
The extension's engaged. Would you like to hold?

Monsieur Coutras ne répond pas.
Mr Coutras isn't answering.

J'essayerai un autre numéro. Ne quittez pas.
I'll try another number. Hold the line, please.

(iii) An operator or secretary wishing to put a call through to a given person will say:

Il y a un appel avec préavis pour Mademoiselle Richard.
There's a personal / person-to-person call for Miss Richard.

Madame Garnier vous appelle de Genève. Est-ce que vous acceptez la communication?
Mrs Garnier is calling from Geneva. Will you take the call?

Vous avez Monsieur Le Fustec en ligne.
Mr Le Fustec is on the line for you.

101 Leaving a message

(i) To ask someone to phone you:

Tu veux <u>me passer un coup de fil</u> ce soir? < coll. >
Could you give me a ring this evening?

Vous pourriez <u>demander à</u> Madame Barre <u>de me rappeler</u> plus tard?
Could you ask Mrs Barre to ring me back later?

Votre collègue <u>pourra me contacter</u> cet après-midi. <u>Je vous donne mes coordonnées.</u>
Your colleague can get in touch with me this afternoon.
I'll give you my number.

(ii) Taking a message for someone:

> *Je lui dirai que c'est de la part de qui?*
> Who shall I say rang?

> *Vous voulez laisser un message?*
> Would you like to leave a message?

> *Je peux lui faire une commission?* < informal >
> *Je peux lui transmettre un message?* < formal >
> Can I leave a message for him / her?

> *Est-ce que je dois leur dire de vous rappeler?*
> Shall I get them to ring you back?

> *Au bip sonore, laissez votre message.* (answering machine)
> Please speak after the tone.

102 Ending a conversation

Many French phone conversations are brought to an end by one party (or both) saying *Allez . . .*:

> *Allez, je vous laisse. Au revoir.*
> Well, I must ring off. Bye.

> *Allez, salut. Je t'embrasse.* < coll. >
> Cheerio. All my love.

> *Allez, je vous dis au revoir.*
> Well, goodbye then.

> *Allez. A dimanche!*
> Bye till Sunday then!

103 The operator and reporting problems

(i) Reporting faults:

> *La ligne est très mauvaise.*
> The line is very bad.

> *J'entends très mal. Vous pouvez parler plus fort?*
> It's a bad line. Can you speak up?

> *On nous a coupés. / La communication a été coupée.*
> We were cut off.

Renseignements téléphoniques

vous cherchez, si votre correspondant réside hors du département, si vous ne savez pas comment appeler votre correspondant ou si vous souhaitez connaître le prix d'une communication téléphonique, et que vous n'avez pas trouvé ces renseignements dans les pages bleues :

Si vous n'êtes pas sûr du numéro de votre correspondant, consultez l'annuaire. Si vous n'avez pas trouvé le numéro que

pour la métropole, les DOM, Andorre et Monaco : **composez le 12**

Dérangements

Si votre poste entretenu par l'administration, fonctionne mal ou « reste muet », **composez le 13** à partir d'une cabine ou du poste d'abonné le plus proche (appel gratuit).

Dans le cas où la défaillance concerne un appareil acheté dans le commerce, adressez-vous à votre revendeur.

(ii) Directory enquiries (*renseignements*):

Je voudrais le numéro du Crédit Agricole à Agen.
I'd like the number of the Crédit Agricole bank at Agen.

Quel est l'indicatif pour les Pays-Bas, s'il vous plaît?
What's the code for the Netherlands please?

Je regrette, mais cet abonné est sur la liste rouge.
I'm sorry, but the customer is ex-directory.

Il n'y a pas d'abonné à ce nom.
We have no person listed under that name.

(iii) Official recorded messages:

Le numéro que vous demandez n'est pas en service actuellement.
The number you have dialled is not available.

Par suite d'encombrements, nous ne pouvons pas donner suite à votre appel. Veuillez rappeler plus tard.
We regret that all the lines are engaged. Please try again later.

WRITING LETTERS

Correspondence is subject to convention in most languages, and particularly so in French, where the formulae for opening and closing a letter are plentiful. The choice is rarely arbitrary: how you address your correspondent, and how you sign off, is indicative of how you see your relationship with the other person. Below you will find detailed guidance on the appropriate form for the context. You may well come across subtle variations in letters you receive from French correspondents: remember that letter writing still remains a delicate art for the French, who have not forgotten the example of literary forebears such as Madame de Sévigné.

In common types of correspondence – requests, complaints, making a reservation and so forth – there are set phrases which most writers will use. To demonstrate how these work in an authentic context, examples are given in the form of short letters on key subjects. With some adaptations, these should serve as basic models. You may observe that the tone of correspondence is generally more formal in French than in English, and also that conventional phrases tend to be longer in French – especially the equivalents of 'Yours sincerely' and 'Yours faithfully'.

104 Beginning and ending letters

(a) Heading official letters

For formal correspondence, it is normal either to use headed notepaper or to put your own name and address (including the postcode) at the top of the letter.

Below this, on the right-hand side, put the title, name and address of the person to whom the letter is addressed. The titles *Monsieur / Madame / Mademoiselle* should be given in full here. If you are writing to a department within a firm, use the expression *Service de* .... When giving an address in France, note that *rue* is usually written with a small letter.

The date should be put on the right-hand side, below the address of your correspondent. Remember that dates are preceded by *le*, and months are written with a small letter. It is usual to write the day of the month and the year in figures, but the month as a word. (For the form of dates, see section 143b.)

Below the date, on the left (or, if you prefer, immediately below the letter heading, on the left), you can include:

> *Vos réf.* . . . Your ref. . . .
> *Nos réf.* . . . Our ref. . . .
> *Objet:* . . . Re: . . .

> *Mademoiselle Christine Pearce*
> *43 Southport Road*
> *Redhill, Surrey RH2 6XJ (G.-B.)*
>
> *Monsieur Alain Lecercle*
> *Service Commercial*
> *Faïences de la Cornouaille*
> *Vos réf. AL / F.D. 503*   *25 rue du Port*
> *Objet: demande de documentation*   *29000 Quimper (France)*
>
> *le 23 juillet 1992*

(b) Addressing your correspondent

For any official letter (e.g. business, to hotels) addressed to a person who is not known to you personally, or only in a formal capacity, use just:

> *Monsieur* Dear Sir
> *Madame* Dear Madam
> *Mademoiselle* Dear Madam (if you know the recipient is an
> unmarried woman)

If you are writing to a person in an important position, whom you do not know personally, or only formally, it is preferable to use *Monsieur / Madame le / la* + title (on the problem of genders and professions, see section 9a):

> *Monsieur le maire* Dear Sir (addressed to the mayor)
> *Madame la directrice* Dear Headmistress

For professional correspondence, when writing to a colleague or counterpart whom you know a little, it is common to use:

> *Monsieur et cher Collègue / Madame et chère Collègue* < formal >
> *Cher Collègue / Chère Collègue* < less formal >

For a colleague or personal acquaintance whom you normally address by title + surname, use:

Cher Monsieur Dufour Dear Mr Dufour
Chère Mademoiselle Pignon Dear Miss / Ms Pignon

For informal letters to personal friends with whom you are on Christian name terms, use:

Chers Jean-Luc et Marie
Chère Michèle

A variant on this, particularly appropriate when writing to friends with whom you have a slightly more formal relationship (e.g. friends of an older generation) is:

Cher Ami / Chère Amie / Chers Amis

(c) Ending letters

The myriad of formulae used to end French correspondence can seem bewildering, so this section offers examples of the most important ones for different contexts.

For a formal (business) letter which began *Monsieur / Madame / Mademoiselle*, the equivalent to 'Yours faithfully' is:

Je vous prie d'agréer, Monsieur / Madame / Mademoiselle, l'expression de mes sentiments distingués.

For a formal letter to someone in an important official position (M.P., Director, etc.), a more respectful equivalent of 'Yours faithfully' is:

Je vous prie d'agréer, Monsieur le député / Madame la directrice, l'assurance de ma courtoise considération / l'assurance de mes sentiments respectueux.

For a formal letter to a person with whom you have had some professional contact, the equivalent of 'Yours sincerely' is:

Croyez, cher Monsieur / chère Madame / cher Collègue / chère Collègue, à l'expression de mes sentiments les meilleurs / à l'assurance de mes sentiments très cordiaux.

For a personal letter to acquaintances or friends whom you do not know closely (or of an older generation) – in other words, those you would address as *vous* in French – equivalents of 'Yours ever' / 'All good wishes' include (in descending order of formality):

> *Très cordialement*
> *Bien à vous*
> *Je vous adresse mon très amical souvenir*
> *Toutes mes / nos amitiés*
> *Amicalement*

For personal letters to close friends or family – those you would address as *tu* in French – equivalents of 'love' / 'love and best wishes' include:

> *Je t'embrasse / Nous vous embrassons*
> *Bons baisers*
> *Grosses bises*

105 Informal letters

When you are writing a general 'newsy' letter to friends, the style can be informal, and the content will obviously depend on the situation. The example below gives ideas for some standard phrases for thanks, good wishes, and so forth.

Oxford

Chère Julie,

Merci bien de la lettre que tu m'as envoyée de Chamonix. J'ai été très contente d'avoir de tes nouvelles, et d'apprendre que tu passes un bon moment dans les Alpes. Excuse-moi de te répondre avec un peu de retard, mais depuis un mois j'ai été vraiment débordée au travail. En plus, je devrai déménager d'ici l'été, alors j'ai passé pas mal de temps à chercher un nouvel appartement. Une copine m'a proposé de partager sa maison, qui se trouve au nord d'Oxford, mais ça fait un peu cher. En tout cas, je ne manquerai pas de t'envoyer ma nouvelle adresse, et peut-être que tu viendras me voir en juillet? Ça me ferait très plaisir.

Avec Adam, on garde un excellent souvenir de nos vacances chez toi. Adam m'a dit d'ailleurs de t'embrasser de sa part, et bien sûr nous envoyons le bonjour à tes parents, sans oublier ta grand-mère.

A bientôt, et grosses bises,

Catherine

---

translation overleaf

Oxford

Dear Julie,

Many thanks for your letter from Chamonix. It was very good to get your news, and to hear that you're having a good time in the Alps. I'm sorry it's taken me a while to reply, but I've been snowed under at work for the last month. Also, I've got to move house by the summer, so I've spent quite a lot of time looking for a new flat. A friend's suggested that I can share her house – to the north of Oxford – but it's a bit expensive. Anyway, I'll certainly send you my new address, and perhaps you'll come to see me in July? I'd be delighted if you could.

Adam and I had a wonderful time when we were on holiday with you. I mustn't forget that Adam said to send you his love, and of course we send our greetings to your parents, and your grandmother.

Hope to hear from you soon.

With love from
Catherine

106 Making reservations and bookings

(a) To the Tourist Office for a list of hotels and campsites

> *Office de Tourisme*
> *3 avenue Jean-Laigret*
> *41000 Blois, France*
>
> *Monsieur ou Madame,*
>
> *En vue d'un séjour dans votre belle région au mois de septembre, je vous serais obligé(e) de bien vouloir m'adresser une liste des hôtels et des campings à proximité de Blois. J'aimerais également me renseigner sur la possibilité d'excursions touristiques en car à partir de Blois.*
>
> *Avec mes remerciements pour votre obligeance, je vous prie de croire, Monsieur ou Madame, à l'expression de mes sentiments distingués.*

Dear Sir or Madam,
I am planning to visit your charming region in September, and would be grateful if you could send me a list of hotels and campsites near Blois. I would also like some information about the possibility of excursions by coach from Blois.
Thanking you for your advice,
Yours faithfully,

226

(b) To a hotel to ask about the availability of rooms

Hôtel Atlantique
33 boulevard de la Mer
33120 Arcachon, France

Monsieur ou Madame,

Avec ma famille, j'aimerais passer huit jours à Arcachon, du 1er au 8 août. Pourriez-vous me faire savoir s'il vous reste deux chambres avec douche et WC (une chambre avec grand lit, une avec deux lits) pour cette période? Nous préférerions des chambres qui donnent sur la cour. Nous aimerions recevoir aussi vos tarifs de demi-pension et de pension complète.

Dans l'attente de vous lire, je vous prie d'agréer, Monsieur ou Madame, l'expression de mes sentiments distingués.

Dear Sir or Madam,

I intend to spend a week with my family in Arcachon, from 1 to 8 August. Please could you advise me whether you have two rooms (one double and one twin) with shower and toilet for this period? We would prefer rooms looking onto the courtyard. Please could you also send us your prices for half-board and full-board?

Looking forward to hearing from you,

Yours faithfully,

(c) To confirm a hotel booking and pay a deposit

Monsieur A. Meunier
Hôtel Beaufort
17 rue A. Favier
13260 Cassis, France

Monsieur,

Ayant bien reçu le dépliant et les tarifs de votre hôtel, je vous écris pour confirmer la réservation d'une chambre pour une personne pour les quatre nuits du 23 au 26 juin. Vous m'avez proposé une chambre avec salle de bains et W.C. Je la prendrai en demi-pension, donc au tarif de 440 francs par jour. Je compte arriver le premier soir vers 18 heures.

Veuillez trouver ci-joint 500 francs d'arrhes.

Je vous prie de croire, Monsieur, à l'expression de mes sentiments distingués.

Dear Sir,

I received the brochure and prices for your hotel, and am writing to confirm my reservation of a single room for four nights from 23 to 26 June. You offered me a room with bathroom and toilet. I would like to stay half-board, at the daily rate of 440 francs. I expect to arrive at about 6 p.m. on the first evening.
Please find enclosed a deposit for the sum of 500 francs.

Yours faithfully,

(d) To reserve a place on a campsite

> *Le Gestionnaire*
> *Camping Municipal*
> *9 rue Baudry*
> *14000 Caen, France*
>
> *Monsieur ou Madame,*
>
> *Nous désirerions séjourner dans votre région du 1er au 15 juillet. Pourriez-vous donc nous réserver un emplacement dans votre camping pour cette période, et nous faire savoir vos tarifs actuels? Nous serons cinq personnes, dont trois enfants, avec une caravane, une tente et une voiture.*
>
> *Dans l'espoir d'une réponse favorable, nous vous prions de croire, Monsieur ou Madame, à l'expression de nos sentiments distingués.*

Dear Sir or Madam,

We would like to visit your region from 1 to 15 July. Please could you reserve us a pitch at your campsite for this period, and send us your current prices? We shall be a party of two adults and three children, with a caravan, tent and car.

Hoping to receive a favourable reply.

Yours faithfully,

(e) To book furnished holiday accommodation

> *Madame M. Lagny*
> *24 rue La Villette*
> *46200 Souillac, France*
>
> *Madame,*
>
> *Votre adresse m'a été communiquée par l'Office de Tourisme de Souillac. A cet effet, je vous serais obligé(e) de bien vouloir me dire si votre maison serait libre pour la première quinzaine de mai. Dans l'affirmative, quel en serait le prix? Nous serions trois personnes: moi-même, mon frère et ma belle-soeur.*
>
> *Je désirerais avoir éventuellement quelques précisions: nombre de pièces, fourniture des draps, équipement de la cuisine, avec ou sans jardin.*
>
> *Dans l'espoir d'une réponse favorable, je vous prie d'agréer, Madame, l'expression de mes sentiments distingués.*

Dear Mrs Lagny,

I have received your address from the Tourist Office in Souillac, and am writing to ask whether your house would be available to rent for the first two weeks in May. If so, please could you let me know the price? We would be a group of three adults: myself, my brother and my sister-in-law.

Could I also ask you for some further information on the number of rooms, the provision of bed-linen, kitchen facilities, and whether there is the use of a garden?

Hoping to receive a favourable reply,

Yours sincerely,

107 Letters of complaint

(a) To a shop in respect of an unsatisfactory purchase

> La Boutique du Ménage
> 17 place Saint-Jacques
> 29000 Quimper
>
> Monsieur ou Madame,
>
> *J'ai le regret de vous signaler que je suis mécontent(e) de la nappe en coton (ligne 'Fleurs du Printemps') que j'ai achetée dans votre magasin la semaine dernière.*
>
> *L'ayant utilisée une première fois, je l'ai lavée dans ma machine à laver, suivant scrupuleusement les consignes indiquées. Néanmoins, la nappe a déteint, de sorte que je ne pourrai plus m'en servir.*
>
> *Je me permets de solliciter un remboursement du prix intégral de l'article, qui était de 240 francs.*
>
> *Je vous prie de croire, Monsieur ou Madame, à l'expression de mes sentiments distingués.*

Dear Sir or Madam,

I regret to inform you that I am dissatisfied with the cotton tablecloth (from the 'Spring Flowers' range) which I bought from your shop last week.

After using it once, I put it through my washing-machine, taking great care to follow the washing instructions. However, the colours ran, with the result that I am unable to use the tablecloth again.

I would ask you for a refund of the full price of the article, i.e. 240 francs.

Yours faithfully,

231

(b) To an estate agent in respect of unsatisfactory (holiday) accommodation

---

L'Agence Martin
34 place de la Croix Rousse
69000 Lyon

Monsieur ou Madame,

J'ai le regret de vous informer que j'ai été très déçu(e) par l'appartement que vous m'avez proposé dans la Résidence des Mimosas (6 rue du 4 septembre). J'avais précisé que je voulais un F3 dans une rue bien calme. Or, sans me prévenir, vous m'avez donné un F2, de dimensions très limitées, et dans un quartier fort bruyant, surtout le soir.

J'ai essayé de vous signaler mon mécontentement dès mon arrivée, mais en raison des vacances votre agence était fermée pendant toute la semaine que j'ai passée à Lyon.

Il me semble que votre agence a fait preuve d'une désinvolture peu acceptable à mon égard. Je me vois donc obligé(e) de vous demander de me rembourser au moins 50 pour cent de la location que je vous ai versée.

Je vous prie de croire, Monsieur ou Madame, à l'expression de mes sentiments distingués.

Dear Sir or Madam,

I regret that I must register my disappointment in respect of the flat you provided for me in the Résidence des Mimosas (6 rue du 4 septembre). I had specified that I wanted a two-bedroom flat, in a quiet road. However, without warning me, you gave me a very small one-bedroom flat, in an area which was distinctly noisy, especially in the evenings.

Upon my arrival, I attempted to contact you to express my dissatisfaction, but your agency was closed for holidays for the whole of the week I stayed in Lyons.

I consider that your agency has failed to treat my booking with the care I would expect. I must therefore ask you to refund at least 50 per cent of the rent I paid you.

Yours faithfully,

(c) To an individual in respect of unacceptable / unneighbourly behaviour

> *Monsieur A. Leroux*
> *38 rue de la Paix*
> *59500 Douai*
>
> *Monsieur,*
>
> *Vous me voyez quelque peu gêné(e) de vous écrire.*
>
> *J'ai loué la maison en face de la vôtre pour le mois de septembre, espérant y passer des vacances paisibles. Or, vos deux fils ont la malheureuse habitude de passer des heures devant notre maison à réparer leurs motos, tout en écoutant de la musique très bruyante. Je leur ai signalé à plusieurs reprises que leurs activités nous gênaient, mais ils n'ont pas modifié leur comportement.*
>
> *Pourrais-je compter sur vous pour appuyer mes demandes? En l'occurrence, une solution à l'amiable me semble nécessaire.*
>
> *Je vous prie de croire, Monsieur, à l'expression de mes sentiments distingués.*

Dear Mr Leroux,

It is with some hesitation that I write to you.

I have rented the house opposite your own for September, hoping to enjoy a quiet holiday. However, your sons have unfortunately taken to spending hours outside our house repairing their motorbikes and listening to very loud music. On several occasions I have pointed out to them that this was disturbing us, but my complaints have had no effect.

Could I ask you to reinforce my request? In the situation, we need to find a neighbourly solution.

Yours sincerely,

(d) To a public body in respect of an unsatisfactory service

> *Office de Tourisme*
> *98300 Avers*
>
> *Monsieur ou Madame,*
>
> *J'ai le regret de vous signaler que les brochures sur la ville d'Avers que vous m'avez envoyées au mois de mars donnent des renseignements qui sont pour le moins trompeurs.*
>
> *En effet, votre brochure indique qu'il existe trois campings municipaux à Avers, alors qu'en réalité il n'en existe plus qu'un seul – comblé, évidemment. D'autre part, l'exposition sur les 'Trois Siècles de Viticulteurs Avernois', chaleureusement recommandée par votre brochure, a fermé ses portes en 1988!*
>
> *Il faut constater que notre passage à Avers nous a déçus. Du moins l'Office de Tourisme devrait-il se donner la peine de remettre à jour ses informations touristiques.*
>
> *Je vous prie de croire, Monsieur ou Madame, à l'expression de mes sentiments distingués.*

Dear Sir or Madam,

I regret to inform you that the information in the brochures on Avers which you sent me in March is, to say the least, misleading.

Your brochure says that Avers has three public campsites, whereas in fact there is now only one – which is obviously oversubscribed. Furthermore, the exhibition on 'Three Centuries of Wine Production in Avers', which your brochure warmly recommends, closed in 1988!

I am forced to say that we were disappointed by our stay in Avers. At the very least, the Tourist Office should take the trouble to update its guides.

Yours faithfully,

108 Letters concerning employment

For a sample C.V. see section 109.

(a) Seeking vacation / short-term employment

> *Société Internationale des Libraires*
> *Service du Personnel*
> *16 avenue Bethelot*
> *75004 Paris, France*
>
> *Objet: demande d'emploi de vacataire*
>
> *Monsieur ou Madame,*
>
> *Souhaitant travailler en France pendant les vacances universitaires, je vous serais reconnaissant(e) de me faire savoir si votre Société propose des postes de vacataires. Je serais libre à partir du 1er juillet jusqu'au 15 septembre, et serais prêt(e) à assumer les fonctions de secrétaire, réceptionniste ou employé(e) de bureau.*
>
> *A toutes fins utiles, voici mon curriculum vitae, avec les noms de deux personnes voulant bien me recommander.*
>
> *Dans l'espoir d'une réponse favorable, je vous prie d'agréer, Monsieur ou Madame, l'expression de mes sentiments distingués.*

Dear Sir or Madam,

Re: application for a vacation post

I should like to work in France during the university vacation, and should be grateful if you could inform me whether your firm offers any temporary posts. I am available from 1 July until 15 September, and am willing to work as a secretary, receptionist, or in a clerical post.

In the hope that you may be interested in my application, I enclose my C.V., together with the names of two referees.

Yours faithfully,

235

(b) Applying for a job as an au pair

> *Madame Y. Rudler*
> *17 avenue Lattré*
> *41400 Montrichard, France*
>
> *Madame,*
>
> *Dans le journal du Courrier de la Loire j'ai relevé la petite annonce dans laquelle <u>vous demandiez une jeune fille au pair</u> pour le mois de juillet. Le poste me conviendrait parfaitement, car j'aime beaucoup les petits enfants, et je suis désireuse de séjourner en France pour perfectionner mon français.*
>
> *Je vous prie de trouver <u>ci-joint mon curriculum vitae</u>, ainsi que les noms de deux personnes voulant bien me recommander.*
>
> *Dans le cas où vous aimeriez me recevoir, pourriez-vous me donner des précisions sur le montant de l'argent de poche dont je pourrais bénéficier, ainsi que sur les heures de travail?*
>
> *Dans l'attente de votre réponse, je vous prie d'agréer, Madame, l'expression de mes sentiments distingués.*

Dear Mrs Rudler,

I saw your advertisement in the *Courrier de la Loire* for an au pair for July. The post would be ideal for me, since I am very fond of small children, and would like to stay in France to improve my French.

I enclose for your attention my C.V. and the names of two personal referees.

If you are interested in my application, might I ask you for information about the allowance you would pay, and the hours I would be expected to work?

Hoping to receive a favourable reply,

Yours sincerely,

236

(c) Applying for a post advertised in the press

La Banque Nationale de Normandie
Service du Personnel
32 rue Gemare
14000 Caen, France

Objet: demande d'emploi de traducteur

Monsieur ou Madame,

En réponse à votre annonce parue dans le journal du Monde, j'ai l'honneur de solliciter ma candidature pour ce poste actuellement vacant dans votre Banque.

Ci-joint mon curriculum vitae.

Je serais éventuellement libre pour me rendre à vos bureaux à Londres ou à Caen pour une entrevue.

Je vous prie d'agréer, Monsieur ou Madame, l'expression de ma courtoise considération.

Dear Sir or Madam,

Re: application for the post of translator

In response to your advertisement in *Le Monde*, I would like to apply for the above vacancy in your Bank. Please find enclosed my C.V.

If you wished, I should be available for interview at your offices in London or Caen.

Yours faithfully,

(d) Accepting a written offer of a post

> *Galeries Martin*
> *Service du Personnel*
> *4 rue Mirabeau*
> *18000 Bourges, France*
>
> <u>*A l'attention de Madame Gilbert*</u>
>
> *Madame,*
>
> *Je vous remercie de votre lettre du 29 avril, me proposant le poste de secrétaire-bilingue dans votre établissement à partir du 1er juin. <u>Je trouve toutes les conditions que vous m'avez proposées parfaitement satisfaisantes, et je serai heureux / heureuse d'accepter le poste</u> aux Galeries Martin.*
>
> *Je vous prie d'agréer, Madame, l'expression de mes sentiments distingués,*

Dear Mrs Gilbert,

Thank you for your letter of 29 April, offering me the post of bilingual secretary in your firm, with effect from 1 June. All the conditions outlined in your letter are perfectly satisfactory, and I am pleased to accept the post with the Galeries Martin.

Yours sincerely,

(e) Letter of resignation

> *Hôtel Les Tilleuls*
> *20 rue de Port-Vendres*
> *66190 Collioure, France*
>
> *A l'attention de Monsieur Hély*
>
> *Monsieur,*
>
> *Ayant décidé de rentrer en Grande-Bretagne pour reprendre mes études, j'ai l'honneur de vous informer de ma démission du poste de veilleur de nuit que j'occupe dans votre hôtel.*
>
> *Je serai heureux de travailler jusqu'à la fin du mois, à moins que vous ne trouviez d'ici-là un remplaçant.*
>
> *Veuillez agréer, Monsieur, l'assurance de mes sentiments respectueux.*

Dear Mr Hély,

I have decided to return to Britain to continue my university course, and so must ask you to accept my resignation from the post of night porter at your hotel. I shall be happy to work until the end of the month, unless you find a replacement in the meanwhile.

Yours sincerely,

109 Curriculum vitae

Applications for jobs in France will usually require a C.V. to be submitted. The example below gives the standard headings, and some indications of appropriate information.

CURRICULUM VITAE

NOM DE FAMILLE: *Luce*

PRENOMS: *Jean-Marie Christophe*

ADRESSE: *21 rue de la Paix, 83600 Fréjus*

NUMERO DE TELEPHONE: *93.99.50.47 (bureau)*
93.98.81.27 (domicile)

NATIONALITE: *Français*

DATE ET LIEU DE NAISSANCE: *le 17 mars 1959, à Brignoles*

SITUATION DE FAMILLE: *célibataire*

EDUCATION ET ETUDES UNIVERSITAIRES:

Lycée de Batignoles (1970-1977): baccalauréat C

Université de Nice (1977–1981): D.E.U.G., licence et maîtrise en sciences naturelles

EXPERIENCE PROFESSIONNELLE:

Chercheur dans l'Entreprise Fignon (Nice, 1982–1988)

Directeur des recherches, Institut de la Santé (Fréjus, 1988–)

CENTRES D'INTERET ET PASSE-TEMPS:

Le cyclisme, le tennis, la lecture, le cinéma russe

REFERENCES:

(1) Monsieur R. Breton, Directeur de l'Institut de la Santé, 24 rue Fabre, 83600 Fréjus

(2) Madame Y. Moine, Professeur à l'Université de Nice, 11 rue Rivoli, 06000 Nice

---

240

CURRICULUM VITAE

SURNAME: Luce

FIRST NAMES: Jean-Marie Christophe

ADDRESS: 21 rue de la Paix, 83600 Fréjus

TELEPHONE NUMBER: 93-995047 (work)
93-998127 (home)

NATIONALITY: French

DATE AND PLACE OF BIRTH: 17th March 1959, at Brignoles

MARITAL STATUS: single

SECONDARY AND UNIVERSITY EDUCATION:
Lycée de Batignoles (1970–1977): baccalauréat (section C)
University of Nice (1977–1981): B.Sc. and M.Sc. in Biology

PREVIOUS EMPLOYMENT:
Researcher in 'Entreprise Fignon' (Nice, 1982–1988)
Head of Research, Institute for Health (Fréjus, 1988–)

OUTSIDE INTERESTS:
Cycling, tennis, reading, Russian films

REFERENCES:
(1) Monsieur R. Breton, Director of the Institute for Health, 24 rue Fabre, 83600 Fréjus
(2) Professor Y. Moine, University of Nice, 11 rue Rivoli, 06000 Nice

110 Testimonials, references and authorizations

(a) Brief testimonials

> *A qui de droit*
>
> *Je soussigné, Henri Martin, Directeur de l'Institut des Beaux-Arts, certifie que Mademoiselle Claire Evry a été à mon service en qualité de Conservatrice du 1ᵉʳ janvier 1986 au 30 septembre 1991, et qu'elle m'a donné toute satisfaction.*
>
> *Fait à Dijon, le 30 septembre 1991.*

To whom it may concern

I, Henri Martin, Director of the Institute of Fine Arts, confirm that Miss / Ms Claire Evry has been employed under me as a Keeper from 1 January 1986 to 30 September 1991, and that she has fulfilled her duties satisfactorily.

Dijon, 30 September 1991.

> *A qui de droit*
>
> *Je soussignée, Anne Labaudy, Professeur à l'Université de Tours, certifie que Monsieur Anthony Forth a suivi assidûment les cours de première année sur la littérature française contemporaine, et qu'il a été reçu à l'examen avec la mention 'Bien'.*
>
> *Fait à Tours, le 7 juillet 1991.*

To whom it may concern

I, Anne Labaudy, Professor of Tours University, declare that Mr Anthony Forth regularly attended the first-year classes on contemporary French literature, and that he passed the examination with a distinction.

Tours, 7 July 1991.

242

(b) Personal references

> *La Directrice*
> *L'Agence de Voyages 'Est-Ouest'*
> *33 rue des Petits Champs*
> *75001 Paris*
>
> Madame,
>
> <u>Je suis heureux / -euse de vous recommander vivement</u> Madame Béatrice Chartier, que je connais depuis cinq ans en qualité de collègue. Elle est d'une personnalité morale exemplaire, et mérite toute votre confiance.
>
> Quant à ses qualités professionnelles, je devrais souligner sa longue expérience dans le secteur du tourisme, sa parfaite maîtrise de l'allemand, et l'exactitude dont elle fait preuve dans toutes ses tâches.
>
> Je vous prie d'agréer, Madame, l'expression de mes sentiments distingués.

Dear Madam / Dear Ms . . .,

I am pleased to recommend Mrs Béatrice Chartier to you most warmly. I have worked with her for five years. Her moral character is exemplary, and you may have every confidence in her.

In respect of her professional qualities, I should like to underline her long experience in tourism, her perfect command of German, and the attention to detail which she shows in all her work.

Yours faithfully / sincerely,

(c) Giving an authorization to a proxy

Je soussignée, Simone Lenoir, donne pouvoir par la présente à
Madame Jeanne Bourgne de conclure au mieux l'achat de l'Agence
Immobilière Lochoise actuellement en cours de réalisation.

Fait à Loches, le 29 novembre 1991.

I, Simone Lenoir, hereby authorize Mrs Jeanne Bourgne to act on my behalf
in concluding the current purchase of the Agence Immobilière Lochoise.

Loches, 29 November 1991.

Je soussigné, Alexandre Mâcon, actionnaire de la Société des Amis de
Gruissan, ne pouvant me rendre personnellement à l'Assemblée
Générale de la dite Société, donne ma procuration à Monsieur
Charles Hubert.

Fait à Paris, le 17 octobre 1991.

I, Alexander Mâcon, shareholder of the Société des Amis de Gruissan, being
unable to attend the Annual General Meeting of the said society in person,
give my vote by proxy to Mr Charles Hubert.

Paris, 17 October 1991.

244

111 Commercial correspondence

(a) Enclosing brochures and information for a client

> *La Société des Artisans*
> *9 place d'Etain*
> *86000 Poitiers*
>
> *Messieurs,*
>
> *Nous vous remercions de votre lettre du 29 mai. Vous trouverez ci-joint une documentation sur nos magasins en Angleterre et en Ecosse. Si vous désirez recevoir des informations complémentaires sur nos partenaires aux Etats-Unis, nous serons heureux de vous les fournir.*
>
> *Nous aimerions travailler avec la Société des Artisans, et espérons recevoir un courrier de votre part dans les prochaines semaines.*
>
> *Nous vous prions de croire, Messieurs, à l'expression de nos sentiments distingués.*

Dear Sirs,

Thank you for your letter of 29 May. Please find enclosed a brochure about our shops in England and Scotland. If you would like to receive further information, concerning our American partners, we shall be happy to furnish it.

We would be delighted to work with the Société des Artisans, and hope that we may hear from you in the near future.

Yours faithfully,

(b) Asking for a quotation

> *Le Directeur*
> *Installations Electriques*
> *43 route de Brest*
> *29210 Morlaix*
>
> *Monsieur,*
>
> *A la suite de notre entretien du 2 courant, portant sur l'installation de deux cuisines dans notre restaurant, je vous serais obligé(e) de m'envoyer au plus tôt votre devis.*
>
> *Veuillez croire, Monsieur, à l'expression de mes sentiments distingués.*

Dear Sir / Dear Mr . . .,

Following our discussion of 2nd inst. concerning the installation of two kitchens in our restaurant, I should be grateful if you could send me your quotation as soon as possible.

Yours faithfully / sincerely,

(c) Placing an order

> *La Directrice*
> *Les Porcelaines Rustiques*
> *19 avenue Baudin*
> *87000 Limoges*
>
> *Madame,*
>
> *Nous vous remercions de votre catalogue de cette année. Nous serons heureux de vendre vos produits dans nos magasins, comme l'année précédente.*
>
> *Pour le mois de mars, nous aimerions commander 500 services de table du modèle 'Campagne Rustique'. Comme d'habitude, nous réglerons à la livraison la moitié de l'expédition, et le reste par versements sur quatre mois.*
>
> *Par ailleurs, il est possible que nous nous intéressions à votre collection 'Vie Champêtre'. Pourriez-vous nous faire savoir quel rabais vous seriez prête à nous accorder sur 350 services à petit déjeuner?*
>
> *Veuillez croire, Madame, à l'expression de nos sentiments distingués.*

Dear Mrs / Ms . . .,

Thank you for sending us your current catalogue. We shall be happy to sell your products in our shops, as we did last year.

We should like to order 500 dinner sets in the 'Campagne Rustique' line for March. As usual, we shall pay half the invoice upon delivery of the order, and the remainder in four monthly instalments.

It is also possible that we may wish to stock your collection 'Vie Champêtre'. Could you advise us what discount you would be prepared to allow us on an order of 350 breakfast sets?

Yours sincerely,

(d) Apologizing for a delayed order

Le Directeur
La Co-opérative des Viticulteurs
82 boulevard Mistral
11100 Narbonne

Monsieur,

Nous accusons réception de votre lettre du 12 avril, et regrettons vivement que votre commande n'ait pas encore été honorée. Nous n'avons pas actuellement en stock l'article réclamé. Cependant, nous en disposerons dès le mois prochain, et nous vous l'expédierons immédiatement.

Nous vous prions de nous excuser pour ce retard inattendu, dû à des circonstances indépendantes de notre volonté.

Veuillez agréer, Monsieur, l'expression de nos sentiments les plus dévoués.

Dear Sir,

We acknowledge receipt of your letter of 12 April, and apologize for the fact that your order has not yet been expedited. The article you request is currently out of stock. However, it will be available as from next month, and we shall forward it to you without further delay.

We would ask you to accept our apologies for this unexpected delay, which is due to circumstances beyond our control.

Yours faithfully,

(e) Asking for an urgent reply to an earlier letter

Le Service Commercial
Le Journal de l'Ouest
33 Cours des Dames
17000 La Rochelle

Monsieur ou Madame,

Sauf retard dans l'acheminement du courrier, vous semblez ne pas avoir répondu à ma lettre précédente, du 17 février, concernant les droits de reproduction de certaines photos parues dans votre journal.

Comme il s'agit d'une affaire urgente, je vous serais obligé(e) de bien vouloir me répondre dès réception de la présente.

Je vous prie de croire, Monsieur ou Madame, à l'expression de mes sentiments distingués.

Dear Sir or Madam,

Unless there has been a delay in the postal services, you would appear not to have replied to my letter of 17 February, concerning the right to reproduce certain photos which appeared in your newspaper.

As this is a matter of some urgency, I should be most grateful if you could reply by return of post.

Yours faithfully,

112 Press announcements

Official announcements in the press follow set patterns:

(a) Births

Naissances M.et Mme Le Blanc Le Docteur et Mme Durand ont la joie d'annoncer la naissance de leur petit-fils François chez Caroline et Jean-Yves Durand Amboise, le 17 juillet.	**Births** Mr and Mrs Le Blanc Dr and Mrs Durand have the pleasure of announcing the birth of their grandson François to Caroline and Jean-Yves Durand Amboise, 17th July.

(b) Engagements

Fiançailles On nous prie d'annoncer les fiançailles de Mlle Christine Gérard avec M. Alain Millou le 15 juin, Auxerre.	**Engagement** We are asked to announce the engagement of Miss/Ms Christine Gérard to Mr Alain Millou 15th June, Auxerre.

(c) Marriages

Mariages François-Régis SAUVY et Béatrice QUIGNARD ont le plaisir d'annoncer leur mariage, qui a été célébré dans l'intimité le 26 octobre.	**Marriage** François-Régis SAUVY and Béatrice QUIGNARD are pleased to announce their marriage, which was celebrated quietly on 26th October.

(d) Deaths

Deuils M. Jean Drouin, son époux, Mlle Marie-Claude Drouin, M. Bernard Drouin, ses enfants, ont la très grande tristesse de faire part du décès de **Mme Jean DROUIN,** **née Madeleine Merson,** survenu à Paris, le 23 octobre. La cérémonie religieuse a été célébrée dans l'intimité familiale, suivant les volontés de la défunte. 19 rue du Port 24100 Bergerac	**Deaths** Mr Jean Drouin, her husband, Miss/Ms Marie-Claude Drouin, Mr Bernard Drouin, her children, are sad to announce the death of **Mrs Jean DROUIN,** **née Madeleine Merson,** in Paris, 23rd October. The funeral service was a private family occasion, as requested by the departed. 19, rue du Port 24100 Bergerac

(e) Seasonal greetings

La Maison du Cadeau vous présente ses meilleurs voeux à l'occasion du Nouvel An.
The Maison du Cadeau wishes you a Happy New Year.

Nous souhaitons un joyeux Noël et une bonne et heureuse année à tous nos clients.
We wish all our customers a Merry Christmas and a very Happy New Year.

(f) Opening of a new firm

La Galerie du Prêt-à-Porter est heureuse de vous inviter à l'inauguration de sa nouvelle boutique, le lundi 22 octobre: 34 rue de Montpellier.

The Galerie du Prêt-à-Porter is pleased to invite you to the opening of its new boutique / shop, on Monday 22 October: 34 rue de Montpellier.

(g) Change of address

La Société Angevine vous prie de bien vouloir noter sa nouvelle adresse, qui sera, à partir du Iᵉʳ décembre: 2 avenue Leclerc, 49000 Angers.

As from 1 December, the Société Angevine will be relocated at the following address: 2 avenue Leclerc, 49000 Angers.

113 Official invitations and replies

The examples in this section are all based on formal written usage. For inviting friends, family, or informal acquaintances, see sections 96–8.

(a) Issuing an invitation to a reception or function

Monsieur et Madame Jean-Yves Tessier prient Madame Yvette Rastagnac de leur faire l'honneur d'assister à leur réception le vendredi 30 mars à 18 heures.

Mr and Mrs Jean-Yves Tessier are pleased to invite Mrs Yvette Rastagnac to a reception on Friday 30 March, at 6 p.m.

A l'occasion de l'ouverture de notre nouvelle agence du Crédit Mutuel, nous vous prions de nous faire l'honneur d'assister à un cocktail, le mardi 22 avril, à 11H 30.

To mark the opening of our new branch of the Crédit Mutuel, we are pleased to invite you to a cocktail party on Tuesday 22 April, at 11.30 a.m.

(b) Accepting an invitation

Madame Yvette Rastagnac remercie Monsieur et Madame Jean-Yves Tessier de leur aimable invitation pour le 30 mars, à laquelle elle se rendra avec grand plaisir.

Mrs Yvette Rastagnac thanks Mr and Mrs Jean-Yves Tessier for their kind invitation for 30 March, which she will be pleased to accept.

C'est avec le plus grand plaisir que le Directeur d'Euromagasin se rendra au cocktail à l'occasion de l'ouverture de la nouvelle agence du Crédit Mutuel.

The Manager of Euromagasin will be very pleased to attend the cocktail party to mark the opening of the Crédit Mutuel's new branch.

(c) Declining an invitation

Madame Yvette Rastagnac remercie Monsieur et Madame Jean-Yves Tessier de leur aimable invitation, mais regrette de ne pouvoir accepter en raison d'une obligation antérieure.

Mrs Yvette Rastagnac thanks Mr and Mrs Jean-Yves Tessier for their kind invitation, but regrets that she is unable to accept due to a prior engagement.

Le Directeur d'Euromagasin remercie le Crédit Mutuel de son aimable invitation au cocktail du 22 avril, mais regrette qu'il ne pourra pas s'y rendre en raison d'un autre engagement.

The Manager of Euromagasin thanks the Crédit Mutuel for their kind invitation to the cocktail party on 22 April, but regrets he will be unable to attend due to another engagement.

(d) Wedding invitations and replies

Monsieur et Madame Alain Cesbron

ont la joie de vous faire part du mariage de Mademoiselle Catherine Cesbron, leur fille, avec Monsieur Marc Fontaine, et vous prient d'assister à la messe qui sera célébrée le 15 juillet prochain en l'église Sainte Anne à 11 heures, ainsi qu'au lunch qui aura lieu à l'Hôtel des Glycines à 13 heures.

Mr and Mrs Alain Cesbron

have the pleasure of announcing the forthcoming marriage of their daughter, Catherine, to Mr Marc Fontaine, and request the pleasure of your company at the Nuptial Mass at St Anne's Church on 15 July at 11 a.m., and thereafter for a buffet luncheon at the Hôtel des Glycines at 1 p.m.

Monsieur Olivier Péroux adresse ses chaleureuses félicitations à Monsieur et Madame Alain Cesbron à l'occasion du prochain mariage de leur fille, Catherine, et accepte avec joie leur aimable invitation.

Mr Olivier Péroux offers Mr and Mrs Alain Cesbron his warmest congratulations on the forthcoming marriage of their daughter, Catherine, and is pleased to accept their kind invitation.

Monsieur Olivier Péroux adresse ses chaleureuses félicitations à Monsieur et Madame Alain Cesbron à l'occasion du prochain mariage de leur fille, Catherine, mais regrette de ne pouvoir accepter leur aimable invitation en raison des vacances familiales.

Mr Olivier Péroux offers Mr and Mrs Alain Cesbron his warmest congratulations on the forthcoming marriage of their daughter Catherine, but regrets that he is unable to accept their kind invitation because of family holidays.

(e) Inviting business associates / new clients to a trade fair or exhibition

'Logiciel 2001' est heureux de vous inviter à la Foire de l'Informatique, qui se déroulera du 2 au 5 mai à la Salle des Expositions, Villepinte. Notre stand se trouvera à gauche de l'entrée principale de l'exposition. Des prospectus et des fiches techniques sur nos services informatiques seront à votre disposition.

'Software 2001' is pleased to invite you to the Computing Fair, which will be held from 2 to 5 May at the Exhibition Centre, Villepinte. Our stand will be situated to the left of the main entrance to the exhibition. Prospectuses and spec sheets will be available, giving details of our computing services.

WRITING ESSAYS

Students of French may be required to write an essay on a topical or literary subject. This section offers some 'skeleton' structures for constructing a cogent and well-expressed argument. For vocabulary appropriate to specific topics, see sections 142–51. Sections 80–3 provide useful further material on expressing different viewpoints, and section 130 treats key synonyms.

It is worth remembering that the quality of an essay will be judged on three criteria: relevant and well-informed content; incisive and well-organized argument; and idiomatic and correct use of French. On the first two points, the most essential key to success is to read the question closely, so that you answer it precisely, and then construct a balanced and thorough plan. Obviously, different types of essays require different approaches, but in almost all cases a plan (and essay) will work through the following stages:

(1) Brief general introduction to the subject (*amener le sujet*)

(2) Interpretation of the precise implications of the question (*cerner l'enjeu*)

(3) Indication of how the essay will proceed (*annoncer le plan*)

(4) The main body of the argument, subdivided as appropriate, e.g. For / Against
(*le développement: par exemple, thèse et antithèse*)

(5) General conclusions, related back to the question (*présenter les conclusions*)

In general, the style of an essay in French needs to be formal (*style soutenu*). This means avoiding over-colloquial expressions, and becoming familiar with the idiom of formal written French – as demonstrated, for example, throughout this section. You may initially find this register of French rather impersonal, even pompous, but remember that in French the distinction between the informal spoken language and formal written style tends to be more pronounced than in English. With practice, you should be able to select some of the 'skeletal' phrases you find particularly useful, and make them part of your own active vocabulary.

114 General introduction

(i) For a direct approach to the terms of the question:

La constatation ci-dessus soulève une question fondamentale.
The observation in the title raises a basic question.

L'affirmation de Camus pose avec netteté le problème de l'injustice.
The statement by Camus raises very clearly the problem of injustice.

Cette citation tirée de la publication des 'Amis de la Terre' nous met en face du grave problème qu'est le rapport entre l'homme et son environnement.
This quotation from the document by 'Friends of the Earth' confronts us with the serious problem of the relationship between man and the world in which he lives.

A l'origine de la réflexion de cet auteur est une idée profondément pessimiste en ce qui concerne la condition humaine.
The observation by this author is based on an essentially pessimistic view of man's condition.

Le libellé auquel nous nous trouvons confronté met en valeur la notion du devoir civique.
This title is phrased in a way which emphasizes the idea of civic duty.

(ii) For a more general introduction to the subject, before coming on to the terms of the question:

Toute analyse des qualités d'un roman se heurte à la question du rôle du lecteur.
Any analysis of the strengths of a novel begs the question of the role of the reader.

Le développement des transports collectifs est un problème fort important dans la mesure où il nous touche dans notre expérience quotidienne.
The development of public transport is a crucial problem since it affects / impinges on our everyday lives.

Nous vivons dans un monde / à une époque où toutes les valeurs traditionnelles sont remises en question.
We are living in a world / at a time when all the traditional values are being called into question.

Les sources de l'énergie font l'objet de plusieurs recherches actuelles.
Sources of energy are currently the object of research.

255

L'affaire Pérec a défrayé la chronique / a fait la Une pendant plusieurs mois.
The Pérec affair was in the headlines for several months.

Il y a vingt ans un artiste a jeté un pavé dans la mare en déclarant que les musées étaient inutiles.
Twenty years ago an artist created an outcry when he declared that museums were useless.

115 Interpreting the question

(i) Defining the essence of the question:

On peut reformuler la question ainsi: quel est le rôle du travail dans le monde actuel?
The question can be reinterpreted as follows: what is the role of work in the world today?

Le problème se résume donc à ceci: la C.E.E. existera-t-elle toujours d'ici un siècle?
In short, what we need to ask is whether the E.E.C. will still exist in a hundred years from now.

Les diplômes sont-ils survalorisés: voici le noeud du problème.
Are academic qualifications overvalued: this is the heart of the problem.

La question est donc de savoir dans quelle mesure la censure peut se justifier.
The question is therefore one of how far censorship can be justified.

Cette remarque nous amène à nous interroger sur l'avenir de l'industrie informatique.
This remark invites us to question the future of the computer industry.

(ii) Stating what aspects are / are not relevant:

Pour aborder le thème de la solitude, il importe de considérer les poèmes de Verlaine.
If we wish to examine the theme of solitude, it is important to look at the poems of Verlaine.

Cette opinion mérite d'être examinée de plus près.
This point of view deserves closer consideration.

Il convient d'approfondir la notion du progrès.
We need to examine more closely the notion of progress.

Il faut préciser la nature de ces réserves.
We need to give a precise account of these reservations.

On laissera de côté la situation des Etats-Unis, qui est un cas particulier.
We shall leave aside the situation of the U.S.A., which is a special case.

Dans le contexte de ce sujet, nous nous abstiendrons de parler de l'histoire de l'époque entre les deux guerres.
In the context of this title, we shall not refer to the history of the period between the two wars.

Nous ne nous arrêterons que sur le cas des grandes villes.
We shall only take into account the case of cities.

En traitant ce sujet, il faut éviter de tomber dans les poncifs.
In discussing this subject, we must avoid the trap of falling into clichés.

116 Outlining the plan and transitions

(i) To introduce a first section:

Il faut tenir compte de plusieurs facteurs: tout d'abord, l'état actuel des choses; ensuite, l'évolution éventuelle de nos besoins; et enfin, les enjeux politiques.
Several factors must be taken into consideration: first, the present state of things; secondly, the likely development of our needs; and finally, the political stakes.

Premièrement, il convient de peser les avantages pour les ouvriers.
First we should weigh up the advantages for the workers.

En premier lieu, il faut constater la perte des forêts tropicales.
We should first of all note the loss of tropical rain forests.

Dans un premier temps, nous nous interrogerons sur le statut de la femme.
We shall start by investigating the position of women.

La première question qui se pose, c'est celle de la sécurité.
The first question to be raised is that of safety.

On ne saurait évoquer cette controverse sans poser une question préalable.
It would be impossible to speak of this controversy without raising a preliminary question.

257

Cette réserve reste fondamentale, comme nous aurons l'occasion de le voir plus en détail par la suite.
This remains a principal objection, as will be shown later in more detail.

(ii) To draw a logical consequence from an argument:

Il s'ensuit que la télévision par satellite offre bien des avantages.
It follows that satellite television offers many advantages.

Aussi est-il que la plupart des cinéphiles préfèrent les films en version originale.
Thus most regular cinema-goers prefer films in the original language.

Il faut ainsi admettre l'importance du groupe de pression / du lobby écologique.
We must therefore recognize the importance of the ecological lobby.

Ce système coûte donc trop cher.
This system is therefore too expensive.

Or, ce projet comporte un certain nombre de risques.
Now, this plan contains / holds a number of risks.

(iii) To move on to another complementary argument:

Mais notre discussion resterait incomplète si nous négligions de considérer un autre de ses aspects fondamentaux.
But our treatment of the subject would be incomplete if we did not look at another fundamental aspect.

A ce stade, il faut passer en revue un deuxième critère.
At this point a second criterion must be examined.

A cet égard / A ce propos, un deuxième argument s'impose.
In this respect there is a second argument which we must take into account.

Pour ce qui est des jeunes / En ce qui concerne les jeunes / Quant aux jeunes, nous observons une tendance pareille.
As far as young people are concerned, there is a similar tendency.

De même, les Hollandais ont subi un échec.
Similarly, the Dutch experienced a setback / defeat.

De plus, l'entretien de ces machines s'avère compliqué.
Furthermore, these machines are complicated to service.

Il en va de même pour les personnes du troisième âge.
The same is true for retired people.

D'ailleurs, nous pourrions citer également le cas d'Amiens.
Moreover / Besides, we could also cite the case of Amiens.

(iv) To move on to an opposing argument:

Cependant, il convient de nuancer ce point de vue.
However, this point of view cannot be entirely accepted.

Pourtant / Néanmoins / Toutefois, deux tendances opposées s'affrontent dans l'interprétation de cette situation.
However, there are two opposing schools of thought on the interpretation of this situation.

D'une part, les importations ont augmenté, mais d'autre part les exportations n'ont pas baissé.
On the one hand, imports have gone up, but on the other hand exports have not fallen.

D'un côté, on a besoin de plus de professeurs, mais de l'autre côté il n'existe pas assez de candidats diplômés.
On the one hand we need more teachers, but on the other hand there are not enough qualified candidates.

Par ailleurs, on pourrait envisager une réduction du nombre de véhicules particuliers.
Alternatively, we might envisage a reduction in the number of private vehicles.

Or, il faut contester une telle interprétation de ces statistiques.
However, we should challenge such an interpretation of these statistics.

Ayant exposé ces deux points de vue, nous tenons à démontrer qu'il ne s'agit pas d'une opposition irrémédiable.
After considering these two points of view, we should observe that they are not irreconcilable.

117 Defining key terms

(i) Explaining the need for definition:

Les termes 'citoyen' et 'état' devront retenir notre attention.
The terms 'citizen' and 'state' require closer analysis.

Il nous appartient de définir l'expression employée par Racine.
We need to define the expression used by Racine.

'Liberté' est un mot clé, qu'il faudra commenter.
'Freedom' is a key word and one which requires analysis.

Il est nécessaire de nous arrêter sur la phrase 'chacun, selon son expérience.'
The phrase 'each according to his experience' needs further comment.

Nous constatons donc que la définition de 'l'amitié' proposée dans la citation est incomplète.
Thus we should note that the definition of 'friendship' offered in the title / quotation is incomplete.

(ii) Establishing various meanings of a term or expression:

Dans la formule à discuter, l'appellation 'européen' peut être prise à son sens premier.
In the wording of the title, the term 'European' can be understood in its primary sense.

Il convient de prendre ce terme dans un sens large.
This term should be understood in its wider / broader meaning.

Cette locution s'emploie aussi bien au sens propre, qu'au sens figuré.
This expression is used in both a literal and a figurative sense.

Dans ce contexte, il faudra entendre le mot 'fou' au sens propre.
In this context, the word 'mad' should be understood in its literal meaning.

Or, c'est au second de ces deux sens que le sujet se rapporte.
And it is the second of these two meanings which is implied by the title.

(iii) Giving synonyms and antonyms:

L'expression 'l'union libre' désigne l'état civil de deux personnes qui vivent en concubinage, c'est-à-dire sans se marier.
The expression 'union libre' refers to the status of two people who are living together, that is to say, who are not married.

Il s'agit des écoles libres, soit confessionnelles.
It is a question of private schools, i.e. religious establishments.

Nous pensons aux Français qui ont vécu en Algérie, autrement dit, les pieds-noirs.
We mean the French who lived in Algeria, otherwise known as the 'pieds-noirs'.

Le mot 'vert' est essentiellement synonyme d'écologiste.
The word 'green' is effectively synonymous with 'ecologist'.

Cette formule se rapproche de la définition proposée par Malraux.
This phrase / formula comes close to the definition suggested by
Malraux.

Il faut se garder de confondre ces deux termes.
It is important not to confuse these two terms.

*'Généreux' et 'avare' peuvent être considérés comme des épithètes
antinomiques.*
The adjectives 'generous' and 'mean' can be considered as direct
opposites / antonyms.

Cette définition se distingue de celle retenue par notre premier écrivain.
This definition is different from that given by the first author under
consideration.

L'interprétation philosophique s'oppose ici au sens courant du mot.
The philosophical interpretation is here different from the usual
meaning of the word.

118 Giving examples

★ Remember the spelling and gender of *un exemple*!

Par exemple, Edith Piaf est connue de tous les Français.
For example, all French people have heard of / know of Edith Piaf.

Il y a plusieurs régions concernées, à savoir l'Anjou et la Normandie.
This concerns various regions, for example, Anjou and Normandy.

Citons à titre d'exemple les romans de Marguerite Duras.
Take, for example, the novels of Marguerite Duras.

Les usines Peugeot offrent un exemple frappant / remarquable.
The Peugeot factories offer a striking / notable example.

La littérature contemporaine nous fournit maints exemples.
Contemporary literature offers numerous examples.

*Nous pourrons approfondir cet argument en nous appuyant sur
l'exemple des films de Claude Chabrol.*
We can support / develop this argument by reference to the films of
Claude Chabrol.

261

Prenons comme hypothèse un bachelier qui désire s'inscrire en faculté de droit.
Let us take the hypothetical case of a student who has passed the 'bac' and who wants to enrol to study law at university.

Il suffit de citer l'exemple des Jeux Olympiques.
We can simply cite the example of the Olympic Games.

Ce poème illustre le désespoir de Rimbaud.
This poem illustrates Rimbaud's despair.

La croissance de l'économie allemande démontre l'importance d'une politique centralisée.
The growth of the German economy shows the importance of centralized policy.

A l'appui de cette affirmation, on peut évoquer le cas de Van Gogh.
The case of Van Gogh confirms this claim / statement.

119 Supporting an argument

On peut déclarer à juste titre que cette époque ne reviendra plus.
It is legitimate to say that this period will not recur.

Il est exact de dire que la qualité de vie parmi les personnes âgées constitue un sujet de préoccupation.
It is fair to say that the quality of life experienced by old people gives cause for concern.

Nous sommes en droit d'affirmer que ce projet ne se fera jamais adopter par le gouvernement actuel.
We are entitled to say / can be sure that this plan will never be adopted by the present government.

L'optimisme des industriels est confirmé par les faits.
The optimism of the industrialists is supported by the facts.

Toutes les évidences nous permettent de soutenir cette opinion.
All the evidence supports this point of view.

Que l'enfant ait (subj.) *besoin de ses parents, c'est un fait incontestable.*
It is undeniable that a child needs its parents.

Je tiens à insister sur le fait que ce sont les jeunes qui ont initié cette réforme.
I would like to underline the fact that it was young people who introduced this reform.

120 Opposing an argument

Il y a aussi le revers de la médaille.
There is also the other side of the coin.

Il serait injuste d'accepter d'emblée tous ces arguments.
It would be unfair to accept all these arguments immediately.

Il n'est plus raisonnable dès lors de prétendre que seule la femme doit s'occuper des enfants.
It is no longer reasonable to claim that only women should care for children.

Le grand reproche qu'on peut faire à certains urbanistes, c'est leur manque d'imagination.
The most serious reproach we can level against certain town-planners is their lack of imagination.

On est obligé de reconnaître le bien-fondé des mises en garde de ce groupe.
We are forced to accept that this group's warnings are justified / well founded.

Nous devons émettre nos réserves quant à cette solution.
We must confess to some reservations as far as this solution is concerned.

Un certain nombre d'éléments s'oppose à une réponse trop simple.
A certain number of factors make it impossible to give a simple answer.

Approuver une telle dépense relèverait d'une naïveté qui ne s'accorde pas avec les réalités.
To approve such an expenditure would be to show a naive disregard for the reality of the situation.

Cette constatation a été globalement réfutée.
This claim has been totally disproved.

Certains savants ont récusé ce jugement.
Certain scholars / scientists have rejected / refused to accept this judgement.

Les résultats de l'enquête ont démenti cette observation.
The results of the inquiry disproved this observation.

Un tel raisonnement entraîne une condamnation sans appel.
Such an argument must be totally dismissed.

263

121 Conclusions

En conclusion . . . / En fin de compte . . . / Tout compte fait . . .
In conclusion . . . / Finally . . . / In the last analysis . . .

En dernière analyse, nous tenons à approuver la citation de Sartre.
In the last analysis, I think we should concur with the words of Sartre.

Au terme de notre analyse, il convient de faire le bilan.
In conclusion, we should weigh up the arguments.

De ces remarques, on peut déduire que nous ne partageons pas le point de vue de Butor.
From these remarks, it may be inferred that I do not share Butor's point of view.

Avec cette réserve – qui est de taille, certes – nous admettrons l'opinion de Balzac.
With this reservation, which it must be said is an important one, I would accept Balzac's opinion.

Cette mise au point nous permet d'insister sur l'importance de l'art moderne.
This summary underlines the importance of modern art.

FORMAL REPORTS AND ADDRESSES

This section covers writing reports on projects, research, business achievements and so forth. The register of language is also suitable for formal verbal reports – e.g. a report to a board meeting, or a lecture at a conference. For reports on more formal academic research, many of the phrases indicated in sections 114–21 are also appropriate.

122 Reporting observations

(a) Key verbs and verbal phrases

Nous avons remarqué / observé une baisse du chômage.
We have noticed / observed a drop in unemployment.

Le Président a fait remarquer que la situation ne pouvait pas durer.
The President pointed out that the situation could not continue.

On a assisté à un ralentissement de la croissance économique.
We have witnessed a slowdown in economic growth.

Plusieurs équipes ont constaté le même phénomène.
Several teams have noted the same phenomenon.

Mon collègue a déjà indiqué que nous souhaitons poursuivre ces recherches.
My colleague has already indicated / suggested that we hope to continue this research.

On ne peut pas manquer de signaler l'importance de cette découverte.
The importance of this discovery deserves to be underlined.

Le chercheur a déclaré que l'investigation ne pourrait nullement nuire aux plantes.
The researcher declared that the investigation could in no way be harmful to plants.

Le chef de l'entreprise a précisé qu'il était prêt à adopter de nouvelles mesures.
The head of the firm made it clear / explained that he was ready to adopt new measures.

Le docteur a fait état de cette évolution dans son dernier rapport.
The doctor recorded / noted this development in his last report.

Le physicien a exposé sa thèse sur l'origine de cet effet.
The physicist explained his thesis on the cause of this effect.

Mon livre cherche à expliquer pourquoi ce secteur de la population est défavorisé.
My book seeks to explain why this sector of the population is deprived.

Il convient d'analyser tous les résultats.
We should analyse all the results.

Nous voulons regarder à la loupe ce cas qui fait exception à la règle.
We want to examine in detail this case, which is an exception to the rule.

Il serait difficile de résumer les acquis de cette année en deux mots.
It would be difficult to summarize what we have achieved this year in just a few words.

Le secrétaire a voulu retracer l'histoire de l'association.
The secretary undertook to recount the history of the association.

(b) Key nouns

La direction a fait / établi un rapport sur l'année 1992-3.
The management has written / composed a report on the year 1992–3.

C'est le ministre de l'Environnement qui fera le discours ce soir.
The Minister for the Environment will be making the speech tonight.
(*discours* official speech)

A l'occasion de l'Assemblée Générale, elle a fait une communication sur les fouilles.
At the Annual General Meeting, she gave a paper on the excavations.
(*communication* conference paper)

Dans le communiqué du Préfet, vous avez sans doute remarqué la première observation.
In the Prefect's report / circular, you will probably have noticed his first observation / remark. (*exposé* official circular / report)

266

Chaque étudiant devra préparer un exposé qu'il présentera devant la classe.
Each student will be required to prepare a paper which he will deliver to the class (*exposé* paper delivered orally by students)

Le Secrétaire nous lira le procès-verbal de la dernière réunion des chercheurs.
The Secretary will read us the minutes of the last meeting of the researchers. (*procès-verbal* official minutes)

Ma collègue nous a offert une mise au point du problème.
My colleague has given us an outline / a summary of the problem.

La constatation va certes surprendre certains professionnels.
Of course the observation will surprise some professionals.

La déclaration du Président a été applaudie.
The President's statement / declaration was applauded.

Il faudra que je donne (subj.) *des précisions sur ce point.*
I must give some more details on this point.

Les actionnaires s'attendront à une analyse détaillée des données.
The shareholders will expect a detailed analysis of the facts / data.

L'étude approfondie du groupe danois a fourni des indications favorables.
The full / detailed study by the Danish group offered some favourable findings.

123 Reporting conclusions

Je veux faire le bilan de la situation financière.
I wish to give a summary / resumé of the financial situation.

Dans la conjoncture actuelle, toute mise au point devrait être considérée comme provisoire.
In the present situation / climate, any summary / analysis can only be considered provisional.

Quelles conclusions peut-on tirer de ces faits?
What conclusions can be drawn from these facts?

La police doit <u>conclure à</u> un attentat commis par des terroristes.
The police must conclude that it was a political murder carried out by
terrorists.

<u>Il en résulte que</u> l'Occident devra freiner sa consommation du pétrole.
As a consequence, the West must reduce its oil consumption.

*<u>Il en découle / s'ensuit que</u> chaque demande doit être considérée en
fonction de nos ressources.*
It follows that each request must be considered in the light of our
resources.

*<u>Il est d'ores et déjà acquis que</u> la médecine parallèle peut servir dans
certains cas.*
By now it is clearly established that alternative medicine can help in
certain cases.

Ce graphique <u>traduit</u> deux tendances opposées.
This graph / diagram shows two opposing trends.

Les résultats <u>ont révélé</u> une nouvelle tendance inquiétante.
The results have shown a disturbing new trend.

*Des enfants de quatre ans <u>se sont révélés</u> capables de déchiffrer ces
cryptogrammes.*
Some four-year-old children have shown themselves capable of solving
these puzzles.

Cette expérience <u>va s'avérer</u> inutile.
This experiment will prove to be worthless.

*Le projet <u>aura pour effet</u> d'améliorer le cadre de vie des habitants des
cités.*
The project will serve to improve the environment in which residents of
housing estates live.

124 Methods of research

(i) People involved in carrying out research

un(e) chercheur / -euse	a researcher
un cobaye / un cochon d'Inde	a guinea pig
un(e) enquêteur / -euse	a person leading an inquiry

une personne interrogée	a person interviewed
un(e) savant (e)	a scholar / scientist
un(e) scientifique	a scientist
un(e) universitaire	an academic (i.e. holding a university post)

(ii) Forms of research

une analyse	an analysis
une enquête	an inquiry
une épreuve	a test
une expérience	an experiment
des recherches (f.) (usually plural)	research
un sondage	an opinion poll

(iii) Methods of research

un appareil	a piece of equipment / apparatus
une consigne (de sécurité)	a (safety) instruction
une démarche (à suivre)	a step (to follow)
un dispositif	a device / collection of apparatus
un échantillon	a sample
le matériel	material / apparatus
un procédé	a procedure / a process (general term)
un processus	a process (especially scientific)
une technique	a technique

125 Making predictions

Les spécialistes ont annoncé <u>une prévision</u> alarmante concernant le nombre d'accidents de la route.
Specialists have made a disturbing prediction about the number of road accidents.

Selon <u>les projections</u> de l'Institut de la Santé, on mangera moins de viande d'ici l'an 2000.
According to the predictions of the Institute for Health, we shall eat less meat by the year 2000.

Nous n'osons guère nous lancer dans <u>les pronostics</u>.
We scarcely dare to risk any predictions.

Il ne faut pas se perdre <u>en conjectures</u>.
We must not get lost in hypotheses.

Pour ce qui est de l'évolution de ce marché, nous en sommes réduits aux hypothèses.
As far as the evolution of this market is concerned, we can only make hypotheses.

A court / long terme, on pourrait prévoir une amélioration de notre chiffre d'affaires.
In the short / long term, we might expect an improvement in our turnover.

Désormais, on pourrait envisager deux scénarios.
From now on / Henceforth, we might envisage / imagine two possible scenarios.

Le médecin estime que le problème disparaîtra au bout de six mois.
The doctor reckons that the problem will disappear within six months.

PART 3

Word power

SELECTIVE GLOSSARIES OF IDIOMS AND SYNONYMS

126 Building on verbs

Verbs are the backbone of a language – and one of the greatest sources of worry to foreign speakers. Part 1 reviewed the uses of the different tenses and moods in French (sections 36–47). This section lists idiomatic structures and expressions based on common verbs, together with key compound forms. Irregular verbs are marked *, referring you to the table of conjugation of common irregular verbs in the Appendix (pp. 504–19).

accrocher to hang up, hook (e.g. on wall, coatpeg), to catch and tear (clothing on a nail)

accrocher quelqu'un < coll. > to catch someone (i.e. their attention)
accrocher l'ennemi < military > to immobilize the enemy
accrocher sa montre / des bijoux < slang > to pawn one's watch / jewels
accrocher une station to tune in to a radio station
s'accrocher à quelqu'un / à quelque chose to hang on to someone / something

décrocher (1) to take off a hook or peg
(2) to land (e.g. a good job) < slang >

raccrocher (1) to hang back up
(2) to hang up the phone:
Ne raccrochez pas! Hold the line!

acheter* to buy (note accents in some tenses)

acheter quelque chose à quelqu'un to buy something for someone, or, sometimes, to buy something from someone (the context should make it clear):
Ma voisine était malade, alors je lui ai acheté des fruits.
My neighbour was ill, so I bought some fruit for her.
Comme mon voisin est fermier, je lui achète mes oeufs.
As my neighbour's a farmer, I buy my eggs from him.

acheter comptant / au comptant to pay cash
acheter à credit to buy on credit
acheter d'occasion to buy second-hand
acheter à prix d'or to pay a ridiculous price for
acheter chat en poche to buy a pig in a poke

s'acheter to be bought / to buy for oneself:

> *Ce n'est pas un produit qui s'achète couramment.*
> It's not a product which is often bought / people often buy.

racheter (1) to buy back, buy up
         (2) to redeem (especially in a religious context):

> *La Société Vincent rachètera l'entreprise qui a fait faillite.*
> The Société Vincent will buy up the firm which went bankrupt.

agir to act, operate

agir en (ami) to act as (a friend)
agir en dessous to act in an underhand manner
agir de concert avec quelqu'un to act together with someone
agir sur to have an effect upon (a situation)

s'agir de to be a question of

★ Note that *s'agir* is only used with the impersonal subject *il*:

> *De quoi s'agit-il dans ce roman?* What's this book about?

réagir to react

aller* to go, fit, suit

Remember that compound tenses are conjugated with *être*.

> *Ce manteau vous va bien.*
> This coat suits you / is a good fit.

> *Ça vous va?* Does that suit you?

> *Allez, . . .* Well, . . .
> *Allez donc!* Come on! / Come off it!
> *Vas-y! / Allez-y!* Go on! / Go ahead!
> *Vous y allez un peu fort!* < coll. > That's a bit much!
> *Ça ne va pas comme ça!* That's not on / not right!
> *Il va de soi que . . .* It goes without saying that . . .
> *Il y va de (la vie).* It's a question of (life and death).
> *Il en va de même de (lui).* It's the same with (him).

aller chercher to go and fetch
aller au devant de (son ami) to go to meet (his / her friend)
aller droit au but to get straight to the point
aller son train to go along at one's own pace
aller son petit bonhomme de chemin to jog along
ne pas y aller par quatre chemins not to beat about the bush
ne pas y aller avec le dos de la cuillère not to pussy-foot / not to mince
  words

s'en aller to go away:

> *Va-t'en! / Allez-vous-en!* Go away! / Clear off!

avoir* to have

A particularly important structure with *avoir* is
avoir (quelque chose) à (faire):

> *J'ai trois voitures à réparer.*
> I have three cars to repair.

cf. the idiomatic phrase:
n'avoir qu'à (+ infinitive) to have only to:

> *Elle n'a qu'à me demander.* She has only to ask me.
> *Qu'est-ce que tu as / vous avez?* What's the matter?

en avoir pour (+ time) to need (time):

> *J'en ai pour dix minutes.* I need ten minutes.

Il y a (1) There is / are
       (2) ago: *il y a un an* a year ago

(N.B. *Il y a* always remains singular.)

avoir beau (+ infinitive) to do in vain / there's no point in (doing):

> *Vous avez beau lui parler.* There's no point in talking to him.

avoir quelqu'un < coll. > to catch someone out:

> *Je t'ai eu!* Got you!

en avoir assez / marre < coll. > to be fed up:

> *J'en ai assez / marre.* I'm fed up.

avoir l'air (+ adjective) to look (+ adjective)
avoir (20) ans to be (20)
avoir besoin de to need

275

avoir le cafard < coll. > to be depressed
avoir chaud / froid to be / feel hot / cold (of a person)
avoir de la chance to be lucky
avoir envie de (+ infinitive) to feel like (doing)
avoir faim to be hungry
avoir l'habitude de (+ infinitive) to be used to (doing)
avoir hâte de (+ infinitive) to be in a hurry (to do)
avoir honte (de quelque chose) to be ashamed (of something)
avoir lieu to take place
avoir la parole to have the floor (to speak)
avoir peur de to be afraid of
avoir raison to be right (of a person)
avoir soif to be thirsty
avoir des soucis to be worried
avoir tort to be wrong (of a person)

se faire avoir to be taken in / caught out

battre* to beat, strike, whip (e.g. eggs)

battre de l'aile to be in bad way (literally: like a wounded bird)
battre la campagne to scour the countryside
battre les cartes to shuffle (at cards)
battre des mains to clap / applaud
battre le pavé to walk up and down the street
battre son plein < coll. > to be in full swing (e.g. party)
battre en retraite to beat a retreat

se battre to fight (each other)
se battre avec / contre (quelqu'un) to fight (someone)

abattre to knock down, dishearten

combattre *(quelqu'un / contre quelque chose / pour quelque chose)* to fight (someone / against something / for something)

débattre *(un sujet)* to debate (a subject)
se débattre contre (quelque chose) to fight against (something)

rabattre to knock down (prices), turn down (sheets)
se rabattre sur (quelque chose) to fall back on (something)

chercher to look for, seek

chercher à (+ infinitive) to try to (do):

> *Vous cherchez à le voir?* Are you trying to see him?

> *Ça va chercher dans les mille francs.* < coll. > It'll fetch about 1000 francs.

aller chercher (quelque chose / quelqu'un) to go and get (something / someone)
envoyer chercher (quelqu'un) to send for someone
venir chercher (quelqu'un) to call for (someone)

chercher une aiguille dans une botte de foin to look for a needle in a haystack
chercher la petite bête to split hairs / be over-critical
chercher des ennuis to be looking for trouble
chercher midi à quatorze heures to be looking for difficulties for the sake of it
chercher querelle (à quelqu'un) to pick a fight (with someone)

rechercher to endeavour to obtain, look hard for, research

courir* to run

courir à toutes jambes to run like mad

> *par le temps qui court* nowadays
> *Un mot en courant sur . . .* A quick word about . . .
> *Le bruit court que . . .* Rumour has it that . . .

courir après des chimères to chase after illusions
courir les filles < coll. > to be a womanizer

> *Il me court sur le haricot.* < slang > He gets on my nerves.

courir deux lièvres à la fois to try (and fail) to do two things at once
courir les rues to be common knowledge

accourir (vers quelqu'un) to run up (to someone)

parcourir (1) to travel through, cross
(2) to skim through, read cursorily

recourir à to have recourse to

cueillir* to pick, gather

cueillir des lauriers to win laurels
cueillir (un voleur) < slang > to nab (a thief)

277

accueillir to welcome, greet, invite as a guest

> *Les parents de mon correspondant m'ont accueilli chez eux.*
> My penfriend's parents had me to stay.

recueillir to gather, harvest:

> *J'ai recueilli dix exemples de cette phrase chez Proust.*
> I've found / gathered ten examples of that phrase in Proust.

> *Le Parti Socialiste a recueilli 40 pour cent des voix.*
> The Socialist Party won 40 per cent of the vote.

se recueillir (1) to gather one's thoughts quietly
                (2) to pay one's respects (at a grave)

dire* to say, tell

dire à quelqu'un de (+ infinitive) to tell someone to (do)

> *c'est-à-dire* that is to say / i.e.
> *à ce qu'on dit* apparently
> *à vrai dire* to tell the truth
> *sans mot dire* without a word

> *Dis donc! / Dites donc!* Hey! / Look here!
> *Qui l'aurait dit?* Who'd have thought that?
> *Dire que (je la connais!)* And to think that (I know her!)
> *Comment dirais-je?* How shall I put it?

> *C'est beaucoup dire.* I wouldn't say that much.
> *Ça vous dit?* < coll. > Does it appeal to you?
> *Ça ne me dit rien.* < coll. > I don't feel like it.
> *Ça me dit quelque chose.* That rings a bell.
> *Cela en dit long sur son attitude.* It says a lot about his attitude.

dire un mot en faveur de to put in a good word for
dire ses quatre vérités à quelqu'un to tell someone a few home truths

se dire to be said, be called

> *Comment est-ce que ça se dit en italien?*
> How do you say that in Italian? / What's it called in Italian?

entendre dire que to hear that (i.e. hearsay)
vouloir dire to mean

contredire to contradict

dédire to contradict, withdraw (a statement)

interdire to forbid

interdire quelque chose à quelqu'un not to allow someone something

médire to speak ill of, slander

prédire to predict

redire to repeat

trouver quelque chose à redire to find something to criticize

donner to give, deal (at cards)

> *étant donné que* given that
> *donner dans (un piège)* to fall into (a trap)
> *donner sur (le jardin)* to look out onto (the garden)
>
> *C'est donné!* < coll. > It's a bargain!
> *C'est donnant donnant.* It's a fair exchange.
> *Quel âge est-ce que tu lui donnes?* How old do you think he is?

donner le change à quelqu'un < coll. > to throw someone off the
 scent / mislead someone
donner un coup d'oeil sur / à to take a look at
donner libre cours à to give free rein to
donner le feu vert to give the go-ahead
donner lieu à (des plaintes) to give rise to (complaints)
donner rendez-vous à quelqu'un to make an appointment with
 someone
donner de la tête (contre) to bump one's head (against) / bump into

se donner (à) to give oneself, abandon oneself (to)
se donner du mal pour (faire) to take pains (doing)
se donner en spectacle to make a spectacle of oneself

s'adonner (à) (1) to devote oneself to
              (2) to become addicted to

redonner to restore, return (but for returning things, *rendre* is far more
 common)

dormir* to sleep

dormir debout hardly to keep one's eyes open
un conte à dormir debout a cock-and-bull story

dormir à la belle étoile to sleep out in the open
dormir sur les deux oreilles to sleep soundly

dormir à poings fermés to sleep soundly
dormir comme une souche to sleep like a log

endormir to put / send to sleep, anaesthetize

s'endormir to fall asleep
se rendormir to go / fall back to sleep

être* to be

⭐ Note the two basic structures:

- *Il est* (+ adjective) *de* (+infinitive):

  Il est difficile de vous répondre.
  It's difficult to give you an answer.

- *C'est* (+ adjective) *à* (+ infinitive)
  (Noun) *être* (+ adjective) *à* (+ infinitive)

  C'est facile à réparer.
  It's easy to repair.

  La maison est à vendre.
  The house is for sale.

  Soit! < formal / literary > Agreed! / So be it!

  Il en est ainsi. That's how it is.
  Il n'en est rien. That's not true at all.
  toujours est-il que < formal / literary > none the less

être à quelqu'un to belong to someone:

  C'est à toi? Is it yours?

en être to be up to (a point):

  Où en êtes-vous dans le livre?
  Where are you up to in the book?

y être (1) to understand / get it:

  Ah! J'y suis! Ah! I get it!

  (2) to be (hard) at it:

  Mon fils y est déjà. My son's already hard at it.

y être pour quelque chose / rien to be / not to be responsible:

  Quant à sa décision, je n'y suis pour rien.
  As for his decision, it's nothing to do with me / I'm not responsible.

être sur le point de (+ infinitive) to be about to (do)
être en train de (+ infinitive) to be (doing) / in the process of (doing)

être d'accord avec to agree with
être au courant de to be up to date on / informed about
être en état / mesure de to be in a position / able to
être en panne to be out of order (machines)
être de retour to return / get back / be back

faire* to do, make

Faire occurs in many common expressions about the weather:

> *Il fait beau.* It's fine.
> *Il fait bon.* It's lovely weather / just right.
> *Il fait chaud.* It's hot.
> *Il fait doux.* It's mild.
> *Il fait frais.* It's chilly / cool.
> *Il fait froid.* It's cold.
> *Il fait jour.* It's daylight.
> *Il fait lourd.* It's close / sultry.
> *Il fait mauvais.* It's bad weather.
> *Il fait nuit.* It's dark / night-time.
> *Il fait orageux.* It's stormy.
> *Il fait du soleil.* There's sunshine.
> *Il fait du tonnerre.* It's thundering.
> *Il fait du vent.* It's windy.
> *Il fait un temps* (+ adjective). It's (adjective) weather.

Faire is used with the partitive article (*du, de la*) for most individual sports, meaning 'to play / go in for':

> *Je fais de la natation depuis six ans, et l'année prochaine je ferai du tennis.*
> I've gone in for swimming for six years now, and next year I'll play tennis.

faire (+ infinitive) to get / have something done:

> *J'ai fait repeindre la maison.* I've had the house redecorated.
> *Il a fait venir la police.* He called the police.

> *Que faire?* What's to be done?
> *Cela ne fait rien.* That doesn't matter.
> *Ça ne me fait ni chaud ni froid.* < coll. > I don't care one way or the other.
> *Cela vous fait 40 francs.* That will be 40 francs.

> *C'en est fait de (lui).* He's had it (of people).

en faire autant to do the same:

>*Puisque tu te sers, alors j'en fais autant.*
>Since you're helping yourself, I'll do so too.

faire en sorte que . . . to see to it that . . .:

>*Elle a fait en sorte que chaque invité recevait un cadeau.*
>She saw to it that each guest received a present.

>*Le directeur fera en sorte que tu sois* (subj.) *récompensé.*
>The manager will see to it that you are rewarded.

faire exprès (+ infinitive) to do on purpose / deliberately:

>*Il a fait exprès de t'agacer.*
>He deliberately annoyed you. / He annoyed you on purpose.

faire bon accueil (à quelqu'un) to welcome (someone)
faire attention (à) to be careful (about)
faire de l'autostop to hitch-hike
faire des bêtises to mess around / play around
faire comme chez soi to make oneself at home
faire des courses / des achats to go shopping
faire la cuisine to cook / do the cooking
faire face à to face up to / oppose
faire des histoires < coll. > to make a big fuss
faire la grasse matinée to have a lie-in / sleep through
faire de son mieux to do one's best
faire part de quelque chose à quelqu'un to inform someone of
    something (especially weddings, deaths)
faire partie de to be part of
faire de la peine à quelqu'un to hurt someone's feelings
faire peur à quelqu'un to frighten someone
faire plaisir à quelqu'un to please someone
faire une promenade to go for a walk
faire la queue to queue / line up
faire savoir (à quelqu'un) que to inform (someone) that
faire semblant de (+ infinitive) to pretend to (do)
faire suivre to forward (mail)
en faire à sa tête to go one's own way / not to listen to advice
faire voir quelque chose à quelqu'un to show something to someone

se faire (+ infinitive) to get oneself (+ past participle):

>*L'enfant s'est fait renvoyer de l'école.*
>The child got himself / herself expelled from the school.

il se fait que it happens that
Comment se fait-il que . . ? How come that . . .?
Cela se fait? Is that done / acceptable?

se faire à (+ noun) to get used to / become resigned to:

Je me suis fait à l'idée. I've got used to the idea.

s'en faire to worry:

Ne t'en fais pas! Don't worry / get upset!
Il ne s'en fait pas! < coll. > He's got a nerve!

se faire fort de (+ infinitive) to be confident of (doing)
se faire des illusions to delude oneself
se faire une raison to resign oneself / accept philosophically
se faire du mauvais sang to get upset / worried
se laisser faire to submit passively / to go along

défaire to undo, unmake, rout

se défaire de to get rid of

refaire to redo, remake

falloir* to be necessary
Remember that *falloir* is only ever used with the impersonal subject *il*.
Il me faut I need:

Il me faut plus de temps. I need more time.
Il me faut le voir. / Il faut que je le voie (subj.). I have to see him.

comme il faut correctly / in an acceptable manner
une personne comme il faut a well-bred / very proper person

ce qu'il faut what's necessary / what's needed

s'en falloir to be lacking / missing:

Il s'en faut de la moitié. We're missing half. / Half is missing.

peu s'en faut very nearly / almost:

J'ai tous les noms, ou peu s'en faut.
I've got almost all the names.

tant s'en faut a long way from it / far from it:

Je n'ai pas encore terminé le rapport, tant s'en faut.
I haven't finished the report yet, far from it.

il s'en faut de peu que (+ subj.) almost to / very nearly to:

> *Il s'en est fallu de peu que je ne lui dise la vérité.*
> I very nearly told him the truth.

 il s'en faut de beaucoup que (+ subj.) to be far from:

> *Il s'en faut de beaucoup que je sois prêt à partir.*
> I'm far from ready to leave.

se fier to trust

Note that this verb is normally only found in the reflexive form.

se fier à quelqu'un to trust someone

confier *quelque chose à quelqu'un* to entrust something to someone
se confier à quelqu'un to confide in someone

défier to defy, brave

défier les dangers to face / brave dangers
défier quelqu'un de (+ infinitive) to challenge someone to (do)
se défier de (quelque chose) to lack confidence in (something)
se défier de soi-même to be lacking in self-confidence

se méfier *de quelqu'un / quelque chose* to mistrust someone /
  something

jeter* to throw (note double *t* in some tenses)

jeter l'ancre to cast anchor
jeter l'argent par les fenêtres to throw money away
jeter un coup d'oeil sur / à to glance at / take a look at
jeter un cri to shout / give a cry
jeter son dévolu sur to set one's sights on / be out to catch (with
  marriage in view)
jeter sa gourme to sow one's wild oats
jeter de l'huile sur le feu to fan the flames (of trouble)
jeter le manche après la cognée to throw in the towel
jeter aux orties to do away with / discard (especially old-fashioned ideas
  or practices)
en jeter plein la vue to put on a big show
jeter de la poudre aux yeux de quelqu'un to pull the wool over
  someone's eyes

jeter un sort sur to cast a spell over

se jeter to throw oneself, flow (of rivers):

> *La Garonne se jette dans l'Atlantique.*
> The Garonne flows into the Atlantic.

projeter to plan, project

rejeter to reject

jouer to play

> *A vous de jouer.* It's your turn / move.
> *Qu'est-ce qu'on joue au cinéma?* What's on at the cinema?

★ Note the distinction:

- *jouer au / à la / aux* + sport / game
- *jouer du / de la / des* + musical instrument

> *On peut jouer au football ou aux cartes, comme tu veux.*
> We can play football or play cards, you choose.

> *Est-ce que tu joues de la guitare ou du piano?*
> Do you play the guitar or piano?

jouer au / à la (+ profession) to play at being
jouer au plus fin avec quelqu'un to try to outwit someone
jouer cartes sur table to play fair / above board
jouer des coudes to push and shove
jouer double jeu to double-cross
jouer gros jeu to play for high stakes
jouer la comédie to put on an act / show off
jouer les trouble-fêtes to rock the boat
jouer pour la galerie to play to the audience
jouer serré to play it close to one's chest
jouer la surprise to feign surprise
jouer au plus sûr to play safe
jouer un tour à quelqu'un to play a trick on someone

se jouer de quelqu'un to make a fool of someone

faire jouer (les boiseries) to warp (wood)
faire jouer une clé (dans la serrure) to jiggle a key around (in the lock)

déjouer to foil, frustrate
déjouer un complot to foil a plot

lever* to raise, lift (note the accent in certain tenses)

lever les bras au ciel to throw up one's hands (in horror)
lever le camp to break up camp
lever une interdiction to raise a ban
lever un lièvre to raise a sticky point
lever le pied < coll. > to take off / clear off
lever la séance < formal > to dissolve a meeting

se lever to get up:
> *Le temps se lève.* The weather's clearing up.

se lever du pied gauche to get out of bed on the wrong side

élever (1) to raise (buildings, obstacles)
> (2) to bring up (children), keep animals

s'élever to rise (intransitive), to be raised:
> *Les prix s'élèvent tous les jours.* Prices rise daily.

enlever *quelque chose à quelqu'un* to remove, take away something
from someone
enlever un enfant to kidnap a child

prélever to deduct at source (e.g. tax)

relever (1) to raise again, lift back up
> (2) to accentuate, emphasize
> (3) to find, note

> *La robe relevait sa beauté.*
> The dress accentuated her beauty.

> *Le bibliothécaire a relevé dix articles sur le théâtre.*
> The librarian found ten articles on the theatre.

relever la garde to relieve the guard
relever (une jupe) to turn up / tuck up (a skirt)

se relever to get up again, to recover

soulever (1) to raise, excite (problems, emotions)
> (2) to rouse to indignation

> *Cela me soulève le coeur.* It sickens me.

se soulever to rise up (e.g. in indignation)

mener* to lead, take (note accents in some tenses)

Cela te mènera loin. That will get you a long way.

mener (un projet) à bien to carry out (a plan) successfully
mener bien sa barque to manage one's affairs well
mener (deux activités) de front to do (two things) simultaneously
mener grand train to live it up / live in style
mener la grande vie to live in style
mener quelqu'un par le bout du nez to twist someone round one's little finger
mener quelqu'un tambour battant to give someone a firm lead
mener une vie to lead a life

amener to lead, take (especially people going to a place)
★ Note that *mener une personne* means literally 'to lead / show the way', whereas *amener* is used to translate 'to take':

amener quelqu'un (en voiture) to give a lift to someone
amener quelqu'un à (+ infinitive) to induce someone to (do)

s'amener < coll. > to turn up

emmener to lead away, take away (especially of things)
être emmené à to be able to (of people)

promener to take for a walk (of dogs and children)

se promener to go for a walk

envoyer promener quelqu'un < coll. > to send someone packing

ramener to take back (person or thing)

ramener à la maison to bring home
ramener quelqu'un à (son devoir) to recall someone to (his / her duty)

se ramener à < coll. > to amount to / add up to:

Toutes ses idées se ramènent à ceci. All his ideas add up to this.

mettre* to put, place, turn on (electrical appliances)

Mettez que ... Suppose that ...

mettre bas to give birth (only of animals)
mettre en cause to question / call into question
mettre quelqu'un en colère to make someone angry
mettre de côté to put aside / save
mettre quelqu'un au courant to bring someone up to date
mettre fin à to put an end to

287

mettre en lumière to bring out / emphasize
mettre en marche to start up / set going (engines)
mettre au monde to give birth to (a child)
mettre en ordre to tidy up
mettre les pieds dans le plat (1) to put one's foot in it
                                               (2) to put one's foot down
mettre au point to clarify / resume, to perfect
mettre quelqu'un à la porte < coll. > to kick someone out / sack
  someone
mettre en relief to emphasize / accentuate
mettre en scène to stage
mettre la table / le couvert to lay the table

se mettre to put oneself:

> *Je me suis mis(e) à sa place.* I put myself in his / her place.

se mettre à (+ infinitive) to start to (do)
se mettre à table to sit down to eat
se mettre à (+ noun) to set to / turn oneself to:

> *Il se met au bricolage.* He turns his hand to D.I.Y.

se mettre en colère to get angry
se mettre en marche to start up (engine)
se mettre en route to set off
se mettre en tête de (+ infinitive) to take it into one's head to (do)

admettre to admit, acknowledge, let in

commettre to commit

démettre (1) to dislocate, put out of joint
                 (2) to dismiss (from work)

se démettre to resign

émettre to emit, give off (a noise), to broadcast (radio, T.V.)

omettre to omit, leave out

promettre to promise
promettre à quelqu'un de (+ infinitive) to promise someone to (do)

se promettre de (+ infinitive) to promise oneself to (do)

remettre to put back, replace
remettre à (plus tard) to put off until (later)
remettre en question to call into question

soumettre to submit, subject
se soumettre à quelque chose to submit oneself to something

mordre to bite

mordre à quelque chose to take to something:

    Elle a bien mordu à ce travail. She's really taken to this job.

mordre à (l'appât) to bite into (the bait)
mordre à belles dents to bite right into (of fruit, etc.)
mordre sur (la ligne de départ) to step over (the starting line)
mordre la poussière to bite the dust

se mordre les doigts de quelque chose to kick oneself for something

démordre to let go one's hold, yield

ne pas en démordre < coll. > to refuse to budge an inch
faire démordre quelqu'un to make someone shift

perdre to lose, ruin, waste

    à mes moments perdus in my spare time

perdre son argent to waste one's money
perdre la boussole < slang > to go off one's rocker
perdre l'habitude to be out of practice
perdre son latin not to be able to make head or tail of something
perdre la main to lose one's touch
perdre le nord to lose one's bearings
perdre son temps to waste one's time
perdre la tête to panic
perdre (quelque chose) de vue to lose sight of (something)

se perdre to get lost
se perdre de vue to lose touch
s'y perdre to get confused
se perdre dans to lose oneself in / be absorbed in

porter to carry, bear

porter sur (quelque chose) to concern / treat something:

    Mes enquêtes portent sur une tribu africaine.
    My research concerns an African tribe.

être porté à (+ infinitive) to be inclined to (do)

289

porter atteinte à to strike a blow at
porter le nom de to bear the name of
porter quelqu'un aux nues to praise someone to the skies
porter plainte to lodge / register a complaint
porter remède à to remedy
porter secours à quelqu'un to help someone

se porter bien to be well (state of health)
se porter comme un charme to be as fit as a fiddle

se porter candidat to stand as a candidate

apporter to bring

comporter to comprise, consist of
se comporter to behave

emporter to take away, carry away

l'emporter sur (1) to outweigh (something)
              (2) to beat (someone)
    Qui l'a emporté? Who won?

s'emporter to fly into a rage
s'emporter contre to rail against

exporter to export

importer (1) to import
          (2) to matter (used only in third person)
    Cela vous importe beaucoup?
    Is it very serious for you? / Does it matter a lot to you?

    N'importe. Never mind.
    n'importe quel livre any book
    Peu importe. It's not serious.
    Peu importe lequel! It doesn't matter which!

rapporter to bring back, yield, bring in money
s'en rapporter à quelqu'un to rely on someone's version of events

reporter to carry back
se reporter à quelqu'un to refer back to someone

supporter to put up with, tolerate

pouvoir *   to be able, to be possible

être on ne peut plus (+ adjective) to be as (adjective) as you could hope
   to find / as possible:

   C'est un homme on ne peut plus charmant.
   He's as charming a man as you could hope to find.

n'en pouvoir plus to be unable to carry on:

   Je n'en peux plus! I can't take any more! / I can't carry on!

n'y pouvoir rien not to be responsible / to be unable to do anything:

   Je n'y peux rien. I can't do anything about it. / I'm not responsible.

se pouvoir to be possible:

   Cela se peut. That may be so.
   Il se peut que . . . (+ subj.) It is possible that . . .

prendre *   to take, capture

★ *prendre quelque chose à quelqu'un* to take something from someone

à tout prendre all in all

   Je prendrais volontiers (un café). I could just do with (a coffee).
   Qu'est-ce qui te prend? What's got into you?

être pris to be occupied / engaged / busy

prendre quelqu'un pour to take someone for
prendre quelque chose sur soi to take responsibility for
prendre quelqu'un de court to catch someone short
prendre quelqu'un au dépourvu to catch someone off guard / when
   they are not expecting you
prendre fait et cause pour to stand up for
prendre quelqu'un sur le fait to catch someone in the act / red-handed
prendre feu to catch fire
prendre fin to come to an end
prendre garde to watch out
prendre quelque chose en grippe < slang > to take a strong dislike to
prendre ses jambes à son cou < coll. > to take to one's heels
prendre le large to go out to sea (of boats)
prendre en main to take charge of
prendre des mesures to take steps
prendre la mouche < coll. > to fly off the handle
prendre naissance to originate, arise (of things)
prendre la parole to speak / have the floor

prendre le parti de (1) to speak up for someone
                     (2) to decide to take a course of action

prendre au pied de la lettre to take literally
prendre du poids / des kilos to put on weight
prendre position to make a stand
prendre la retraite to retire
prendre au sérieux to take seriously
prendre quelqu'un à témoin to call someone as a witness
prendre quelque chose de travers to take something amiss
prendre des vessies pour des lanternes to believe any old story / to
   believe the moon is made of green cheese

se prendre à quelque chose to tackle something
s'en prendre à quelqu'un to attack / blame someone
se prendre à (+ infinitive) < literary > to begin to
se prendre pour to take oneself for
se prendre d'amitié pour quelqu'un to take to someone

apprendre to learn

comprendre (1) to understand
                (2) to comprise, include

   Je n'y comprends rien. I can't make anything of it.
   Cela se comprend. That's understandable.

entreprendre to undertake

s'éprendre *(de)* to fall in love (with)

se méprendre < literary > to be mistaken (especially mistaking one
   person for another)

reprendre to take back, resume, correct (someone)

reprendre quelqu'un à quelque chose to catch someone doing
   something again:

   Vous ne m'y reprendez pas. You won't catch me doing that again.

reprendre connaissance to recover consciousness
reprendre le dessus to regain the upper hand
reprendre ses forces to recover one's strength
reprendre haleine to catch one's breath

se reprendre to recover oneself, correct oneself

rire* to laugh

rire de (quelque chose) to laugh at (something)

pour rire as a joke / for fun
sans rire . . . seriously

> *Vous voulez rire!* You're joking! / You must be joking!

faire rire to be funny:
> *Tu me fais rire.* You are funny.

avoir le fou rire to have a fit of giggles
rire dans sa barbe to laugh up one's sleeve
rire de bon coeur to laugh heartily
éclater de rire to burst out laughing
rire aux éclats / rire à gorge déployée to laugh loudly / roar with
   laughter
rire jaune to give a forced laugh
rire au nez de quelqu'un to laugh in someone's face

se rire de to make fun of

sourire *(à quelqu'un)* to smile (at someone)

savoir* to know
> *Je ne sais pas trop.* I don't really know.
> *Je ne sais que faire.* I don't know what to do.

> *Vous n'êtes pas sans savoir que . . .* < formal / literary >
> You are well aware that . . .

> *Sachez que* < especially journalistic >
> Remember that . . . / You may like to know that . . .

à savoir i.e. / namely
> *C'est à savoir.* That remains to be seen.

Autant que je sache. As far as I know.
> *Pas autant que je sache.* Not as far as I know.

faire savoir à quelqu'un que (+ indicative) to inform someone that
Reste à savoir si . . . It remains to be seen whether . . .

en savoir long sur quelque chose to be in the know about / know more
   than one is letting on:
> *Il en sait long sur cette affaire.* He's in the know about that matter.

dieu sait qui / où / comment (etc.) goodness knows who / where / how
  (etc.)

savoir gré à quelqu'un to be grateful to someone
savoir mauvais gré à quelqu'un to be displeased with someone
ne pas savoir sur quel pied danser not to know which way to turn
ne plus savoir à quoi s'en tenir not to know what to think any longer
ne pas savoir à quel saint se vouer to be at one's wits' end

se savoir to be known:

> *Tout se sait dans cette ville.*
> Everything is known / gets around in this town.

sortir* (1) to go out, come out (intransitive: compound tenses
          conjugated with *être*)
          (2) to get out, bring out (transitive: compound tenses
          conjugated with *avoir*)

un sujet qui sort (à l'examen) a question which comes up (at an exam)

sortir avec (quelqu'un) to be going out with (someone)

être sorti de l'auberge to be out of the woods

> *Cela m'est sorti de l'esprit / de la tête.* It's slipped my mind.

sortir de ses gonds < coll. > to fly off the handle
sortir du lit to get out of bed
sortir un livre to bring out / publish a book
sortir d'une maladie to be recovering from an illness
sortir de l'ordinaire to be out of the ordinary
sortir de table to leave the table

se sortir de (la situation) to get out of (the situation)
s'en sortir to manage / cope with difficulties:

> *Comment veux-tu qu'il s'en sorte maintenant?*
> How do you expect him to cope now?

assortir to match, pair

deux choses bien assorties two things which are a good match

ressortir (1) to go out again, go back out
          (2) to stand out, be thrown into relief

ressortir de quelque chose (1) to result from something
                      (2) to be dependent on / under
                          jurisdiction of

faire ressortir (quelque chose) to throw into relief / emphasize (something)

tenir* to hold, possess, keep

Tiens! / Tenez! (1) Look! (especially with surprise)
      (2) Here you are!

tenir à quelque chose to be keen on something
tenir à ce que (+ subj.) to insist that
  Il ne tient qu'à (vous). It's up to / all depends on (you).
  Je n'y tiens pas. I don't mind if not. / I'm not particularly keen.
  Je n'y tiens plus. I can't hold on any longer.
  Qu'à cela ne tienne. < formal > That need not be a problem.

tenir de (son père) to take after (his / her father)

tenir l'affiche to have a long run (of film, play)
tenir bon to hold one's ground / stand fast
tenir jusqu'au bout < coll. > to stick it out to the end
tenir compte de (quelque chose) to take (something) into account

  Cela (lui) tient au coeur. It's very important (to him / her).

tenir le coup < coll. > to last out (of people)
tenir (quelqu'un) au courant to keep (someone) up to date
tenir debout to make sense / hold water
tenir (quelqu'un) à distance to keep (someone) at arm's length
tenir la dragée haute à quelqu'un to keep someone waiting for something / hold out on someone
tenir (quelqu'un) en haleine to keep (someone) in suspense
tenir lieu de to take the place of
tenir de la place to take up space
tenir le haut du pavé < coll. > to lord it / take pride of place
tenir parole to keep one's word
tenir rigueur à quelqu'un de quelque chose to hold something against someone
tenir (quelque chose) de bonne source to have it on good authority
tenir tête à quelqu'un to stand up to someone

se tenir (1) to take place (location of events)
      (2) to behave (especially of children)

savoir se tenir to know how to behave oneself

se tenir à quelque chose to abide by / follow (e.g. idea)

ne pouvoir se tenir de (+ infinitive) < literary > to be unable to stop
   oneself (doing)
se le tenir pour dit to take it as said / to get the message
se tenir coi to lie low / keep quiet
se tenir debout to remain standing
se tenir sur ses gardes to be on one's guard

s'abstenir *de* (+ infinitive) to abstain, refrain from (doing)

appartenir *à* to belong to

   Il vous appartient de (+ infinitive) . . . < formal >
   It is your duty to / you should (do) . . .

contenir to contain, consist of, keep in check

se contenir to restrain oneself

retenir (1) to hold back, withhold, restrain
         (2) to delay, give detention to a child (school)
         (3) to book (e.g. a seat)
se retenir (*de* + infinitive) to hold oneself back (from doing)

soutenir to uphold, support, defend
soutenir la conversation to keep the conversation going

tirer to pull, drag, fire

être tiré par les cheveux to be far-fetched (e.g. of an explanation)
être tiré à quatre épingles to be dressed up / dressed to kill

   La peau (me) tire. My skin feels tight / irritable.

tirer sur (quelqu'un) to fire on (someone)

tirer les cartes to read fortunes (in cards)
tirer au clair to clear up (a mystery)
tirer à la courte paille to draw lots / straws
tirer le diable par la queue < coll. > to be hard up
tirer son épingle du jeu to get out while the going's good
tirer à sa fin to draw to an end
tirer la langue to stick out one's tongue
tirer un livre / un journal à x exemplaires to print *x* copies of a
   book / newspaper
tirer le meilleur parti de to make the best of
tirer profit de quelque chose to profit from something
tirer au sort to draw lots
tirer les vers du nez (à quelqu'un) < coll. > to worm secrets out (of
   someone)

se tirer (1) to pull oneself, haul oneself
            (2) < slang > to clear off

se tirer d'affaire to get out of trouble
se faire tirer l'oreille pour (+ infinitive) to have to be pushed to (do)

s'en tirer to pull through
s'en tirer avec to get away / off with (e.g. of thieves)
s'en tirer à bon compte to get off lightly

attirer to attract, entice

étirer to stretch, lengthen
s'étirer to stretch one's limbs (of people and cats)

retirer to withdraw, retract, pull back
retirer sa parole to go back on one's word
se retirer to retreat, withdraw, ebb (sea)

tomber to fall
Remember that compound tenses are conjugated with *être*.

tomber bien (juste) to come at (just) the right moment
être bien tombé to have made a lucky choice

tomber sur to run into / come across

faire tomber to knock down / to push over
laisser tomber quelque chose to drop something
laisser tomber quelqu'un < coll. > to drop someone

tomber amoureux de to fall in love with
tomber à l'eau to fall flat / be unsuccessful (of projects)
tomber dans un guêpier to stir up a hornet's nest
tomber malade to fall ill
tomber raide mort to drop dead
tomber des nues to come back down to earth with a bump
tomber en panne to break down / suffer a breakdown
tomber dans les pommes < coll. > to pass out
tomber en ruines to be in ruins (of buildings)
tomber à la renverse to fall over backwards / do a double take
   (i.e. with surprise)
tomber par terre to fall down / fall right over
tomber à plat ventre to fall flat on one's face

retomber to fall back down, to have a relapse
retomber malade to fall ill again

venir* to come
Remember that compound tenses are conjugated with *être*.

à venir to come / future:

>   *les générations à venir* future generations

venir à (+ infinitive) (1) to get to a stage of (doing)
>   (2) to happen to (do)

venir de (+ infinitive) to have just (done):
>   *Je viens de revoir ce film.* I've just seen that film again.

faire venir to send for
venir chercher to call for

venir comme un cheveu sur la soupe to turn up when least needed
venir à l'esprit to come into one's mind / have the idea
venir au monde to come into the world / be born

en venir à (+ infinitive) to get to the point of (doing):

>   *Où voulez-vous en venir?* What are you getting at?

en venir à bout de quelque chose to get to the end of / cope with
en venir aux mains to come to blows

advenir to happen, come about (used only in third person
   singular: *il advient*)

>   *Qu'est-il advenu de lui?* < formal > What's become of him?

convenir to agree, acknowledge, suit

>   *Ça vous convient?* Does that suit you?
>   *Il convient que . . .* (+ subj.) It is fitting / proper that . . .

prévenir *quelque chose* to anticipate / forestall something
prévenir quelqu'un to warn someone

provenir *de* to originate from, spring from

revenir to come back, return
revenir sur ses pas to retrace one's steps

revenir à quelque chose to amount to / cost:

>   *Cela revient à la même chose.* It comes down to the same thing.
>   *Cela revient cher.* It works out expensive.

revenir à la charge to return to the fray
revenir à ses moutons to get back to the matter in hand

ne pas en revenir to be surprised

faire revenir to brown, cook lightly (meat)

se souvenir *de quelque chose / de quelqu'un* to remember
  something / someone

survenir to happen (unexpectedly), befall

voir to see

> *Voyons!* Let's see! / Now look here! / Come, come!
> *Vois-tu . . . / Voyez-vous . . .* Yes, but . . . / The thing is . . .
> *C'est à voir.* That remains to be seen.

voir quelque chose de ses propres yeux to see something with one's
  own eyes

voir à quelque chose to see to something
voir à ce que (+ subj.) to see to it that

avoir quelque chose à voir avec to have something to do with / be
  related to
n'avoir rien à voir avec to have nothing to do with:
> *Ça n'a rien à voir.* < coll. > That's irrelevant.

en voir de belles < coll. > to see some right things / right goings-on
n'y voir que du bleu not to smell a rat
voir trente-six chandelles to see stars
y voir clair <coll. > to get the idea / see clearly
voir le jour to be born / see the light of day
voir quelque chose (venir) de loin to see something coming / have
  thought as much
voir quelque chose du même oeil to see eye to eye on something
voir trouble to have blurred vision / not to see clearly
voir la vie en rose to be optimistic / look on the bright side of things

faire voir to show
faire voir de quel bois on se chauffe < coll. > to show what one is
  made of
en faire voir de toutes les couleurs à quelqu'un to give someone a hard
  time

laisser voir to reveal / give away

se voir to see oneself, see each other, be seen:
> *Cela se voit.* That's evident.
> *Ils ne peuvent pas se voir.* < coll. > They can't stand each other.

299

entrevoir to catch a glimpse of

pourvoir to provide, see to
pourvoir à un emploi to fill a vacancy
se pourvoir de to provide oneself with

prévoir to foresee, provide (in advance), plan
Note: conjugated like *voir* **except** in future and conditional *je prévoirai*, etc.

revoir to see again, revise, reconsider

*vouloir** to want, wish, mean to
(For *vouloir que* + subjunctive, see section 44c (ii).)

> *Que veux-tu? / Que voulez-vous?* What do you expect?
> *Veuillez* (+ infinitive) . . . < public notices or formal correspondence> Please (do) . . .
> *Voulez-vous / Veux-tu* (+ infinitive) . . .? < polite request > Would you (do) . . .?

vouloir bien (+ infinitive) to be willing to / keen to
en vouloir à quelqu'un to hold it against someone / bear a grudge against someone:
> *Tu m'en veux?* Are you cross with me?

s'en vouloir to be cross with oneself

vouloir de quelque chose to be interested in something / willing to accept something:
> *Tu veux de son argent?* Will you accept his money?

vouloir dire to mean:
> *Cela ne veut rien dire.* It's meaningless.

vouloir du bien à quelqu'un to wish someone well

127 Building on nouns

You will probably be familiar with the literal meaning of most of the nouns given below. This section lists some of the common idiomatic expressions in which they are also used, and which are a key to word power in French.

abord (m.) approach

Au premier abord / De prime abord, ça paraît difficile.
At first sight, it looks difficult.

Dès l'abord, il se méfiait. < literary >
From the outset, he was suspicious.

Il s'arrêta aux abords de la ville.
He stopped on the outskirts of the town.

Il faut trouver un garage d'abord.
We must find a garage first.

Mon directeur est d'un abord difficile.
My manager is not very approachable.

affaire (f.) business, matter, deal

Ce n'est pas mon affaire.
That's nothing to do with me.

Mêlez-vous de vos affaires. < coll. >
Mind your own business.

La belle affaire!
What a lot of fuss about nothing!

Vous aurez affaire à mon collègue.
You'll be dealing with my colleague.

Voilà, ça devrait faire ton affaire. < coll. >
There you are, that should be what you need.

C'est l'affaire d'une petite demi-heure.
It won't take half an hour.

Vouz avez fait une bonne affaire?
Have you struck a good deal / got a bargain?

Le propriétaire était impliqué dans une affaire.
The owner was involved in a lawsuit.

Le gamin s'est tiré d'affaire en sautant par le mur. < slang >
The kid got out of trouble by jumping over the wall.

Son affaire est faite. < slang >   He's done for.

Il connaît le ministre des Affaires étrangères.
He knows the Foreign Minister.

Je devrais mettre de l'ordre dans mes affaires.
I should sort out my finances.

Il laisse ses affaires traîner partout à la maison. < coll. >
He leaves his things lying all over the place at home.

301

bout (m.) end, bit

Mettez les tables bout à bout.
Put the tables end to end.

C'est comme si on habitait au bout du monde.
It's like living in the middle of nowhere.

Elle a parcouru la ville d'un bout à l'autre.
She's been right through the town (from end to end).

Je suis complètement à bout ce soir. < slang >
I'm absolutely shattered / all in this evening.

Nous sommes à bout d'arguments. < coll. >
We've run out of arguments.

Vous êtes venus au bout du problème?
Did you get over the problem?

Le soldat a tiré sur lui à bout portant.
The soldier fired on him at point-blank range.

Il le répète à tout bout de champ.
He keeps repeating it every five minutes.

Les enfants répondirent du bout des lèvres. (with verbs of
    speaking)
The children answered half-heartedly.

Elle ne savait pas par quel bout le prendre. (usually negative)
She didn't know how to handle him.

Nous avons toujours du mal à joindre les deux bouts.
We always have trouble making ends meet.

bras (m.) arm

Ils se promenaient bras dessus, bras dessous.
They were going for a walk arm in arm.

Il a saisi son cousin à bras le corps.
He grabbed his cousin round the waist.

En été il est toujours en bras de chemise.
In summer he's always in shirt sleeves.

Elle, c'est quelqu'un qui a le bras long. < coll. >
She's someone who has influence / pull.

Il a quatre enfants sur les bras.
He's got four children to look after / support.

Mon voisin est mon bras droit.
My neighbour's my right-hand man.

L'usine manque de bras ce mois-ci.
The factory's short of workers this month.

Les bras m'en tombent! < coll. >
I'm amazed!

coeur (m.) heart

Ils ont appris le poème par coeur.
They learned the poem by heart.

Comme enfant, il avait toujours du coeur au ventre.
As a child, he always had plenty of guts.

C'est un homme adorable, qui a le coeur sur la main.
He's a wonderful man, very big-hearted / kind-hearted.

Il ne sait pas dissimuler ses émotions; il a le coeur sur les lèvres.
He can't hide his feelings; he wears his heart on his sleeve.

Nous n'avons pas le coeur à sortir après cette triste nouvelle.
We're not in the mood to go out after that sad piece of news.

C'est un sujet qui me tient à coeur.
It's a subject which is close to my heart.

C'est un enfant délicat, qui a souvent mal au coeur.
He's a delicate child, and often feels sick.

Ça m'a fait mal au coeur de le voir dans un tel état.
It upset me to see him in that state.

Que tu as le coeur gros!
You are unhappy!

compte (m.) account, reckoning, report

un compte bancaire a bank account
un compte à rebours countdown (satellite launch)
un laissé pour compte a down-and-out (person)
un règlement de comptes a settling of scores

Son compte est bon.
He / She is done for.

Vous l'avez acheté à bon compte.
You bought it cheaply. / You got it at a good price.

Cette erreur ne devrait pas entrer en ligne de compte.
That mistake shouldn't be taken into account.

Je le prendrai sur mon compte.
I'll take responsibility for it.

Sur le compte de la fermeture annuelle, il n'y a rien à dire.
As far as the annual period of closure is concerned, there's nothing
more to say.

Au bout du compte, ça ne me concerne pas.
When all's said and done, it's nothing to do with me.

L'affaire a été réglée en fin de compte.
The business was sorted out in the end / anyway.

Tout compte fait, je ne peux pas l'accepter.
All things considered, I can't accept it.

Vous avez lu le compte rendu de ce livre dans Le Monde?
Have you read the review of this book in *Le Monde?*

Le maire devait rendre compte de ses décisions.
The mayor had to account for / give an account of his decisions.

Je viens de me rendre compte de ce que tu as dit.
I've just realized what you said.

On tiendra compte de votre assiduité.
Your regular attendance will be taken into account.

*Compte tenu de vos excellents résultats, notre collège sera heureux
de vous accueillir.*
Given your excellent results, our college will be delighted to have
you.

corps (m.) body

le corps enseignant teaching profession / staff

Ce vin a du corps.
This is a full-bodied wine.

Les deux soldats luttaient corps à corps.
The two soldiers were fighting hand to hand.

Je ne lui ai fait mal qu'à mon corps défendant.
I only hurt him / her against my will.

Ils ont fait corps avec la nouvelle équipe.
They've merged with the new team.

C'est quelqu'un qui fait toujours corps à part.
He's always a loner. / He always goes his own way.

Elle s'est jetée à corps perdu dans la foule.
She threw herself recklessly / headlong into the crowd.

Le projet prend corps.
The project / plan is taking shape.

304

côté (m.) side

Note that, with the exception of the phrase *à côté de*, meaning 'beside, next to', *côté* is normally preceded by the preposition *de*. *De ce côté* means both 'from this side' and 'on this side'.

La traduction est un peu à côté.
The translation's a bit off target.

Elle vit à côté de ma mère.
She lives next to my mother.

C'est dans la chambre d'à côté.
It's in the next / adjoining bedroom.

De mon côté, il n'y a aucun problème.
For my part / As far as I'm concerned, there's no problem.

Il y a eu des malentendus de côté et d'autre.
There have been misunderstandings on both sides.

Ils habitent du côté d'Amiens.
They live near / in the direction of Amiens.

Ils marchaient à mes côtés.
They walked beside me.

Aïe! J'ai un point de côté.
Ow! I've got a stitch.

Il faut laisser de côté cette question.
You have to leave that question aside.

Combien d'argent as-tu mis de côté?
How much money have you put aside / saved?

Les experts se sont rangés du côté de la victime.
The experts sided with the victim.

Elle m'a regardé de côté.
She looked askance at me.

coup (m.) blow

This is one of the most frequent constituents of French idioms, especially in colloquial usage. The list below is necessarily selective.

un coup d'essai a go / stab
un coup de feu a (gun) shot
un coup de foudre love at first sight
un coup de fusil a rifle shot
un coup de pied a kick

un coup de soleil sunburn
un coup de téléphone a phone call
les trois coups three raps (given in the theatre before the start of the
     performance)
tout à coup suddenly
tout d'un coup suddenly (marking stronger surprise)
C'est lui, à coup sûr. That's him, without a doubt.

Après coup, je m'en suis souvenu. < coll. >
After the event, I remembered it.

Il était vexé, alors du coup il est parti.
He was annoyed, so as a result he left.

Elle est dans le coup?
Is she in on the secret?

Ils sont partis sur le coup de minuit.
They left at exactly / on the stroke of midnight.

Nous l'avons acheté sur un coup de tête.
We bought it on impulse.

Quand son fils ne revenait pas, elle était aux cent coups.
When her son didn't come back, she was really worried.

Cet artiste a fait les quatre cents coups pendant sa jeunesse.
This artist led a dissolute life during his youth.

J'avais le coup de pompe à cinq heures.
I felt really tired / drained at five o'clock.

Tu as eu un coup de veine. < coll. >
You were lucky / had a lucky break.

Vous voulez que je vous donne un coup de main?
Would you like me to give you a hand?

Tu m'as fait un mauvais coup.
You did me a bad turn.

Elle en a pris un coup. < coll. >
She took it hard. / It affected her badly.

Il ne peut pas tenir le coup. < coll. >
He can't keep up / keep going (i.e. lacks stamina)

dent (f.) tooth

faire ses dents to be teething
serrer les dents to grit your teeth

J'ai / Je garde une dent contre ton frère.
I've got a grudge against your brother.

306

Ma tante a la dent dure.
My aunt is sharp-tongued / very critical.

Il est sur les dents aujourd'hui.
He's very edgy today.

Les reporters l'ont déchiré à belles dents.
The reporters tore him to pieces. < metaphor >

Cet enfant ne mange jamais que du bout des dents.
That child only ever plays with his / her food.

diable (m.) devil

Expressions with *diable* tend to be colloquial in register.

C'est un bon diable. < coll. > He's a good-natured chap.

Que diable se passe-t-il? < coll. >
What on earth's going on?

Sa maison est au diable vert. < coll. >
His / Her house is miles out in the country.

L'homme s'est sauvé comme s'il avait le diable au corps.
The man ran away as fast as the wind.

Les étudiants ont fait le diable à quatre jusqu'à ce que la police arrive. < coll. >
The students kicked up a row until the police arrived.

C'était dur, il fallait tirer le diable par la queue. < coll. >
It was tough, we were very hard up.

esprit (m.) mind, spirit, wit

le Saint-Esprit Holy Spirit / Holy Ghost
avoir de l'esprit to be witty
croire aux esprits to believe in ghosts
perdre l'esprit to go mad
rendre l'esprit to give up the ghost

Je m'excuse. J'avais l'esprit ailleurs.
I'm sorry. I was miles away. / I was thinking about something else.

Cet homme a trop l'esprit de clocher pour accepter les réformes.
This man is too narrow-minded to accept the reforms.

J'aurais dû le lui dire tout de suite. Maintenant ça ferait trop l'esprit de l'escalier.
I should have said it to him / her earlier: it's too late for it to be funny now. (Used when you think of a funny reply too late – when you're on the way downstairs!)

fait (m.) fact, deed

au fait by the way / incidentally
de fait indeed / certainly
en fait as a matter of fact / indeed (to express agreement with
    previous speaker)
par le fait in point of fact
un fait divers a (local / human interest) news report

En fait de sports, vous ne pouvez pas le coller.
You can't catch him out on the subject of sport.

Elle n'a pas été réélue du fait de ce scandale.
She was not re-elected because of this scandal.

Il m'a mis au fait des négociations.
He brought me up to date with the negotiations.

Mon voisin avait pris fait et cause pour eux.
My neighbour sided with them.

Le voleur a été surpris sur le fait.
The thief was caught in the act.

feu (m.) fire

In classical literature, especially poetry, *les feux* is used for 'love'.

'Au feu!' 'Fire!'
prendre feu to catch fire
un feu d'artifice a firework display
un feu rouge a set of traffic lights

Il faut faire fondre le beurre à feu doux.
The butter must be melted over a low heat.

Cette assiette va au feu.
This plate is ovenproof.

J'y mettrais ma main au feu.
I'd swear to it.

Pardon, Monsieur, avez-vous du feu?
Excuse me, do you have a light?

Il a le feu au derrière! < coll. >
He's in a hurry!

L'armée a fait feu sur les fugitifs.
The army fired on the runaways.

Ce projet a fait long feu.
This plan misfired.

Pendant la guerre on a appris à faire feu de tout bois.
During the war we learned to manage with whatever we had.

Mon patron m'a donné le feu vert.
My boss gave me the go-ahead.

Le feu est aux poudres!
The fat's in the fire!

fond (m.) bottom, foundation

le fond du tableau the background of the picture
à fond thoroughly
au fond basically, in the last analysis
un article de fond a (newspaper) leader
une course de fond long-distance race
le ski de fond cross-country skiing

Il est parti à fond de train.
He left at top speed.

Ils ont cherché la maison de fond en comble.
They searched the house from top to bottom.

J'ai fait fond sur sa contribution.
I relied on his contribution.

Il ne nous restait que le fond du panier.
We were left to scrape the barrel.

garde (f.) guard, watch, safe-keeping

Garde-à-vous! < military > Attention!

Est-ce que vous êtes le médecin de garde aujourd'hui?
Are you the doctor on call today?

Il faut être sur ses gardes avec cette personne.
You have to watch out for / keep a sharp eye on that individual.

Je l'ai mis(e) en garde contre les vendeurs de produits de beauté.
I warned him / her against people selling cosmetics.

Ils n'avaient garde de vous déranger. < literary / archaic >
They had no intention of disturbing you. / Far be it from them to
have disturbed you.

Je me suis éloigné du chemin sans y prendre garde.
I wandered away from the path without noticing.

Prenez garde de ne pas tomber dans le fossé.
Take care not to fall into the ditch.

309

heure (f.) hour, time

une bonne heure a good hour / an hour or more
une petite heure not more than an hour
une heure d'affluence / de pointe rush hour / peak hour
une heure creuse off-peak time
une heure supplémentaire overtime
de bonne heure early

A tout à l'heure! See you later! / Bye for now!

A la bonne heure! Well done! / Right!

Il est toujours à l'heure. He's always on time.

Elle est poète à ses heures.
She writes poetry when she feels like it.

Ça ne sert à rien de chercher midi à quatorze heures.
There's no point in making unnecessary complications.

Vous allez passer un mauvais quart d'heure.
You're in for a bad time.

histoire (f.) history, story

la petite histoire the human / anecdotal side of history

Quelle histoire! < coll. > What a fuss!
Pas d'histoires! < coll. > Don't make a fuss! / Don't get into trouble!

Quand il est malade, c'est toute une histoire.
When he's ill, he makes such a fuss.

Il lui est arrivé une drôle d'histoire.
Something funny / odd happened to him / her.

Il leur a raconté une histoire à dormir debout.
He told them a cock-and-bull story.

Ce n'était pas sérieux. Histoire de nous amuser un peu.
It wasn't serious. We just wanted a bit of fun.

idée (f.) idea

une idée reçue a prejudice / a platitude

J'ai changé d'idée depuis hier.
I've changed my mind since yesterday.

Tu as besoin de vacances pour te changer les idées.
You need a holiday to give you a break / take your mind off things.

Ma soeur a toujours beaucoup d'idées.
My sister's always very imaginative / creative.

Ils ont des idées très arrêtées.
They've got very set ideas.

Il lui est venu à l'idée de m'inviter au théâtre.
He had the idea of inviting me to the theatre.

Elle s'est fait l'idée que je suis difficile.
She's got the idea that I'm difficult.

Tu ne me l'ôteras pas de l'idée. < coll. >
You can't change my mind on that point.

jambe (f.) leg

Cet enfant est toujours dans mes jambes.
That child is always under my feet.

Lui, il a toujours des jambes de quinze / vingt ans.
He's still got a good pair of legs on him.

Quand il a vu l'agent de police, il a couru à toutes jambes.
When he saw the policeman, he ran like the wind.

Elle a pris ses jambes à son corps.
She made a hasty retreat / took to her heels.

Ça me fait une belle jambe! < coll. >
A fat lot of use that will be!

Ça ne sert à rien de leur faire des ronds de jambe.
It's no use bowing and scraping to them.

Il l'a traité par-dessus la jambe.
He treated him in a very offhand / careless way.

langue (f.) tongue, language

la langue verte slang
une mauvaise langue a gossip
tirer la langue to stick out one's tongue

Je l'ai sur le bout de la langue.
It's on the tip of my tongue.

Il ne faut pas avoir la langue liée.
You mustn't be tongue-tied.

Il a la langue bien pendue.
He's a real chatterbox. / He's got the gift of the gab.

Ce n'est pas ce que je voulais dire. La langue m'a fourché.
That's not what I meant to say. I made a slip of the tongue.

Tu donnes ta langue au chat?
Do you give up? (guessing)

ligne (f.) line

une belle ligne a good figure (especially of women)
En ligne! < military > Fall in!

Là, vous allez à la ligne.
You need to start a new paragraph there.

Voici une question qui vient en première ligne.
This is a fundamental question.

Cela n'entre pas en ligne de compte.
That doesn't come into consideration.

Il s'est écarté de la ligne droite.
He went off the straight and narrow.

main (f.) hand

à la main by hand
fait à la main handmade
la main dans la main hand in hand
un coup de main < coll. > help
en un tour de main in a twinkling / flash

J'avais cette lettre sous la main tout à l'heure.
I had that letter here a moment ago.

Je ne peux pas mettre la main sur le rapport tout de suite.
I can't lay my hands on the report straight away.

Ma fille a des mains de beurre.
My daughter's a butterfingers.

Nous ne voulons pas arriver les mains vides.
We don't want to arrive without anything / without a gift.

Quelqu'un doit les prendre en main.
Someone should take them in hand.

J'espère qu'ils n'en viendront pas aux mains.
I hope they won't come to blows.

Il n'y est pas allé de main morte.
He attacked viciously. / He laid it on too thick.

Cette équipe a gagné haut la main.
That team won hands down.

Il a essayé de passer la main dans le dos de sa collègue.
He tried to butter up / flatter his colleague.

J'ai perdu la main pour ce genre de choses.
I'm out of practice at this sort of thing.

Mon père était toujours prêt à mettre la main à la pâte. < coll. >
My father was always ready to put his shoulder to the wheel / get his hands dirty.

mise (f.) bet, placing, manner of dress

The idioms below derive from verbal phrases with *mettre*; see pp. 287–8.

la mise au net making a fair copy
la mise au point (1) perfecting / putting final touches
                    (2) summary / review to date
la mise au tombeau entombment / burial

la mise en bouteille bottling
la mise en cause calling into question
la mise en liberté release (of prisoner / hostage)
la mise en oeuvre putting into effect / introduction
la mise en page lay-out (of book / printed document)
la mise en place installation
la mise en pli set (at hairdresser's)
la mise en scène the staging / decor (of a play)
la mise en vente sale / putting up for sale
la mise en vigueur application / introduction (of a law)

nez (m.) nose

avoir bon nez pour quelque chose to have a good nose for something
avoir le nez creux to be canny
saigner du nez to have a nosebleed

On m'a fermé la porte au nez.
They shut the door in my face.

Il l'a sorti au nez et à la barbe du garde.
He took it out right under the guard's nose.

Elle le mène par le bout du nez.
She can twist him round her little finger.

Il a fait un pied de nez au directeur.
He cocked a snook at the headmaster / manager.

Après le déjeuner mon grand-père a piqué du nez. < coll. >
After lunch my grandfather had a little snooze.

J'ai ces gens-là dans le nez. < slang >
I'm sick of those people.

Arrête de fourrer le nez dans mes affaires! < slang >
Stop sticking your nose into my business!

Il faut que tu lui tires les vers du nez. < coll. >
You'll have to pump him / her (for information).

oeil (m.) eye (plural: **yeux**)

Mon oeil! A likely story!
un oeil au beurre noir / un oeil poché a black eye
un clin d'oeil a wink
en un clin d'oeil as quick as a flash

Aux yeux de l'Eglise, le mariage est un sacrement religieux.
According to / In the eyes of the Church, marriage is a holy
sacrament.

Je veux jeter un coup d'oeil dans ce magasin.
I want to have a quick look in that shop.

La petite fille a ouvert de grands yeux.
The little girl looked amazed.

Vous pourriez garder l'oeil sur mes affaires?
Could you keep an eye on my things?

Mon patron a fermé les yeux sur mon absence.
My boss turned a blind eye to my absence.

Nous ne voyons pas la situation du même oeil.
We don't see eye to eye over the situation.

J'ai eu ce canapé à l'oeil. < coll. >
I got this settee for nothing.

Ça nous a coûté les yeux de la tête.
It cost us the earth.

La réponse sautait aux yeux.
The answer was staring us in the face.

Tu lui as donné / tapé dans l'oeil. < slang >
You've made a hit. / He / She's taken a fancy to you.

Je m'en bats l'oeil. < slang >
I couldn't care less.

oreille (f.) ear

Elle est devenue un peu dure d'oreille.
She's become a bit hard of hearing.

J'ai préféré faire la sourde oreille.
I preferred to turn a deaf ear.

S'il a de l'oreille, je lui ferai apprendre le piano.
If he's got a musical ear, I'll make sure he has piano lessons.

Les oreilles doivent vous tinter.
Your ears must be burning.

Tu me casses les oreilles avec ta musique. < coll. >
You're deafening me / driving me mad with your music.

Il m'a rebattu les oreilles de son histoire.
I got tired of hearing his story.

Ma soeur s'est fait tirer l'oreille pour m'accompagner.
I had a hard time persuading my sister to come with me.

Les journalistes avaient la puce à l'oreille.
The journalists had their suspicions / their ears to the ground.

pas (m.) step, rhythm

pas à pas step by step / little by little
au pas (1) at a walking pace
          (2) in step / in rhythm
de ce pas directly / at once

Il descendit l'allée à grands pas.
He strode down the driveway.

J'ai marché à pas de loup.
I crept along stealthily.

Comme il était tard, ils pressèrent / hâtèrent le pas.
As it was late, they walked quickly / speeded up.

Fatiguée, elle ralentit le pas.
She was tired and slowed down.

On s'est trompés, il vaut mieux retourner sur nos pas.
We've gone wrong, we'd better retrace our steps.

En attendant, il faisait les cent pas.
He was pacing up and down as he waited.

Elle a progressé à pas de géant.
She progressed by leaps and bounds.

Il fallait deux semaines pour les convaincre de franchir le pas.
It took two weeks to convince them to take the decisive step.

En s'adressant à lui, il a fait un pas de clerc.
He made a blunder / faux pas in approaching him.

pied (m.) foot

un casse-pied < coll. > a nuisance (of people)
au pied levé (1) at the drop of a hat
              (2) unawares (catching someone)
un coup de pied a kick

Vous n'avez jamais mis le pied chez ta belle-soeur? < coll. >
You've never been to your sister-in-law's?

C'est le pied! < slang > It's brilliant / fantastic!

Il a joué comme un pied. < slang > He played terribly.

!! *Il a pris son pied.* < slang >
He had it off / had sex / had a really good time.

Vous avez le pied marin? Are you a good sailor?

Vingt ouvriers ont été mis à pied.
Twenty workers have been laid off.

Je crois qu'il lui a marché sur les pieds.
I think he upset him / her.

Vous me cassez les pieds sur cette histoire. < coll. >
You're giving me a lot of trouble / being a pain over this.

Je faisais le pied de grue pendant une demi-heure en t'attendant.
I was standing around / kicking my heels waiting for you for half an hour.

Il ne faut pas interpréter ce vers au pied de la lettre.
This line shouldn't be taken / interpreted literally.

Cette affaire a mis le Premier ministre au pied du mur.
This affair left the Prime Minister with his back to the wall.

point (m.) point, full stop, stitch

un point d'interrogation a question-mark
un point-virgule a semi-colon
deux points a colon
un point de repère a landmark / meeting-point
à point medium (for cooking steak)
au point perfect, ready (e.g. cooking)
au point nommé at the right moment
au point du jour at the crack of dawn

Non, un point c'est tout! No, and that's final!

Nous sommes sur le point de sortir.
We're just about to go out.

Je vais faire le point sur nos discussions.
I'll sum up our discussions.

Notre journaliste fera le point sur la crise aux Etats-Unis.
Our journalist will bring the latest information on the crisis in the States.

Elle voulait mettre les points sur les 'i'.
She insisted on getting all the little details sorted out / getting things straight.

prise (f.) taking, grasp, plug / socket

Many of the idioms below derive from verbal phrases with *prendre*; see pp. 291–2.

la prise de la Bastille the storming of the Bastille
une prise de bec < coll. > a quarrel
une prise de sang a blood sample
une prise de son a sound recording
une prise de vue a shot (photo / film)
la prise en charge (1) taking care of / responsibility for
                    (2) minimum charge (e.g. taxi fare)

En écrivant cet article, il donna prise à la critique.
By writing this article, he laid himself open to criticism.

Le chat lâcha prise, et l'oiseau s'envola.
The cat dropped / let go of the bird and it flew away.

Je n'ai pas vraiment prise sur elle.
I haven't really got much influence over her.

L'entreprise est aux prises avec ses concurrents.
The firm is struggling against its competitors.

queue (f.) tail, queue

!! *la queue* < slang > penis / cock
un piano à queue a grand piano

Nous avons fait la queue devant le cinéma.
We queued up in front of the cinema.

Il m'a raconté une histoire sans queue ni tête.
He gave me a very confused story / cock-and-bull story.

Ils ont dansé à la queue leu leu.
They danced in a long line / one behind another.

Leur procès a fini en queue de poisson.
Their trial fizzled out.

Ce chauffard m'a fait une queue de poisson.
That roadhog cut me up. (of driving)

Il y a eu une époque où j'ai tiré le diable par la queue. < coll. >
There was a time when I was really hard up.

sang (m.) blood

pur sang thoroughbred

C'est mon propre sang.
She's / He's my own flesh and blood.

Combien de soldats ont versé leur sang dans cette guerre?
How many soldiers shed their blood in this war?

Son histoire me glaçait le sang.
His / Her story made my blood run cold.

Mon sang n'a fait qu'un tour quand il m'a annoncé la nouvelle.
My heart missed a beat when he told me the news.

Il ne faut pas te faire de mauvais sang. < coll. >
You mustn't get upset / worked up.

Les Grecs mirent la ville à feu et à sang.
The Greeks sacked the town.

tête (f.) head

la tête la première head first
de la tête aux pieds from head to toe
un coup de tête whim / impulse
un homme / une femme de tête a man / woman with a good head
  on his / her shoulders
un signe de tête a nod
une grosse tête < coll. > a bighead
à tue-tête at the top of one's voice

Je n'aime pas sa tête. < coll. > I don't like the look of him / her.

Il a la tête d'un officier de l'armée.
He looks like an army officer.

Excusez-moi, j'avais la tête ailleurs.
I'm sorry, my mind was elsewhere.

Après deux verres de champagne, j'ai la tête qui tourne.
After two glasses of champagne, I feel dizzy / giddy.

Quand j'ai refusé d'acheter le jouet, il m'a fait la tête.
When I refused to buy the toy, he sulked.

Tu en fais toujours à ta tête.
You always go your own way / never listen to advice.

Il tenait tête à son père. He stood up to his father.

Tous les compliments lui ont tourné la tête.
All the compliments have gone to his / her head.

C'est à se taper la tête contre le mur. < coll. >
It's enough to drive you mad.

La presse s'est servie de mon voisin comme tête de Turc.
The press made my neighbour into a scapegoat.

tour (m.) turn, trip, trick

le Tour de France the annual French cycle race
le premier / second tour de scrutin the first / second round of voting
tour à tour in turn
en un tour de main in a twinkling / flash

Tu veux faire un tour dans ma nouvelle voiture?
Do you want to come for a ride in my new car?

Vous avez fait le tour de tous les musées?
Have you been round all the museums?

Ils m'ont joué un mauvais tour. They played a dirty trick on me.

Il faut faire le tour de ce problème.
We must look at this problem from all angles.

Il a lancé la balle à tour de bras. He threw the ball with all his force.

Nous avons fait la cuisine à tour de rôle.
We took it in turns to cook.

Elle avait un tour d'esprit très vif. She had a very lively mind.

vie (f.) life

un niveau de vie a standard of living
un train de vie a way of living / lifestyle

Jamais de la vie! Not on your life! / Never!

Tu vas nous donner signe de vie? < coll. >
Will you get in touch with us?

Les vieilles habitudes ont la vie dure. Old habits die hard.

Comment fait-il pour gagner sa vie?
How does he manage to earn a living?

Sa grand-mère lui menait la vie dure.
His / her grandmother gave him / her a hard time / hard life.

319

128 Colourful adjectives

You will be familiar with the main colour adjectives in French used in their literal sense. Many of them also give rise to some idiomatic figurative expressions. Even with the word *couleur*, you have:

jouer dans la couleur to follow suit (at cards)

L'affaire prend couleur.
Things are taking shape.

Elle m'en a fait voir de toutes les couleurs. < coll. >
She led me a merry dance / messed me about.

Il a dit cela sous couleur d'amitié.
He said it under a show of friendship.

Il en parlait comme un aveugle des couleurs.
He held forth about it without knowing anything.

blanc white

In French, white has the traditional image of purity, but also the association of a blank, something non-existent.

être blanc comme neige to be as pure as the driven snow
devenir blanc comme un linge to turn white as a sheet
une copie blanche a blank script
un examen blanc a mock exam
la houille blanche hydroelectric power
un mariage blanc an unconsummated marriage
des vers blancs blank verse
de but en blanc point-blank, without warning
dire tantôt blanc, tantôt noir to say first one thing then another
donner carte blanche à quelqu'un to give someone absolute freedom
faire chou blanc < slang > to be an utter flop
laisser un blanc to leave a gap
passer une nuit blanche to stay up all night

bleu blue

If blue has kept some of its aristocratic overtones in French, it also designates 'raw / fresh' – cf. 'green' in English.

un bleu (1) a bruise
         (2) a new recruit / novice
un bas bleu a bluestocking

320

un bifteck bleu a rare steak
un conte bleu a cock-and-bull story
une peur bleue a terrible fear
le sang bleu blue blood
les bleus de travail working overalls
être bleu de froid to be blue with cold
être bleu de colère to be livid (with anger)
n'y voir que du bleu not to smell a rat

gris grey

Apart from its associations with the brain, grey designates something rather unpleasant.

la matière grise the little grey cells / grey matter
un temps gris overcast weather
en voir de grises to have an unpleasant time of it
faire grise mine à quelqu'un to give someone the cold shoulder

jaune yellow

As in English, yellow is associated with cowardice.

un jaune < slang > a blackleg / scab
le jaune d'un oeuf the yolk of an egg
rire jaune to give a forced laugh / a sickly smile

noir black

As in English, black is primarily associated with unhappiness or misfortune.

noir comme du jais jet black
noir comme dans un four pitch black
une bête noire a pet aversion
le marché noir the black market
une rue noire de monde a road swarming with people
la traite des noirs the slave trade
broyer du noir to be depressed
Il fait noir. It's dark.
mettre noir sur blanc to put in black and white / in writing
porter le noir to be dressed in black (mourning)
regarder quelqu'un d'un oeil noir to look askance at someone
voir la vie en noir to take a gloomy view of things

rose pink

Pink is worth citing because it is the 'happy' colour, opposed to grey and black.

une crevette rose prawn
un flamant rose a pink flamingo
voir la vie en rose to have an optimistic view of life

rouge red

As in English, red is associated with left-wing politics and with anger.

le rouge < coll. > red wine
un rouge à lèvres lipstick
les Rouges the Commies
un compte bancaire en rouge a bank account in the red
voter rouge to vote Communist
devenir rouge comme une cerise to blush / go as red as a beetroot
se fâcher tout rouge < coll. > to get furious
voir rouge to see red

vert green

The ecological overtones of green exist in French as in English. Otherwise, in French idioms, green suggests health and vigour (cf. green shoots) and also daring / risqué humour (cf. 'blue' in English).

les Verts the Greens (Ecologists)
mettre un cheval au vert to put a horse out to grass
employer le vert et le sec to leave no stone unturned
prendre quelqu'un sans vert to catch someone off their guard < literary >
en voir des vertes et des pas mûres to go through a hard time / see a
    strange mixture
des histoires vertes racy stories
au temps de sa verte jeunesse in the first bloom of his / her youth
le langage vert slang / teenage language
une verte réponse a sharp reply
une verte vieillesse robust old age

129 Adverbial nuance

Adverbs qualify verbs, adjectives or other adverbs. The standard formation of adverbs is explained in section 24. This section looks at some common French adverbs which have particular nuances.

On the one hand, there are cases in which knowing the adjective from which the adverb is derived does not necessarily give you the adverb's idiomatic meaning. And then there are a number of adverbs which are close in form to an English adverb, but slightly or notably different in meaning. Where these adverbs derive from an adjective which may be classed as a *faux ami*, they are marked < F.A. > (see sections 132–3 on *faux amis*).

(a) Adverbs used primarily in formal notices

formellement strictly (associated with prohibition) < F.A. >
Il est formellement interdit de donner à manger aux animaux.
Feeding the animals is strictly forbidden.

incessamment immediately
Toute personne non ressortissante de la C.E.E. doit se rendre incessamment au bureau de l'immigration.
All non-E.E.C. residents should report immediately to the immigration office.

instamment urgently / expressly (associated with polite orders)
Les clients sont instamment priés de ne pas toucher aux objets exposés dans la vitrine.
Customers are expressly requested not to touch articles in the window. / Please do not touch articles in the window.

ultérieurement later < F.A. >
Veuillez nous rappeler ultérieurement. (recorded message)
Please call us back later.

(b) Adverbs used in standard written and spoken French

accessoirement in addition
Il existe accessoirement deux piscines en plein air.
In addition there are two open-air swimming pools.

actuellement currently < F.A. >
Le nombre de chômeurs est actuellement en baisse.
The number of people unemployed is currently falling.

alternativement alternately / by turns

Ils se relayaient pour garder les enfants alternativement.
They had a rota to look after the children alternately.

couramment (1) fluently
                (2) commonly

Tu parles le grec couramment?
Do you speak Greek fluently?

C'est quelque chose qui se fait couramment en Egypte.
It's something which is common practice / commonly done in Egypt.

définitivement for good / definitively < F.A. >

Vous avez quitté Paris définitivement?
Have you left Paris for good?

éventuellement possibly < F.A. >
(can be used to translate 'might' or 'may')

Tu auras éventuellement besoin d'argent?
Might you need some money?

forcément necessarily

Je ne viendrai pas forcément moi-même.
I shan't necessarily come myself.

globalement all in all / overall

Les résultats ont été globalement positifs.
Overall the results have been positive.

inversement conversely / alternatively

*Si vous voulez rester ici, j'irai le chercher, ou inversement vous y irez et
moi je resterai ici.*
If you'd like to stay here, I'll go and fetch him, or conversely /
alternatively you go and I'll stay here.

mûrement more closely / at leisure (thinking over something)

J'ai mûrement réfléchi à votre proposition.
I've thought over your suggestion at leisure.

parallèlement also / at the same time

Il travaille à l'hôtel le soir et poursuit parallèlement ses études.
He works at the hotel in the evenings, and is carrying on his studies
at the same time.

ponctuellement irregularly / from time to time < F.A. >

Note that this is a neologism, still contested by some purists.

Cette troupe d'acteurs ne monte des pièces que ponctuellement.
This theatre company only stages performances from time to time.

proprement literally, correctly (concerning definitions)

*Ce bâtiment, proprement dit 'Le Temple d'Adonis', est plus connu
sous le nom de 'La Cachette'.*
This building, whose correct name is 'The Temple of Adonis', is
commonly known as 'The Hideaway'.

scrupuleusement thoroughly / precisely (of work done)

Il a vérifié scrupuleusement tous nos comptes.
He checked all our accounts thoroughly.

sensiblement noticeably / appreciably < F.A. >

La qualité des repas s'est sensiblement améliorée.
The meals have got noticeably better.

strictement absolutely (usually with a negative)

Cette phrase ne veut strictement rien dire.
This sentence means absolutely nothing.

sûrement certainly (with hypotheses, or a negative)

Il sera sûrement parti maintenant.
He'll certainly have left by now. / He must have left by now.

Tu le feras? Will you do it?
Sûrement pas! Certainly not!

uniquement only < F.A. >

J'ai accepté uniquement pour te faire plaisir.
It was only to please you that I accepted.

(c) Adverbs used mainly in colloquial spoken French

(tout) bêtement (quite) simply

Il avait tout bêtement oublié de leur téléphoner.
He'd quite simply forgotten to ring them.

carrément really / honestly

Je ne peux carrément pas rester ce soir.
I honestly / really can't stay this evening.

drôlement not half < slang >

Il est drôlement fort! He isn't half strong!

effectivement precisely / quite right

Ça sera difficile à réparer. It'll be difficult to repair.
Effectivement. Quite right. / Precisely.

Voilà effectivement ce que je voulais vous montrer.
That's precisely what I wanted to show you.

justement exactly / precisely < f.a. >

C'est ce qu'il nous faut, n'est-ce pas? It's what we need, isn't it?
Justement. Exactly.

J'étais justement sur le point de partir.
I was precisely on the point of leaving.

largement ample / plenty

Le petit déjeuner était largement suffisant.
The breakfast was quite ample.

Il y a largement de la place. There's plenty of room.

nettement distinctly / far . . . (used in comparisons)

Elle est nettement plus avancée que sa cousine.
She's far more advanced than her cousin.

passablement quite a lot

Il avait passablement voyagé pendant sa jeunesse.
He'd travelled quite a lot in his youth.

rudement very / really < slang > < f.a. >

Vous vous débrouillez rudement bien.
You manage really well.

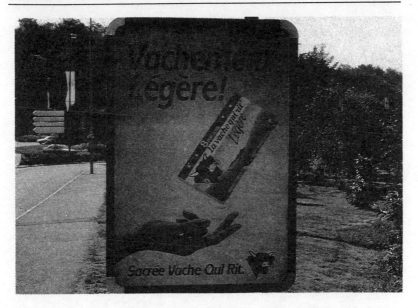

vachement very / bloody < slang and unacceptable in some company >

Ce restaurant est vachement cher!
That restaurant's very / bloody expensive!

130 Key synonyms

Both in speech and in writing, a wide vocabulary is a mark of good style. For that reason alone, it is useful to find synonyms for over-used words. For English learners of French there is the further point that in formal style, e.g. *exposés*, reports and essays, *avoir*, *être*, *dire* and other common verbs simply do not occur as frequently as 'to be', 'to have', 'to say' in English. If you look closely at *Le Monde*, for example, you will find French has a variety of verbs which are more precise and more elegant, whereas English might use other parts of speech to give comparable variety. Cultivating some of the synonyms below will help you to move down the path from 'translationese' to 'real' French.

avoir to have

La Défense comprend un grand centre commercial.
The Défense area has / includes a large shopping centre.

La ville abrite 600 sociétés.
The town has (shelters) 600 firms.

La Suisse dispose de 1000 personnes prêtes à agir.
Switzerland has (at its disposal) 1000 people ready to act.

On compte 67 pour cent des salariés de formation scientifique.
Sixty-seven per cent of the staff have a scientific background.

Le projet comporte trois zones d'activités.
The project has / covers three centres of activity.

Elle possède une maison de campagne dans le Jura.
She has a country house in the Jura.

Notre hôtel jouit d'un panorama exceptionnel.
Our hotel has (enjoys) an exceptional view.

Le quartier bénéficie d'une maison de la culture très active.
The district has / has the benefit of a very active cultural centre.

Cette solution présente trois avantages.
This solution has / offers three advantages.

Le nouveau système offre un certain nombre d'inconvénients.
The new system has / includes a certain number of drawbacks.

beaucoup de lots of / many

Bien des étudiants ont choisi ce parcours.
A good many students have chosen this path / course.

Nombreux sont les citoyens qui se sont plaints. < emphatic >
De nombreux citoyens se sont plaints.
Many citizens have complained.

Il essaya à maintes reprises. < literary >
He tried many times.

Chaque weekend bon nombre de Parisiens quittent la capitale.
Every weekend many Parisians leave the capital.

Ils se quittèrent avec force larmes. < literary / archaic >
They separated with many a tear.

Ils avaient besoin d'une grande quantité de marchandises.
They needed a good supply of wares.

bon good

Ce serait une modification fort souhaitable.
It would be a very good / desirable change.

Vous m'avez donné un conseil très précieux.
You gave me very good / valuable advice.

328

On m'a proposé un placement avantageux.
I've been offered a good investment.

J'ai trouvé le régime très bénéfique.
I found the diet very good / beneficial.

Sa démarche a eu des effets positifs.
His / Her activity had good / positive effects.

causer to cause

(See section 95.)

une chose a thing / **quelque chose** (m.) something

Where possible use a more precise term, and particularly avoid *chose* when referring to something abstract.

Quel est cet objet?
What's that thing / object?

Quel est l'article que vous désirez voir?
Which is the thing / item you wish to see?

C'est un fait qui m'a intrigué.
It's a thing / fact which has intrigued me.

On a constaté un phénomène étrange.
We have noticed something strange. (abstract)

Voici l'élément que nous jugeons le plus significatif.
This is the thing which we consider most significant. (abstract)

comme as / like

En tant que professeur, je devrais recevoir cette revue.
As (in my capacity as) a teacher, I should receive that review.

Il viendra à la réunion en qualité d'arbitre.
He will come to the meeting as (in the capacity of) an arbitrator.

Il a été nommé, ainsi que mon frère.
He was appointed, as was / like my brother.

J'ai invité Florence aussi bien que Denise.
I invited Florence as well as Denise.

J'ai été consulté de même que ma collègue.
I was consulted, as was my colleague.

Elle cherche une maison semblable à la mienne.
She's looking for a house like / similar to mine.

329

Votre réaction est pareille à la mienne.
Your reaction is like / the same as mine.

Elle resta immobile, telle une statue. < literary >
She stood quite still, like a statue

dire to say

Il a annoncé que les troupes se retireraient.
He said / announced that the troops would withdraw.

Le Président a affirmé que le projet coûterait trop cher.
The President said / stated that the project would be too expensive.

Les scientifiques constatèrent qu'il s'agissait d'un accident.
The scientists said / stated that it was an accident.

La société Réal a déclaré qu'elle sortirait une nouvelle série de voitures.
The Réal firm said / announced that it would be bringing out a new range of cars.

Le maire a fait remarquer que les riverains devraient bénéficier d'un tarif préférentiel.
The mayor said / observed that there should be a reduction for local residents.

Le syndicat a indiqué que la direction voulait reprendre les discussions.
The union said / indicated that the management wanted to renew talks.

Vous avez noté que ces modèles sont très demandés.
You said / observed that these models are highly sought after.

L'accusé prétendait que la victime lui était inconnue.
The accused said / claimed that the victim was unknown to him.

Je leur ai signalé que cette mesure serait inefficace.
I said / pointed out to them that this measure would not work.

L'ambassadeur a soutenu que son pays n'avait pas été averti.
The ambassador said / maintained that his country had not been warned.

être to be (*il y a* there is / are)

(i) ' There is / are' + noun   or 'X is / are' + noun

Plusieurs arguments se présentent.
There are a number of arguments.

Il existe des controverses à ce sujet.
There are disagreements on this subject.

★ N.B. *il existe* is always singular.

Ces rapports constituent des documents irremplaçables.
These reports are irreplaceable documents.

Votre livre représente une nouvelle interprétation de l'époque.
Your book is / offers a new interpretation of the period.

Il se produira une catastrophe écologique.
There will be an ecological disaster.

L'industrie des textiles a connu une véritable crise.
There has been a real crisis in the textile industry.

La vie en société implique un certain nombre de contraintes.
There are a number of constraints involved in living in society.

Nous assistons à une évolution des moeurs sociales.
There is / We are seeing a change in social customs.

Son approche relève du socialisme.
His / Her approach has socialist overtones.

(ii) 'X is / are' + adjective

Le directeur s'est montré compréhensif.
The director was understanding.

La réparation s'est trouvée plus facile que prévue.
The repair was / turned out to be easier than expected.

La voiture s'est révélée performante.
The car is / has proved to be impressive / a high-performance model.

Ces solutions se sont avérées inefficaces.
These solutions are / have proved to be ineffectual.

Le Conseil Municipal s'est déclaré outragé.
The Town Council was / claimed to be outraged.

les gens people

In formal style, *personnes* is preferable to *gens*:

Les personnes ayant à se plaindre doivent s'adresser à la direction.
People wishing to complain should speak to the management.

In many cases, it is possible to find a more precise term to replace 'people':

Les citadins oublient trop facilement l'équilibre écologique.
People living in towns too easily overlook the question of ecological balance.

Les responsables des groupes scolaires doivent se présenter à l'accueil.
People in charge of school parties should go to the reception.

important important

L'essentiel, c'est de faire preuve de notre bonne volonté.
What is important is to demonstrate our good will.

La médecine douce pose des problèmes fondamentaux.
Alternative medicine poses some very important / fundamental problems.

Deux points de cet argument me paraissent saillants.
Two points of this argument seem to me particularly important.

La liberté de la presse est un sujet capital.
The freedom of the press is a very important / vital subject.

La question cardinale est celle d'une guerre nucléaire.
The most important / crucial question is that of a nuclear war.

Plus révélateur encore est le cas des villes du sud-est.
The case of towns in the south-east is even more important / significant.

Elle jouit d'une influence considérable.
She is a very important influence / has considerable influence.

mauvais bad

Le directeur a signalé son comportement regrettable.
The headmaster noted his bad behaviour.

Ce produit risque d'avoir un effet nuisible.
This product is likely to have a bad / harmful effect.

Les experts avaient prévu les conséquences néfastes de cet acte.
The experts had foreseen the deadly consequences of this action.

Je crains que cet incident n'ait une suite funeste. < literary >
I fear this incident may have a bad outcome.

un problème a problem

Ils voudraient résoudre l'épineuse question de l'immigration.
They would like to resolve the thorny problem of immigration.

Le cas des chômeurs reste très actuel.
The problem of the unemployed is still important / high on the agenda.

La concurrence et la productivité sont au centre du débat.
Competition and productivity are the main problems / subjects
under discussion.

Les enjeux économiques sont énormes.
The economic risks (stakes) are enormous.

La disparition de cet homme reste un énigme.
The disappearance of this man remains a mystery.

C'est un casse-tête. < coll. / journalistic >
It's an insoluble problem.

Le chef d'état est au pied du mur. < coll. / journalistic >
The head of state is up against it / has his back to the wall.

sérieux serious

La situation est devenue gravissime. < journalistic >
The situation has become extremely serious.

La difficulté de subvenir à ces besoins est de plus en plus aiguë.
The difficulty of meeting these needs is more and more serious / acute.

Son manque d'intérêt est inquiétant.
His / Her lack of interest is serious / worrying.

Aucun pays ne peut se désintéresser de ce débat.
This debate is serious for all countries. / No country can afford to
ignore this debate.

*La question prend toute sa dimension au moment où la nouvelle
loi entre en vigueur.*
The full significance of this question emerges as the new law is applied.

Le conflit a laissé des traces profondes.
The conflict has had serious effects / left deep scars.

131 Popular expressions and slang

Popular expressions and slang (*l'argot*) are a tricky area for foreign
speakers. They may not be familiar with this register of language
from their more formal studies – and in any case slang changes
quite fast. Some of the popular idioms of the de Gaulle generation
may produce laughter or incomprehension among today's teenagers. The use of popular expressions, and more particularly slang,
is often indicative of a sense of group identity (peer groups at
school, close colleagues at work, friends), and foreign speakers

therefore need to be sure they are choosing an appropriate context in which to display their varied vocabulary. In other words, it is helpful to recognize all the expressions listed below, but if in doubt stick to the more formal equivalent in your own speech!

I have indicated by ! or !! expressions which range from the somewhat vulgar to those distinctly liable to shock in some company. I have also highlighted (in **bold type**) popular expressions or slang which are extremely common. It's interesting to note that while some areas of human activity – food, money, sex – are rich in slang in both languages, in other cases French has a common popular term for which there is no real equivalent in English, e.g. *la bagnole, le toubib*. Those who believe languages betray the mentalities of those who speak them may care to think further . . .

SLANG / POPULAR TERM		MORE FORMAL EQUIVALENT
s'amener	to turn up	*arriver*
archi-(+ adjective)	incredibly	*très*
arnaquer	to swindle	*escroquer*
arroser quelque chose	to celebrate / pop a cork	*fêter*
se faire avoir	to be taken for a ride	*se laisser duper*
une baffe	a clout / slap	*une gifle*
une bagnole	a car	*une voiture*
!! *baiser*	to screw	*faire l'amour*
une balade	a walk / drive	*une promenade*
se balader	to go for a walk / drive	*se promener*
balancer	to chuck	*jeter*
(100) balles	(100) francs	*(100) francs*
baragouiner	to talk gibberish	*estropier une langue*
baratiner	to chat up	*faire la cour à quelqu'un*
La barbe!	What a bore!	*C'est ennuyeux.*
le bec	mouth / gob	*la bouche*
bêcheur	toffee-nosed / show-off	*vaniteux*
bidon	sham	*faux*
un bled	a village in the sticks	*un hameau isolé*
la boîte	firm	*une entreprise*
! *le bordel*	balls-up / mess	*le chaos*
bosser	to work (hard)	*travailler (dur)*
la bouffe	grub	*la nourriture*
bouffer	to eat / nosh	*manger*
Ça bouge!	They're getting on with it.	*Ça évolue.*
le boulot	work / job	*le travail*
un bouquin	book	*un livre*

334

	bouquiner	to spend time reading	*lire*
	bourrer	to stuff / cram	*surcharger*
!	*un branleur*	a wanker / berk	*un jeune blanc bec*
	une brique	10,000 francs	*10.000 francs*
	la brioche	pot-belly	*un gros ventre*
	le caïd	gangleader / the chief	*le chef*
	Ça caille.	It's freezing.	*Il fait très froid.*
	Je cale.	I'm absolutely full.	*Merci, je ne peux plus.*
	un casse-pied	a pain	*ennuyeux*
	casser les pieds à quelqu'un	to be a pain	*ennuyer*
	se casser	to clear off	*s'échapper*
	Ça te chante?	Do you fancy it?	*Ça vous intéresse?*
	Chiche!	Dare you!	*Vous n'oseriez pas!*
	avoir du chien	to be sexy / stylish	*avoir du charme*
!!	*faire chier*	to be a bloody pain	*ennuyer*
!!	*les chiottes* (f.)	the bog	*les toilettes*
	chiper	to nick	*voler*
	chipoter	to split hairs	*être mesquin*
	chouette	great / brilliant	*excellent*
	une claque	a clout / slap	*une gifle*
	claquer	to clout / slap	*gifler*
	Ça cloche.	It doesn't fit / go.	*Ça passe mal.*
	une clope	a fag	*une cigarette*
	le petit coin	the bathroom	*les toilettes*
!!	*con(ne)*	bloody stupid	*stupide*
!!	*une connerie*	something bloody stupid	*une bêtise*
	un copain	a (m.) mate / friend	*un ami*
	une copine	a (f.) mate / friend	*une amie*
	un coup de fil	a phone call / ring	*un coup de téléphone*
	crever	to kick the bucket / be knackered	*mourir / être épuisé*
	crever de faim	to be starving	*avoir très faim*
	les croulants	the oldies	*les vieux*
	être cuit	to be done for	*être pris*
!	*le cul*	bum / arse	*le derrière*
!	*le culot*	(bloody) cheek	*l'audace*
!	*culotté*	cheeky / shameless	*éhonté*
	débile	idiotic	*stupide*
	se dégonfler	to chicken out	*manquer de courage*
!	*dégueulasse*	disgusting / foul	*dégoûtant*
!!	*se démerder*	to get out of the shit	*se débrouiller*
	dénicher	to unearth / dig up	*trouver*

335

SLANG / POPULAR TERM		MORE FORMAL EQUIVALENT
dingue	odd / peculiar	*étrange*
Ça te dit?	Do you fancy it?	*Ça t'intéresse?*
draguer	to chat up / pick up	*faire la cour à*
faire dodo	to have a snooze	*dormir*
s'emballer	to be wild over	*s'enthousiasmer*
!! *un emmerdement*	a bloody nuisance / problem	*un ennui*
!! *emmerder*	to be a pain in the arse	*ennuyer*
! *engueuler quelqu'un*	to give someone a rollicking	*réprimander*
éreinté	knackered	*épuisé*
Espèce d'idiot!	You idiot!	*Vous êtes fou!*
extra	brilliant	*excellent*
une faiseuse d'anges	a backstreet abortionist (= a maker of angels)	*un(e) avorteur / -euse*
fauché	broke	*sans le sou*
! *les fesses* (f.)	bum / buttocks	*le derrière*
filer	to rush off / push off	*s'en aller*
Fiche-moi la paix!	Be quiet! / Give over!	*Tais-toi!*
Fiche-moi le camp!	Clear off!	*Va-t'en!*
Je m'en fiche.	I couldn't care less.	*Ça m'est égal.*
fichu	broken / useless	*cassé / inutile*
le fiston	son / my lad	*le fils*
flasher	(1) to be brilliant	*être épatant*
	(2) to go on a trip	*être drogué*
un flic	a cop	*un agent de police*
la flotte	water	*l'eau*
! *Fous-moi la paix!*	Shut up!	*Tais-toi!*
! *Fous-moi le camp!*	Bugger off!	*Va-t'en!*
! *Je m'en fous.*	I couldn't give a shit.	*Ça m'est égal.*
! *foutu*	buggered up	*fichu*
le frangin	brother	*le frère*
la frangine	sister	*la soeur*
le fric	money / cash	*l'argent*
frimer	to bluff	*bluffer*
la fringale	incredible hunger	*très faim*
les fringues (f.)	clothes / togs	*les vêtements*
fumiste	phoney	*fantaisiste*
une gaffe	a slip / boob	*une erreur*
le / la gamin(e)	kid	*un enfant*
! *une garce*	bitch	*une fille*
le gars	lad	*le garçon*

SLANG / POPULAR TERM		MORE FORMAL EQUIVALENT
génial	brilliant	*épatant*
les godasses (f.)	shoes	*les chaussures*
gonflé(e)	full of himself / herself	*orgueilleux / -euse*
le / la gosse	kid	*l'enfant*
! *se gourer*	to make a balls-up	*se tromper*
graisser la patte à quelqu'un	to slip money to someone	*acheter quelqu'un*
! *la gueule*	mouth / face / mug	*la bouche / le visage*
poser un lapin	to stand up (for a date)	*manquer au rendez-vous*
! *un lèche-cul*	a creep / arse-licker	*un lèche-bottes*
une grosse légume	a big-wig / VIP	*un personnage important*
lessivé	all-in / washed out	*épuisé*
le machin	the thingummy	*la chose*
marrant	funny / killing	*amusant*
se marrer	to have fun	*s'amuser*
J'en ai marre.	I'm fed up.	*J'en ai assez.*
un mec	a bloke / guy	*un homme*
! *Merde!*	Shit!	*Mince! / Zut!*
mijoter	to cook up a scheme	*comploter*
le / la minet(te)	cat / kitty	*le / la chat(te)*
moche	ugly	*laid*
le / la môme	infant / kid	*le / la petit(e)*
se mouiller dans	to get mixed up in	*tremper dans*
! *la nana*	woman / bird	*la femme*
les nippes (f.)	clothes / togs	*les vêtements*
l'oseille (f.)	dosh / cash	*l'argent*
la pagaille	mess / a pig-sty	*le désordre*
la patate	spud	*la pomme de terre*
la patte	leg	*la jambe*
paumé	floored	*perdu*
! *pédé* (= *pédéraste*)	gay	*homosexuel*
! *péter le feu*	to be full of beans	*être en forme*
un pépin	a hitch	*un ennui*
un(e) péquenaud(e)	a country bumpkin	*un(e) paysan(ne)*
dans le pétrin	in the soup	*en difficulté*
la piaule	pad	*la maison / chez moi*
C'est le pied.	It's great / brilliant.	*C'est excellent.*
! *prendre son pied*	to have it off / have a good time	*faire l'amour / bien s'amuser*

337

SLANG / POPULAR TERM		MORE FORMAL EQUIVALENT
piger	to get (the point)	comprendre
faire pipi	to spend a penny	aller aux toilettes
piquer	to nick	voler
piquer une colère	to get mad	se mettre en colère
la piquette	plonk	du vin inférieur
le piston	pulling strings	l'influence
planter	to leave high and dry	abandonner
faire du plat	to chat up	flatter / séduire
faire la plonge	to do the dishes	faire la vaisselle
le pognon	dosh / lolly	l'argent
à poil	stark naked	nu
pompette	tipsy	un peu ivre
tomber dans les pommes	to pass out	s'évanouir
prendre un pot	to have a drink	prendre quelque chose à boire
le pote	mate	l'ami
les potins (m.)	gossip	les commérages
le / la prof	teacher	le professeur
‼ une pute	whore	une prostituée
‼ la queue	prick / cock	le pénis
prendre du rab	to take more grub / seconds	se resservir
une râclée	a thrashing / hiding	une correction
radin	stingy	avare
râler	to moan / whinge	se plaindre
J'en ai ras-le-bol.	I'm sick of it.	J'en ai assez.
raseur	boring	ennuyeux
rater	to miss / fail	manquer
rigoler	to laugh / have fun	rire / s'amuser
rigolo	funny / killing	amusant
ringard	out of the ark	démodé
les ripoux	crooked cops	des agents malhonnêtes
roupiller	to snooze	dormir
! sacré	bloody	maudit
! un salaud	bastard	un sale type
se faire du mauvais sang	to fret	s'inquiéter
passer un savon	to tick off	réprimander
sécher	to skive / cut	manquer à
faire suer quelqu'un	to drive someone mad	irriter quelqu'un
faire un tabac	to be a big hit	faire un grand succès

338

SLANG / POPULAR TERM		MORE FORMAL EQUIVALENT
passer quelqu'un à tabac	to do someone over	*agresser quelqu'un*
le tapage	a din	*le bruit*
C'est de la tarte.	It's a piece of cake / a push-over.	*C'est très facile.*
la taule	nick / clink	*la prison*
pas terrible	not much cop	*pas très fort*
le toubib	doctor	*le médecin*
Ça tourne.	Business is good.	*Ça va bien.*
le toutou	doggy	*le chien*
du toc	fake	*du faux*
tracasser quelqu'un	to drive someone mad	*ennuyer quelqu'un*
‼ tringler	to screw / have it off	*faire l'amour*
‼ se faire tringler	to get laid	*faire l'amour*
la trouille	a real scare	*très peur*
le truc	the thingummy	*la chose*
le type	the chap / guy	*l'homme*
❗ vachement	bloody	*très*
virer	to sack	*renvoyer*
zigouiller	to do in	*tuer*
❗ le zizi	penis / willy	*le pénis*

FAUX AMIS

Faux amis – or false friends – are words which look almost or completely identical in two languages, but have different meanings in each. For example, to describe a friend as 'versatile' in English is usually a compliment, but *versatile* in French is reserved for those you have reason to distrust – as changeable and fickle.

True *faux amis* do not share the same meaning in both languages (section 132); in other cases (partial *faux amis*), there is some degree of overlap, but also some distinction (section 133). The most common *faux amis* are listed, except those which are examples of *franglais* (for which, see sections 134–5). The most common meanings are given, but if there are *faux amis* which you have not met before, check their full range of meanings in one or more large dictionaries.

132 True *faux amis*

True *faux amis* are words which have a different meaning in English and French.

abusif incorrect, illegal, unauthorized
    (abusive *injurieux*)

académique related to an Académie / the Académie Française
    (academic *universitaire* – if related to higher education;
    intellectuel – more generally)

actuel present, current
la situation actuelle the present situation
    (the actual situation *la situation elle-même*)

actuellement at present, currently
    (actually *en fait, à vrai dire*)

les actualités (f.) the (T.V.) news

un(e) adepte keen supporter, follower
    (to be adept at *être doué pour / savoir très bien faire*)

adhérer à to join (e.g. club)
   (to adhere to *s'attacher à* – to stick to; *s'en tenir à* – to stay with, not to change)

un agenda a diary
   (agenda *ordre du jour* (m.))

l'agonie (f.) death throes
   (agony *une souffrance atroce*)

agréer (1) to recognize formally, give approval to
centre d'équitation agréé approved riding centre
       (2) to accept (greetings) < formal >
Veuillez agréer mes sentiments distingués. Please accept my sincere wishes. / Yours faithfully.
       (to agree *approuver quelque chose, être d'accord sur quelque chose*)

une allée an avenue
   (an alley *une ruelle*)

alléger to relieve, lighten
   (to allege *alléguer*)

une allocation an allowance (government money)
   (an allocation *une attribution*)

une apologie praise
faire l'apologie de quelqu'un to sing someone's praises
   (an apology *les excuses* (f.pl.); to apologize *faire ses excuses, s'excuser*)

apte à (+ infinitive) capable of / fit to (do)
   (to be apt to *avoir tendance à* + infinitive)

l'assistance (f.) audience, public

l'assistance sociale social welfare
   (assistance *aide* (f.))

assister à quelque chose to attend something
   (to assist *aider, donner un coup de main*)

attendre to wait for
   (to attend *assister à*)

un(e) auditeur / -trice a member of the audience
un auditeur libre student following course without taking exams
   (an auditor *un expert-comptable*)

avertir to warn
 (to advertise *faire de la publicité pour*)

un avertissement a warning
 (an advertisement *une publicité, une petite annonce*;
 an ad / advert *une pub*)

un axe an axis
 (an axe *une hache*)

un bail a lease
 (bail *la caution*; on bail *sous caution*)

une balance a pair of scales; Libra (zodiac)
 (balance *l'équilibre* (m.); to lose one's balance *perdre son*
 équilibre)

balancer to weigh; to chuck < slang >
 (to balance two things *tenir en équilibre*)

bénévole voluntary, charity (work)
 (benevolent *bienveillant*)

blesser to hurt
 (to bless *bénir*)

une brassière (*de sauvetage*) a life-jacket
 (a bra *un soutien-gorge*)

brave fine, splendid (of people)
C'est un brave garçon! He's a fine lad!
 (brave *courageux*)

une bribe a fragment
 (a bribe *un pot-de-vin*)

une caméra a film / T.V. camera
 (a camera *un appareil-photo*)

un canapé a settee, sofa
 (a canopy *un dais*; canopy over bed *un baldaquin*)

candide gullible, credulous
 (candid *franc*; candidly *franchement*)

un car a coach, bus
 (a car *une voiture*)

une case (1) a box, compartment
   (2) a hut, cabin
 (a case *un cas*; a piece of luggage *une valise*; a trial *un procès*)

une casserole a saucepan
    (a casserole *une marmite, un fait-tout*)

une caution a deposit, bail
    (caution *la prudence*)

une cave a cellar
    (a cave *une caverne, une grotte*)

le change exchange (foreign money)
le taux de change the exchange rate
    (a change *un changement*; change / loose money *la monnaie*)

chasser to hunt
    (to chase *poursuivre*)

communal belonging to the Commune (administrative area)
    (communal *collectif, public*)

la commodité convenience, comfort
    (a commodity *un article, un produit*)

complaisant affable; tolerant of partner's extra-marital affairs
    (complacent *suffisant, content de soi-même*)

une conférence a lecture, speech
    (a conference *un colloque, un congrès*)

une confidence a secret
faire une confidence à quelqu'un to entrust a secret to someone
    (confidence *la confiance*)

conséquent (1) consistent
            (2) sizeable, important
    (consequent *qui s'ensuit*)

un cours a lesson
une course a race
    (a training course *un stage*)

les crudités (f.) raw (salad) vegetables
    (crudity *la grossièreté*)

une cure taking the waters, spa treatment
    (a cure *une guérison*)

décevoir to disappoint
    (to deceive *tromper*)

le défiance mistrust
    (defiance *un refus absolu, la désobéissance*)

343

un délai time limit, expiry date
dans un délai de huit jours within a period of a week
    (a delay *un retard*)

délayer to dilute (liquids)
    (to delay *retarder, remettre à plus tard*)

un député an M.P.
    (the deputy . . . *le sous-*. . .; the deputy mayor *le maire-adjoint*)

détenir to exercise (power, authority)
    (to detain *retarder, arrêter*)

une devise a motto
les devises foreign currency
    (a device *un procédé, un stratagème*)

dilapider to fritter away, dissipate
    (dilapidated *vétuste* – especially buildings)

disgracieux awkward, ugly
    (disgraceful *honteux*)

draguer < vulgar slang > to chat up
    (to drag *traîner, tirer*)

un éditeur a publisher
une maison d'édition a publishing house
    (an editor *un rédacteur en chef*)

les effectifs members of staff, number of people involved
    (effective *efficace*)

l'emphase (f.) bombastic rhetoric
    (emphasis *l'accent mis sur quelque chose*)
emphatique bombastic
    (emphatic *qui insiste sur quelque chose*)

énergétique energy, related to energy (scientific)
les ressources énergétiques energy resources
    (energetic *énergique* – of people)

l'équipement (m.) facilities
    (equipment *le matériel*)

éventuel possible, future
une date éventuelle a possible date
    (the eventual date *la date définitive*)

344

éventuellement possibly, in the event
    (eventually *tôt ou tard*)

une fabrique a factory
    (fabric *le tissu, une étoffe*)

fastidieux tiresome, irksome
un travail fastidieux a tiresome task
    (fastidious *pointilleux*; a choosy eater *difficile*)

une figure a face
    (a figure *un chiffre*)

formel strict, categorical
    (formal *officiel, cérémonieux*)

formidable < slang > great / wonderful
    (formidable *redoutable*)

génial < slang > brilliant, clever
    (genial *aimable, sympathique*)

gai lively (no homosexual overtones)
    (gay *homosexuel*; *pédé* < slang >)

une grappe a bunch (e.g. of grapes)
    (a grape *un raisin*)

un grief a grievance, grudge
    (grief *la tristesse, la douleur, le chagrin*)

hardi bold, daring
    (hardy *robuste*)

ignorer not to know
J'ignore son nom. I don't know his / her name.
    (to ignore *ne pas faire attention à*)

incessamment very soon
    (incessantly *sans cesse, sans arrêt*)

un inconvénient a disadvantage
    (inconvenient *pas commode*)

une injure an insult
    (an injury *une blessure*)
injurier to insult
    (to injure *blesser, faire du mal à*)

une instance entreaty, insistence
avec instance earnestly
    (an instance *un cas, un exemple*; for instance *par exemple*)

une intoxication poisoning
    (intoxication *ivresse* (f.))

l'isolation (f.) insulation
l'isolation sonore sound-proofing
    (isolation *l'isolement* (m.))

une issue a way out, exit
voie sans issue one-way street
    (an issue *un sujet, un enjeu*)

labourer to plough
    (to labour *travailler dur*)

large wide
    (large *grand*)

la lecture reading
    (a lecture *une conférence*)

une librairie a bookshop
    (a library *une bibliothèque*)

le local / les locaux premises
    (my 'local' *le bistrot du coin*)

la location renting, hire; booking (tickets)
    (a location *un emplacement, un lieu*)

la malice mischief
    (malice *la méchanceté*)

mince thin, slim
    (mince *la viande hachée*)

misérable poor; wretched
    (miserable *malheureux*)

la monnaie small change
    (money *l'argent* (m.))

un moraliste someone who studies human behaviour
(e.g. La Rochefoucauld, La Bruyère)
    (a moralist / moralizer *un moralisateur*)

une nappe a tablecloth
    (a nap *une sieste*)

une nouvelle a short story
    (a novel *un roman*)
les nouvelles (f.pl.) news

une part a share
    (a part *une partie*; *un rôle* – in a play)

une partition a musical score
    (a partition wall *une cloison*)

passer un examen to take an exam
    (to pass an exam *être reçu à un examen*)

la peine sadness
avoir de la peine à (+ infinitive) to have trouble (doing)
à peine scarcely
    (pain *la douleur*)

un pet a fart
    (a pet *un animal domestique*)
péter to fart
    (to pet *caresser*)

le pétrole crude oil
    (petrol *l'essence* (f.); but when filling up car, ask for *super*
    or *sans plomb* 4-star / lead-free)

une phrase a sentence
    (a phrase *une locution, une expression*)

un physicien a physicist
    (a physician *un médecin*)

une pièce a room; a document
une pièce d'identité I.D.
    (a piece: *une part* share; *une partie* proportion)

une pile a battery
    (a pile *un tas*)

un préjudice a wrong (done to someone)
    au préjudice de quelqu'un to someone's disadvantage
    (a prejudice *un préjugé, un parti pris*)

un préservatif a condom / sheath
    (preserves *les conserves;* a preservative *un agent de conservation*)

prétendre to claim, assert
(to pretend *faire semblant de, faire mine de*)

prévenir to warn, to avert
(to prevent *empêcher*)

une prime a bonus, free gift
(prime *capital, primordial*)

un procès a trial
(a process *un procédé, un processus*)

la propriété property; ownership
(propriety *la bienséance*)

une prune a plum
(a prune *un pruneau*)

un raisin a grape
(a raisin *un raisin sec*)

la recette a recipe
(a receipt *un reçu, une facture*)

la rente unearned income (on letting property)
(rent *le loyer*)

un repaire a den, hideout
(a repair *une réparation*)

résumer to summarize
(to resume *reprendre, poursuivre*)

le sanitaire bathroom fittings
(sanitary *hygiénique*)

sensible sensitive (person); marked, notable
une augmentation sensible a marked increase
(sensible *raisonnable, sensé*)
sensiblement markedly, notably
(sensibly *raisonnablement, sagement*)

un stage a (training) course
(a stage *une étape; une scène* – theatre)

un standard a telephone exchange
(a standard *une norme*)

un store a blind, shutter
(a store *un magasin, un grand magasin*)

supplier to beg, beseech
    (to supply *fournir*)

sympathique nice, friendly
    (sympathetic *compatissant*)

un trouble disturbance, anxiety
    (a trouble *un ennui, une difficulté*)
troubler to disturb (especially psychologically)
    (to trouble *déranger*)
trouble (adjective) unclear
eau trouble unclear / murky water
voir trouble to have blurred vision

ultérieur later, subsequent
    (an ulterior motive *une arrière-pensée*)

user to wear out
    (to use *employer, se servir de*)

les usuels (m.) reference works (in library)
    (usual *habituel*)

versatile fickle, unreliable
    (versatile *avoir des aptitudes diverses*)

une veste a jacket
    (a vest *un gilet de corps*)

un vicaire a curate
    (a vicar *un curé*)

virtuel potential
    (virtual *presque certain*)

un wagon a car, coach (of train)
    (a wagon *une charrette*)

133 Partial *faux amis*

Partial *faux amis* are those which only sometimes have the same meaning in English and French.

accommoder (1) to prepare (culinary)
           (2) to suit, accommodate
    (to accommodate / put up *loger, héberger*)

349

accuser (1) to acknowledge (receipt)
Nous accusons réception de votre lettre.
We acknowledge receipt of your letter.
(2) to accuse / make an accusation

une action (1) a share (Stock Exchange)
(2) an action

une addition (1) bill (in restaurant)
(2) addition

affecter (1) to affect for the worse
Sa mort l'a beaucoup affecté. His / her death affected him (badly).
(2) to appoint someone to a post
Je serai affecté dans le nord l'année prochaine.
I shall be appointed / posted in the north next year.

un agent (1) a policeman (*un agent de police*)
(2) an agent
(an agent / representative *un représentant*; an agent / dealer
un concessionnaire)

un(e) amateur / -trice (1) a lover, devotee
(2) an amateur, non-professional

l'application application / dedication / practical use
(an application – for a job *la candidature, la demande*; an
application letter *une lettre de candidature*)

apprécier (1) to pass judgement on
(2) to appreciate
une appréciation (1) a judgement
(2) appreciation

un argument (1) plot of play
(2) an argument, justification, reason
un argument en faveur de quelque chose an argument in favour of
something
(an argument / quarrel *une discussion*)

assumer to assume, take on (responsibility, task)
(to assume / suppose *supposer*)

assurer (1) to insure (person / object)
(2) to provide service / cover
Les services de transport seront assurés tout le mois d'août.
Transport services will be provided throughout August.
(3) to assure

une assurance (1) an insurance policy
                (2) assurance

une bombe (1) an aerosol can
                (2) a bomb

un caractère psychological character
        (a fictional character *un personnage*)

la chance (1) good luck
avoir la chance de to have the good luck to
                (2) chance, good fortune
courir sa chance to try one's luck, take one's chance
        (chance / fate *le hasard, le sort*; by chance *par hasard*)

la circulation (1) traffic
                    (2) circulation (of blood)

un comédien (1) an actor < formal >
                    (2) a comedian

composer (1) to dial
                (2) to compose

la confusion (1) embarrassment
                    (2) confusion, bewilderment
        (confusion / mess *le chaos, le désordre*)
confus (adjective) (1) embarrassed
                        (2) confused, bewildered
        (confused / chaotic *chaotique*; confused / muddled *embrouillé*,
        peu clair)

un contrôle (1) an inspection, check
                    (2) control, restriction
        (control / command *la direction*; self-control *la maîtrise de soi*)
contrôler (1) to check
            (2) to control, restrain
        (to control, manage *diriger, maîtriser*)
un contrôleur an inspector

la correspondance (1) connection (travel), onward flight / train
                        (2) correspondence

le crédit credit
les crédits government funding

défendre (1) to forbid (*défendre à quelqu'un de* + infinitive)
                (2) to defend

351

un degré a degree (measurement of temperature, etc.)
   (a university degree *un diplôme universitaire*)

une discussion (1) an argument, quarrel
                 (2) a discussion
discuter de quelque chose (1) to argue over
                            (2) to discuss

disposer de to dispose of, have at one's disposal
   (to dispose of / get rid of *se débarrasser de*)

un engagement an engagement, commitment
   (an engagement for marriage *les fiançailles* (f.pl.))

une évidence (1) a clear fact
               (2) evidence
   (legal evidence *un témoignage, une pièce à conviction*)

exciter (1) to arouse sexually
          (2) to excite (but beware unintentional *double-entendre* in
          view of (1))
   (to excite a person *passionner* – no dubious overtones; to excite
   emotions *susciter, éveiller*)
Ce chanteur me passionne. I find that singer really exciting / wonderful.

une expérience (1) an experiment
                 (2) an experience

expérimenté (adjective) experienced

la facilité ease, facility for doing something
   (facilities *les installations, l'équipement; les facilités* can occur, but
   is rare)

femelle female (of animals)
   (female – for people *féminin*)

une galerie (1) a car roof-rack
              (2) a gallery

un habit (1) clothing
un habit de soirée evening dress
           (2) a habit (nun / monk)
   (a habit / way *une habitude*)

un hangar (1) a shed
            (2) an aircraft hangar
   (a clothes hanger *un cintre*)

important (1) large, big (especially numbers)
un nombre important de visiteurs a large number of visitors
           (2) important

un indicatif (1) a telephone code
               (2) indicative (mood of verb)

une information (1) a piece of news (especially on T.V.)
les informations the T.V. news
                 (2) a piece of information
     (information, details *les renseignements* (m.))

intéressant (1) profitable, earns money
Cette entreprise n'est pas intéressante.
This undertaking isn't profitable.
           (2) interesting
intéresser quelqu'un (1) to be profitable for someone
                     (2) to interest someone

une intervention (1) an operation (medical)
                   (2) a speech (at meeting, conference)
                   (3) an intervention

une intrigue (1) a plot (of play, novel)
               (2) an intrigue

juste (1) correct, right (*la juste réponse*)
       (2) a tight fit / squeeze < coll. >
C'est trop juste. It's too tight. / It won't fit.
       (3) just, fair
       (to have just done something *venir de* + infinitive)

mâle male (of animals)
       (male – for people *masculin*)

une mutation (1) a professional relocation, new appointment
Il a demandé une mutation. He's asked to be relocated.
               (2) mutation (biological)

une nomination (1) an appointment, posting
                 (2) a nomination
nommer quelqu'un (1) to appoint someone
                   (2) to name someone

une note (1) a mark, grade
           (2) a note
           (a note / message *un petit mot*)

un office (1) (Church) service, a duty
        (2) an office, post
exercer un office to hold office
    (an office / study *un bureau*)

l'opportunité (1) good fortune
            (2) opportunity, good chance
    (to have an opportunity to *avoir l'occasion de*)

un parc (1) a fleet, chain
un parc de cinémas a chain of cinemas
        (2) a park

les parents (m.) (1) relations, relatives
                (2) parents

un pavillon (1) a ship's flag
            (2) a suburban house
            (3) a pavilion

une pension (1) a boarding school
            (2) a government pension
une pension d'invalidité an invalid pension
    (old-age pension *la retraite*)
un(e) pensionnaire a boarder
    (an old-age pensioner *un(e) retraité(e)*)

la permission (1) leave of absence
être en permission to be on leave (e.g. from army)
            (2) permission

un(e) photographe a photographer
BUT *une photo* a photo (abbreviated form of
une photographie a photograph)

une pomme de pin a pine cone
    (a pineapple *un ananas*)

pratiquer to go in for, practise (hobbies)
    (to practise / train *s'entraîner, (se) perfectionner*)

la rage (1) rabies
        (2) rage, anger

les relations (f.) relations, relationship
    (relations / relatives *les parents* (m.) / *la famille*)

le reste the remainder, the rest
le reste des adultes the rest of the adults
les restes (m.) leftovers (of food)
    (rest, break *le repos*)
rester to remain, rest
    (to rest, relax *se reposer*)

rude coarse, harsh, rude
    (rude / impolite *grossier, impoli*)

sauvage (1) unofficial
une grève sauvage an unofficial / wildcat strike
       (2) savage, wild

séculaire age-old, secular (i.e. 100 years old)
    (secular, non-religious *laïque*)

une sentence (1) a proverb, saying
           (2) a penal sentence
    (a grammatical sentence *une phrase*)

le sexe (1) male or female sexual organs
       (2) sex

une société (1) a firm
         (2) a society

spirituel (1) witty, clever
       (2) spiritual

le sujet (1) topic of study
       (2) subject of discussion
       (3) subject, person
    (a school subject *une matière*; a university subject *une discipline*)

supporter to put up with, bear, support
    (to support – financially / morally – *soutenir*)

susceptible (1) likely to (*susceptible de* + infinitive)
          (2) susceptible, touchy

le temple (1) a Protestant church
       (2) a temple

la tension (1) blood pressure, high blood pressure
       (2) tension

un terme (1) a term, word
        (2) a term, end (*mettre terme à* to put an end to)
(a school term *un trimestre*)

un thème (1) a translation into a foreign language
        (2) a theme

un traitement (1) salary
          (2) treatment
le traitement de texte word-processing

une union a union (act of joining)
    (a trade union *un syndicat*)

unique (1) only, single
C'est l'unique exemplaire qui me reste. It's the only copy I have left.
        (2) unique

l'usage (m.) (1) usage, custom
          (2) wear and tear
    (usage, use of something *l'emploi* (m.))
un usager a user (especially of public transport)

le vers (1) line of poetry
        (2) verse (as opposed to prose)
en vers in verse
    (a verse of poetry *une strophe*; a verse of the Bible *un verset*)

une version (1) a translation from a foreign language
         (2) a version

un voyage (1) a journey, trip
         (2) a voyage by sea
    (a voyage on a boat *une croisière, une traversée*)

FRANGLAIS

134 Rise and domains of *franglais*

With the passage of time it is common for one language to be influenced by another, and particularly for items of vocabulary to be borrowed. The Norman Conquest led to a strong French influence on the English of the Middle Ages. Now, in the late twentieth century, the tables are turned, as French is constantly bombarded by the influence of English – or, more often, American English. The phenomenon is not new: *le shampooing* was noted in French in 1899. However, as the incidence of *franglais* has increased over the last thirty years, it has given rise to polemical debate. Some official French quarters seek to prevent new terms becoming accepted, and try to suggest acceptable Gallic neologisms. Take the case of videos: *la vidéo* (or *la vidéocassette*) is widely used for the video tape, but the machine is known as *le magnétoscope*, by analogy with *le magnétophone* (tape-recorder) – both the latter being coined from respectable Greek roots. The verb *réaliser* is another interesting test case; purists still use *se rendre compte* for 'to realize' and only accept *réaliser* in the sense of 'to achieve', but many French speakers use *réaliser* in both senses.

Not surprisingly, *le franglais* enjoys particular popularity amongst the younger generation, and sections of the press. An English / American term may sound more 'with it' – e.g. *Elle est très cool!* – and at least denotes a veneer of international culture. Compare the way some English speakers casually drop the odd French phrase into their conversation! And newspaper headlines with a foreign term are eye-catching: *Le baby boom* stands out, demanding that you read on.

135 Common *faux amis* of *franglais*

To list all current examples of *franglais* would require a full dictionary, so the list below is limited to common cases where the French form or use of the term is somewhat or wholly different from the English, i.e. is a type of *faux ami*. In quite a few cases, the *franglais* term is an abbreviation of a longer English form, e.g. *le living* from 'living room'.

If you wish to collect further examples of up-to-date *franglais*, look particularly in teenage magazines, sports reports, and adverts. Remember also the world of computers is a hotbed of *franglais* (see section 149).

N.B. Pronunciation of *franglais* is often unpredictable, hence it is advisable to check the phonetic transcription in a good dictionary.

le baby-foot	table-football, bar-football
les baskets (m.)	trainers (shoes)
un bermuda	a pair of (bermuda) shorts
le bifteck	steak (originally: *le beefsteack*)
une boum	a disco, party
la boxe	boxing
le break	estate car
le bristol < archaic >	visiting card
le caddie (or *caddy*)	(supermarket) trolley
le cake	fruitcake
la caméra	film camera
le camping	camping, campsite
le camping-car	camper-van
le car	coach, bus
le car-ferry	ferry
le catch	wrestling
un cocktail	a cocktail, a cocktail party
le cross	cross-country (whence, *le cyclo-cross* cross-country cycle event; *le moto-cross* scrambling)
le dancing	dance-hall
le dogue	bulldog (used in French since the fourteenth century)
le dopage	drug-taking (especially in connection with sports)
le duplex	split-level flat
un express	a fast train / a black coffee
le five o'clock < old-fashioned >	afternoon tea
le flash	T.V. / radio news bulletin
le foot	football
le footing	jogging (*le jogging* is more recent)
gay	gay, homosexual (usually with English spelling, and pronounced *à l'anglaise*, distinct from *gai*)

le grill	grill, steak-house
un gangster	an armed robber
un happening	a happening, event (especially in the 1960s)
un hold-up	an armed robbery, hold-up
le houligan	hooligan
un job	a casual / part-time job
le jury	jury, selection board, panel of examiners
le kangourou	kangaroo
le kiwi	kiwi (bird), kiwifruit
le klaxon	horn
klaxonner	to hoot, toot
le leader	political leader
le lifting	face lift
le living	living room (or *la salle de séjour*)
le lunch	luncheon, buffet, wedding breakfast
le mailing	mail-shot
le management	American-style management (if no American reference implied, use *la gestion*)
les medias	the media, mass media (as in English, the un-Latinate singular *un media* occurs)
le micro	microphone (*X est au micro.* We are speaking to X live.)
le mixage	editing (radio / T.V. / cinema)
une nurse < archaic >	a governess, nanny
le parking	car park, parking space
la performance	performance (of racehorses, athletes, and especially cars)
performant (adjective)	high-performance (especially of cars)
le ping-pong	table-tennis (official term)
le pique-nique	picnic
le / la politicien(ne)	political wheeler and dealer, a politician (often pejorative, but can be simply a synonym of *homme / femme politique*)
le pongiste	table-tennis player
le pressing	dry-cleaner's
la pub, la publicité	an ad, advert, advertisement
un pull	a pullover
un puzzle	a jigsaw puzzle
le pyjama	pyjamas
un racket	an organized racket, extortion, 'protection'
relax (or *relaxe*) (adjective)	laid-back

le rosbif	roast beef
le scotch	sellotape (from brand name)
le scoutisme	scouting mouvement (cf. *un scout*)
le self	a self-service restaurant
le shampooing	shampoo
faire du shopping	to go round the big shops
un smoking	a dinner jacket
un snack	a snack-bar, cafeteria
(un immeuble de) standing	luxury (block of flats)

le starter	choke (car)
le / la speaker(ine)	radio / T.V. announcer
le stop	stop sign, a junction at which you must stop
faire du stop	to hitch-hike (originally: *l'autostop*)
stopper	to stop (in a car, or other motor vehicle)
le studio	bedsit, studio-flat
un talkie-walkie	a walkie-talkie
le tee-shirt	T-shirt
le ticket	bus, underground or restaurant ticket
le tube	hit (pop song)
la vidéo, la vidéo-cassette	video tape
le volley	volleyball
les W.C. (m.)	toilet (N.B. always plural – cf. *les toilettes*)

PROVERBS

Proverbs encapsulate popular wisdom, which frequently transcends linguistic and cultural barriers. Hence, some proverbs are almost identical in English and French. Others only exist in one language, perhaps reflecting something about the *mentalité* or preoccupations of its speakers.

The list below provides a selection of common proverbs. In each case, there is a literal translation, followed by a more idiomatic rendering, or – where it exists – an equivalent.

136 Deserts and retribution

A chacun son dû.
  Give everyone his due.

Comme on fait son lit, on se couche.
  (How one makes one's bed, one lies on it.)
  You make your bed and you have to lie on it.

Aide-toi et le Ciel t'aidera.
  (Help yourself and Heaven will help you.)
  God looks after those who help themselves.

Qui s'y frotte s'y pique.
  (He who rubs against it pricks himself on it / is stung by it.)
  If you court danger, you're asking for trouble.

Qui aime bien châtie bien.
  (He who loves well punishes well.)
  Spare the rod and spoil the child.

Qui sème le vent, récolte les tempêtes.
  (He who sows wind reaps storms.)
  If you cause trouble, you get what you ask for.

Les bons comptes font les bons amis.
  (Good accounts make good friends.)
  Short reckonings make long friends.

Idleness and work

L'oisiveté est la mère de tous les vices.
 (Idleness is the mother of all vices.)
 The devil makes work for idle hands.

Il ne faut pas courir deux lièvres à la fois.
 (It is no good chasing two hares at once.)
 Take one thing at a time.

A l'oeuvre on connaît l'ouvrier.
 (By the work one knows the workman.)
 A man is known / judged by his work.

Chacun son métier.
 Each to his own job. / Every man to his own way.

Le chat parti, les souris dansent.
 When the cat's away, the mice will play.

Mieux vaut tard que jamais.
 Better late than never.

138 **Age and experience**

Si jeunesse savait, si vieillesse pouvait.
 (If youth knew how, if old age were physically able.)
 If youth had the wisdom of old age, or old age the physical strength
 of youth.

On n'apprend pas à un vieux singe à faire des grimaces.
 (You don't teach an old monkey to pull faces.)
 You can't teach an old dog new tricks.

Chat échaudé craint l'eau froide.
 (A cat who has been scalded is scared of cold water.)
 Once bitten twice shy.

Deux yeux voient mieux qu'un.
 (Two eyes see better than one.)
 Two heads are better than one.

En forgeant on devient forgeron.
 (By working at the forge, one becomes a blacksmith.)
 Practice makes perfect. / You learn what you do.

Dans le royaume des aveugles, les borgnes sont rois.
 In the kingdom of the blind, those with one eye are king.

139 Conditions, suspicions and caution

Avec des 'si', on pourrait mettre Paris en bouteille.
  (With enough 'ifs', you could put Paris in a bottle.)
  Dreaming how things might be does not make them possible.

Il faut battre le fer pendant qu' il est chaud.
  You must strike while the iron's hot.

Il n'y a pas de fumée sans feu.
  There's no smoke without fire.

A bon entendeur, salut.
  (To him who understands clearly, hail!)
  A word to the wise is enough.

Un homme averti en vaut deux.
  (A well-informed man is worth two.)
  Forewarned is forearmed.

Qui ne risque rien n'a rien.
  (He who risks nothing has nothing.)
  Nothing ventured, nothing gained.

L'habit ne fait pas le moine.
  (The habit does not make the monk.)
  Appearances can be deceptive. / Don't judge a book by its cover.

Tout ce qui brille n'est pas d'or.
  All that glitters is not gold.

Qui se ressemble s'assemble.
  (Those who are alike gather together.)
  Birds of a feather flock together.

Tant va la cruche à l'eau qu'à la fin elle se casse.
  (The water-jug goes to the water so frequently that in the end it
  breaks.)
  It will end in tears.

Il ne faut pas mettre tous ses oeufs dans le même panier.
  Don't put all your eggs in one basket.

Il ne ne faut pas vendre la peau de l'ours avant de l'avoir tué.
  (You must not sell the bear's skin before you have killed it.)
  Don't count your chickens before they're hatched.

140 Optimism and pessimism

Après la pluie, le beau temps.
   (After the rain, the fine weather.)
   Every cloud has a silver lining.

Il n'est bois si vert qui ne s'allume.
   (There is no wood so green that it will not light.)
   A little patience goes a long way.

On prend plus de mouches avec une cuillerée de miel qu'avec un tonneau de vinaigre.
   (One catches more flies with a spoonful of honey than with a barrel of vinegar.)
   Being kind gets you further than being harsh.

Un malheur en amène un autre.
   (One misfortune brings another.)
   Trouble always comes in pairs.

141 Food

L'appétit vient en mangeant.
   (Appetite comes with eating.)
   The more you have the more you want.

Dis-moi ce que tu manges et je te dirai qui tu es.
   (Tell me what you eat and I'll tell you who you are.)
   You can tell what a person is like from what they eat.

La faim fait sortir le loup du bois.
   (Hunger makes the wolf leave the woods.)
   Hunger will break through stone walls.

Ventre affamé n'a point d'oreilles.
   (A starving stomach has no ears.)
   A hungry man will not listen to reason.

SPECIAL VOCABULARIES

Sections 142–51 provide selective vocabulary lists for ten important thematic areas. The first five are of general or everyday interest, and are intended to take your vocabulary beyond the basic expressions common to most phrasebooks. Sections 147–51 are more specialized, and depending on whether you want French primarily for business, keeping up with current affairs, scientific research, or literary and cultural studies, you will find one or more sections addressed to your needs. The vocabularies are of course not exhaustive on any topic, but offer you a practical resource for looking up terms you may meet, and for increasing your own word power.

142 Numbers and statistics

(a) Cardinal numbers

1	*un / une*	22	*vingt-deux* (etc.)
2	*deux*	30	*trente*
3	*trois*	40	*quarante*
4	*quatre*	50	*cinquante*
5	*cinq*	60	*soixante*
6	*six*	70	*soixante-dix*
7	*sept*	71	*soixante et onze*
8	*huit*	72	*soixante-douze* (etc.)
9	*neuf*	79	*soixante-dix-neuf*
10	*dix*	80	*quatre-vingts*
11	*onze*	81	*quatre-vingt-un* (etc.)
12	*douze*	90	*quatre-vingt-dix*
13	*treize*	91	*quatre-vingt-onze*
14	*quatorze*	92	*quatre-vingt-douze* (etc.)
15	*quinze*	100	*cent*
16	*seize*	101	*cent un*
17	*dix-sept*	102	*cent deux* (etc.)
18	*dix-huit*	200	*deux cents*
19	*dix-neuf*	300	*trois cents* (etc.)
20	*vingt*	1000	*mille*
21	*vingt et un*	1001	*mille un*

1100 *onze cents*	100.000 *cent mille*
1200 *mille deux cents* (etc.)	1.000.000 *un million*
10.000 *dix mille*	

In Belgium and Switzerland, you may meet the forms *septante* for 70 and *nonante* for 90.

(b) Ordinal numbers

1st *premier / -ière*	8th *huitième*
2nd *second (e)* (if only 2);	9th *neuvième*
deuxième (if 3 or more)	10th *dixième* (etc.)
3rd *troisième*	100th *centième*
4th *quatrième*	101st *cent unième*
5th *cinquième*	102nd *cent deuxième* (etc.)
6th *sixième*	1000th *millième* (etc.)
7th *septième*	

★ Note that with dates, French uses the ordinal number only for the 1st:

> *le 1er janvier / le premier janvier* 1 January

For other dates, use the cardinal number:

> *le 14 avril / le quatorze avril* 14 April

The same rule applies with the names of sovereigns:

> *François 1er / François Premier* Francis the First
> *François II / François Deux* Francis the Second

(c) Round numbers

To give approximations, add *-aine* to numbers between 10 and 60, and 100, e.g.:

une dizaine	about 10
une douzaine	a dozen
une vingtaine	about 20 / a score
une soixantaine	about 60
une centaine	about 100

Note the special meaning of:

une huitaine about a week (*huit jours* a week)
une quinzaine a fortnight (*quinze jours* two weeks)
milliers thousands

Il y avait des milliers de touristes à Paris.
There were thousands of tourists in Paris.

(d) Idiomatic expressions with numbers

C'est à deux pas d'ici. It's only a minute away.
être à deux doigts de faire quelque chose to be on the verge of (doing)
Un tiens vaut mieux que deux tu l'auras. A bird in the hand is worth two in the bush.

les trois quarts du temps most of the time
coûter trois fois rien to cost next to nothing
être haut comme trois pommes < coll. > to be knee-high to a grasshopper

dire ses quatre vérités à quelqu'un to tell someone a few home truths
ne pas y aller par quatre chemins not to beat about the bush
être tiré à quatre épingles to be spruced up / dressed up
couper les cheveux en quatre to split hairs
se mettre en quatre pour faire quelque chose to go to any ends to do something (to help someone else)
un de ces quatre matins < coll. > one of these days
la semaine des quatre jeudis when pigs might fly

être au septième ciel to be over the moon
le septième art the cinema

aujourd'hui en huit a week (from) today

trente-six: the number 36 is used to imply 'a good many / a hundred and one':
   Il n'y a pas trente-six façons de s'y prendre.
   There aren't 101 ways to do it.
en voir trente-six chandelles to see stars

(e) Statistics and percentages

Un écolier sur cinq quittera l'école sans diplôme.
One pupil in (every) five will leave school without a qualification.

Trente pour cent des employés préfèrent ce système.
Thirty per cent of employees prefer this system.

Il faut tenir compte de la part croissante des femmes salariées.
We must take into account the increasing percentage (literally: share) of women out at work.

Où se situe la moyenne?
What is the average?

La fourchette / L'écart entre ces deux groupes se rétrécit.
The gap between these two groups is narrowing.

Les prévisions se situent entre 5000 et 6000 francs.
The estimates vary between 5000 and 6000 francs.

Le nombre de cas sera compris entre 700 et 800 par an.
There will be between 700 and 800 cases a year.

Les investissements dépasseront 100.000 francs.
Investments will top / rise above 100,000 francs.

Le montant évoluera entre 2000 et 2500 francs.
The sum will reach between 2000 and 2500 francs.

Le nombre de voyageurs est passé de 5000 à 7500.
The number of travellers has risen from 5000 to 7500.

Il faudra revoir ces chiffres à la hausse / à la baisse.
These figures will have to be revised upwards / downwards.

143 Times, dates and temporal expressions

(a) Giving the time

Remember that the 24-hour clock is used in all official timetables in France. Even in conversation someone may suggest:

On se retrouvera à dix-neuf heures.
Let's meet again at 7 p.m.

With the 24-hour system, to express minutes past the hour use the number of minutes (not *quart / demi*):

à vingt et une heures quarante-cinq at 9.45 p.m.
but
à dix heures moins le quart

à dix-sept heures trente at 5.30 p.m.
but
à cinq heures et demie

Note the following abbreviations in conversation:

Il est moins cinq / dix (etc.)
It's five / ten to.

Il est le quart / la demie.
It's a quarter / half past.

To give an approximate time:

Ils doivent arriver vers six heures.
They should arrive at about six o'clock.

(b) Dates

(See section 142a and b for use of cardinal and ordinal numbers.)

Note the word order in French if you are giving a day and date:

le lundi 19 juillet Monday, 19 July

To ask the date:

Quelle est la date?
On est le combien aujourd'hui? < coll. >

To refer to years:

Il est né en 1960.
He was born in 1960.

Cet événement se passa en l'an 1654.
That event took place in the year 1654.

L'an 2000 approche.
The year 2000 is drawing near.

les années 20 / 30 (etc.) the 1920s / 1930s (etc.)

(c) Referring to the past

hier	yesterday
avant-hier	the day before yesterday
la veille	the previous day, the day before
l'avant-veille	the previous day but one
l'année dernière	last year
l'année précédente	the previous year, the year before
alors	then, at that time
d'antan < literary / archaic >	of yesteryear
auparavant	previously, beforehand
autrefois	formerly, in earlier times
jadis < literary >	formerly
précédemment	previously

369

(d) Referring to the present

aujourd'hui	today
ces jours-ci	these days
à l'époque actuelle	at the present time
par le temps qui court	at the present

actuellement	at present, currently
déjà	already
d'ores et déjà < literary >	already
jusqu'ici	up until now
parfois	sometimes, occasionally

(e) Referring to the future

demain	tomorrow
après-demain	the day after tomorrow
le lendemain	the next day
le surlendemain	two days later, the next day but one
d'ici (à) trois jours	in three days' time / from now

bientôt	soon
désormais	henceforth, from now on
dorénavant < formal >	henceforth
à partir de maintenant	from now on
sous peu < literary >	soon, in a short time

The weather

For the more common expressions relating to the weather based on the verb *faire*, see section 126.

(a) Expressions common in conversation

Tu as entendu la météo? Have you heard the weather forecast?

Nous avons eu une vraie canicule. We've had a real heatwave.

Il fait un froid de canard. < coll. > It's freezing cold.

Il y aura un risque de verglas. There will be a danger of ice on the roads.

Ça tourne à l'orage. < coll. > There's a storm brewing.

Le temps s'est gâté. The weather's turned bad.

Le temps commence à se lever.
It's beginning to brighten up. / The sky's beginning to clear.

Le fond de l'air est frais. < coll. > It feels nippy today.

Nous avons été surpris par l'averse. We weren't expecting the shower.

(b) Expressions used in weather reports

Le temps n'évoluera guère. There will be little change in the weather.

Les précipitations seront abondantes. There will be heavy rainfall / snowfall.

De rares averses s'annoncent pour le nord-ouest.
There will be occasional showers in the north-west.

Les nuages deviendront plus nombreux sur la moitié nord.
Cloud will increase in the north.

Le sud-est aura des passages nuageux plus fréquents.
The south-east will have more frequent cloudy periods.

Les brumes se dissiperont en fin de matinée.
The mist will clear by late morning.

Des éclaircies se développeront.
Bright spells will develop.

Vous aurez une journée bien ensoleillée.
You will have a very sunny day.

Un vent faible soufflera sur l'ensemble de la France.
There will be a light wind in the whole of France.

MÉTÉOROLOGIE

Les orages se cantonneront dans les régions montagneuses.
Storms will be confined to mountain areas.

Ce sont des températures inférieures / supérieures aux normes pour la saison.
The temperatures are lower / higher than we would expect for this time of year.

(c) Long-term climatic changes

Les climatologues craignent un réchauffement de la terre.
Climatologists fear a global warming effect.

On parle d'un renforcement de l'effet de serre.
There is talk about an increase in the greenhouse effect.

La couche d'ozone est menacée.
The ozone layer is threatened.

Faudrait-il craindre une nouvelle période glaciaire?
Should we fear a new ice-age?

Les problèmes liés à la sécheresse s'aggravent.
The problems linked to the prolonged dry spell / drought are growing worse.

 145 Travel

(a) Cars

un amortisseur	shock-absorber
une batterie	battery
une boîte de vitesses	gearbox
une bougie	spark plug
un capot	bonnet
une clé de contact	ignition key
un clignotant	indicator
un cric	jack
la direction	steering
un essuie-glace	windscreen wiper
un frein	brake
un moteur	engine
un pare-brise	windscreen

un phare	headlight
un pneu crevé	puncture
une portière	door (of car)
un rétroviseur	rear-view mirror
une soupape	valve
une vitesse	gear, speed
un volant	steering wheel
caler	to stall
clignoter	to indicate
débrayer	to declutch, let out the clutch
démarrer	to set off
écraser	to run off
embrayer	to engage the clutch
entrer en collision avec	to collide with
faire le plein	to fill up (with petrol)
freiner	to brake
se heurter	to collide
tamponner	to bang into / collide with
tomber en panne	to break down
l'alcootest (m.)	the breathalyser
un bouchon	traffic jam / tailback
brûler / griller un feu rouge	to go through a red light
un carambolage	multiple pile-up
une ceinture de sécurité	seatbelt
le code de la route	the highway code
un contrôle de vitesse	speed test / trap
un embouteillage	traffic jam
la sécurité routière	road safety
une autoroute à péage	motorway with toll
un boulevard périphérique	ring road / bypass
une route nationale	A-road / main road
une route départementale	B-road / secondary road
une route à quatre voies / une voie express	dual carriageway
une rocade	ring road / bypass

Reports on road conditions may advise you to check with *Bison Futé* (the Smart Bison) – a government-sponsored motoring advisory service, giving advice on radio, T.V. and by phone.

La ville est belle en autobus Renault

(b) Bus

In most French towns, books of bus tickets can be bought in advance. A ticket is valid for a set time (e.g. 45 minutes / one hour), even if you change buses, but must be time-stamped when you get on the first bus.

un arrêt de bus	bus stop
un arrêt facultatif	request stop
un carnet de tickets	book of tickets (e.g. ten)
faire l'appoint	to give the exact money
oblitérer le ticket	to time-stamp ticket in a machine
un tarif réduit	reduced price ticket (e.g. for children)

(c) Train and underground

Train tickets can be purchased in advance, and for certain trains (especially *T.G.V.*), reservation is compulsory. When you go on to the platform to catch your train, you must date-stamp (*composter / valider*) your ticket in one of the orange machines – otherwise you will be travelling illegally. There are various *réductions* applicable if you are travelling as a couple, family, group, or are a child or Senior Citizen *(le troisième âge)*, and these usually apply to foreign tourists as well as French nationals. Ask for advice before purchasing your ticket.

Tickets for the Paris underground can be bought in advance. One ticket is valid for a single journey within the *zone urbaine* however many times you change trains.

une consigne	left-luggage office
une consigne automatique	automatic luggage locker
une fiche horaire	timetable (leaflet)
un guichet	ticket office
composter un billet	to date-stamp (and validate) a train ticket in a machine
descendre du train	to get off the train
monter dans le train	to get on the train
valider un billet	to date-stamp (and validate) train ticket in a machine
un carnet de tickets	book of ten metro tickets
une carte orange	monthly season ticket (for metro and buses)
une correspondance	change (of trains)
une station de métro	metro station

(d) Plane

une aérogare	airport terminal
une boutique hors taxe	duty-free shop
une carte d'accès à bord	boarding pass
l'embarquement (m.)	boarding
l'enregistrement (m.) *des bagages*	checking in
une navette	shuttle
la Police de l'Air	(French) passport check

| une porte | departure gate |
| un satellite | boarding area (within terminal) |

atterrir	to land
décoller	to take off
enregistrer les bagages	to check in
récupérer les bagages	to get back / reclaim luggage

146 Shopping

(a) Types of shops

un atelier	studio, workshop (e.g. pottery)
une boutique	(small) shop
un atelier / une boutique d'artisan	craft shop
un centre commercial	shopping centre (in or out of town)
un commerce	shop, business
tenir un commerce	to run a shop / business
une foire	occasional / special market
les halles (f.)	covered market
un hypermarché	hypermarket / superstore
un grand magasin	department store
une grande surface	shopping centre (usually out of town)
un supermarché	supermarket
la vente par correspondance	mail-order shopping

(b) Departments within stores

The general term for 'a department' is *un rayon*, e.g. *le rayon de papeterie* (stationery department).

l'alimentation (f.)	food
les articles de ménage (m.)	household items
le bricolage	D.I.Y.
la caisse	checkout, till
l'électroménager	electrical goods
le jardinage	gardening
la librairie	books
les meubles (m.)	furniture
la papeterie	stationery
la pharmacie	chemist's

la quincaillerie	ironmongery, hardware
le service après vente	customer services
la vaisselle	china and glass
les vêtements (m.)	clothing

(c) Methods of payment

un avoir credit note
une facture bill
un ticket de caisse till receipt

payer en argent liquide / en liquide to pay cash

> *Vous n'avez pas les 30 centimes / une pièce de 10 francs?*
> Would you have the 30 centimes / a 10-franc coin?

payer par carte bancaire / par VISA to pay by credit card / VISA (often
referred to generically as *la carte bleue*, the name of the French credit
card system)

taper son code secret to key in one's PIN number (for identification)

payer par chèque to pay by cheque

> *C'est à l'ordre de qui?*
> To whom should I make it out?

377

mettre quelque chose sur son compte to put something on account
verser un acompte to pay a deposit / make a down payment
effecter des versements échelonnés to make regular payments
une traite mensuelle, une mensualité a monthly payment

(d) Sales and reductions

une braderie annual day of sales
   (in many towns, there is an annual one-day *braderie*, during which
   shops have stalls on pavements)
fin de série end of line
une liquidation du stock clearance sale
des prix massacrés enormous reductions
les soldes (f.) the sales

un rabais de 10 pour cent
une réduction de 10 pour cent } 10 per cent reduction
une remise de 10 pour cent

147 Commerce and finance

(a) Government spending and revenue

les coffres (m.) *de l'Etat*	the state coffers
les crédits	government funding
les dépenses publiques	public spending
dégager quatre milliards de francs	to release four billion francs
geler les crédits	to freeze government funding
verser une subvention à quelqu'un	to give someone a subsidy
les charges fiscales	the tax burden
les charges sociales	National Insurance contributions
un(e) contribuable	a taxpayer
les droits (m.) *de succession*	death duties
le fisc	the Inland Revenue (French equivalent)
la fiscalité	the tax system
l'impôt foncier	property tax
l'impôt sur le revenu	income tax
les impôts locaux	local taxes (cf. Poll Tax / rates)
le prélèvement	deduction at source
prélever des impôts	to levy taxation
les rentrées fiscales	tax revenue
le revenu imposable	taxable income
le seuil minimum d'imposition	tax threshold
la tranche d'imposition	tax bracket
la T.V.A. (Taxe sur la valeur ajoutée)	V.A.T.

(b) Salaries and income

If you are enquiring about French salaries, be prepared for the fact that the French usually quote their monthly (rather than annual) salary: either *brut* (gross) or *net* (net).

There is a minimum rate of pay, authorized by the government, known as *le S.M.I.C. (salaire minimum interprofessionnel de croissance)*, which is frequently referred to in discussions of pay.

There are various words for wages / salary:

la feuille de paie	payslip
les gages (m.) < old-fashioned >	wages
le revenu	income
le salaire	pay, salary
le traitement	salary (usually when paid monthly into a bank)

379

Other factors which affect pay:

l'ancienneté (f.)	length of service with employer
l'augmentation (f.) *des salaires*	pay rise / pay award
le barème	(salary) scale
un échelon	a point (on salary scale)
la grille des salaires	salary structure
la prime	bonus
le salaire de base	basic salary

Unearned income can derive from:

les actions (f.)	shares
les rentes (f.)	unearned income (investment, property)
une rente foncière	ground rent
une rente viagère	a life annuity

(c) Banking and investment

une caisse d'épargne	savings bank (cf. building society in England)
les capitaux	capital
un carnet de chèques / un chéquier	cheque book
une carte de crédit	credit card
un chèque en bois < coll. > ⎱ *un chèque sans provision* ⎰	cheque which will bounce
un compte bancaire	(current) bank account
un compte d'épargne	savings / deposit account
un montant	amount, sum
un plan-logement	savings account for home loan
un point retrait-argent	cashpoint machine
un prêt bancaire	bank loan
un prêt au logement	mortgage, home loan
un relevé de compte	bank statement
les remboursements (m.)	repayments
un retrait (d'argent)	withdrawal (of money)
un solde	balance (of bank account)
un taux d'intérêt	interest rate
le taux de l'inflation	the inflation rate
un versement	paying in (money)
un virement bancaire	credit transfer
emprunter (de l'argent) à quelqu'un	to borrow (money) from someone
encaisser un chèque	to cash a cheque
être à découvert	to be overdrawn
prêter (de l'argent) à quelqu'un	to lend money to someone

retirer de l'argent	to withdraw money
verser de l'argent sur son compte	to put money into one's account
une action	share
un(e) actionnaire	shareholder
un agent de change	stockbroker
la Bourse des valeurs	the French Stock Exchange
un cambiste	exchange broker
la corbeille	stockbrokers' central enclosure (Paris)
la cotation	quoting (on the Stock Exchange)
le cours (du franc)	the value / rate (of the franc)
les devises étrangères	foreign currency
le marché des changes	the foreign exchange markets
les marchés boursiers	the stock markets
une obligation	bond
une offre publique d'achat	takeover bid
un placement sûr	safe investment
un portefeuille	portfolio
un taux de change	exchange rate
les titres (m.)	stocks, securities
les transactions boursières	share dealings
les valeurs mobilières	securities, stocks and shares
un investissement foncier	investment in land and property
le marché de l'immobilier	the property market
un placement immobilier	property investment

(d) Production

une chaîne	production line
une chaîne de montage	assembly line
un contremaître	foreman
un fabricant	manufacturer
une main d'oeuvre	workforce
un ouvrier	a worker
un ouvrier spécialisé	a skilled worker
un robot	robot
un sous-traitant	subcontractor
un atelier	workshop
un chantier	building site
les coûts de production	production costs
un entrepôt	warehouse
les matières premières	raw materials
une pièce détachée	component part
une pièce de rechange	spare part
un procédé de fabrication	manufacturing process

un produit	product, commodity
la production en (grande) série	mass production
le rendement	output
une usine	factory, plant

(e) Sales and marketing

un acheteur	buyer
un(e) client(e)	customer
un concessionnaire	recognized dealer
un(e) concurrent(e)	competitor
un(e) consommateur / -trice	consumer
un démarcheur à domicile	door-to-door salesman
un(e) détaillant(e)	retailer
un distribueur	dealer
un fournisseur	supplier
un grossiste	wholesaler
un intermédiaire	middle-man
un(e) représentant(e)	sales representative
un vendeur au porte-à-porte	door-to-door salesman

un chiffre d'affaires	turnover
un chiffre de vente	sales figure
un commerce de détail	retail trade
un commerce de gros	wholesale trade
un débouché	outlet
un démarchage	door-to-door sales, canvassing opinion

distribuer	to market, distribute
un échantillon	sample
un éventail	range
lancer un produit	to launch a product
une marque	brand
une part du marché	share of the market
la planification	(forward) planning
la recherche commerciale	market research
la société de consommation	consumer society
se tailler une part du marché	to win a share of the market

(f) Advertising and public relations

une agence de publicité	advertising agency
un annonceur	advertiser
un chef de produit	product manager
un(e) conseiller / -ère	consultant

une affiche	hoarding, poster
une annonce publicitaire	an advertisement
faire passer une annonce	to run an advert
un concepteur	designer
un étalage	window display
une fourchette d'âge	age bracket
une légende	caption
un message publicitaire	advertisement, blurb
une mise en page	lay-out
un programme	schedule
une publicité	advertising, an advertisement
les relations publiques	public relations

148 Politics and current affairs

(a) Government

le Président de la République	the President of France
le chef de l'Etat	the head of state (i.e. the President)
l'Elysée	official residence of the President (used by journalists to indicate the President, e.g. *L'Elysée a déclaré que . . .* cf. '10 Downing Street said . . .')
le Premier ministre	French Prime Minister
le chef du gouvernement	the head of the government (i.e. the Prime Minister)
Matignon	official residence of the Prime Minister (and therefore used by journalists to indicate the Prime Minister)
un ministre d'Etat	(senior) Minister
un ministre délégué / chargé de . . .	deputy Minister
un secrétaire d'Etat	Minister (lower ranked)
le Conseil des ministres	weekly ministerial meeting (cf. Cabinet Meeting)
le ministre des Affaires étrangères	Foreign Secretary
le Quai d'Orsay	the Foreign Office
le ministre de l'Intérieur	Home Secretary
le ministre des Finances	Chancellor of the Exchequer
l'Administration publique	Civil Service
l'Assemblée nationale	National Assembly (lower house)
un(e) député(e)	M.P.
la fonction publique	civil service (i.e. all employees of the state)

un(e) fonctionnaire	employee of the state / civil servant (groups such as teachers are *fonctionnaires* in France, being paid by the state)
un haut fonctionnaire	senior civil servant
un ministère	ministry
le Parlement	Parliament
le Sénat	Senate (upper house)
le Préfet	Prefect (chief administrator, appointed by government, for a region or department)
la Préfecture	offices of the Prefect
un conseil municipal	town / city council
un(e) conseiller / -ère municipal(e)	town / city councillor
un élu local	local councillor
l'Hôtel de Ville / la mairie	Town Hall
un maire	mayor
un maire-adjoint	deputy / assistant mayor

(b) Elections

les (élections) européennes	elections for European Parliament
les (élections) législatives	general / parliamentary election
les (élections) municipales	local (town / city) council elections
les (élections) présidentielles	presidential election
être candidat(e) à (la présidence)	to be a candidate for (the presidency)
une circonscription	constituency
une cote (de popularité)	(popularity) rating / standing
se démettre	to resign
une démission	resignation
se désister	to stand down, withdraw
élire	to elect
entrer en lice	to enter the arena / fray
la majorité	the government
l'opposition	the opposition
une plate-forme électorale	election manifesto
un raz-de-marée	landslide (literally: tidal wave)
recueillir x pour cent des voix	to win x per cent of the vote
la représentation proportionnelle	proportional representation
le scrutin	voting
le scrutin majoritaire	first-past-the-post system
un sondage	opinion poll
un taux de participation	turnout

le premier / deuxième tour de scrutin	first / second round of voting
les urnes (f.)	ballot boxes
aller aux urnes	to go to the polls
une voix	a vote

(c) Political debate

un(e) adhérent(e)	(party) member
le centre	the centre
la droite	the right
être de droite	to be right-wing
la gauche	the left
être de gauche	to be left-wing
les militants de base	grassroots militants
un parti politique	political party
la cohabitation	'cohabitation' (e.g. Socialist President and right-wing Prime Minister / government)
déposer une motion de censure	to put down a motion of censure
s'engager pour (une mesure)	to fight for, be politically active for (a measure)
faire une intervention à l'Assemblée	to make a speech in Parliament
une manifestation	protest march
mettre à l'étude (un projet)	to study (a project)
l'ordre du jour	the agenda, business of the day
poursuivre des discussions	to continue discussions
prendre des mesures en faveur de (quelqu'un)	to act for (someone)
rompre des négociations	to break off negotiations
une séance parlementaire	parliamentary sitting
un sommet	summit

(d) Home affairs

une allocation	allowance
les allocations familiales	family allowances (i.e. child benefit, etc.)
un(e) assistant(e) social(e)	social worker
l'assurance invalidité	disability payment
l'assurance maladie (f.)	sick-pay
l'assurance maternité (f.)	maternity benefit
l'assurance vieillesse (f.)	(state) pension scheme
la cotisation	National Insurance contribution
l'Etat-providence	the Welfare State

une famille nombreuse	large family (three or more children, officially)
une prestation	benefit payment
une retraite	retirement pension
un(e) retraité(e)	retired person
la Sécurité sociale	(French system of) National Insurance
le troisième âge	retired people, Senior Citizens
le chômage	unemployment
un débrayage	stoppage (of work)
une embauche	taking on staff
une force ouvrière	workforce
une formation	training
une grève (sauvage)	(wildcat) strike
un licenciement	redundancy
le marché de l'emploi	employment market
un mouvement de grève	strike action
la population active	working population
la préretraite	early retirement
le recyclage	retraining, in-service training
un stage de reconversion	retraining course
un syndicat	trade union
l'aménagement du territoire	town-planning (on a national scale)
un boulevard périphérique / une rocade	ring road / bypass
un cadre de vie	life-style, the residential character of a place
une cité	housing estate
un espace vert	open space, park
les H.L.M. (f.) (habitations à loyer modéré)	council housing / council flats
un logement social	local authority housing
un réaménagement	(re)development
les taudis (m.)	slums
un terrain vague	wasteland
l'urbanisme (m.)	town-planning
un(e) urbaniste	town-planner

(e) Foreign affairs

la C.E.E. (Communauté economique européenne)	E.E.C.
les DOM-TOM	overseas French *départements* and territories
l'ONU	United Nations
l'OTAN	NATO
l'outre-Manche	Great Britain

un pays sous-développé	underdeveloped country
un pays en voie de développement	developing country
le perfide Albion < ironic / pejorative >	Great Britain
le Tiers Monde	Third World
une ambassade	embassy
un blocus naval	naval blockade
un boycott / un boycottage	boycott
un consulat	consulate
un(e) homologue	counterpart
un(e) immigré(e) clandestin(e)	an unofficial immigrant
un(e) otage	hostage
la politique extérieure	foreign policy
un porte-parole du gouvernement	government spokesperson
les pourparlers (m.)	discussions
reserrer les liens	to forge closer links
un ressortissant (étranger)	(foreign) resident / national
rompre les relations diplomatiques	to break off diplomatic relations

(f) The law and legal matters

abroger une loi	to repeal a law
adopter un projet de loi	to vote through a bill
déposer un projet de loi	to table a bill
entrer en vigueur	to come into force (law)
un projet de loi	a bill
une proposition de loi	a private bill
voter (un projet de) loi	to pass a law
l'avocat de la partie civile	counsel for the prosecution
le box des accusés	the dock
comparaître	to appear (in court)
la cour d'assises	Assize Court (i.e. Crown Court)
écrouer	to consign to prison
inculper quelqu'un de	to accuse someone of
intenter un procès contre	to take out a lawsuit against
un juge d'instruction	investigating magistrate
un(e) juriste	lawyer
un non-lieu	case dismissed
le Palais de Justice	the law courts
le parquet	office of public prosecutor, court
la partie de la défense	counsel for the defence

poursuivre (quelqu'un) en justice	to prosecute (someone)
le / la prévenu(e)	the accused
le procureur (de la République)	public prosecutor
rendre un verdict	to return a verdict
traduire (quelqu'un) en justice	to bring (someone) to court
le tribunal de police	police court (for petty offences)
le tribunal d'instance	magistrates' court
le tribunal de grande instance	High Court
un agresseur	mugger
une agression	mugging
un attentat	political assassination attempt
un bandit	(armed) robber
une contravention	parking ticket / fine
un crime	crime, murder
un criminel	criminal, murderer
un délit	(petty) crime
un(e) détenu(e)	prisoner
détourner un avion	to hijack a plane
enfreindre une loi	to break a law
un hold-up	armed robbery, raid
une infraction	offence
un malfaiteur	criminal
un pirate de l'air	hijacker
un ravisseur	kidnapper
un(e) récidiviste	re-offender
le trafic des stupéfiants	drug trafficking
un viol	rape
un violeur	rapist
un voyou	yobo, hooligan
la B.R.B. (Brigade de la répression du banditisme)	anti-crime squad
le commissariat de police	police station
les C.R.S. (Compagnie républicaine de sécurité)	special riot police
les forces de l'ordre	police authorities
un gardien de la paix	police officer
les pouvoirs publics	the authorities
le R.A.I.D. (Recherche-Assistance-Intervention-Dissuasion)	crack police squad (cf. role of S.A.S.)
les ripoux < slang >	crooked policemen

149 Computers and technology

(a) Computers

Much of the language of computers is international – or *franglais*. *Un P.C.* is used, as in English, for a personal computer; *le logiciel* exists for 'software', but *le software* is also heard.

un homme-système	systems analyst (even if a woman!)
un(e) informaticien(ne)	computer specialist
l'informatique (f.)	computing / computer science
un ingénieur	(computer) engineer
la programmation	programming
un programmeur	programmer
une imprimante	printer
une machine à traiter le texte	word-processor
(or *un ordinateur*)	
un micro-ordinateur	micro-computer
un ordinateur	computer
un ordinateur central	central computer
une banque de données	database
un clavier	keyboard
un composant	component
un disque	hard disk
une disquette	soft / floppy disk
les données (f.)	data
un écran	screen
un fax	fax
un fichier central	databank
le logiciel	software
le matériel informatique	hardware
un octet	byte
un programme	computer program
une puce	microchip
un réseau	network
une souris	mouse
un terminal (des terminaux)	terminal
connecté	on-line
non connecté	off-line
effacer	to delete
informatiser	to put on computer, computerize
mettre en page / en forme	to format
traiter	to handle, process

(b) Computer-related technology

You may have noticed in France the widespread *Minitel* service, run by the *P.T.T. (Postes et Télécommunications)*. It provides telephone subscribers with a range of services, from directory enquiries, to details of flight availability, to getting the latest information on school examinations.

une carte à puce	magnetic card
une piste magnétique	magnetic strip
un point retrait-argent	cash-point machine (bank)
une télécarte	phone card
une télé-commande	remote control

(c) Domestic technology

un appareil électroménager	domestic appliance
un C.D.	compact disc, C.D. player
une chaîne stéréo / hifi	stereo / hifi system
un congélateur	freezer
un four à micro-ondes	microwave oven
un lave-vaisselle	dishwasher
une machine à laver / un lave-linge	washing-machine
un magnétoscope	video recorder
un mixer	mixer, blender
un répondeur téléphonique	answering machine

(d) Other recent technology

une antenne parabolique	satellite dish
une centrale nucléaire	nuclear power station
la désintégration de l'atome (m.)	the splitting of the atom
une fusée	rocket
une navette (spatiale)	(space) shuttle
la télévision par câble	cable television
la télévision par satellite	satellite television

(e) Some 'green' issues and technology

Products or machines which are ecologically sound are designated *propre* or *vert*, e.g. *la voiture propre*. On commercial products, you will see *respecte l'environnement*, the equivalent of 'environmentally friendly'.

les changes pour bébé non blanchis au chlore	nappies not artificially bleached
l'essence sans plomb	lead-free petrol
la lessive sans phosphate	phosphate-free washing-powder
le papier recyclé	recycled paper
les piles sans mercure	mercury-free batteries
le recyclage des déchets	recycling of waste
la reprise des vides	collection of empty bottles

150 Cinema and the fine arts

(a) Cinema

The cinema is known affectionately as *le grand écran* (the big screen) as opposed to *le petit écran* (i.e. the T.V.).

le cinéma d'art et d'essai	experimental / avant-garde films
un court-métrage	short film (especially documentary)
un dessin animé	cartoon
un documentaire	documentary
un film en exclusivité	new release
un film en version originale	foreign film (not dubbed)
l'industrie cinématographique	the cinema industry
un(e) acteur / -trice	actor, actress
un cinéaste	famous film director
un(e) cinéphile	keen cinema-goer

391

un(e) figurant(e)	extra / walk-on part
un metteur en scène	director
un réalisateur	producer
une star	star
une vedette	star
le générique	credits
le gros plan	close-up
le mixage	sound editing
le montage	editing
le tournage	filming, shooting
doubler	to dub
interpréter un rôle	to play a role
passer	to be showing (Ce film passe à dix cinémas.)
porter (un roman) à l'écran	to make a film of (a novel)
sortir un film	to bring out a film
tourner un film	to shoot, make a film
tourner un film en extérieur	to shoot a film on location

(b) Fine arts

une aquarelle	water-colour
les bandes dessinées (les b.d.)	cartoons
la broderie	embroidery
un dessin	drawing
une ébauche	rough / outline sketch
une exposition	exhibition
une maquette	model (to scale)
une peinture	painting
une peinture à l'huile	oil painting
une sculpture	sculpture
un(e) architect	architect
un(e) artiste	artist
un graveur	engraver
un mécène	patron
un peintre	painter, artist
un(e) sculpteur / -trice	sculptor
un aménagement	design / redesigning (architectural)
l'arrière-plan (m.)	background
un cadre	(1) frame; (2) setting
une esquisse	sketch
une gravure	engraving
le premier plan	foreground
un tableau	picture
une toile	canvas

151 Literature

(a) Writers and their craft

(Unless a separate feminine form is given, the masculine form of the noun is used for both men and women.)

un auteur	author
un biographe	biographer
un conteur	short-story writer
un critique	critic
un dramaturge	playwright, dramatist
un écrivain	writer
un fabuliste	writer of fables
un historien	historian
un philosophe	philosopher
un poète	poet
un(e) romancier / -ère	novelist
un(e) lecteur / -trice	reader
un(e) liseur / -se	avid reader
composer	to compose
créer	to create / write
dépeindre	to depict, paint
écrire	to write
évoquer	to conjure up
raconter	to tell, relate
rédiger	to write up (e.g. articles)

(b) Genres and works

★ Note that *l'oeuvre* (m.) = the complete works of an author, but *une oeuvre* = one work.

une autobiographie	autobiography
une biographie	biography
un chef d'oeuvre	masterpiece
un compte-rendu	critical review
un conte	short story / tale
un conte de fées	fairytale
un écrit	piece of writing
une fable	fable
une histoire	story, history
un livre de poche	a paperback
une nouvelle	short story / novella
une pièce de théâtre	play

393

un poème	poem
une poésie < literary >	poem, poetry
un récit	an account, tale
un recueil (de poésie)	collection (of poetry)
un roman	novel
un roman à l'eau de rose	sentimental novel (e.g. Mills and Boon)
un roman policier	detective story

(c) Plays and acting

★ Contrary to many students' attempts to coin a new item of *franglais*, *le drame* does not mean 'drama / theatre'. *Le drame* refers exclusively to (i) a hybrid form of tragedy and comedy (*le drame bourgeois*), popular in the eighteenth century, or (ii) 'drama' in the sense of dramatic events in everyday life.

un(e) acteur / -trice	actor
les acteurs	the cast
un(e) cabotin(e) < coll. >	ham actor
un(e) comédien(ne)	(1) actor, (2) comic actor
la distribution des rôles	the cast list / *dramatis personae*
un metteur en scène	producer
une pièce de théâtre / une pièce	play
le public	the audience
un régisseur	stage manager
une représentation	performance
une reprise	revival (of an earlier performance)
un souffleur	prompter
un spectacle	play, performance
un(e) spectateur / -trice	spectator
le théâtre	drama, theatre
une troupe (de théâtre)	(theatre) company
un(e) tragédien(ne)	tragedian
une vedette	star
les accessoires	props
un costume	costume
la création d'une pièce	(first / new) staging of a play
un décor	set
les rampes (f.)	footlights
une scène	stage
créer (+ name of play)	to perform / stage (of new performance)
interpréter un rôle	to play a part / role
monter une pièce	to put on a play
faire relâche	(of theatre) closed for annual holidays
tenir le rôle de	to play the part of

(d) Prose writing

★ Note the distinction between *le caractère* (psychological character / nature) and *le personnage* (a fictional character).

un climat	climate, atmosphere
le fond et la forme	form and content
un héros (N.B. *le héros*)	hero
une héroïne (N.B. *l'héroïne*)	heroine
une intrigue	plot
un personnage principal	main character
un personnage secondaire	minor / secondary character
un thème central	main theme
la thématique (de la violence)	the theme (of violence)
un traitement	treatment, handling (of a subject)
un calembour	pun
une histoire rocambolesque	swashbuckling / incredible tale
une image	image
une métaphore filée	extended metaphor
un jeu de mots	play on words
un poncif	hackneyed / well-worn theme
un style ampoulé	overblown style
un style emphatique	bombastic style
un style pittoresque	colourful style

> *L'histoire se déroule en Algérie.*
> The story takes place / is set in Algeria.

> *La nouvelle a pour toile de fond la société mexicaine.*
> The short story is set against the backdrop of Mexican society.

> *La pièce nous transporte au Moyen Orient.*
> The play takes us to the Middle East.

> *L'historien nous fait revivre les années 60.*
> The historian re-creates the 60s for us.

> *Le roman suscite chez le lecteur un sentiment d'inquiétude.*
> The novel provokes a feeling of unease in the reader.

> *Les propos de l'auteur remettent en cause nos certitudes.*
> The author's remarks challenge our certainties.

(e) Poetry

une chanson	song
une épopée	epic (poem)
une strophe	verse, stanza
un vers	line of poetry
un alexandrin	alexandrine (12-syllable line)

la césure	caesura (pause in middle of line)
une cheville	padding (to provide required number of syllables)
une coupe	pause / break within a line
un rythme	rhythm
une rime	rhyme
des rimes plates	rhyming couplets (aa bb cc)
des rimes croisées	rhyme scheme: abab cdcd
des rimes embrassées	rhyme scheme: abba cddc
en vers libres	in blank verse

PART 4

Exercises

152 Omission of the article

(See S2)   p. 6

A   *Translate into French:*

1. My grandfather, a great lover of olive oil, couldn't bear English cooking.
2. We have met with new problems.
3. School groups and students can obtain a reduction.
4. Roquefort is made from ewes' milk.
5. What a waste of money!
6. Haven't you got any seats?
7. These women have made enormous sacrifices.
8. Are you a civil servant?
9. Add some good brandy to the cake.
10. I've received various answers.
11. The stationer's hasn't got any more files.
12. Certain excavations indicate that it was a Roman forum.

B   *Compléter le texte suivant avec un article défini ou indéfini (ou mettre × s'il ne faut pas d'article):*

____ France qui se targue d'être ____ perle touristique de l'Europe est-elle guettée par ____ laideur?

____ routes, ____ autoroutes, ____ rues commerçantes, ____ entrées d'agglomérations et ____ franges villageoises sont jalonnées par ____ multitude de panneaux publicitaires, qui sollicitent ____ attention de l'automobiliste ou du piéton, masquent ____ paysages et donnent de l'Hexagone ____ bien piètre image.

____ responsables de l'équipement ont eux-mêmes multiplié ____ panneaux réglementaires presque jusqu'au délire: sur ____ 60 derniers kilomètres de l'autoroute du Nord arrivant à Paris, on dénombre ____ 350 dispositifs d'information. ____ sociétés d'autoroute croient bien faire en signalant ____ points ____ plus remarquables surgissant à l'horizon. ____ régions, ____ départements et ____ communes rivalisent d'imagination pour vanter par ____ affiches leurs atouts.

Mais comme chacun veut étaler son message et crier plus fort que ____ autres, c'est ____ cacophonie. ____ touristes étrangers en sont choqués et ____ Français commencent à s'irriter. Au ministère de l'équipement, ____ ministre et ____ chefs de service conviennent que ____ seuil du supportable a été dépassé. Ils envisagent de 'paysager

399

3___ autoroutes' et de reconquérir _32_ entrées d'agglomération. Le ministre de l'environnement admet que _33_ paysages urbains et ruraux requièrent _34_ protection législative. Celle-ci devra comporter, à l'évidence, _35_ nettoyage des routes et des boulevards, ces vitrines de la France.

(excerpted from *Le Monde*)

 ## Uses of the definite and indefinite articles

(See S3 and S4)

A *Translate into French:*

1. On Sundays the baker's is only open in the morning.
2. Shut your eyes!
3. We left Germany on Wednesday and arrived in Portugal on Friday.
4. The English like sparkling wines.
5. He looked at the old suit with disdain.
6. How much a kilo is the goat's cheese?
7. Tolerance is a rare quality.
8. She's gifted with incredible imagination.
9. In Israel most people speak Hebrew and English.
10. King Francis the First invited Leonardo da Vinci to Amboise.
11. He broke his leg last year while skiing.
12. What are you doing for Whitsun?
13. Little Anne will be two in May.
14. Hungarian is a difficult language.

B *Compléter les blancs par une forme de l'article défini ou une forme de l'article indéfini:*

Nouveau record du tour du mont Blanc
Brigitte Chambon, trente-trois ans, a établi ____ nouveau record du tour du mont Blanc en ____ étape: elle a parcouru près de 170 kilomètres en 22 heures 59 minutes et 22 secondes.

Chaque année, 20.000 à 25.000 randonneurs s'engagent dans ____ tour du mont Blanc, course classique qui traverse ____ vallée de Chamonix et ____ Val Ferret italien et suisse. ____ parcours se situe essentiellement à ____ étage subalpin, entre 1500 et 2000 mètres d'altitude. ____ principales difficultés sont ____ col de la Croix du Bonhomme, ____ col de la Seigne et ____ col Ferret. ____ dénivelée

totale à _____ montée est de 7670 mètres. A _____ allure normale, _____
marcheur chargé de _____ sac de _____ dizaine de kilos met environ 5 à 7
jours pour boucler _____ tour.

(excerpted from *Le Monde*)

Uses of the partitive article and *de* + article

(see S5 and S6)

A *Translate into French:*

1. The journalist emphasized the bad quality of TV quiz shows.
2. Have you got your student card?
3. Are there tables and chairs in the garden?
4. The number of jobs offered to the long-term unemployed has doubled.
5. You've put in too much garlic and not enough lemon juice.
6. The electrical department sells hairdryers.
7. I've still got a litre of the milk we bought yesterday.
8. On the 14th July the road was blocked with cars.
9. The head of state has just resigned.
10. I'd like two kilos of the apples over there.
11. Word-processing is taught in primary schools now.
12. The beach was covered with the seaweed brought up by the high tide.

B *Compléter les blancs dans ces publicités avec du, de l', de la, des, de, d':*

(i) Le fleuve, source de notre histoire, ressource de notre avenir
De tous temps, les fleuves ont éte les témoins _____ vie _____ peuples.
Sources _____ vie et _____ richesses agricoles et énergétiques, sources _____
échanges économiques ou culturels, ils sont à la fois une sève
nourricière, un axe _____ développement et le symbole _____ civilisations
entières. Les grands fleuves _____ monde sont en eux-mêmes _____
formidables conteurs.
   Aujourd'hui fragilisés, menacés dans leur intégrité, ils n'en portent
pas moins les interrogations _____ notre époque et les espoirs _____ avenir
que nous souhaitons léguer à nos enfants. Le Rhône est de ceux-là.
Aménagé, géré, mais aussi préservé par la Compagnie Nationale _____
Rhône, le fleuve né _____ coeur _____ Alpes, source _____ histoire _____

toute une région, représente l'une ＿＿ principales ressources ＿＿ notre avenir.

(excerpted from *Publicité de la Compagnie Nationale du Rhône*)

(ii) Médecin: passionné de communication

Si vous recherchez un métier alliant vos connaissances ＿＿ médecine et votre goût de les partager, notre laboratoire pharmaceutique peut vous proposer ＿＿ postes au développement ou à la promotion ＿＿ nos médicaments à fort potentiel international. Aussi, nous souhaitons rencontrer ＿＿ médecins, anciens internes, ou ayant une première expérience ＿＿ industrie pharmaceutique.

Une bonne connaissance ＿＿ anglais serait un atout supplémentaire.

Si vous êtes intéressé par ces postes basés à Paris, merci d'envoyer lettre manuscrite avec photo et c.v.

155 Plural forms of nouns and adjectives

(See S8 and S17c, d, e)

A *Translate into French:*

1. Spaghetti with tomato sauce is an Italian dish.
2. Have you invited the Mondons for this evening?
3. There are roadworks on the Nationale 23.
4. *Le Monde* offers detailed articles on international problems.
5. On the 14th July there are dances in the streets of Paris.
6. The stained-glass windows in the cathedral at Chartres are among the finest in Europe.
7. In large shopping centres you often see graffiti.
8. The club 'Action 2000' meets in these premises.
9. It took six firemen to control the fire.
10. They are both accountants.
11. You need to change two tyres.
12. In the farmyards there were geese and peacocks.
13. The children were collecting pebbles.
14. Where have you put the corkscrews?
15. In the Middle Ages castles were surrounded by moats.

B *Mettre les mots soulignés qui le permettent au pluriel en faisant attention à l'accord des adjectifs et des verbes:*

Le Pont du Gard, la beauté retrouvée
<u>Le plan d'aménagement conçu</u> par l'architecte Jean-Paul Viguier redonne au site son authenticité: du haut des 50 mètres du Pont du Gard, on ne distinguera plus ni toit, ni tente et encore moins les voitures, seulement le Gardon et la forêt cévénole. <u>Tout ce qu'un voyageur est</u> en droit d'attendre, se garer, se restaurer, se reposer ou <u>confier ses enfants à la halte-garderie</u>, sera repoussé dans <u>une zone spécifique</u>, loin des yeux. Parkings à plus de 800 mètres des berges, bâtiments ne dépassant pas 5 mètres de hauteur et coupés par <u>un mur-promenade qui meurt</u> dans la garrigue. <u>Ligne pure, matériel léger</u>, verre, toile.

Les architectes n'ont pas l'intention de guider de force les visiteurs. Ils espèrent seulement les prendre par la main pour leur faire comprendre la <u>prouesse technique</u> de la Rome antique. Les accompagner dans <u>un réseau</u> de sentiers réhabilités ou nouvellement créés. Un pari difficile que <u>l'architecte-paysagiste espère</u> gagner.

(excerpted from *Marie France*)

 156 **Gender according to meaning: people, animals, occupations**
(See S9 and S10a)

A *Translate into French:*

1. The zoo has two female zebras.
2. The name of the victim has not been revealed.
3. The woman pianist was playing Chopin.
4. All the girls on the course got diplomas.
5. Professor Martine Pasteur will chair the round table.
6. Male candidates sat on the right, female candidates on the left.
7. The person I spoke to had a blue hat.
8. Male guinea pigs are more aggressive.
9. The new recruits are waiting in the yard.
10. There is only one woman engineer in the company.
11. The sentry woke up with a start.
12. The stags and does had been separated.

B *Compléter les blancs avec un article (défini ou indéfini), et faire l'accord des mots indiqués entre parenthèses:*

(i) Pression des banques

La crise de l'immobilier fait ____ victime de plus. M. Michel Deville, l'____ des promoteurs les plus (connu) de la place, doit, sous la pression de ses banquiers (international) céder les rênes de sa société de promotion immobilière. Il sera remplacé par Madame Henriette Boisset, (directeur) de la société Matisse depuis 1987. 'Ironie du sort', commente Marie Gournet, ____ des collègues proches de Monsieur Deville, 'car Madame Boisset était elle-même sous ____ tutelle de sa banque il y a trois ans.'

(ii) La saison théâtrale de janvier se prépare

Clotilde Debayser répète *Marie* d'Isaac Babel, qui date de 1933. Elle dit qu'elle éprouve le besoin d'être entourée, et c'est pour cette même raison qu'elle est devenue (comédien). Elle a été reçue au concours du Conservatoire, puis, 'J'ai travaillé un peu, j'ai eu ____ bébé' (elle a aujourd'hui trois filles). Puis elle est retournée dans la classe de Jean-Pierre Vincent, ____ (excellent) professeur. Ce que Clotilde Debayser attend d'____ metteur en scène, c'est une ligne à suivre. Au théâtre, elle cherche ____ famille. 'Je suis l'' (aîné) de dix enfants. J'aime retrouver une ambiance qui bouge beaucoup, tout le temps ____ personne qui arrive, ____ autre qui disparaît. Le plus grand bonheur, je l'éprouve dans le remue-ménage des répétitions.'

(excerpted from *Le Monde*)

 Gender according to meaning: things

(See S10b)

A *Translate into French:*

1. Which is her native language, Portuguese or Greek?
2. Cucumber can be indigestible.
3. The Queen has visited Japan, New Zealand and Mexico.
4. They've had to cut down all the elms.
5. Phosphate and calcium are essential minerals.
6. For this recipe I need a cabbage, a carrot and a turnip.
7. Autumn is milder in the south-west.
8. Granite is a very difficult stone to work.
9. The vine was killed by the snow.

10. On Fridays I finish at 2 p.m.

11. The diamond was surrounded by an emerald and a ruby.

12. Cambodia has announced a ceasefire.

B *Compléter les blancs avec un article (défini, indéfini ou partitif):*

Émincé de légumes au riz

Porter à ébullition dans ____ wok un peu de sauce de soja, 2 c. à s. d'huile d'olive, autant de vin blanc et de saké. Ajouter les légumes coupés en dés ou en julienne. On commence par ceux qui poussent dans ____ terre – ____ fenouil, ____ carotte, ____ pomme de terre, ____ oignon – et on continue avec ceux qui poussent hors de ____ terre – ____ céleri, ____ poivron rouge, ____ poireau. On repousse vers ____ haut du wok les légumes qui sont cuits et on rajoute les nouveaux légumes crus au centre du wok. Faire cuire ____ riz à l'eau.

158 Gender according to ending of noun: always masculine endings

(See S11a)

A *Translate into French:*

1. The spy was wearing dark glasses.
2. In the holidays my sister does babysitting to earn some money.
3. The cat was sitting in the armchair.
4. The owl was hunting a mouse.
5. This is a very rare jewel.
6. His advice helped me.
7. For this cake you need two very ripe pears and some plain chocolate.
8. A third assassination has been carried out in New York.
9. I have a very sensitive skin.
10. Someone has stolen her bag.
11. The bird had a broken wing.
12. You've forgotten to tie your laces.
13. The role of this union depends on the future of socialism.
14. The pavement was strewn with wet leaves.

B *Compléter les blancs avec un article (défini, indéfini ou partitif) et faire l'accord des adjectifs indiqués entre parenthèses:*

Les trains touristiques de la Suisse normande
De Caen à Clécy, ____ train touristique de la Suisse normande, ____ autorail des années 50, a remporté ____ (tel) succès que l'on a dû lui adjoindre cette année ____ (nouveau) avec 5 remorques. Sur ____ ligne archi-pittoresque, qui, sans l' (excellent) idée de ses promoteurs, aurait disparu, ____ train roule à ____ allure paisible de 30 km à l'heure, avec arrêts (facultatif), obligatoires ou même à la demande. On peut contempler des auberges, de (petit) campings, des gîtes (rural) tout au long ____ voyage: tout incite à la détente.
   Il y a de (nombreux) départs et retours entre 10h30 et 19h40 à 70F ____ trajet pour les adultes et 45F pour les enfants. Pour (tout) renseignement, tél. 31.79.02.02.

(excerpted from *Côte Fleurie Magazine*)

159 Gender according to ending of noun: mainly masculine endings (See S11a (i, ii))

A *Translate into French:*

1. Antenne 2's report on the Sudan was excellent.
2. The letter is in the file.
3. Can you speak to Mrs Lefèvre on the phone?
4. The index is on page 78.
5. The Minister's career was destroyed by his brother's suicide.
6. Explain the problem to me.
7. There's a mistake in the last paragraph.
8. France has the shape of an irregular hexagon.
9. The first picture in the book showed a castle.
10. The milk and cream have gone off.
11. She lives in a small village and her son has to cycle to college.
12. Until recently meat was forbidden in Lent.
13. The scientists observed a strange phenomenon.
14. Where's the seat of the European parliament?

B *Compléter les blancs avec un article (défini/indéfini/partitif) et faire l'accord des adjectifs indiqués entre parenthèses:*

Le désir de voir ____ (fameux) château de Rochambeau, dont ____ propriétaire donnait parfois ____ laitage aux élèves nous rendit tous sages. Le lendemain, après ____ dîner, nous partîmes à midi et demi, tous munis d' ____ cubique morceau de pain que l'on nous distribuait d'avance pour ____ goûter.

Quand nous fûmes arrivés sur ____ colline, Louis Lambert me dit, 'Mais j'ai vu cela cette nuit en rêve!' Il reconnut et ____ bouquet d'arbres sous (lequel) nous étions, et ____ disposition des feuillages (vert), enfin (tout) les détails du site qu'il apercevait pour la première fois. (Ce) événement, dont l'analogue peut se retrouver dans les phénomènes du sommeil de beaucoup d'hommes, fera comprendre les (premier) talents de Lambert; en effet, il sut en déduire (tout) ____ système, en s'emparant d' ____ fragment de pensée pour reconstruire (tout) ____ création.

(excerpted from H. de Balzac, *Louis Lambert*)

160   Gender according to ending of noun: mainly feminine endings

(See S11b)

A   *Translate into French:*

1. The white chalk of the distant cliffs was barely visible.
2. The disappearance of various traditional trades has changed this quarter of Paris.
3. Tomorrow there will be ice on the roads in the north.
4. Did you see the film *Dangerous Liaisons*?
5. Within the sphere of religion, teenagers have been more active.
6. His ignorance was shocking.
7. At the holiday village you can go swimming and take advantage of an introduction to water skiing.
8. The syllabus for the English classes seems inadequate.
9. The delay was the cause of fresh concern.
10. Rome was a bastion of Christian civilization.
11. He has an annoying tendency to ask superfluous questions.
12. The wolf disappeared without leaving the slightest trace.
13. The group of tourists was watching the Greek dances with such admiration.
14. This text defies literal translation.

B *Compléter les blancs avec un article (défini / indéfini / partitif), et faire l'accord des adjectifs indiqués entre parenthèses:*

LES VOIES DE L'APPRENTISSAGE AU XVIe SIECLE

Le cas de Thouars peut être considéré comme _____ exemple de portée plus générale: l'activité (professionnel) des femmes est souvent (révélateur) d'_____ situation économique ou (familial) précaire. Le destin normal d'une fille, dans _____ milieu des métiers, est de rester au foyer jusqu'au moment de (son) mariage.

Si, dans _____ plupart des cas, l'apprentie est orpheline de père ou de mère elle est engagée, de préférence, chez un homme marié, pour apprendre _____ métier (exercé) par son épouse. Dans le faubourg Saint-Marcel, on ne s'étonne pas de voir les fillettes s'initier auprès des femmes qui confectionnent bonnets et chaperons (revendu) à Paris, au grand dam des maîtres bonnetiers, souffrant _____ concurrence. Celles dont les parents exercent _____ profession un peu plus (spécialisé) s'engagent plutôt pour apprendre _____ métier de lingère. Pour ce quartier de Paris, _____ débouché presque (exclusif) reste _____ domaine _____ (petit) confection vestimentaire, sauf à s'engager comme 'servante-apprentie' chez _____ marchande de poissons ou _____ marchande de beurre.

(from E. Berriot-Salvadore, *Les femmes dans la société française de la Renaissance*)

161 # Gender according to ending of noun: words ending in *-eur/-é* (See S11c, d)

A *Translate into French:*

1. How many households have a personal computer?
2. Sicilians fear dishonour more than death.
3. The cafe had old photos of some famous actors.
4. Plougastel produces an excellent strawberry liqueur.
5. Do I have to apply to the tax inspector or the collector of taxes?
6. By ministerial decree, flower markets are allowed on Sundays.
7. The rarest quality is discretion.
8. Her mother gave them a vacuum-cleaner for Christmas.
9. You've got to throw the dice before you take a card.
10. In her private life, Simone Signoret knew both happiness and unhappiness.
11. Medieval chroniclers were surprised by the grandeur of the city.

12. To tell you the truth, the committee should not have approved the treaty.

B *Compléter les blancs avec un article (défini ou indéfini) et faire l'accord des adjectifs indiqués entre parenthèses:*

PUISSANTE, PORTABLE ET CONVIVIALE, L'INFORMATIQUE DU FUTUR CHANGERA NOTRE FAÇON DE VIVRE

Les fabricants des (grand) et (petit) ordinateurs ont désormais une idée assez claire de la manière dont devraient évoluer leurs machines. Ils disposent d'ores et déjà de 'neutrones' aux performances (impressionnant). Reste à imaginer comment les connecter, les faire travailler ensemble. L'Institut national de recherche en informatique et automatique a récemment convié à Paris 28 chercheurs (étranger) à se pencher sur ＿＿ question. La miniaturisation aide ＿＿ rapidité, critère essentiel en informatique. Mais, 'Hélas! on ne peut aller plus vite que la nature,' soulignait ＿＿ professeur au Collège de France.

En attendant de surmonter (certain) difficultés, les chercheurs tentent de concilier plusieurs systèmes. Est-ce que les (grand) processeurs en parallèle doivent effectuer (chacun) une seule opération, une suite d'opérations, ou fonctionner indépendamment sur ＿＿ même programme divisé en 'tâches' spécifiques? 'C'est un peu ＿＿ problème du travail à la chaîne', explique ＿＿ ingénieur. 'On fractionne plus ou moins l'ouvrage afin de concilier au mieux ＿＿ rapidité d'exécution, ＿＿ production des ouvriers et ＿＿ communication dans l'entreprise.'

(excerpted from *Le Monde*)

162 Gender according to ending of noun: common masculines ending in *-e*

(See S12)

A *Translate into French:*

1. There was a photo of the campsite in the brochure.
2. I left my umbrella and briefcase on the bus.
3. This gîte isn't on my list.
4. The main character had to speak in all the acts of the play.
5. She hung out the washing to dry on the line.
6. Shall I send the letter to your private address?
7. I'm on a diet, so I can eat only the green vegetables and the meat.

8. One marriage in three ends in divorce.
9. I'll look in the advertisements for second-hand cars.
10. They had to close the laboratory because of the risk of a plutonium leak.
11. Don't pour too much mineral water in my glass.
12. Do you have the new train timetable?
13. The safety instructions were very precise.
14. He'd forgotten the secret code to open the safe.
15. The magazine had published an article on the birth of the princess.
16. We have the choice between a television set and a washing machine.

B *Compléter les blancs avec un article (défini ou indéfini) et faire l'accord des adjectifs indiqués entre parenthèses:*

LA CHASSE AUX MELOMANES EST OUVERTE

Cette année ne sera pas plus facile dans ____ monde des spectacles, et singulièrement dans le landernau musical, que dans (celui) de l'économie. (Tout) les services de relations publiques s'apprêtent à lancer des questionnaires en direction de la clientèle, notamment sur le choix des (meilleur) horaires. Voilà ____ bien (heureux) initiative.

Cependant, il ne suffira pas de modifier les horaires pour résoudre ____ crise de la musique. On ne fera pas l'économie de la question de l'argent. Déjà certains organisateurs ont pris le taureau par les cornes et ____ tendance est à la baisse. ____ très aristocratique Théâtre des Champs-Elysées, (dépourvu) de (tout) subvention (public), a augmenté ____ nombre des places meilleur marché. ____ célèbre Orchestre de Paris a eu ____ surprise de ne pas voir ses caisses (pris) d'assaut pour certains concerts. ____ programme Mozart et Dvorak n'étant pas en cause, c'est le prix des places les plus (cher) qu'il faut incriminer.

(excerpted from *Le Figaro*)

163 Gender according to ending of noun: common feminines not ending in -e
(See S13)

A *Translate into French:*

1. This time we'll choose a quieter place.
2. What's the price of a single ticket?

---

3. Our bedroom looked out on to the courtyard.

4. Rachel cut her first tooth yesterday.

5. By law, smoking on the underground is forbidden.

6. My new flat is close to the Louvre.

7. Charles sold one warehouse after his father's death.

8. Would you like some tea or a cold drink?

9. I can't revise for all the exams.

10. Do you know the real reason why they're not coming?

11. The Old Testament is above all the history of the Jewish religion.

12. When was the Eiffel Tower built?

B *Compléter les blancs avec un article (défini ou indéfini) et faire l'accord des adjectifs indiqués entre parenthèses:*

(i) Sans doute la femme qui se tenait devant moi, comme devant un juge, avait réellement vécu bien des années dans ____ paix terrible des âmes (refusé), qui est ____ forme ____ plus atroce, ____ plus incurable, ____ moins (humain) du désespoir. J'avais voulu réchauffer d'____ coup (ce) coeur (glacé), porter ____ lumière au dernier recès d'une conscience que ____ pitié de Dieu voulait peut-être laisser encore dans de miséricordieuses ténèbres.

C'est alors – non! cela ne peut s'exprimer – tandis que je luttais de (tout) mes forces contre ____ doute, ____ peur, que l'esprit de prière rentra en moi.

(excerpted from G. Bernanos, *Journal d'un curé de campagne*)

(ii) Ils commencèrent à attendre. ____ fois qu'on l'avait décelé, ____ grondement du canon ne se perdait plus de l'oreille, où qu'on allât; il n'y avait plus que lui. Quand Grange un instant se bouchait les oreilles de ses doigts, l'allée (entier) n'était qu' ____ coulée (printanier) et (doux), tiède déjà sous ____ brume (doré), qui fuyait merveilleuse-ment vers les lointains (bleu). A mesure que ____ temps passait, Grange sentait grandir en lui ____ sentiment de sécurité (irréel). L'air fraîchissait délicieusement; ____ poudroiement de la lumière rasante sur ____ forêt du soir était si riche, si insolite, qu'____ envie brusque, irrésistible, lui venait de s'y baigner, de s'y retremper.

(excerpted from J. Gracq, *Un Balcon en forêt*)

164 Gender of compound nouns
(See S14)

A *Translate into French:*

1. She bought herself a pied-à-terre in Budapest.
2. The workforce has accepted the new working conditions.
3. Is the Mona Lisa Leonardo's masterpiece?
4. There was a bat in the attic.
5. Profitability is the keyword of this decade.
6. His former fiancée has been invited too.
7. Is the stationery department on the ground floor or in the basement?
8. I don't eat peas or cauliflower.
9. Why have you put the corkscrew in the dishwasher?
10. We've been window-shopping in the town centre.
11. My mother-in-law bought the children a kite.
12. Subletting is forbidden according to the contract.

B *Compléter les blancs dans ces publicités avec un article (défini ou indéfini) et faire l'accord des adjectifs indiqués entre parenthèses:*

(i) Prix club
_____ filtre à eau électrique. Avec l'Ultrascreen de Kenwood vous disposerez en permanence d'une eau présentant une garantie maximale de pureté.

(ii) Les promos d'Aquarius
Les clubs Aquarius annoncent des prix promotionnels pour les vacances d'hiver, en chambre double, pension (complet). _____ mini-séjour aux Deux-Alpes vous est (proposé) pour 1200F par personne.

(iii) Baladeur sans fil
D'une sophistication sans pareille, ce baladeur comporte _____ casque sans fils d'une grande fidélité, avec _____ (petit) émetteur-récepteur (intégré). Un bel exercice de style!

(iv) Vous avez la gueule de bois . . .
Vous êtes du style royal: _____ trône-toilettes est l'endroit au monde qui vous rassure le plus quand vous vous sentez patraque. La Boldoflorine,

la bonne tisane pour le foie, traite merveilleusement la constipation passagère. ＿＿ ou deux cuillerées à café par tasse d'infusion chaque jour.

(v) Berlin
La capitale allemande est devenue plus incontournable que jamais. Ne négligez pas l'apparat désuet du Pergamonmuseum qui présente ＿＿ légendaire chef-d'oeuvre hellénistique, la fameuse porte d'Ishtar et la voie des Processions de Babylone.

165 Nouns taking two genders and words identical in form but different in gender and meaning
(See S15 and S16)

A *Translate into French:*

1. *Le Père Goriot* is one of Balzac's best known works.
2. Should we give a tip to the guide?
3. The critic gave his verdict when it came to his turn.
4. I wanted to give you a little something to say thank you.
5. I paid an enormous amount of money for that picture.
6. Nobody has stopped to help them.
7. Put the flowers in the blue vase.
8. All the people we spoke to were tourists.
9. In the kitchen they found an old stove and a broken clock.
10. Only eat the mussels which are open.
11. Long skirts have come back into fashion.
12. People were moved by the tragedy.

B *Compléter les blancs avec un article (défini ou indéfini) et faire l'accord des adjectifs entre parenthèses:*

(i) Les services de tourisme du pneu Michelin vous présentent leur guide (vert) de la Bretagne.

(ii) ＿＿ **voile.** Le découpage des côtes offre des baies bien abritées très favorables à la navigation.

(iii) Les cures marines. Les propriétés de l'eau de mer et la douceur du climat permettent de soigner certaines affections. Des centres de thalassothérapie sont situés sur ＿＿ Manche et l'Atlantique.

(iv) Huîtres et coquillages
Grande région productrice d'huîtres plates, la Bretagne a également développé ses parcs d'huîtres creuses et surtout de moules (délicieux).

(v) La vie littéraire
Henri Queffélec, né à Brest en 1910, est de nos jours un des auteurs ayant le plus célébré la Bretagne: parmi ses oeuvres bien (connu), *Un Recteur de l'Ile de Sein*. Autre écrivain breton actuel, Pierre Jakez Hélias, avec *Le Cheval d'orgueil*, _____ livre qui évoque les traditions du pays bigouden.

(vi) Quimper: cathédrale
La cathédrale possède une remarquable collection de vitraux du 15e siècle. En faisant _____ tour du beau vaisseau, on verra, dans les chapelles, des tombeaux, des autels, des statues, oeuvres (ancien) et modernes, et une Mise au Tombeau dans la chapelle sous _____ tour de droite.

(excerpted from *Guide Michelin: Bretagne*)

 # Forms and agreement of the adjective
(See S17 and S18)

A *Translate into French:*

1. Naval exercises will start tomorrow.
2. These are brand-new shoes.
3. The new hotel is located near the municipal gardens.
4. His private fortune is estimated at 30 million.
5. Pupils must wear brown skirts and pullovers.
6. Public opinion has hardly changed.
7. Turn right, then go straight on to the church.
8. The Greek navy and the Turkish army are training.
9. I have an old uncle who lives in Toulouse.
10. Your clothes are wet through.
11. Eastern countries are the favourite destination for young people this year.
12. We don't sell half-bottles.
13. I'm looking for a light green jacket.
14. Could you leave the windows wide open?

B *Faire l'accord des adjectifs indiqués entre parenthèses:*

CRISE DES BANLIEUES

Certains événements (survenu) dans les banlieues conduisent à s'inter-roger; des 'Minguettes' en 1981, aux violences de 1990–1 à Vaulx-en-Velin, pourquoi y a-t-il récurrence des explosions (social), alors que les politiques (engagé), les solutions (prôné) au cours de ces dix années font globalement consensus? Conseils (communal) de prévention de la délinquance, missions (local) pour l'insertion des jeunes ... (quel) que soient les gouvernements, la couleur (politique) des villes est (banalisé). Certes, on peut souligner l'insuffisance des moyens (mis) en oeuvre, la complexité des interventions (public); on peut aussi, à juste titre, rappeler l'amplification des difficultés (social) qui affecte la société (français) dans son ensemble, lorsqu'il s'agit de traiter, au-delà des inégalités (social), l'exclusion.

N'est-on pas tenté en fait – faute de pouvoir traiter cette question (persistant) des inégalités (social) – de la dissoudre dans la question (urbain)? On instaure ainsi un perpétuel jeu de chaises (musical): reconquête sociale (effectif) des (centre) -villes, (premier) indices d'une réinsertion des (grand) ensembles les mieux (situé) ... au prix d'une translation (spatial) sans fin de leurs habitants d'un quartier de la ville à un autre.

(excerpted from *La France 1992*)

 Position of adjectives
(See S19)

A *Translate into French:*

1. In your opinion was de Gaulle a great statesman?
2. The vineyards stayed in the same family down to the fifteenth generation.
3. We've had an exceptionally cold dry winter.
4. This brief meeting in Bruges was the last time they saw each other.
5. He was wearing a brown tie and white trousers.
6. In a small dirty cupboard we found some real treasures.
7. The poor dog hides under the bed when there's a storm.
8. It's a really enormous garden.
9. It's a question of public safety.
10. In the Latin Quarter there are lots of Italian and Greek restaurants.

11. It's too long a walk for the children.

12. Les Tourettes is such a beautiful place.

13. In a large poplar-lined avenue stood a statue of Napoleon.

14. This is a well-written, exciting novel.

B *Compléter ce texte journalistique en introduisant les adjectifs suivants pour qualifier les mots qui sont soulignés. Attention à la position et à l'accord des adjectifs!*

suprême, petit, célèbre, sublime, victorien, tropézien, cannois, centenaire, épais, gorgé, rare, prestigieux, luxuriant, léger, automatiques

LE CAP FERRAT: LA PRESQU'ÎLE DES MILLIARDAIRES

Un environnement préservé, c'est aujourd'hui le luxe sur la Côte d'Azur. Le bourg de Saint-Jean-Cap-Ferrat, à peine 2.500 âmes, est donc devenu la presqu'île aux milliardaires.

Emancipé seulement depuis le début du siècle, Saint-Jean n'était jusqu'en 1900 qu'un quartier de Villefranche-sur-Mer, ouvrant majestueusement vers le large sa rade frequentée par des yachts et dominée par les maisons du cap de Nice et du Mont-Boron. Loin de l'esbroufe ou de la frime, la 'presqu'île aux milliardaires', qui s'étend sur 232 hectares, s'élance vers la mer à mi-chemin entre Nice et Monaco. A l'abri de ses pinèdes et des haies clôturant des parcs de fleurs, le Cap Ferrat accueille discrètement célébrités et fortunes. Les riches – les vrais – viennent ici se réfugier épisodiquement. Difficile d'entrevoir leurs demeures. Qu'elles se nomment Les Cèdres, Le Trianon ou La Serena, tout juste les devine-t-on au travers d'une végétation et de la brume vaporisée par les systèmes d'arrosage.

(excerpted from *L'Evénement du jeudi*)

168 Comparative and superlative forms of adjectives
(See S21)

A *Translate into French:*

1. This poster is worse than the other one.

2. She's as absent-minded as her brother.

3. Have you seen the biggest villas?

4. I can't accept this quotation. It's even worse!

5. The climate in Nice is so much milder than in Paris.

6. It's the worst motorway I know.

7. Is the suburb as noisy as the town?

8. She's the best pianist I've ever heard.

9. The young rabbit is smaller than the guinea pig.

10. This film isn't as funny as the last one.

11. He'll give up the project if there's the least obstacle.

12. The house prices on the Riviera are the most expensive in France.

13. The turnover is better than last year's.

14. These examples of Renaissance art are of less importance.

B *Mettre les adjectifs soulignés à la forme superlative:*

Five o'clock tea

Balzac le consommait bien fort, importé de Russie; nos romancières anglaises le sirotent avec élégance, en imaginant les crimes pervers. Chaud ou glacé, vert ou parfumé, le thé est en tout cas l'une des boissons désaltérantes. Et symboliques. Déguster une tasse, c'est d'emblée adhérer à un certain art de vivre et déclarer la guerre au mauvais 'fast-drink'. Encore faut-il en respecter les petites règles, que nous livre le président du nouveau Club des buveurs de thé.

Noir ou vert?

Vous pouvez l'aimer vert, comme le thé de Chine, ou noir, comme le thé de Ceylan qui est fort, et peu recommandé pour les insomniaques après 16 heures.

Infusion

Aux cuillers-passoires en aluminium, qui vous laisseront un goût détestable, préférez les petites chaussettes en tissu; elles permettent à la feuille de s'épanouir juste avant la fin. Faites infuser le bon thé de l'Inde pendant 3 minutes ou le thé vert pendant 6 minutes.

(excerpted from *Le Figaro*)

169 Demonstrative and possessive adjectives

(See S22 and S23)

A *Translate into French:*

1. These knives and spoons belonged to my grandmother.

2. Who's her lawyer?

3. This domestic appliance doesn't use much electricity.
4. They've left their car and bikes at our house.
5. This owl has been living here for two years.
6. Have you hurt your hand?
7. This law only applies to those resident in France.
8. I've twisted my ankle.
9. That helicopter is about to land.
10. Is that his bag? No, it's hers.
11. This train stops at Orléans, but that one is direct.
12. He collects stamps, so he knows their value.
13. Give me your names and address.
14. My aunt and uncle are in Greece.
15. His positive attitude helped me.

B *Compléter le texte suivant avec les formes son, sa, ses, ce, cet, cette, ces:*

Maintenant la nuit était venue tout à fait. Pierre Chemin avait remis _____ pipe dans _____ poche; Adèle Genoud avait été coucher _____ enfant; les chauves-souris avaient été se coucher aussi.

On entendit les portes se fermer l'une après l'autre, mais on n'avait plus besoin de tourner la clé dans la serrure.

Il n'y avait plus non plus une seule de _____ lumières, comme autrefois. Est-ce qu'on se souvient? Quand on entrait dans les villages il y avait toujours _____ deux ou trois points de feu à des maisons qu'on ne distinguait pas, et ils faisaient penser à des étoiles tombées. Et quelquefois, les nuits d'orage, voilà qu'elles s'allumaient toutes à l'imitation des éclairs, et tout le monde s'habillait, parce qu'il n'y avait de sécurité pour personne, et la vie de chacun de nous pouvait lui être reprise à chaque heure, comme _____ biens.

Le veilleur de nuit faisait _____ tournée avec _____ lanterne; c'était une lumière de plus, et celle-ci se promenait.

Par les nuits les plus tranquilles, il fallait qu'on fût sur _____ gardes.

(excerpted from Charles-Ferdinand Ramuz, *Joie dans le ciel*)

170 Form and position of adverbs
(See S24 and S25)

A *Translate into French:*

1. They haven't appointed her successor yet.
2. I'm not sufficiently up to date on this project.

3. The decision will be taken independently.

4. Alternatively, you could cancel the booking.

5. I'll try to explain the system to you briefly.

6. Paradoxically, he now regrets his departure.

7. Perhaps you'd do better to call us back tomorrow?

8. We were deeply shocked by your behaviour.

9. We looked everywhere for the letter.

10. He prepared himself badly.

11. Fortunately, my father was at home.

12. They enjoyed themselves enormously.

13. He listened patiently to the story.

B *Remplacer les locutions soulignées par un adverbe. Attention à la position de l'adverbe!*

BAR ROTI

Faites vider et écailler les bars par le poissonnier. Pratiquez des incisions profondes et espacées avec régularité sur l'un des flancs des poissons.

Coupez des citrons en rondelles fines. Avec soin disposez les deux bars tête-bêche dans un plat allant au four. Insérez une rondelle de citron et une branchette de thym frais dans chaque entaille des poissons.

Répartissez des tomates en quartiers autour. Salez, poivrez, et à la fin arrosez d'un filet d'huile d'olive. Préchauffez le four et faites cuire le bar à une température douce pendant 35 minutes. A mi-cuisson, versez un verre de vin blanc dans le plat (mais pas de façon directe sur les poissons). Servez avec des pommes de terre à la vapeur ou des salicornes.

(excerpted from *Marie-France*)

171 Comparative and superlative forms of adverbs
(See S27)

A *Translate into French:*

1. You'd do better to take a scheduled flight.

2. The more one learns, the more one forgets.

3. When did you start to feel worse?

4. Students work much harder before exams.

5. I'm not earning as much as last year.

6. The more you ski, the fitter you'll be.

7. He hasn't mastered the system as well as you.
8. They repaired the wall as best they could.
9. You'll know better than he does.
10. If you want to make progress you'll have to revise more.
11. The less I think about it, the less it bothers me.
12. I don't have the chance to see them as often as I'd like.
13. Never mind if you've got another meeting.
14. Come and see us as often as possible.

B *Lire le texte suivant, puis compléter les phrases avec une forme d'un adverbe comparatif ou superlatif:*

LES RURALES FONT MOINS D'ENFANTS QUE LES CITADINES

Les femmes des villes ont aujourd'hui plus d'enfants que les femmes des champs: c'est le grand changement concernant la fécondité en France au début des années 90, selon une récente étude de l'INSEE. Désormais, alors que la moyenne nationale est de 1,78 enfant par femme, elle n'est que de 1,75 en zone rurale, mais de 1,82 dans l'agglomération parisienne. Chez les agriculteurs, la fécondité est en baisse parce que la population agricole diminue en nombre, mais remonte dans l'échelle sociale.

Exemple de cette fécondité citadine, l'Ile-de-France se distingue aussi par la disparité entre ses départements. En Seine-Saint-Denis et dans le Val-d'Oise, les presque 2 enfants par femme s'expliquent par l'importance des populations ouvrières et étrangères. A Paris, les femmes vivent souvent seules, et le nombre d'enfants diminue fortement. A l'inverse, le nombre de 1,95 enfant par femme de la Seine-et-Marne et des Yvelines est peut-être dû au cadre de vie, à la taille des logements de la grande banlieue résidentielle.

L'âge moyen des mères à leur premier enfant est de 28,2 ans. Il est plus bas dans le Nord (27,5 ans), et plus élevé en Ile-de-France, surtout pour les Parisiennes (30,3 ans). Cette augmentation est générale et s'explique évidemment par l'allongement des études supérieures, qui retarde la première maternité.

(excerpted from *Le Figaro*)

1. Le taux de natalité baisse _____ en zone rurale.
2. Désormais la population agricole vit presque _____ bien _____ la population citadine.
3. On constate en général que dans les milieux où les femmes vivent _____ _____ _____ , souvent elles n'ont pas plus de deux enfants.

4. _____ les femmes vivent seules, _____ le nombre d'enfants diminue.

5. Le taux de natalité ne baisse pas _____ sensiblement en Seine-et-Marne _____ dans le reste de l'Ile-de-France.

6. _____ les femmes font des études supérieures, _____ elles retardent leur première maternité.

172 Personal pronouns: conjunctive forms

(See S28)

A *Translate into French:*

1. I've got to do it. I promised him I would.
2. Why have you sent them a card?
3. Do you like the furniture? It's new.
4. Don't take that case. It's too heavy.
5. I'd like to speak to them about it.
6. You know she has some pieces of antique furniture. She showed them to us.
7. They're going to build blocks of flats. They'll be council housing.
8. Where are the keys? They're in the car.
9. What happens if an inspector stops you?
10. Leave her alone. She's tired.
11. We're spending four nights at St Paul. It's a medieval village.
12. They've suggested a picnic. What do you think about it?
13. I'm being sent to Geneva. Have you been there?
14. People get lost in the town centre.
15. I'm doing potatoes. How many will you eat?
16. Go away!
17. Don't worry, I'll take care of you.
18. He thought it strange that we had changed our bank.
19. I'm going to get my hair cut.
20. Don't put them in the bin.

B *Remplacer les mots soulignés par des pronoms, en faisant attention à l'ordre des mots et à l'accord éventuel des participes passés:*

DANS LA VIE PRODIGIEUSE DE MADEMOISELLE CHANEL, L'EPISODE ROMANESQUE DE SA MISSION SECRETE EN 1943 RESTE MYSTERIEUX

En effet, j'ai très bien connu Mlle Chanel et passé plus d'un an à la suivre pour tenter, avec son accord, de mettre noir sur blanc le récit de sa vie. Au cours de nos innombrables conversations, elle n'a jamais fait allusion à sa 'mission', mais elle m'a bien dit qu'elle était allée à Madrid pendant un bon mois en 1943. Elle n'aimait guère les Espagnols. Ceux-ci ont probablement mal accueilli Mlle Chanel, la pressant de regagner Paris. L'origine de ce voyage doit venir de sa liaison avec un officier allemand en poste à Paris pendant l'Occupation. Ce baron Hans Gunther von Dincklage était censé s'occuper de l'industrie textile française. En réalité, c'était un agent du service de renseignement, sans doute de longue date puisqu'il avait vécu à Paris avant la guerre.

C'est Spatz qui fit rencontrer Schellenberg et Mlle Chanel. Elle plut beaucoup à Schellenberg. Il fut séduit par la proposition de Mlle Chanel: rencontrer secrètement son ami Churchill à Madrid, le convaincre que le vrai danger était à l'Est, que la Grande-Bretagne et l'Allemagne étaient vouées à s'entendre et à se partager l'Europe. Projet tout à fait chimérique.   (excerpted from *Enquête sur l'histoire*)

173 Personal pronouns: disjunctive forms (See S29)

A *Translate into French:*

1. Like you, I prefer to send a fax if it's urgent.
2. I was thinking about both of you yesterday.
3. You and I have the same tastes.
4. 'Each for himself', that's today's society.
5. Claire and Véronique wallpapered the sitting-room themselves.
6. It was they who made the mistake the first time.
7. Personally I would have left, but I know that *he* would have stayed.
8. We prefer to see clients ourselves.
9. You'll be able to explain better than him.
10. Who can walk? She and I can.
11. Can the trainees leave or will you need them later?
12. *They* don't even say hello.
13. Everyone should have a pencil on them.
14. You and your neighbour, do you get on well?

15. Alain and Huguette have a lot of experience. You can rely on them.

16. If Emilie is away I'll have to call on you.

17. No-one can do everything on their own.

18. Was it you who rang this evening?

19. Who does the bike belong to, you or her?

20. He and my sister have known each other for years.

B **(i)** *Ajouter un pronom disjonctif pour mettre en relief chaque nom ou chaque pronom souligné dans le texte:*

<u>Vitardo</u> a posé sa valise et sa serviette noire sur la banquette arrière de la voiture, puis il s'est assis à côté de Louis.

– Je suis vraiment désolé, Louis . . .

– Mais non, mais non . . . <u>On</u> est à la gare en cinq minutes . . . <u>Louis</u> démarre lentement. Au bout d'un instant il coupe le moteur. <u>La voiture</u> descend la petite route droite en silence.

– <u>Vous</u> revenez quand? demande Louis.

– Le prochain weekend. J'espère passer le mois d'août ici avec Martine et les enfants. <u>Vous</u> avez de la chance de rester toute l'année à la montagne. Ça fait à peine six ans que <u>nous</u> avons acheté notre chalet.

– J'avais l'impression que vous étiez là depuis plus longtemps.

<u>Vitardo</u> a le même âge que Louis. Il travaille à Paris dans une société d'import–export. <u>Martine et lui</u> viennent chaque année skier à Noël.

(excerpted from P. Modiano, *Une Jeunesse*)

(ii) *Compléter ce dialogue en utilisant il / l' / le / lui:*

INES: J'accepte de devoir mépriser l'univers entier, mais non mon fils. Je crois que je serais capable de ____ tuer si ____ ne répondait pas à ce que j'attends de ____

FERRANTE: Alors, tuez-____ donc quand ____ sortira de vous. Donnez-____ à manger aux pourceaux. Car il est sûr que, autant par ____ vous êtes en plein rêve, autant par ____ vous serez en plein cauchemar. Cauchemar pour vous. Cauchemar pour ____ aussi. Un jour on ____ déchirera, on dira du mal de ____ . Oh! je connais tout cela.

INES: Est-il possible qu'on puisse dire du mal de mon enfant!

FERRANTE: On ____ détestera.

INES: On ____ détestera, ____ qui n'a pas voulu être!

FERRANTE: ____ souffrira, ____ pleurera.

INES: Vous savez l'art des mots faits pour désespérer! Comment retenir ses larmes, les prendre pour moi, les faire couler en moi? Moi, je puis tout supporter: je puis souffrir à sa place, pleurer à sa place. Mais ____!

423

Oh! Que je voudrais que mon amour eût le pouvoir de mettre dans sa vie un sourire éternel! Déjà cependant on _____ attaque, cet amour.

(excerpted from H. de Montherlant, *La Reine morte*)

 ## Demonstrative and possessive pronouns
(See S30 and S31)

A *Translate into French:*

1. Are you borrowing your neighbour's trailer? No, theirs is too small, this is ours.
2. This seems to me the most important question.
3. The wood has rotted. It's because of the damp.
4. We shan't do a mailshot. It's not worth it.
5. Is this your bag? No, it's hers.
6. It's difficult to give a precise answer.
7. I'll call round later if it suits you better.
8. It was last year that they went bankrupt.
9. I can't come. It's impossible.
10. Are they your brothers in the photo?
11. My washing machine isn't working. Could I use yours?
12. It's a quarter to nine.
13. I like all his films, especially those of the fifties.
14. What surprises me is not his attitude.
15. It was not without emotion that they parted.
16. We interviewed twenty air stewardesses. Those who worked part-time earned less.
17. You see that balcony? It's my flat.
18. We don't know who will take early retirement. It's yet to be decided.
19. Is it tomorrow that the estate agent is due to inspect the house?
20. It's unfortunate that he did not contact us earlier.

B *Compléter les blancs avec un pronom demonstratif, ou il / elle:*

LES AVENTURIERS DE LA B.D.

S'_____ est un genre où l'aventure est reine, c'est certainement _____ de la B.D. _____ est que l'aventure est, dans la B.D., la loi du genre: _____ est le moteur d'un récit court, toujours lu avec précipitation, toujours relu ensuite, vignette à vignette, avec délice. Les bonnes B.D. sont _____ que l'on relit comme l'on savoure une pipe. Relire le même *Tintin*, le même *Gil Jourdan*, à un an, cinq ans, et dix ans de distance et _____ est se remémorer sa fraîcheur d'âme à la première lecture.

Le miracle Hergé, _____ est que, toutes générations confondues, des milliers et millions de lecteurs à travers le monde se soient identifiés à Tintin et à sa lutte contre _____ qui sont les 'banksters'. Le miracle Hergé _____ est qu'aucun auteur de B.D. n'aura eté aussi commenté, étudié, exposé que _____ qui a créé Tintin, et qu'aucune B.D. autre que _____ née de son imaginaire n'a fini par s'enraciner autant dans le réel.

_____ est sûr en tout cas que cette année sera, une fois encore, une grande année Tintin!

(excerpted from *Enquête sur l'histoire*)

175 Relative pronouns

(See S32)

A *Translate into French:*

1. Do you know the woman whose address he gave you?
2. What you were saying yesterday made me change my mind.
3. The questions I asked seemed to surprise her.
4. One morning when it was fine we set out early.
5. They're showing the film we were talking about.
6. The car he parked next to had a puncture.
7. I want to know what you are all doing.
8. This is the spare part I needed.
9. The figures he used were very recent.
10. The person whom you spoke to made a mistake.
11. The suitcases we lost were old in any case.
12. I was about to leave when the letter arrived.
13. The building they were heading towards was an old priory.
14. That's the woman whose photo we saw in the newspaper.
15. What worries me is that she can't swim.
16. The papers which are on the table are confidential.
17. The card is valid for only six months, which I've never understood.
18. That's the reason why we don't use the cellar.
19. The friends I do yoga with are coming to dinner this evening.
20. There will be six of them, which complicates things.

425

B *Remplir les blancs avec un pronom relatif:*

(i) Les circonstances de la mort de Bertet, ____ semblaient d'abord aller dans le sens d'un accident – comme l'affirmait Thérèse –, tournèrent après examen à sa confusion et à son inculpation. En effet Bertet était mort dans son bain, électrocuté par son rasoir électrique. Or l'enquête montra ____ il ne se rasait qu'avec un rasoir mécanique – ____ l'on retrouva – et ____ l'appareil ____ avait provoqué sa mort était du type 'pour dames' et appartenait à Thérèse. Mais le plus grave pour Thérèse et son amant, c'était une lettre ____ Bertet avait adressée à sa soeur quelques jours avant sa mort et ____ celle-ci s'empressa de verser au dossier. Dans cette lettre, Bertet accusait sa femme et le jeune Anglais de chercher à l'éliminer. Thérèse l'avait obligé à signer une assurance ____ ferait d'elle une veuve millionnaire s'il venait à disparaître. Il prétendait avoir déjà par deux fois échappé par hasard à des accidents organisés par eux et ____ auraient dû être mortels. Bref, il avertissait sa soeur ____ s'il mourait accidentellement, il s'agirait d'un assassinat ____ Thérèse et son amant seraient les auteurs.

(excerpted from M. Tournier, *Théobald, ou le crime parfait*)

(ii) Ainsi nous nous taisions tous deux dans un massif silence ____ n'entamaient point nos quelques paroles, l'écoutant nous faire remarquer ____ , dans le roman policier, le récit est fait à contre-courant, puisqu'il commence par le crime, aboutissement de tous les drames ____ le détective doit retrouver peu à peu, ____ est à bien des égards plus naturel que de raconter sans jamais revenir en arrière. Dans le roman policier le récit explore peu à peu des événements antérieurs à celui par ____ il commence, ____ peut déconcerter certains, mais ____ est tout à fait naturel, puisque, dans la réalité, c'est évidemment seulement après l'avoir rencontré que nous nous intéressons à ____ a fait quelqu'un.

(excerpted from M. Butor, *L'Emploi du temps*)

176 Indefinite pronouns

(See S33)

A *Translate into French:*

1. Several of the new employees have already received a bonus.
2. What do the children do at lunchtime? Some eat in the canteen, others go home.

3. The two brothers have very little contact with each other.

4. Something marvellous has happened!

5. She has three daughters and each has had health problems.

6. The site is out of bounds to anyone who is not wearing a safety helmet.

7. Various employees are displeased. I interviewed some of them yesterday.

8. My colleague is a very shy person.

9. Some drivers take the motorway, others prefer the scenic route.

10. No, this doesn't fit. You'll need something else.

11. You want some folding chairs? We've got some in the attic.

12. Perhaps someone else has used the photocopier.

13. He's generous, he's always ready to help others.

14. The teacher didn't say very much.

B *Lire le texte suivant, puis compléter les phrases avec un pronom indéfini:*

Pour qu'une démocratie existe:
– Tout le monde doit avoir le droit de voter. Seules conditions imposées: l'âge et la nationalité. En France le suffrage universel est, pour les hommes, une réalité depuis 1844, pour les femmes depuis 1944.
– Plusieurs partis doivent pouvoir exposer librement leurs conceptions et leurs programmes. Pour permettre au citoyen de choisir, ces partis doivent avoir accès à tous les moyens de communication: presse, radio, télévision . . .
– Le vote doit être secret. En France, les bulletins de vote doivent obligatoirement être imprimés sur du papier blanc et mis sous enveloppe, par chaque électeur, dans le secret de l'isoloir. Il y a un isoloir pour 300 inscrits.

(excerpted from Nathan, *Les Institutions de la France*)

1. ____ reçoit un bulletin de vote doit le remplir et le mettre sous enveloppe.

2. Certains électeurs lisent les programmes des candidats, ____ se reportent sur la télévision ou la radio.

3. ____ a le droit de voter en France à partir de 18 ans.

4. Lorsqu'un électeur remplit son bulletin de vote il ne doit pas regarder le bulletin d' ____ .

427

5. Les femmes réclamaient le droit de vote bien avant 1944 et ___ se sont battues pour l'obtenir.

6. ___ qui ne sait pas pour qui voter peut lire les programmes des candidats.

7. Tous les citoyens ont le droit de voter mais un certain nombre ne comprennent pas ___ aux élections.

8. Les partis politiques ont accès à plusieurs moyens de communication: ___ préfèrent la télévision, ___ ciblent la presse écrite.

177 Agreement of subject and verb: impersonal verbs

(See S34a)

A *Translate into French:*

1. There existed several species of this reptile.
2. It turned out that we needed a new car.
3. The play's about a young girl who arrives in New York.
4. There have been two accidents this week.
5. To change a car registration number one must contact the prefecture.
6. In the past it often happened that sons were apprenticed at fourteen.
7. There was a frost last night.
8. What's it about?
9. It's autumnal weather today.
10. It's possible that we may have a change of staff.
11. It follows that we shall no longer be able to finance this operation.
12. It would be better to reply in writing.

B *Voici quelques affiches qui utilisent une locution impersonnelle. Ré-écrire les phrases en utilisant les mots entre parenthèses:*

1. Il est recommandé aux étudiants de fermer à clé leur porte de chambre même pour une absence de courte durée. (devoir)
2. Il est rappelé qu'aucun prélèvement sur bourse n'est effectué. (nous)
3. Il est interdit de fumer dans la zone non-fumeur. (on)
4. Il est conseillé de ne laisser aucun objet de valeur dans le car. (nous)
5. Il est défendu de marcher sur la pelouse. (on)

178 Agreement of subject and verb: composite and collective subjects

(See S34b, c)

A *Translate into French:*

1. Leili and I are getting married in August.
2. There were several groups, each of which had a flag.
3. A substantial number of those on the course had worked for a TV station.
4. Only employees and their children will be admitted.
5. The managing director or her secretary will contact you.
6. The firm has opened a branch in Rouen.
7. Most of the houses were destroyed during the war.
8. What are you and your brother doing?
9. The 'Casino' and the 'Manoir' are both luxury hotels.
10. The majority of visitors to EuroDisney were foreigners.
11. Most of the posts left vacant will be abolished.

B *Mettre les verbes entre parenthèses à la forme qui convient:*

(i) Déchets domestiques: toujours plus!
Chacun _____ (être) producteur de déchets. Le Parisien _____ (rejeter) 620 kilos de déchets par an, contre 400 kilos pour la moyenne nationale. Niveau et rythme de vie _____ (obliger), il achète davantage de journaux et de revues et _____ (consommer) beaucoup plus de plats cuisinés emballés. En 1991, les boissons, les légumes et les fruits _____ (produire) plus de 60% du poids des déchets alimentaires. Bien qu'inférieure, la part des déchets non alimentaires n'en _____ (être) pas moins préoccupante.

Parmi tous les détritus, il faut aussi, bien sûr, comptabiliser la montagne d'emballages qui nous _____ (envahir) chaque année: bouteilles en tout genre, contenants multiples des produits de beauté, boîtes de chaussures ... Toutes catégories confondues, ils _____ (représenter) 40% du volume total des déchets des ménages. A elle seule, l'utilisation des produits et articles de toilette _____ (provoquer) un tiers des déchets d'emballage issus de la consommation non alimentaire; mais 73% des emballages jetés _____ (provenir) des produits alimentaires.

(excerpted from *L'Etat de la France 1992*)

(ii) Pays de l'Est: cars et sandwiches

Difficile de comptabiliser avec précision ces nouveaux touristes venus des pays de l'Est. La plupart d'entre eux ne _____ (dormir) pas à l'hôtel, ni même sous la tente sur un terrain de camping, et ne _____ (dépenser) pas un sou en France. Ils _____ (consacrer) leur maigre budget vacances à payer le car, dans lequel ils _____ (passer) la nuit. Sandwiches fournis au début du voyage. La Société des autoroutes du Nord et de l'Est de la France _____ (voir) passer 300 de ces cars en dix jours, l'été dernier.

Certains _____ (aller) jusqu'en Bretagne et _____ (loger) leurs occupants dans les campings. La majorité des Polonais _____ (traverser) toute la France sans s'arrêter, pour se précipiter sur Lourdes. Seuls les Hongrois _____ (avoir) les moyens de s'offrir des séjours prolongés dans des hôtels. On en _____ (dénombrer) 60.000 dès 1990 entre Paris, la Côte d'Azur et même les stations de sports d'hiver.

(excerpted from *Le Point*)

179 Active and passive voices

(See S35a, b)

A *Translate into French:*

1. The role of Hamlet was played by Michel Sourdin.
2. The house had been destroyed by a fire in 1756.
3. The letters will be published in tomorrow's paper.
4. We were disturbed by the same noise.
5. The letter would have been sent to your address in Paris.
6. The child was found just before midnight.
7. We've been asked to attend the reception. (*on*)
8. The new trainee was dismissed after two days. (*se faire*)
9. This product is sold in all the Rallye hypermarkets.
10. Smoking is forbidden inside the building. (impersonal verb)
11. That isn't done in France. (reflexive verb)
12. You'll be sent a contract next week. (*on*)

B *Mettre les verbes entre parenthèses au passif, au temps qui convient:*

(i) RISQUES D'EMBOUTEILLAGES AUTOUR D'EURODISNEY

Le secrétaire d'Etat aux transports routiers et fluviaux a annoncé des mesures exceptionnelles pour la semaine prochaine. Un dispositif (mettre en place) le jour de l'ouverture du parc de loisirs EuroDisney pour éviter l'engorgement des réseaux routiers dans l'est de l'Ile-de-France. Quatre itinéraires (prévoir) déjà pour accéder au parc d'attractions. Les automobilistes (informer) de l'état de la circulation de la zone par des panneaux électriques à message variable. Plus d'un millier d'hommes (CRS, gendarmerie mobile et sapeurs-pompiers de Paris) (mobiliser) tout au long de la journée du 12 avril pour faciliter l'accès au site d'EuroDisney.

(excerpted from *Le Figaro*)

(ii) L'AFFAIRE DES DEPANNEURS: TRENTE-CINQ POLICIERS INCULPES

Trente-cinq gardiens de la paix ou brigadiers de police parisiens (inculper) dans le cadre de l'affaire 'des dépanneurs'. Les inculpations (prononcer) par le premier juge d'instruction au tribunal de Paris. Les dépanneurs intervenaient sur la voie publique pour enlever un véhicule en infraction ou accidenté. En contrepartie, il était fréquent que de petits cadeaux ou la somme de 100 francs (remettre) aux commissariats. Un policier parisien (suspendre) récemment après avoir reçu une telle somme d'un dépanneur.

(excerpted from *Le Figaro*)

(iii) *Réécrire les locutions soulignées dans ce fait divers en utilisant les structures suivantes pour éviter les emplois du passif: on/se faire/se laisser.*

INCULPATION POUR VOL SOUS LA MENACE D'UNE ARME

Mercredi dernier Serge Badinter a été arrêté chez lui. Il a été inculpé jeudi de vol sous la menace d'une arme, de séquestration de personne, de contrefaçon et falsification de chèques et autres faux. On lui reproche l'agression, le vingt mars dernier, d'un comptable près de Bordeaux. Celui-ci a été ligoté et dévalisé par trois hommes qui se faisaient passer pour des policiers, avant d'emporter quelques chéquiers. Les chéquiers volés ont été retrouvés chez des commerçants, où un client de haute taille et bien vêtu a effectué ses achats, laissant la photocopie d'un faux permis de conduire ... qui porte la photo de Serge Badinter.

180 Present indicative

(See S37)

A *Translate into French:*

1. We're irritating the person over there.
2. Why are you running?
3. If you open the door again, I'll put the files away.
4. They're removing the chairs.
5. What you're saying is incredible!
6. When we throw the ball the dog brings it back to us.
7. When you sit down, the cat's going to come onto your lap.
8. What are you buying for tomorrow?
9. What's that called?
10. Which do you both prefer?
11. Tell me if he gives the book back to you.
12. People in Normandy drink cider with meals.
13. I receive a bonus twice a year.
14. Do you think he's exaggerating?
15. Do you feel better today, David?
16. The jewels are worth more than the pictures.
17. How much sugar do you take, Madame Meunier?
18. The au pair cleans the kitchen on Fridays.

B **(i)** *Mettre les verbes entre parenthèses au présent:*

Généralement après l'apéritif nous _____ (rentrer) jusqu'à l'avenue
Wester Wemys par le chemin du bas, entre le mur et la voie ferrée. C'est
l'itinéraire que je _____ (préférer): on _____ (se sentir) protégé.
Nous _____ (se tenir) la main et je _____ (marcher) au milieu:
Anne à gauche, côté Méditerranée, Clara à droite, côté voie ferrée.
Gabriel leur _____ (jeter) des coups d'oeil ravis. Elles le _____
(dépasser) d'une bonne tête. De temps en temps elles _____
(décider) de jouer, elles le _____ (balancer) par les bras comme s'il
était un enfant sous ses cheveux blancs. Elles _____ (rire). Ils _____
(faire) tous les trois la joie des passants.

Gabriel _____ (détester) ces moments. Mais il ne _____ (dire)
rien. Il _____ (savoir) que les femmes _____ (détester) les rabat-
joie. Alors il _____ (prendre) son mal en patience, _____ (crier)

chaque fois vive la France, ce qui (accroître) encore la gaieté d'Anne et de Clara.

(excerpted from Erik Orsenna, *L'Exposition coloniale*)

(ii) *Voici une publicité qui raconte une histoire au passé. Mettre les verbes soulignés au présent:*

LA 205 GENTRY DE PEUGEOT EST SI LUXUEUSE QU'ELLE PEUT VOUS FAIRE CROIRE QUE GEORGE VA VOUS RAMENER A LA MAISON (alors que c'est vous, George)

Monsieur Fox fut le premier client à descendre le grand escalier de l'hôtel. Il régla sa note et me demanda de porter ses bagages jusqu'à sa voiture. Juste devant l'hôtel, sa 205 Gentry l'attendait. Elle était très luxueuse, sa peinture nacrée, ses jantes en alliage et sa silhouette fluide me procuraient une sensation d'élégance, cela devait être un modèle exclusif. En m'approchant je vis les larges sièges en cuir et la ronce de noyer, je mis les bagages dans la malle arrière de la 205 Gentry et donnai les clés à Monsieur Fox. C'est à ce moment que tout devint étrange. Je lui ouvris la porte côté conducteur, il bascula le siège et s'installa confortablement sur la banquette arrière. Il tendit les clés devant lui, comme pour les donner au conducteur, et dit, 'George, ramenez-nous à la maison s'il vous plaît.'

181 Perfect indicative: forms, agreement of past participle

(See S38a, b)

A *Translate into French:*

1. Have you washed your hair, Sophie?
2. The people I spoke to told us to turn right.
3. The swans flew away.
4. The numbers you asked for are engaged.
5. Where are the keys? Have you left them in the car?
6. The plane landed at eight o'clock.
7. Which dress have you chosen?
8. We got lost at Angers.
9. My secretary sent them a fax yesterday.

10. The sculptures we saw were on display in the park.

11. Have you still got the binoculars? No, I've given them back to François.

12. Martine broke her leg when she was skiing.

13. Did you know there was an explosion? Yes, they talked about it this morning on the radio.

14. The horse fell into a ditch.

15. Have you put the geraniums outside?

16. The samples you supplied are too small.

17. My grandfather's grown a lot older this year.

18. She went up the stairs on her own.

19. Which wines did you taste at Saint-Emilion?

20. They came in through the kitchen door.

B (i) *Mettre les verbes entre parenthèses au passé composé:*

Mais je _____ (faire) un pas, un seul pas en avant. Et cette fois, sans se soulever, l'Arabe _____ (tirer) son couteau qu'il me _____ (présenter) dans le soleil. La lumière _____ (gicler) sur l'acier et c'était comme une longue lame étincelante qui m'atteignait au front. Au même instant, la sueur amassée dans mes sourcils _____ (couler) d'un coup sur les paupières et les _____ (recouvrir) d'un voile tiède et épais. C'est alors que tout _____ (vaciller). La mer _____ (charrier) un souffle épais et ardent. Il me _____ (sembler) que le ciel s'ouvrait sur toute son étendue pour laisser pleuvoir du feu. Tout mon être _____ (se tendre) et je _____ (crisper) ma main sur le revolver. La gâchette _____ (céder), je _____ (toucher) le ventre poli de la crosse et c'est là, dans le bruit à la fois sec et assourdissant, que tout _____ (commencer).

(excerpted from Albert Camus, *L'Etranger*)

(ii) *Mettre les verbes soulignés au passé composé:*

Tout a commencé à la fin du siècle dernier. En ce temps-là, Saint-Tropez, port actif, vivait de la construction navale, du commerce du vin, de l'industrie du bouchon et de la pêche. En 1887, un sous-préfet inspiré, Stephen Liégeard, invente la 'Côte d'Azur', à laquelle il consacre un livre. Au passage, il salue Saint-Tropez. La même année, Guy de Maupassant promène son âme mélancolique à bord de son yacht, et découvre à son tour le port. Mais c'est le peintre Paul Signac qui lance la mode. En 1892 il pénètre dans le golfe à bord de son bateau et s'amarre définitivement jusqu'en 1914. Séduit par la lumière de Saint-Tropez, par son port, orienté au nord, Signac <u>fait</u> venir tous ses amis peintres. Ils <u>séjournent</u> à La Hune, ou <u>s'installent</u> dans la région.

Une élite esthète et cultivée <u>descend</u> à son tour vers le golfe. On <u>commence</u> à enfreindre avec délice le sacro-saint tabou de l'exposition au soleil. L'écrivain Colette la première, qui <u>se baigne</u> nue dans la baie des Canoubiers. Elle <u>tombe</u> amoureuse de Saint-Tropez, où elle <u>s'installe</u> à La Treille muscate. En 1932, elle <u>stigmatise</u>, rageuse, le Saint-Tropez des foules. Puis, elle <u>se fâche</u>: 'Quel pays! L'envahisseur <u>le dote</u> de villas et de garages, de faux mas où l'on danse . . .'

(excerpted from *L'Express*)

182 Past historic: forms

(See S38d, e, g)

A *Translate into French:*

1. She returned from the station on foot.
2. We wrote to each other twice.
3. The cousins blushed.
4. They had the car repaired.
5. We stopped in front of the town hall.
6. I sold the farm at the end of the war.
7. She opened her eyes in surprise.
8. He replied absent-mindedly.
9. I shut the door quietly.
10. She handed back the newspaper to her neighbour.
11. They sat down by the window.
12. He repainted the garage.
13. We came back at the beginning of May.
14. They looked out of the window.
15. He held her hand.
16. We opened a small shop in Bordeaux.
17. I chose the first book.
18. They went down the narrow path.
19. She died in Biarritz.
20. They finished speaking at the same time.

B *Mettre les verbes entre parenthèses au passé simple:*

(i) A la fin de l'hiver, il _____ (se produire) un phénomène auquel ils n'avaient jamais assisté: gonflé par les pluies, l'Erne _____ (grossir), les terrains gorgés n' _____ (absorber) plus l'excès des eaux, d'un seul coup les prairies _____ (être) inondées. Alexis photographiait la surface ridée par le vent de ces étangs improvisés. Cependant, un soir qu'il triait des clichés sur la table de l'atelier, il _____ (voir) autour de lui l'alignement des toiles vierges contre le mur et, leur tournant le dos, il _____ (faire) rapidement glisser le reste des négatifs dans un carton. Du reste, les eaux _____ (baisser); il _____ (cesser) de faire des photographies, et ils _____ (passer) quelques jours à cueillir des pissenlits. (excerpted from Danielle Sallenave, *Un Printemps froid*)

(ii) Le troisième jour, elle (exiger), malgré mes refus, que je montasse un des chevaux de son mari. 'Vous m'accompagnerez,' me _____ (dire) -elle, 'j'ai besoin d'aller vite et de me promener très loin.'

Elle _____ (courir) s'habiller et _____ (faire) seller un cheval que M. de Nières avait dressé pour elle. A peine arrivée sous bois, elle _____ (prendre) le galop. Je _____ (faire) comme elle, et je la _____ (suivre). Elle _____ (hâter) le pas dès qu'elle me _____ (sentir) sur ses talons, _____ (cravacher) son cheval, et sans motif le _____ (lancer) à fond de train. Je _____ (se mettre) à son allure, et j'allais l'atteindre quand elle _____ (faire) un nouvel effort qui me _____ (laisser) derrière. Cette poursuite irritante, effrenée me _____ (mettre) hors de moi. (excerpted from Eugène Fromentin, *Dominique*)

183 **Imperfect: forms, and contrast with perfect / past historic** (See S35a and S38c, f, g)

A *Translate into French:*

1. The town was destroyed in 1942.
2. As I started writing, the telephone rang.
3. The young Proust would read for hours.
4. The field was surrounded by a ditch.
5. We used to have lunch together every Thursday.
6. As he stood up, he noticed the hole.
7. In the afternoon the weather was even hotter.
8. As students, we would go to the theatre regularly.

9. They were loading the car before leaving.

10. The burglars were arrested by the police.

11. While the soldiers besieged the castle, the inhabitants took refuge in the cellars.

12. She was injured in the course of the match.

B *Mettre les verbes entre parenthèses au passé composé ou à l'imparfait:*

(i) La vie de Pascal Lino, superstar du Tour de France, est réellement devenue un conte de fées:

Je _____ (avoir) dix ou onze ans, je _____ (vouloir) que mes parents m'achètent le vélo que j'avais repéré dans une boutique de mon village. Un vélo d'occase, un 'Raymond-Poulidor' rouge avec des garde-boue valant 150 francs. Ils _____ (être) d'accord, mais il _____ (falloir) pour ça que je le mérite. Alors tous les jours je _____ (aller) cueillir des framboises et des haricots. Ma mère _____ (venir) avec moi parce que je _____ (etre) petit. Je _____ (bosser) comme un dingue jusqu'à ce que je réunisse la somme. Après, dès que je _____ (avoir) le vélo, je _____ (plaquer) tout, framboises et haricots. Ma mère me rappelle souvent cette histoire.

(excerpted from *France-Soir*)

(ii) *Mettre les verbes entre parenthèses au passé simple ou à l'imparfait:*

Le jour suivant, ou bien à quelques jours de là, je la _____ (rencontrer) de nouveau. Ce _____ (être) sur la hauteur, colline au moins, que le rocher dresse au-dessus de la mer sur la côte ouest, dans un raccourci que je _____ (prendre) pour gagner du temps quand je m'étais attardé au bain. Nul ne _____ (passer) jamais par là, car il _____ (falloir) monter des marches taillées à peine, dans un ravin aveuglant comme un four à chaux, avant de redescendre à travers une broussaille déchirante, et la chaleur _____ (être) si forte, au début de l'après-midi, que des lions lâchés dans ce maquis n'eussent pas fait davantage pour l'interdire aux promeneurs. Aussi d'y entendre des pas sur les cailloux et une voix qui _____ (chantonner), je _____ (avoir) grande surprise. Bonne surprise un peu plus tard quand je _____ (voir) surgir entre deux buissons de lentisques celle qui m'avait émerveillé la veille. Je _____ (se jeter) gauchement dans les épines, pour lui laisser l'étroit sentier; alors elle _____ (sourire).

(excerpted from André Pieyre de Mandiargues, *Feu de braise*)

184 Pluperfect indicative and past anterior

(See S39)

A *Translate into French (using the past historic, rather than the perfect, where appropriate):*

1. After the visitors had left, the count poured himself a large whisky.
2. The dentist asked for another copy of the brochure you'd sent him.
3. They had made up their minds to complain to the garage.
4. We settled in Marseilles a few months after I closed the office in Paris.
5. The gallery was displaying the new paintings it had bought.
6. As soon as she realized the danger, she went back in to phone the police.
7. I wanted to check I hadn't made a mistake.
8. Scarcely had the old lady died before her nephews sold the farm.
9. We remembered we had forgotten to turn off the lights.
10. As soon as she had paid the bill she started to worry.
11. I hadn't looked at my mail when you phoned me.
12. They had scarcely fallen asleep when a car set off.

B (i) *Mettre les verbes entre parenthèses au passé simple, à l'imparfait, ou au plus-que-parfait:*

Adrienne _____ (descendre) la rue sans rencontrer personne. Parvenue à la place du marché, elle _____ (s'arrêter), saisie à la vue du changement que l'heure _____ (apporter) à cet endroit qui lui _____ (paraître) d'abord si morne et si laid. Toutes les baraques des merciers et des marchands de légumes _____ (être) enlevées; les voitures _____ (partir). La place _____ (être) vide, couverte de grandes mares dans lesquelles la lune _____ (voyager) lentement. La beauté du lieu la _____ (saisir) et lui _____ (procurer) un moment de paix pendant lequel elle _____ (oublier) ses soucis. Une minute elle _____ (se tenir) immobile pour ne pas rompre du bruit de ses pas le merveilleux silence de la nuit. Et, par un subit retour sur elle-même, elle _____ (se souvenir) de certaines journées d'enfance. Il _____ (y avoir) des jours où elle _____ (être) heureuse, mais il _____ (falloir) qu'elle attendît cet instant de sa vie pour le savoir.

(excerpted from Julien Green, *Adrienne Mesurat*)

(ii) *Mettre les verbes entre parenthèses au plus-que-parfait:*

EN 1984, LA POLICE AVAIT LAISSE FAIRE

Le mouvement de 1984 va-t-il se reproduire? Dernier exemple en date d'une longue mobilisation des routiers, à l'époque le mouvement de colère des transporteurs _____ (paralyser) en pleine période de sports d'hiver les vallées des Alpes. Des barrages _____ (être installés) également dans toute la France.

A l'époque le gouvernment _____ (parier) sur la lassitude des chauffeurs. Les barrages _____ (s'effilocher) effectivement au bout de huit jours et un accord _____ (intervenir).

Paul Quilès semble aujourd'hui s'inspirer d'une stratégie identique à celle de son prédecesseur. Gaston Deferre qui _____ (ne pas employer) les grands moyens pour rétablir la 'liberté de circulation'.

(excerpted from *Le Figaro*)

185 Future and future perfect
(See S40)

A *Translate into French:*

1. When you're in Mexico, shall we send on your mail?
2. In five years the investments will be worth a million.
3. When you arrive at the airport, go to the basement level and my secretary will give you the keys.
4. I'll know if I have the job on Monday.
5. Someone's taken the car. It must be Thierry.
6. This weekend it will rain most of the time.
7. Once you've tried the software, we'll talk about the new databases.
8. Someone's ringing at the door. It must be the postman.
9. When the children go away on holiday we'll go windsurfing.
10. The plants will die if the drought continues.
11. The dog will run to the end of the field.
12. Will you send me a quotation automatically?
13. Come and see us next week when you've got time.
14. I shall acquire my uncle's shares.

B *Mettre les verbes entre parenthèses au futur:*

(i) Horoscopes

CANCER

Vous _____ (échapper) aux histoires soli-lunaires, _____ (être) bien disposé, et _____ (pimenter) de belles amours d'un peu plus de brio. Les frôlements de la Pleine Lune _____ (accuser) des émotions décuplées, mais vous n'_____ (avoir) rien à craindre. Vos cieux sont beaux.

POISSONS

Encore auréolé d'envies de prestige, vous _____ (aller) vers des gens qui vous en (imposer) un peu. Vous _____ (se sentir) débordé par l'organisation, les détails à régler, mais vous y _____ (arriver). Tout juste . . .

(ii) Météo

1. BORD DE MER: MANCHE

Les nuages _____ (être) nombreux, donnant encore un temps quelque peu maussade. Quelques petites pluies _____ (se produire) l'après-midi au nord de la Seine. Le vent d'ouest _____ (faiblir).

2. MONTAGNE

Sur tous les massifs, le soleil _____ (faire) un retour de force. Quelques brumes _____ (se former) localement en fond de vallée au lever du jour, mais le soleil les _____ (dissiper) rapidement. Les sommets _____ (se détacher) nettement sur fond de ciel bleu. Le vent _____ (être) faible.

3. EUROPE: SCANDINAVIE, DANEMARK, ILES BRITANNIQUES

Journée très maussade. Le ciel _____ (être) gris et il _____ (pleuvoir) fréquemment. Il _____ (faire) au mieux de 16 à 18 degrés.

186 Non-finite forms of the verb (See S41)

A *Translate into French:*

1. I prefer driving an automatic car.
2. After reading the article he phoned his lawyer.
3. Launching a new product is difficult during a recession.

4. To tell the truth, we're worried about David.

5. To hire a car, you need your driving licence.

6. Yes, but where can you find a new car at the same price?

7. I feel like taking a day off.

8. Protecting the seashore is the area's priority.

9. To read the local press, you'd think all landlords are dishonest.

10. After finishing her studies, she went to work in the States.

11. By abolishing this allowance, the government will save money.

12. He brought up the children on his own while still working.

13. Before leaving Italy, why not buy a pair of leather shoes?

14. I was watching him park the car.

15. They left the motorway, going in the direction of Soissons.

16. Why sell off this building?

17. The life-guard, seeing a child in difficulty, got into the water.

18. After looking at each other for a long time, the dogs sniffed each other.

19. Ask them a favour? Never!

20. I've got the date changed.

B (i) *Compléter le texte en mettant les verbes suivants à la forme qui convient (infinitif précédé ou non d'une préposition, participé présent, participé passé):*
bénéficier, perdre, venir, appeler, décliner, s'adapter, promettre, épauler, multiplier, nommer

BOURGOGNE: LES CAVES SE VISITENT

_____ d'un nom connu sur la terre entière ne dispense pas de soigner sa publicité. La Bourgogne en a fait l'expérience, au milieu des années 80, _____ subitemement le tiers de ses visiteurs _____ de Belgique, L'électrochoc fut salutaire. Après _____ à la rescousse l'ancien directeur du tourisme irlandais à Paris, la Bourgogne multiplie ses affiches et ses annonces de presse, _____ sa nouvelle image de marque. Mais il fallait aussi persuader les Bourguignons _____ à la demande étrangère. 264 viticulteurs ont signé une véritable charte touristique _____ d'ouvrir leurs caves à heures fixes. _____ les efforts des professionnels, le conseil régional du tourisme s'est transformé en agence de marketing, _____ les études de marché. Le maire de Mâcon, fraîchement _____ président du comité régional du tourisme, entend bien poursuivre l'action de ses prédecesseurs.

(excerpted from *Le Point*)

(ii) *Compléter les phrases qui suivent l'article:*

APRES LE PASSAGE DU TOUR DE FRANCE

Le parc national de la Vanoise dépose une plainte contre la société française de production

Lors de la traversée du parc national de la Vanoise par le Tour de France, le 18 juillet, un hélicoptère de la société française de production (SFP) s'était 'égaré' à l'intérieur de la zone centrale du parc, interdite aux 'aéronefs civils' volant à moins de mille mètres du sol. La directrice du parc, qui avait renouvelé son interdiction aux organisateurs du Tour, quelques jours avant le passage de l'épreuve, a déposé plainte contre la SFP auprès du Procureur de la République d'Albertville.

Elle a d'autre part remis au magistrat trois procès-verbaux dressés à l'encontre des véhicules de la caravane publicitaire, représentant les sociétés Coca-Cola, Fiat et l'Institut Géographique National. Ceux-ci avaient distribué des tracts et utilisé leurs avertisseurs sonores lors de leur passage dans la réserve naturelle des vallons de l'Iseran. Cet espace protégé est lui aussi soumis à une réglementation stricte destinée à préserver la tranquillité des espèces animales qui y vivent.

(excerpted from *Le Monde*)

1. Un hélicoptère s'était égaré en _____ pendant le Tour de France.
2. Après _____ aux 'aéronefs civils' volant à moins de mille mètres du sol, la directrice a renouvelé son interdiction aux organisateurs du Tour.
3. La directrice a déposé plainte contre la SFP, tout _____ trois procès-verbaux.
4. _____ des tracts est interdit dans la réserve naturelle.
5. _____ des avertisseurs sonores on risque de déranger les espèces animales qui vivent dans la réserve.

187 Tenses of the subjunctive

(See S44a)

A *Translate into French:*
(Where it is appropriate to use the imperfect or pluperfect subjunctive, also give an alternative non-literary form – i.e. present / perfect subjunctive.)

1. Although he was a famous author, he was not buried in the Panthéon.
2. We had asked that you should be reimbursed.
3. The passengers waited for both the trains to leave.

4. The only play which had been performed in that theatre before *L'Avare* was *Le Cid*.

5. It was necessary for the king to speak to the nobles.

6. The spokesman denied that protestors had threatened local residents.

7. Poor though I was, I had never begged.

8. Whatever may happen, I would prefer you to stay here.

9. Before the countess left, her daughter's engagement was announced.

10. It was unlikely that they had finished the harvest.

11. He wanted his children to come and see him one last time.

12. The widow refused to see anyone.

B *Voici des extraits littéraires où les auteurs ont utilisé l'imparfait ou le plus-que-parfait du subjonctif. Compléter les phrases avec les verbes indiqués entre parenthèses, et ensuite substituer une forme plus courante du subjonctif:*

(i) Donc j'avais dix ans et j'aimais ma maîtresse. J'étais prêt à toutes les manoeuvres pour entrer dans ses grâces. Comme j'étais un élève médiocre, ni brillant ni cancre, aucunement remarquable en quoi que ce _____ (être), la tâche n'était pas aisée. Or si j'avais eu par deux fois l'occasion de me rendre dans l'ancienne maison de garde-barrière qu'habitaient Lucie et les siens, c'était en vain que j'avais attendu que Sophie _____ (prononcer) le mot magique, véritable 'Sésame, ouvre-toi' de cette famille.

(excerpted from M. Tournier, *Lucie, ou la femme sans ombre*)

(ii) La vue de la petite madeleine ne m'avait rien rappelé avant que je n'y _____ (goûter) . . . Et dès que j'eus reconnu le goût du morceau de madeleine trempé dans le tilleul que me donnait ma tante (quoique je ne _____ (savoir) pas encore et _____ (devoir) remettre à bien plus tard de découvrir pourquoi ce souvenir me rendait si heureux), aussitôt la vieille maison grise sur la rue, où était sa chambre, vint comme un décor de théâtre s'appliquer au petit pavillon donnant sur le jardin.

(excerpted from M. Proust, *Du côté de chez Swann*)

(iii) Elle était un peu pâle, c'est-à-dire que son fard évident dessinait sur ses joues deux lunes ovales. Elle affectait l'air distrait, comme elle l'_____ (faire) sous un regard humain. . . . Elle contraignit la chatte, que son pied allait meurtrir, à regagner d'un saut son étroit observatoire puis à se coller contre la porte. Saha s'était reprise et _____ (être) morte plutôt que de jeter un second cri.

(excerpted from Colette, *La Chatte*)

188 Subjunctive (after conjunctions)

(See S44, especially S44c (i))

A *Translate into French:*

1. He's the best candidate although he is so young.
2. You'll have to complete the form so that we can check your account number.
3. We've moved house, so we're nearer to the town centre.
4. We can offer you two free seats provided you collect the tickets before six o'clock.
5. Le Lavandou is a well-known seaside resort. Not that there are as many tourists as at Cannes.
6. You'd better remove the stain before she notices.
7. We've borrowed another computer while I'm working at home.
8. I'll take care of it, unless you prefer to go to the Town Hall yourselves.
9. Suppose the strike were declared tomorrow.
10. Don't forget to turn off the electricity before you leave.
11. The service is suspended until the lifts are repaired.
12. After waiting for half an hour she decided to phone them.
13. He filled up the petrol tank without his father asking him to.
14. She shut the door without waking up the dog.

B *Compléter le texte en utilisant les verbes indiqués entre parenthèses:*

DEMOCRATISATION DE L'ENSEIGNEMENT SUPERIEUR

Bien que la population étudiante _____ (augmenter) de 20% entre 1989 et 1992, cette progression ne s'est pas traduite par une forte démocratisation de l'enseignement supérieur. La proportion de fils d'ouvriers à l'Université a augmenté de 1 point (de 8% à 9%), sans que le nombre de fils de professions supérieures _____ (diminuer) pour autant. Les enfants d'enseignants ont de fortes chances de faire des études supérieures, puisqu'ils _____ (constituer) 16% des effectifs, alors que leurs parents ne _____ (faire) que 4.9% de la population active.

La sélection sociale joue de façon très sensible dans la répartition des étudiants entre les universités. Un cadre supérieur ferait des efforts pour que son enfant _____ (s'inscrire) dans une université parisienne, tandis que les fils d'ouvriers _____ (être) présents surtout dans les universités des régions en difficulté.

Ce phénomène, toutefois, ne doit pas en cacher un autre. Les effectifs vont croître de sorte qu'un plus grand nombre de jeunes n'ayant pas d'héritage social ou culturel _____ (pouvoir) accéder à l'enseignement supérieur. Aujourd'hui 58% des étudiants appartiennent à une famille où le père n'a pas fait d'études supérieures.

(excerpted from *Le Monde de l'éducation*)

189 Subjunctive (wishing, emotions, fear, orders, purpose)

(See S44, especially S44c (ii–vi))

A *Translate into French:*

1. I regret that we only accept cheques for 100 francs or more.
2. Are you afraid of failing your driving test?
3. My parents would like us to stop over at their house.
4. The ski instructor insisted we stayed in a group.
5. I'm surprised you haven't seen Marianne again.
6. Do you wish to move to another table, madam?
7. We're afraid the journey will tire my grandfather.
8. The inhabitants of the town expected the town council to react.
9. The government hopes the number of people out of work will start to fall.
10. We'll wait until the road is cleared before we set off.
11. I can quite understand your being disappointed.
12. The police demanded that the witness be questioned again.
13. She was delighted that we had thought of her.

445

B (i) *Compléter le texte en utilisant les verbes indiqués entre parenthèses:*

– Ecoute, Jérôme, c'est ma croix d'améthystes que j'ai là; depuis trois soirs je l'apporte parce que je voulais depuis longtemps te la donner.
– Que veux-tu que j'en _____ (faire)? fis-je assez brusquement.
– Que tu la _____ (garder) en souvenir de moi, pour ta fille.
– Quelle fille? m'écriai-je en regardent Alissa sans la comprendre.
– Ecoute-moi bien calmement, je t'en prie; non, ne me _____ (regarder) pas ainsi; déjà j'ai beaucoup de mal à te parler; mais ceci, je veux absolument te le dire. Ecoute, Jérôme, un jour tu _____? (se marier) Non, ne me _____ (répondre) pas, ne m'_____ (interrompre) pas, je t'en supplie. Je voudrais tout simplement que tu _____ (se souvenir) que je t'aurai beaucoup aimé . . .

(excerpted from A. Gide, *La Porte étroite*)

(ii) *Voici un extrait d'un reportage sur Avignon et son festival de théâtre. Compléter les phrases en dessous en utilisant les mots indiqués entre parenthèses:*

Si les artistes du Festival connaissent leur rôle, les Avignonnais savent leur donner la réplique: la pièce dure depuis maintenant plus de cinquante ans. Les restaurateurs étalent leurs terrasses et n'arrivent plus à fermer leurs congélateurs. Les consommateurs de spectacles ont réservé leurs places avant tout le monde et les adolescents du coin ont dégoté un job pour l'été. Restent ceux qui continuent à se lever tôt pour se rendre au bureau et ne peuvent fermer l'oeil avant 3 heures du matin. En bas de chez eux, les festivaliers rythment un temps qui n'est pas le leur. Les commentaires passionnés, assaisonnés de pastis et de vin couleur locale – une fois le rideau tombé – les agressent sans même qu'ils puissent en profiter. Ils n'ont qu'un souhait . . . dormir comme d'habitude. L'exaspération et la fatigue accumulées engendrent alors des sketches plus vrais que sur scène. Sans Shakespeare, la tempête se déclenche.

(excerpted from *L'Evénement du jeudi*)

1. Les restaurateurs sont heureux que les spectateurs _____ . (réserver leurs places)
2. Les adolescents du coin se félicitent qu'on _____. (proposer un job)
3. Ceux qui continuent à se rendre chaque matin au bureau voudraient que les touristes _____ . (faire moins de bruit)
4. Les Avignonnais souhaiteraient que les festivaliers _____ . (laisser dormir)

5. Les festivaliers ne comprennent pas très bien que certains Avignonnais _____ . (être fatigué et exaspéré)

190 Subjunctive (saying / thinking, possibility, impersonal expressions)

(See S44, especially S44c (vii–ix))

A *Translate into French:*

1. It is probable that the result will appear in the newspaper tomorrow.
2. We think that you may have to wait a week.
3. You must lock the door.
4. Excuse me, do you think this ticket is still valid?
5. The office manager doubted whether we could supply all the materials immediately.
6. The prison officer denied that two prisoners had blackmailed him.
7. It's natural that you should be shocked by his behaviour.
8. It's possible that we may rent a house in the Var.
9. I've no doubt the new shopping centre will be a great success.
10. It's quite unacceptable for him to come back.
11. It is unlikely that this car can be repaired.
12. I'm not claiming that it's a perfect example.

B *Compléter le texte en utilisant les verbes indiqués entre parenthèses:*

Je crois que nous avons changé. Nous ne croyons plus qu'il _____ (y avoir) dans une cité, dans une nation, des parties nobles et des parties infâmes. Nous pensons qu'un pays _____ (être) un organisme complexe dont chaque organe s'explique par tous les autres. Nous pensons qu'une belle ruine _____ (être) un vestige du passé, mais qu'elle _____ (être) aussi une partie vivante d'une ville moderne. Nous aimerions savoir ce que les habitants pensent d'elle, s'ils _____ (passer) avec indifférence le long de ses murs ou s'ils en _____ (être) fiers.

Et, puisque, comme dit Camus, on connaît un pays quand on sait comment on y aime et comment on y meurt, qu'on nous _____ (donner) quelques renseignements sur les mariages, les naissances, les morts, les rythmes saisonniers de la vie. Cela n'est pas tout encore: une

447

ville, pour moderne qu'elle _____ (être), offre un visage singulier. Les anciens guides, ne parlant que du passé, négligeaient cette physionomie des villes qui fait leur charme ou au contraire leur disgrâce. C'est une chose d'avoir des beautés, c'en est une autre d'avoir de la beauté. Je souhaiterais que les ouvrages plus modernes _____ (pouvoir) nous renseigner.

(excerpted from J.-P. Sartre)

191 Subjunctive (superlatives, indefinites)

(See S44, especially S44c (x–xiii))

A *Translate into French:*

1. The first time we went to Lyons, we ate at Bocuse's restaurant.
2. Our marketing department would prefer to find someone who already knows this sector.
3. It's the prettiest village we visited in the region.
4. She always complains whatever people do.
5. Are these the only pictures the museum has kept?
6. Wherever you hide the bone our dog is sure to find it.
7. I'm looking for a colour which won't show the dirt.
8. Whatever his motives may be, I can't understand him having sold his shares.
9. It's the best package holiday we can suggest to you.
10. That political parties are not in agreement is obvious.
11. Whatever agency you choose, you'll be asked to pay a deposit.
12. There's nothing worth visiting in that region.
13. Here's a photo we took last month.
14. That whale hunting is now forbidden is a step in the right direction.

B *Compléter les phrases pour réécrire les annonces publicitaires:*

(i) Visa Premier. Soyez premier partout

Partout dans le monde, la Visa Premier c'est 320.000 guichets bancaires et 100.000 distributeurs Visa. Retrait de 100.000 francs par semaine en monnaie locale. Ligne de crédit personnalisée. Assurances, assistance médicale pour toute votre famille et envoi d'une carte de dépannage en 48 heures en cas de perte ou de vol à l'étranger. Accueil privilégié dans les plus grands hôtels. Ne soyez pas le dernier à avoir une Visa Premier.

1. Où que vous _____ dans le monde, la Visa Premier c'est 320.000 guichets.

2. _____ la monnaie locale, vous pouvez retirer 100.000 francs par semaine.

3. Vous bénéficiez d'assurances et d'assistance médicale pour _____ dans la famille.

4. Vous cherchez un grand hôtel qui vous _____ bien? Utilisez votre carte Visa.

(ii) Pierre et Vacances

Tout est là et tout est possible, au gré de vos envies. Pierre et Vacances a rassemblé dans ses Villages tout ce qui fait la réussite des vraies vacances, piscines, tennis, golf, animations sportives, clubs pour enfants, spectacles. Tout est là si vous le désirez, quand vous le désirez, et tout est compris dans le prix de la location. Pour en savoir plus sur les Villages Pierre et Vacances et les différentes formules de séjour, n'hésitez pas à demander notre catalogue.

1. _____ vos envies, Pierre et Vacances a tout rassemblé dans ses Villages.

2. Quel que sport que vous _____ , tout est là si vous le désirez.

3. Quoi que vous _____ , tout est compris dans le prix de la location.

4. _____ les formules de séjour qui vous intéressent, n'hésitez pas à demander notre catalogue.

(iii) Canada. Le pays vrai

Le Canada est le pays où tous les rêves se réalisent. Vous souhaitez vous reposer dans un endroit luxueux, profiter de tous les plaisirs de la civilisation, pratiquer un sport qui vous tentait depuis longtemps? Rien de plus facile. Mais si vous souhaitez redécouvrir la nature, contempler des paysages étonnants et tranquilles, d'autres paysages du Canada vous sont offerts, rien que pour vous. Venez, et vous n'aurez qu'une envie: revenir.

1. _____ votre rêve, vous pourrez le réaliser au Canada.

2. Rien de plus facile que de trouver un endroit qui _____ luxueux.

3. Quoi que vous _____ redécouvrir dans la nature, le Canada vous offrira des paysages étonnants et tranquilles.

4. Après avoir visité le Canada, la seule envie qu'on _____ c'est de revenir.

192 The conditional mood

(See S45 and S46)

A *Translate into French:*

1. If we had known there were roadworks, we'd have avoided the ring road.
2. Might you need me this afternoon?
3. The journalist asked if you would give an interview.
4. If the meeting finished by four o'clock, you could catch the flight at six.
5. Can you imagine my doing that sort of thing!
6. If he had resigned, she would have replaced him.
7. When we lived in Provence we would have breakfast outside.
8. Can you imagine her staying in a one-star hotel!
9. Would it be too expensive if we hired a car?
10. You should have renewed your Visa card.
11. I didn't know whether all the guests would come by car.
12. We should pay a visit to your aunt next week.
13. Madame Beauchamp hasn't replied yet. Might she be on holiday?
14. When the children were younger we would ask Anne to babysit for us.

B *Traduire en anglais les phrases soulignées:*

(i) Deux avocats de Montpellier sont suspendus par le Conseil de l'ordre

A l'origine de l'affaire, on trouve une série d'articles relatant dans la presse locale des faits divers traités par le cabinet de M. Philippe Lebrun. Il se murmure que l'avocat paierait certains journalistes pour faire de la publicité aux affaires qu'il a en mains. Une histoire circule même sur une forte somme qu'il aurait reçue d'un client en promettant la libération d'un détunu avec la complicité d'un magistrat.

(excerpted from *Le Monde*)

(ii) Devant ce silence Madame de Séryeuse se dit: 'Il faut que ce soit plus grave encore que j'imagine.' Et, persuadée de ses torts, elle commença, timide, comme si c'était elle qui eût été en faute. Ce qui, dans cette scène, n'eût pas le moins stupéfait Séryeuse, eût été l'attitude de sa mère, qu'il croyait froide. Le spectacle de cette passion réveillait chez elle la femme endormie.

(excerpted from R. Badiguet, *Le Bal du comte d'Orgel*)

 Compléter les phrases en utilisant les verbes indiqués entre parenthèses:

COMBIEN FAUT-IL POSSÉDER AUJOURD'HUI POUR ETRE RENTIER?

Tout dépend du niveau de vos besoins ... Si vous _____ (pouvoir) vous contenter de 10.000 à 12.000 F par mois, il vous suffit actuellement de 1,8 à 2 millions placés en sicav monétaires. Et si quelqu'un _____ (posséder) un patrimoine de 3 millions de francs, il pourrait vivre beaucoup mieux qu'un cadre surmené et surchargé d'impôts et de cotisations sociales, en se reposant. Beaucoup de couples pourraient revendre leur logement à Paris et s'établir en province comme rentiers, s'ils _____ (ne pas être piégé) par la spirale infernale du travail. S'ils louaient une maison à un prix raisonnable, quinze ou vingt ans plus tard, l'héritage leur _____ (permettre) d'ailleurs d'arrondir encore leur patrimoine. En effet, si c'est aussi simple, pourquoi les rentiers ne _____-ils (proliférer) pas dans notre pays!

(excerpted from *L'Evénement du jeudi*)

193 Moods in hypothetical clauses
(See S46)

A *Translate into French:*

1. If you eat in a Breton creperie, order bottled cider.
2. If Mitterand has been elected twice, it's because the voters didn't trust the other candidates.
3. If you trained every day, you would be a good athlete.
4. They would have got married in 1939 if the war hadn't started.
5. If the sea is rough, most passengers prefer to have a cabin.
6. The residents would lodge a complaint if the pollution level rose.
7. If he were arrested and brought to trial, would he be sent to prison?
8. She would have made a fortune if she had settled in the States.
9. If the squatters refused to leave, it was because they knew the house was unoccupied.
10. If the ecologists are elected, the site will be protected.

11. If you buy this product and subsequently have problems, do not hesitate to contact our customer services.

12. The factory would have made 500 workers redundant if Méga hadn't bought it.

13. If I had a son I'd send him to work for a year in the developing countries.

14. If the French Revolution started only in 1789, some writers had already foreseen it.

B *Voici des conseils parus dans le journal pour éviter des coups de soleil. Après chaque indication, complétez la phrase suivante en utilisant les mots indiqués entre parenthèses:*

LE SOLEIL DES PETITS: AVEC MODERATION

(i) Les règles à suivre pour bénéficier uniquement des bons côtés du soleil? Ne pas exposer au soleil un bébé de moins d'un an.

Vous ne devez pas exposer un bébé au soleil si _____ . (avoir)

(ii) A tout âge, évitez les heures chaudes de 11 à 15h.

S'il fait chaud, vous _____ . (devoir)

(iii) Jusqu'à quatre ans, protégez l'enfant avec un écran total et renouvelez l'application toutes les deux heures.

Si j'avais un enfant de moins de quatre ans, je _____ . (protéger, renouveler)

(iv) Après chaque baignade, n'oubliez pas de sécher votre enfant car les gouttes d'eau font loupe sur la peau et la brûlent.

Je n'oublierais pas de sécher mon enfant si _____ . (se baigner)

(v) En cas de coups de soleil, réhydratez la peau de l'enfant avec un après-solaire et évitez de l'exposer durant quelques jours.

Si l'enfant avait pris un coup de soleil, on _____ . (réhydrater, éviter)

194 The imperative mood

(See S47)

A *Translate into French:*

1. Let's leave straight away.
2. Don't fill the box up.
3. Sit down for a minute, Solange.
4. Go away, Jacques.
5. Write your names here.
6. Hurry up, you two!
7. Let's have a coffee.
8. Be careful!
9. Jeanne, explain to me what this means.
10. Don't worry, Madame Rigaud.
11. Call me if you need me.
12. Don't get up, Caroline.

B **(i)** *Voici des conseils adressés aux jeunes bacheliers cherchant à s'inscrire à l'université. Réécrire les phrases soulignées en utilisant l'impératif:*

La réussite de vos études en fac se joue largement lors de l'inscription. Le formulaire que vous avez rempli au lycée, en avril, n'est qu'indicatif. Vous pouvez donc modifier votre choix; mais chaque université a tendance à privilégier les lycéens qui l'ont inscrite en tête de liste.

Une fois votre décision prise, vous devez vous armer d'opiniâtreté et de persévérance. Dès les résultats au premier groupe d'épreuves du bac, il faudra vous présenter à l'université pour retirer un dossier dans la filière que vous avez choisie. Vous aurez intérêt à emporter avec vous, au minimum: l'original du relevé de notes du bac; vos papiers d'identité; une dizaine de photos d'identité; une bonne dose d'amabilité. Le dossier devra être rempli et renvoyé avant les dates indiquées.

Mieux vaut ne pas tout miser sur une seule inscription. On ne peut toutefois s'inscrire, en première année, qu'à deux DEUG différents de la même université. Il est interdit de s'inscrire dans deux universités différentes pour préparer le même diplôme.

Surtout, vous pourrez vous renseigner auprès de la cellule d'information et d'orientation présente dans chaque université.

(excerpted from *Le Monde de l'éducation*)

453

(ii) *Voici une recette culinaire qui a paru dans le journal. Vous en rédigerez une version pour un/e ami/e, en mettant tous les verbes soulignés à l'impératif:*

OEUFS FARCIS A L'OSEILLE

<u>Découper</u> proprement une petite calotte à chaque oeuf, <u>vider</u> le contenu et <u>réserver</u> les coquilles. <u>Laver et équeuter</u> l'oseille, <u>la découper</u> en fines lanières.

Dans une poêle, <u>faire fondre</u> du beurre. <u>Verser</u> l'oseille et <u>laisser cuire</u> une minute en tournant. Puis <u>verser</u> les oeufs battus.

<u>Faire cuire</u> à feu moyen, en remuant, jusqu'à ce que les oeufs soient pris. Hors du feu, <u>ajouter</u> 50g de feta émiettée et un bouquet de ciboulette finement ciselée. <u>Poivrer</u> largement.

<u>Remplir</u> les coquilles d'oeufs de ce mélange. <u>Servir</u> chaud.

(excerpted from *Ouest-France*)

195 Prepositions: position (*à, chez, dans, sur*)

(See S49b)

A *Translate into French:*

1. Did you see Martine in the grocer's?
2. She's got an appointment at the dentist's.
3. There was corruption on all levels.
4. I've got a pain in my knee.
5. Can you buy a ticket on the train?
6. We've been invited to the Guillaumes.
7. He had to pay the fine on the spot.
8. Stop! It's hurting my foot!
9. Fabrice has got married – it's in the newspaper.
10. In Stendhal the characters are more important than the plot.
11. On the sixth floor there's a balcony with a panoramic view over Paris.
12. In the south people eat outside far more often.
13. I nailed the poster to the wall.
14. In her country women can't go out alone.

B *Compléter les blancs en choisissant une des prépositions suivantes: à (avec ou sans article défini), chez, dans, sur*

Ma grand-mère, elle, avait appris _____ l'école des soeurs. Comme les autres femmes du village, elle tissait _____ elle, _____ une pièce sans air.

Elle était propre ____ elle et ____ son ménage, qualité la plus importante ____ village, où les voisins surveillaient la blancheur et l'état du linge en train de sécher ____ la corde. Bien que les maisons soient isolées les unes des autres par des haies et des talus, rien n'échappait ____ regard des gens, ni l'heure ____ laquelle l'homme était rentré du bistrot, ni la semaine où les serviettes hygiéniques auraient dû se balancer ____ vent.

Mon père faisait deux kilomètres ____ pied pour atteindre l'école. L'instituteur enseignait durement, la règle de fer ____ les doigts, respecté. Certains de ses élèves parvenaient ____ certificat ____ les premiers du canton, un ou deux ____ l'école normale d'instituteurs. ____ douze ans, mon père se trouvait ____ la classe du certificat. Mon grand-père l'a retiré de l'école pour le placer ____ la même ferme que lui.

(excerpted from A. Ernaux, *La Place*)

196 Prepositions: 'made of' / 'for' (à, de, en)

(See S49b)

A *Translate into French:*

1. The children are building a sandcastle.
2. In the chemist's I bought a lipstick.
3. The frame was made entirely of gold.
4. Could you give me a plastic bag?
5. The house with the large balcony belongs to the mayor.
6. There's a little shop which sells wicker armchairs.
7. When it's hot I have to wear a cotton shirt.
8. Granite monuments withstand the bad weather.
9. For the part of Cyrano we need an actor with a very long nose!
10. After the death of her husband she dressed in grey or black.
11. He gave me a beautiful leather bag.
12. You can't serve the coffee in teacups!

B *Compléter les blancs avec une des prépositions suivantes: à (avec ou sans article défini), de (avec ou sans article défini), en:*

(i) Le décor réussi

Choisissez un festival de tons bleus. Ci-dessus: dynamique des verres ____ pied élégants et incassables. Ils sont ____ plastique! Et un très grand pichet ___ orangeade, et une coupe ___ fruits ___ faïence. ___ gauche, à l'heure de la sieste: un voile ___ coton tamise la lumière, adoucit les contours des objets. Un plaid frangé ___ soie se coordonne aux lattes ___ bois peint traditionnelles de l'Ile de Ré.

(ii) L'été en beauté: coquetterie

___ puces, on trouve toujours des accessoires pour cheveux qui datent du début du siècle, des peignes et des épingles souvent ___ jais, argent et grenat, sans doute très ___ la mode ___ cette époque-là.

Côté ruban, un magasin japonais à Paris crée de merveilleux métrages irisés, veloutés que l'on peut nouer dans ses cheveux. Plus classiques mais toujours jolis, les rubans ___ satin des grands magasins existent dans des gammes très étendues ___ largeurs et ___ couleurs.

(excerpted from *Marie-France*)

197 Prepositions: transport and manner of action (à, de, en, par)
(See S49b)

A *Translate into French:*

1. She travelled from Brussels to Geneva by coach.
2. My grandfather always travelled first class.
3. When the car broke down I had to come back on foot.
4. They're going to arrive on the night train.
5. Her sister refused to ride a horse.
6. In the summer he likes going for bike rides.
7. By plane it only takes two hours.
8. The children adore boat trips.
9. At that moment I was seized with panic.
10. He strode up the stairs.
11. She was speaking softly.
12. Their representative replied in an off-hand tone.
13. She was running at top speed.
14. She dressed up as a Castilian.
15. The owner looked at them threateningly.
16. The farmer gave him a basket filled with fruit.
17. All our garments are hand-made.
18. The landscape is changing in an alarming fashion.

456

B *Remplir les blancs en choisissant une des prépositions suivantes: à (avec ou sans article défini), de (avec ou sans article défini), en, par:*

(i) Joueurs de boules

On joue ____ boules à peu près partout en France, mais c'est probablement sous le soleil de Provence, ____ Marseille par exemple, que l'affaire prend toute son importance. Drame sous les platanes, à 10h, à midi, au soir pour l'apéro, peu importe: ____ la loyale, bien entendu!

(ii) Val de Loire, Chambord

Noces royales de l'espace et du temps, Chambord ____ 365 fenêtres et ____ l'architecture toute d'équilibre se mirant dans l'immensité de sa pièce d'eau. La Renaissance française, encore émerveillée ____ sa découverte de l'Italie, y réalise son idéal de plaisir et de beauté: François Ier demande à Léonard de Vinci de lui dessiner le plan d'un palais ____ sa mesure. Des chasses ____ courre sont régulièrement organisées dans le grand parc, clos ____ un mur d'enceinte de 32 kilomètres.

(iii) Landes, le TGV

Les trains ____ grande vitesse comptent parmi les réussites les plus spectaculaires de l'industrie française moderne. Dernier-né de cette technologie ____ pointe: le TGV-Atlantique. C'est ainsi, ____ exemple, qu'on peut maintenant rejoindre très rapidement Bordeaux, et prendre ensuite tranquillement la route du sud. Là s'étend la vaste plaine marécageuse des Landes, aménagée ____ la fin du siècle dernier ____ une immense forêt de pins maritimes. Forêt lumineuse, ____ profondeurs légères, aériennes, baignées ____ parfum de la résine encore récoltée aujourd'hui ____ les gemmeurs.

(excerpted from T. Zeldin, *Images de la France*)

198 Prepositions: numbers (*de/que, par, sur*)
(See S49b)

A *Translate into French:*

1. More than half the candidates did not turn up for the exam.
2. At the time, I didn't know what to say.
3. The cost of the retraining course is 560 francs.
4. You should work at least eight hours a day.

457

5. Your brother has eaten twice as much as you.

6. Two out of three farmers said they were dissatisfied.

7. Less than 25% of the patients were on this diet.

8. The bonus is 1000 francs.

9. The nurse will come to see you twice a week.

10. The highest mark was 12 out of 20.

11. It's rained less than last year.

12. The turn-out rate for the election was 72%.

B *Compléter les blancs en choisissant une des prépositions suivantes: à, de, en, par:*

(i) Le stade envahi par des cochons

Plus _____ deux cents porcs hollandais échappés d'un camion ont détruit la pelouse du stade de Carpentras.

(ii) Enchères à la Russe

Dernière folie moscovite: la 'mise aux enchères' de neuf hommes célibataires qui ont été vendus à des femmes. Les 'lots' avaient été triés parmi une soixantaine _____ candidats _____ 22 _____ 52 ans.

(iii) Le vin bon pour les artères

Le taux de mortalité coronarienne en France est _____ 95 décès masculins pour 100.000 habitants, chiffre très inférieur _____ ceux de l'Italie (300 décès), des Etats-Unis (255), de la Grande-Bretagne (300). Selon des experts américains, c'est le vin à faible dose (deux ou trois verres _____ jour) qui protégerait les Français.

(iv) Allemagne – alerte sur la bière

Le président des brasseurs allemands tire la sonnette d'alarme: stagnation de la production et de la consommation (au niveau toutefois honorable _____ 143 litres _____ an _____ habitant) et hausse _____ 76, 9% des importations.

(v) Le bilan de santé des Français

L'espérance de vie de nos compatriotes continue de croître. Plus _____ soixante-dix ans pour les hommes, près de soixante-dix-neuf ans pour les femmes. L'écart entre les deux sexes se creuse _____ plus _____ plus: il était seulement _____ 6,7 ans en 1960.

199 Prepositions: use of *depuis*

(See S49b)

A   *Translate into French:*

1. Have you been waiting long?
2. Since they got married, they've been living with his parents.
3. We had been lost for hours.
4. He hadn't driven since his accident.
5. How long have you been studying astronomy?
6. Had you known the victim for long?
7. I haven't seen my aunt for ten years.
8. The technicians had been on strike for three days.
9. How long is it since you last went back to France?
10. Since last year she's become a vegetarian.
11. I've been looking for that book for ages.
12. From the birth of civilization, man has discovered medicinal plants.

B   *Lire le texte suivant, puis compléter les questions qui correspondent aux réponses fournies:*

Il faut attendre la loi du 29 juillet 1881 sur la liberté de la presse pour que les entreprises éditrices des titres de province (on en compte 179 en 1879) se lancent dans l'aventure industrielle. A la suite de la mise au point de la rotative avec ses rendements de l'ordre de 20.000 exemplaires à l'heure, certains de leurs homologues parisiens s'y étaient déjà engagés. L'essor de la presse française aurait certes pu avoir lieu plus tôt si les investisseurs n'avaient pas été freinés par les dispositions restrictives des régimes antérieurs.

L'entre-deux-guerres entraîne une révolution dans le monde de la communication et de l'information en consacrant la fin de l'ère du média unique avec l'apparition de la radiodiffusion. En 1939, la France compte déjà 5 millions de postes-récepteurs et 32 stations émettrices dont 20 appartenant à l'Etat.

(excerpted from M. Mathien, *La Presse quotidienne régionale*)

1. Depuis quand _____? (se lancer) Depuis 1881.
2. Depuis quand _____? (s'engager) Depuis la mise au point de la rotative.
3. Depuis quand _____? (avoir lieu) Depuis un certain temps déjà si les investisseurs n'avaient pas été freinés.

4. Depuis quand _____? (y avoir une révolution) Depuis l'entre-deux-guerres.

5. Depuis quand _____? (constater la fin) Depuis l'apparition de la radiodiffusion.

6. Depuis quand _____? (compter) Depuis 1939.

200 Prepositions: *entre, d'entre, envers, parmi, vers*

(See S49b)

A *Translate into French:*

1. The spire rose up among the simple houses.
2. Between ourselves, it was a very boring film.
3. This is one example among many others.
4. How many of them have already been to India?
5. They ran towards the old farmhouse.
6. How did you choose between the two candidates?
7. At about three o'clock he went out of the back door.
8. It's a decision which affects several of us.
9. Of these modern authors, which will still be read in a hundred years' time?
10. At about what time did you hear the shots?

B *Compléter les blancs en choisissant une des prépositions suivantes: entre, d'entre, parmi, vers:*

(i) TOXICOMANIE: EN EUROPE, DES LEGISLATIONS DISPARATES

Les législations sur la toxicomanie sont extrêmement disparates en Europe. _____ tous les pays européens qui ont voté des textes répressifs pour lutter contre le trafic, les sanctions prévues varient beaucoup. Un exemple _____ beaucoup: un trafiquant d'héroïne risque une peine maximum de dix ans de prison au Danemark, la perpétuité en Grèce ou en Irlande.

L'hétérogénéité est encore plus marquée en ce qui concerne les usagers. L'Allemagne ne fait pas de distinction _____ les différentes drogues; les usagers ne sont pas poursuivis. Le Royaume-Uni fait une distinction _____ trois niveaux de dangérosité; seul l'usage de l'opium est incriminé.

(excerpted from *Le Monde*)

(ii) CATASTROPHE: PLUS DE CINQUANTE MORTS AU PORTUGAL

Un DC-10 s'est écrasé lundi matin sur l'aéroport de Faro au Portugal. Sur les 340 passagers présents dans l'appareil – 13 _____ eux étaient membres d'équipages – on dénombrait 283 blessés. Le DC-10 avait décollé _____ 5h35 de l'aéroport de Schiphol. Ce vol en direction de Faro, qui dessert les sites touristiques du sud du Portugal, devait atterrir _____ 8h30.

Les deux boîtes noires de l'appareil ont été retrouvées _____ les décombres et le pilote et le copilote figurent _____ les rescapés, ce qui devrait faciliter les recherches.

(excerpted from *Le Monde*)

201 Prepositions: expressions of time
(See S50a)

A   *Translate into French:*

1. She lived in Marseille from 1979 to 1990.
2. He'll be back in two weeks' time.
3. I've cancelled all my appointments for next week.
4. The new law comes into force from today.
5. They saw the whole exhibition in less than an hour.
6. From next week there will be no buses after 10 p.m.
7. She tried to hide her anxiety, but within a few minutes she burst into tears.
8. The field was flooded for several weeks.
9. We'll contact all our clients as soon as our Managing Director is back.
10. If you want to hire a jeep, there's a special rate from Thursday to Sunday.
11. She suffered for years on end.
12. In five years' time there will be twice as many private cars.
13. You've been working for the same agency for four years.
14. The Norwegian team made the journey in five days.
15. From next year the station will have automatic left-luggage lockers.
16. We've got to be back in half an hour.

B   *Compléter les blancs en choisissant une des prépositions suivantes: à, au bout de, à partir de, de, dès, en, pendant:*

(i) Saint Laurent sort sa griffe

Lorsque Christian Dior meurt brutalement _____ 1957, c'est son jeune disciple de 21 ans, Yves Saint Laurent, qui est désigné pour le remplacer.

Mais, _____ 1960, il est licencié par la prestigieuse maison. Le 4 décembre 1961, Yves Saint Laurent ouvre officiellement sa propre maison de couture. _____ la première collection, le 29 janvier suivant, le style Saint Laurent triomphe.

(ii) Le maître de l'antithéâtre

Samuel Beckett est né à Dublin _____ 1906, d'une famille aisée et puritaine. Il manifeste _____ l'adolescence son intérêt pour la littérature française. _____ 1928, séjournant à Paris comme lecteur d'anglais à l'École Normale Supérieure, il se dégagera progressivement du rigorisme et de la foi de son enfance. _____ 1938 _____ 1952 il publie sans succès des romans et des nouvelles. Plus heureux au théâtre, il s'impose à l'attention en France et dans le monde entier, avec *En attendant Godot*. L'ensemble de son oeuvre lui a valu le Prix Nobel _____ 1969.

(iii) Dandy et poète

Né à Paris _____ 1821, Charles Baudelaire était le fils d'un amateur de peinture. Mais sa mère, veuve _____ 1827, se remarie l'année suivante, et l'enfant, révolté par ce mariage, est mis en pension à Lyon. Ensuite, _____ trois ans Baudelaire mène au quartier latin la vie dissipée de la Bohème littéraire. Sa famille l'embarque à Bordeaux sur un voilier en partance pour les Indes, mais pris de nostalgie Baudelaire sera de retour _____ dix mois. _____ son retour Baudelaire exige sa part de l'héritage paternel et se lance dans l'existence dorée de la bohème riche, en écrivant déjà certains poèmes des *Fleurs du Mal*.

202 Prepositions: expressions of geographical place
(See S50b)

A *Translate into French:*

1. We've just spent a month in Switzerland and Luxembourg.
2. People living in Sussex were worried about their beaches.
3. Two prisoners have escaped in Caen.
4. There will be storms in Corsica and Provence.
5. Don't forget to phone them when you're in Brussels.
6. This product is selling well in Japan and the States.
7. The manuscripts are kept in Israel.

8. They're going camping in either Burgundy or the Limousin.

9. I've been posted to Denmark.

10. My parents spent the night at Le Lavandou.

11. The train will stop at Dover and London.

12. Most tourists who come to the United Kingdom stay for less than two weeks.

13. Each year there is a festival at Sarlat.

14. The brochure offers holiday homes in the Lot.

B *Compléter les blancs avec une des prépositions suivantes: à (avec ou sans article défini), dans, en, vers:*

(i) Un dirigeant de l'ETA arrêté

En mai, un des responsables présumés de l'ETA avait échappé de peu à une vaste opération menée _____ Bretagne, contre l'organisation séparatiste. Mais lundi _____ Bordeaux les policiers français ne l'ont pas manqué. Il aurait été le bras droit de l'ancien patron de l'ETA arrêté _____ France en mars.

(ii) Arrivée du super-tanker norvégien

Le super-tanker norvégien a accosté mardi _____ Havre après 15 jours de navigation _____ l'Atlantique et _____ Manche avec un gouvernail avarié. L'accident s'était produit alors que le navire retournait _____ Rotterdam avec 300.000 t de pétrole brut chargées _____ Arabie Saoudite.

(iii) Le pèlerinage des Béatitudes

Pas moins de 5.000 pèlerins sont attendus dès ce matin _____ Lisieux. Jusqu'à dimanche, ils participeront au pèlerinage organisé par la communauté des Béatitudes, près de Lisieux. La communauté compte aujourd'hui 600 membres répartis dans une trentaine de 'maisons' _____ France, mais également _____ Italie, _____ Maroc, _____ Israël et _____ Zaïre.

(iv) L'été en fêtes

Le 17 août _____ Quimper, la création d'un oratorio du Britannique Michael Tippett, sera l'un des événements de l'été musical français. Le grand contemporain de Messiaen et de Chostakovitch, mondialement reconnu, est presque ignoré _____ France. En réparant cette lacune, le festival de Quimper, éclaté _____ divers lieux de la cité, prouve qu'il n'est pas une simple étape dans la migration estivale des interprètes. *A Child*

463

of Our Time, écrite _____ Londres en 1940, c'est Bach au temps des fusées V2.

 ## 203 Compound prepositions before nouns

(See S51)

A *Translate into French:*

1. The bonus is calculated according to the sum invested.
2. This car has a higher performance compared to the others.
3. He started smoking without his parents knowing.
4. I had to buy apricots instead of the cherries.
5. The hospital is closed because of the earthquake.
6. The frontier between France and Italy has changed over the centuries.
7. According to their spokesperson, flights are delayed by six hours.
8. As Charles felt sick they stopped by the side of the road.
9. As for Louis XIV, France scarcely knew peace during his reign.
10. The new boutique has closed because of a lack of customers.
11. Temporary workers are paid at the rate of 50 francs an hour.
12. The museum has few twentieth-century paintings except for the one by Picasso.
13. The water was rising up to the first floor.
14. Thanks to your presence, the evening was a great success.
15. As from 1st January you will need to show your membership card.
16. The couple who live above our flat are very noisy.
17. We've taken a house opposite the park.
18. On the subject of your proposal, please would you complete the enclosed form?
19. The town council is going to plant palm trees along the promenade.
20. I didn't know how to react when faced with his refusal.

B *Compléter les blancs par une phrase prépositive:*

(i) LE GOUVERNEMENT BELGE ANNONCE DES IMPÔTS NOUVEAUX

L'an prochain les Belges verront leurs impôts directs augmenter _____ la suppression, pendant quatre ans, de l'indexation sur les prix des barèmes fiscaux. De nouveaux impôts frapperont, _____ 1er septembre, le fuel lourd et le gasoil de chauffage. Les impôts sur les sociétés productrices d'électricité seront également majorés. Cet alourdissement de la pression fiscale constitue, _____ le porte-parole du gouvernement belge, 'la contribution générale des citoyens à la convergence des finances publiques belges _____ la norme budgétaire européenne'. Le gouvernement s'est engagé à geler les dépenses publiques, _____ celles consacrées au service de la dette.

(excerpted from *Le Monde*)

(ii) LA PROTECTION SOCIALE DES INTERIMAIRES EST RENFORCEE

Cinq syndicats ont décidé de signer un accord cadre pour répondre aux préoccupations sociales des intérimaires avec les deux organisations professionnelles du travail temporaire. _____ protection sociale, les intérimaires ne bénéficiaient pas, _____ présent, d'une prévoyance collective élargie. Désormais, les deux tiers des fonds collectés _____ entreprises de travail temporaire serviront à traiter les conséquences des accidents de travail, de trajet, ou les maladies professionnelles survenues _____ missions.

(excerpted from *Le Monde*)

204 Prepositions governing verbs
(See S52)

A *Translate into French:*

1. When do you hope to see your publisher?
2. Instead of telling the truth, Robert let them believe his father was ill.
3. He won the election by promising not to devalue the franc.
4. The concierge will come and change the bulb.
5. I hesitate to ask you this favour.
6. Is this cottage available to rent?
7. Yesterday we spent three hours laying the carpet.
8. Did you hear them arrive?
9. 'Pizzas to take away'.
10. They ended up by asking her sister-in-law to lend them the money.
11. Mr Dassault is sorry not to be able to accept your invitation.
12. The armed robbers left without taking anything.
13. After reading the letter, she tore it up.
14. The management has forbidden him to speak to the reporters.
15. His mother nearly fainted on hearing the news.

16. I promised them I'd give an answer tomorrow.
17. After watching each other for several minutes, the dogs started to bark.
18. We helped them to move house.
19. I must draw out some money before I collect the car.
20. Teenagers generally prefer to go on holiday with their friends.

B *Compléter les blancs avec une préposition, ou mettre × s'il ne faut pas de préposition:*

Mardi prochain, lorsque vous trouverez Henriette en train ____ coudre ____ vous attendre, vous lui direz avant même qu'elle vous ait demandé quoi que ce soit:

'C'est uniquement pour Cécile que je suis allé à Rome cette fois-ci, pour lui prouver que je l'ai choisie définitivement contre toi, pour lui annoncer que j'ai enfin réussi ____ lui trouver une place à Paris, pour lui demander ____ venir afin qu'elle soit toujours avec moi, afin qu'elle me donne cette vie extraordinaire que tu n'as pas été capable ____ m'apporter et que moi non plus je n'ai pas su ____ t'offrir; je le reconnais, je suis coupable à ton égard, c'est entendu, je suis prêt ____ accepter, ____ approuver tous tes reproches, ____ me charger de toutes les fautes que tu voudras si cela peut t'aider le moins du monde ____ te consoler, ____ atténuer le choc.'

Mais vous savez bien qu'elle ne pleurera nullement, qu'elle se contentera ____ vous regarder sans proférer une parole, qu'elle vous laissera ____ discourir sans vous interrompre.

(excerpted from M. Butor, *La Modification*)

205 Interrogative sentences
(See S54)

A *Translate into French:*
(Give three translations for each sentence, to use each form of the interrogative.)

1. What time does the shop close?
2. Whom did you contact?
3. Is the Town Hall open?
4. Why did you stay so long?
5. Which make does your husband prefer?
6. Can I help myself to salad?

7. What are you giving her for her birthday?

8. When do the sales start?

9. How do you make mayonnaise?

10. Will she have received the letter yet?

B *Lire le texte suivant, puis rédiger des questions qui correspondent aux réponses fournies:*
(Pour chaque question, donner les trois formes interrogatives.)

Orso s'étant retiré dans sa chambre, Colomba envoya coucher Saveria et les bergers, et demeura seule dans la cuisine. De temps en temps elle prêtait l'oreille et paraissait attendre impatiemment que son frère fût couché. Lorsqu'elle le crut enfin endormi, elle prit un couteau, s'assura qu'il était tranchant, mit ses petits pieds dans de gros souliers, et, sans faire le moindre bruit, elle entra dans le jardin.

Colomba ouvrit la porte du jardin avec la même précaution, entra dans l'enclos, et en sifflant doucement elle attira près d'elle les chevaux, à qui elle portait souvent du pain et du sel. Dès que le cheval noir fut à sa portée, elle le saisit fortement par la crinière et lui fendit l'oreille avec son couteau. Le cheval fit un bond terrible et s'enfuit en faisant entendre ce cri aigu qu'une vive douleur arrache quelquefois aux animaux de son espèce. Satisfaite alors, Colomba rentrait dans le jardin, lorsque Orso ouvrit sa fenêtre.

(excerpted from P. Mérimée, *Colomba*)

1. _____
Dans sa chambre.
2. _____
Saveria et les bergers.
3. _____
Que son frère fût couché.
4. _____
Que le couteau était tranchant.
5. _____
Doucement.
6. _____
Le cheval noir.
7. _____
Parce qu'il avait ressenti une vive douleur.
8. _____
Oui, elle y rentrait.

206 Uses of inversion

(See S55)

A *Translate into French:*

1. Perhaps it would be better to say nothing.
2. The nuclear waste is more dangerous than the officials will admit.
3. 'I believe,' Corine continued, 'that the theft will soon be discovered.'
4. I return to the example which my colleague, the mayor of Lille, cited.
5. Doubtless you'll wish to think it over.
6. Nevertheless it is true that the homeless are a special case.
7. Thus one must conclude that this is a passing phenomenon.
8. The plane lost contact, it appears, with the control tower.
9. In vain we sought their help.
10. We've bought a flat nearer the office. Even so, it takes me 20 minutes to get there in the morning.
11. She didn't really understand, it seems, what she had been asked to do.
12. Scarcely had the storm started before the roof collapsed.

B *En introduisant dans le texte les locutions entre parenthèses, réécrivez les phrases où l'inversion est obligatoire ou préférable:*

MAUVAIS SOUVENIRS ET MALENTENDUS

Dans l'histoire des relations difficiles entre l'Espagne et la France, (peut-être) l'invasion napoléonienne de 1808 ouvre le bal des malentendus qui pèsent sur la mémoire collective.

(Sans doute) la mort du Caudillo, en 1975, qui permet a l'Espagne d'entamer un processus démocratique et de sortir du ghetto dans lequel l'avait enfermée le franquisme, est à l'origine d'une nouvelle incompréhension: les Espagnols n'admettent pas (il semble) l'extrême prudence de la France, et encore moins l'opposition à l'entrée de l'Espagne dans la CEE (que Paris manifestera rapidement). (En vain) les Espagnols reprochent à la France de ne pas s'investir vraiment dans la lutte contre les séparatistes basques de l'ETA, notamment en refusant de les extrader, comme si, (on regrette de l'autre côté des Pyrenées), l'Espagne n'était toujours pas un pays démocratique.

(excerpted from *Le Monde*)

468

207 Negation

(See S56)

A *Translate into French:*

1. Nobody remembers an unexpected noise.
2. You should see not the doctor but a physiotherapist.
3. He was afraid I would be angry.
4. They prefer not to be too late to bed.
5. It's three years since I last heard him play.
6. Nothing is worse for your back than a sedentary lifestyle.
7. He's got a motorbike, not a car.
8. The inspector did not doubt that the witness had lied.
9. There are only six guests left.
10. I did not dare to criticize them.
11. Never has a recession lasted so long.
12. There are more glasses than we need.
13. You haven't noticed any change?
14. Children are not admitted unless accompanied by their parents.
15. She reads better than she writes.
16. We've decided not to show the photos to anyone.

B *Compléter les blancs dans le texte suivant par une forme négative:*

'Madame,' dis-je avec une politesse et dignité, 'vous accordez l'honneur de votre visite _____ à un morveux _____ à un rustre, mais bien à un bibliothécaire assez heureux pour vous connaître, et qui sait que jadis vous mettiez le désordre et la gaieté dans la maison. Mais je vous croyais évanouie à _____ depuis trois siècles au moins. Se peut-il, madame, qu'on vous voie en ce temps de chemins de fer et de télégraphes? Ma concierge, qui fut nourrice en son temps, _____ sait _____ votre histoire, et mon petit voisin, que sa bonne mouche encore, affirme que vous _____ existez _____ .'

'Monsieur Sylvestre Bonnard,' me dit-elle, 'vous _____ êtes _____ un cuistre. Savoir _____ est _____ , imaginer est tout. _____ _____ existe que ce qu'on imagine. Je suis imaginaire. C'est exister, cela, je pense. On me rêve et je parais! Tout _____ est _____ rêve, et, puisque _____ _____ rêve de vous, Sylvestre Bonnard, c'est vous qui _____ existez _____ .'

(excerpted from A. France, *Le Crime de Sylvestre Bonnard*)

469

208 Key to exercises

152A

1. Mon grand-père, grand amateur d'huile d'olive, ne supportait pas la cuisine anglaise.
2. Nous avons rencontré de nouveaux problèmes.
3. Les groupes scolaires et les étudiants peuvent obtenir / bénéficier d'une réduction.
4. Le roquefort se fait à partir du lait de brebis.
5. Quelle perte d'argent!
6. Vous n'avez pas de places?
7. Ces femmes ont fait d'énormes sacrifices.
8. Vous êtes fonctionnaire?
9. Ajoutez du bon cognac au gâteau.
10. J'ai reçu diverses réponses.
11. La papeterie n'a plus de classeurs.
12. Certaines fouilles indiquent que c'était un forum romain.

152B

La, la, la, ×, ×, ×, ×, ×, une, l', les, une, Les, les, les, ×, Les, les, les, ×, ×, ×, ×, les, la, Les, les, ×, ×, le, les, les, les, une, le

153A

1. Le dimanche le boulanger n'est ouvert que le matin.
2. Fermez les yeux!
3. Nous avons quitté l'Allemagne / sommes partis d'Allemagne mercredi et nous sommes arrivés au Portugal vendredi.
4. Les Anglais aiment les vins pétillants.
5. Il regarda le vieux complet avec dédain.
6. Le fromage de chèvre fait / coûte combien le kilo?
7. La tolérance est une qualité rare.
8. Elle est douée d'une imagination incroyable.
9. En Israël la plupart des gens parlent hébreu et anglais.
10. Le roi François premier invita Léonard de Vinci à Amboise.
11. Il s'est cassé la jambe l'année dernière en faisant du ski.
12. Qu'est-ce que vous faites pour la Pentecôte?
13. La petite Anne aura deux ans en mai.
14. Le hongrois est une langue difficile.

153B

un, une, le, la, le, Le, l', Les, le, le, le, La, la, une, un, d'un, d'une, le

154A

1. Le journaliste a souligné la mauvaise qualité des jeux télévisés.
2. Tu as ta carte d'étudiant?
3. Il y a des chaises et des tables dans le jardin?
4. Le nombre des postes offerts aux chômeurs de longue durée a doublé.
5. Tu as mis trop d'ail et pas assez de citron.
6. Le rayon électro-ménager vend des sèche-cheveux.
7. Il me reste un litre du lait que nous avons acheté hier.
8. Le 14 juillet la rue était encombrée de voitures.
9. Le chef d'Etat vient de démissionner.
10. Je voudrais deux kilos des pommes là-bas.
11. Le traitement de texte s'apprend maintenant dans les écoles primaires.
12. La plage était couverte des algues que la marée haute avait apportées.

154B

(i) de la, des, de, de, d', de, de, du, de, de, de l', du, du, des, de l', de, des, de
(ii) de la, des, de, des, de l', de l'

155A

1. Les spaghettis à la tomate sont un plat italien.
2. Tu as invité les Mondon pour ce soir?
3. Il y a des travaux sur la Nationale 23.
4. *Le Monde* propose des articles de fond sur les problèmes internationaux.
5. Le 14 juillet il y a des bals dans les rues de Paris.
6. Les vitraux de la cathédrale de Chartres sont parmi les plus beaux d'Europe.
7. Dans les grands centres commerciaux on voit souvent des graffitis.
8. Le club 'Action 2000' se réunit dans ces locaux.
9. Il a fallu six sapeurs-pompiers pour maîtriser l'incendie.
10. Ils sont experts-comptables tous les deux.
11. Vous devez changer deux pneus.
12. Dans les basses-cours il y avait des oies et des paons.
13. Les enfants ramassaient des cailloux.
14. Où est-ce que tu as mis les tire-bouchons?
15. Au Moyen Age les châteaux forts étaient entourés de douves.

155B

Les plans d'aménagement conçus, redonnent aux sites leur authenticité, Tout ce que les voyageurs sont, confier leurs enfants aux halte-garderies, des zones spécifiques, des murs-promenades qui meurent, Lignes pures, matériaux légers, les prouesses techniques, des réseaux, les architectes-paysagistes espèrent

156A

1. Le parc zoologique a deux zèbres femelles.
2. Le nom de la victime n'a pas été révélé.
3. La pianiste jouait du Chopin.
4. Toutes les stagiaires ont obtenu un diplôme.
5. Madame le Professeur Martine Pasteur présidera la table ronde.
6. Les candidats se sont assis à droite, les candidates à gauche.
7. La personne à qui j'ai parlé avait un chapeau bleu.
8. Les cochons d'Inde mâles sont plus agressifs.
9. Les nouvelles recrues attendent dans la cour.
10. Il n'y a qu'une femme ingénieur dans la compagnie.
11. La sentinelle s'est réveillée en sursaut.
12. On avait séparé les cerfs et les biches.

156B

(i) une, un, connus, internationaux, directrice, une, la
(ii) comédienne, un, un, excellent, un, une, aînée, une, une

157A

1. Quelle est sa langue maternelle, le portugais ou le grec?
2. Le concombre peut être indigeste.
3. La reine a visité le Japon, la Nouvelle Zélande et le Mexique.
4. Ils ont dû abattre tous les ormes.
5. Le phosphate et le calcium sont des minéraux essentiels.
6. Pour cette recette j'ai besoin d'un chou, d'une carotte et d'un navet.
7. L'automne est plus doux dans le sud-ouest.
8. Le granit est une pierre très difficile à travailler.
9. La vigne a été tuée par la neige.
10. Le vendredi je finis à 14 heures.
11. Le diamant était entouré d'une émeraude et d'un rubis.
12. Le Cambodge a annoncé un cessez-le-feu.

157B

un, la, le, une, une, un, la, le, un, un, le, le

158A

1. L'espion portrait des lunettes noires.
2. Pendant les vacances ma soeur fait du babysitting pour gagner de l'argent.
3. Le chat était installé dans le fauteuil.
4. Le hibou chassait une souris.
5. C'est un bijou très rare.
6. Son conseil m'a aidé.
7. Pour ce gâteau il vous faut deux poires bien mûres et du chocolat noir.
8. Un troisième assassinat / attentat a été commis à New York.
9. J'ai la peau très sensible.

10. Quelqu'un a volé son sac.
11. L'oiseau avait une aile cassée.
12. Tu as oublié de nouer tes lacets.
13. Le rôle de ce syndicat dépend de l'avenir du socialisme.
14. Le trottoir était jonché de feuilles mouillées.

158B

le, un, un tel, un nouveau, une, excellente, Le, une, facultatifs, petits, ruraux, du, nombreux, le, tout

159A

1. Le reportage d'Antenne 2 sur le Sudan était excellent.
2. La lettre est dans le dossier.
3. Vous pouvez parler à Madame Lefèvre au téléphone?
4. L'index est à la page 78.
5. La carrière du ministre a été détruite par le suicide de son frère.
6. Expliquez-moi le problème.
7. Il y a une erreur dans le dernier paragraphe.
8. La France a la forme d'un hexagone irrégulier.
9. La première image du livre représentait un château.
10. Le lait et la crème ont tourné.
11. Elle habite un petit village et son fils doit aller au collège en vélo.
12. Jusqu'à une époque récente la viande était interdite pendant le Carême.
13. Les scientifiques ont observé / constaté un phénomène étrange.
14. Où est le siège du parlement européen?

159B

le fameux, le, du, le, un, le, la, le, lequel, la, verts, tous, Cet, premiers, tout, un, un, toute, une

160A

1. La craie blanche des falaises lointaines était à peine visible.
2. La disparition de plusieurs métiers traditionnels a changé ce quartier de Paris.
3. Demain il y aura du verglas dans le nord.
4. Est-ce que tu as vu le film *Les Liaisons Dangereuses*?
5. Dans le domaine de la religion, les adolescents ont été plus actifs.
6. Son ignorance était choquante.
7. Au village de vacances on peut faire de la natation et bénéficier d'une initiation au ski nautique.
8. Le programme pour les cours d'anglais semble trop léger.
9. Le retard a causé / a été la cause d'une nouvelle inquiétude.
10. Rome était / été un bastion de la civilisation chrétienne.
11. Il a la fâcheuse tendance de poser des questions superflues.
12. Le loup a disparu sans laisser la moindre trace.

13. Le groupe de touristes regardait les danses grecques avec une telle admiration.
14. Ce texte résiste à une traduction littérale.

160B

un, professionnelle, révélatrice, une, familiale, le, son, la, le, exercé, revendus, de la, une, spécialisée, le, le, exclusif, le, de la, petite, la / une, la / une

161A

1. Combien de foyers ont un ordinateur personnel?
2. Les Siciliens craignent le déshonneur plus que la mort.
3. Le café avait de vieilles photos de certains acteurs célèbres.
4. Plougastel produit une excellente liqueur de fraise.
5. Est-ce que je dois m'adresser au percepteur ou au receveur d'impôts?
6. Par arrêté ministériel, les marchés aux fleurs sont permis le dimanche.
7. La qualité la plus rare est la discrétion.
8. Sa mère leur a offert un aspirateur pour Noël.
9. Il faut jeter le dé avant de prendre une carte.
10. Dans sa vie privée, Simone Signoret a connu et le bonheur et le malheur.
11. Les chroniqueurs médiévaux étaient / ont été surpris par la grandeur de la ville.
12. A la vérité, le comité n'aurait pas dû ratifier le traité.

161B

grands, petits, impressionnantes, étrangers, la, la, un, certaines, grands, chacun, le, le, un, la, la, la

162A

1. Il y avait une photo du camping dans la brochure.
2. J'ai oublié mon parapluie et mon sac dans le bus.
3. Ce gîte n'est pas sur ma liste.
4. Le personnage principal a dû parler dans tous les actes de la pièce.
5. Elle a mis le linge à sécher sur la corde.
6. Est-ce que je dois envoyer la lettre à votre adresse personnelle?
7. Je suis au régime, alors je ne peux manger que les légumes verts et la viande.
8. Un mariage sur trois aboutit au divorce.
9. Je regarderai dans les petites annonces pour les voitures d'occasion.
10. Ils ont dû fermer le laboratoire à cause du risque de fuite du plutonium.
11. Ne verse pas trop d'eau minérale dans mon verre.
12. Est-ce que vous avez le nouvel horaire des trains?
13. Les consignes de sécurité étaient très précises.
14. Il avait oublié le code secret pour ouvrir le coffre.
15. Le magazine avait publié un article sur la naissance de la princesse.
16. Nous avons le choix entre un poste de télévision et une machine à laver.

162B

le, celui, Tous, meilleurs, une, heureuse, la, la, Le, dépourvu, toute, publique, le, Le, la, prises, Le, chères

163A

1. Cette fois-ci nous choisirons un endroit plus calme.
2. Quel est le prix d'un aller simple?
3. Notre chambre donnait sur la cour.
4. Rachel a percé sa première dent hier.
5. Selon la loi, il est interdit de fumer dans le métro.
6. Mon nouvel appartement est près du Louvre.
7. Charles a vendu un entrepôt après la mort de son père.
8. Est-ce que tu voudrais un thé ou une boisson froide?
9. Je ne peux pas réviser pour tous les examens.
10. Est-ce que tu sais la vraie raison pour laquelle ils ne viennent pas?
11. L'Ancien Testament est surtout l'histoire de la religion juive.
12. Quand est-ce qu'on a construit la Tour Eiffel?

163B

(i) la, refusées, la, la, la, la, humaine, un, ce, glacé, la / une, la, toutes, le, la
(ii) Une, le, entière, une, printanière, douce, la / une, dorée, bleus, le, le / un, irréelle, le, la, une

164A

1. Elle s'est acheté un pied-à-terre à Budapest.
2. La main-d'oeuvre a accepté les nouvelles conditions de travail.
3. Est-ce que La Joconde est le chef-d'oeuvre de Léonard de Vinci?
4. Il y avait une chauve-souris dans le grenier.
5. La rentabilité est le mot-clé de cette décennie.
6. Son ex-fiancée a été invitée aussi.
7. Est-ce que le rayon de papeterie est au rez-de-chaussée ou au sous-sol?
8. Je ne mange pas les petits pois ni le chou-fleur.
9. Pourquoi as-tu mis le tire-bouchon dans le lave-vaisselle?
10. Nous avons fait du lèche-vitrine dans le centre-ville.
11. Ma belle-mère a acheté un cerf-volant pour les enfants.
12. La sous-location est interdite selon le contrat.

164B

(i) Le / Un
(ii) complète, Un / Le, proposé
(iii) un, un, petit, intégré
(iv) le, Une
(v) le

165A

1. *Le Père Goriot* est une des oeuvres les plus connues de Balzac.
2. Est-ce qu'on devrait donner un pourboire au guide?
3. Le critique a donné son verdict à son tour.
4. J'ai voulu vous offrir un petit quelque chose pour vous remercier.
5. J'ai payé une somme folle pour ce tableau.
6. Personne ne s'est arrêté pour les aider.
7. Mettez les fleurs dans le vase bleu.
8. Tous les gens / Toutes les personnes à qui nous avons parlé étaient des touristes.
9. Dans la cuisine ils ont trouvé un vieux poêle et une pendule qui ne marchait plus.
10. Ne mange que les moules ouvertes.
11. Les jupes longues sont revenues à la mode.
12. Les gens étaient / ont été émus par la tragédie.

165B

(i) vert, **(ii)** La, **(iii)** la, **(iv)** délicieuses, **(v)** connues, un, **(vi)** le, anciennes, la

166A

1. Les exercices navals commenceront demain.
2. Ce sont des chaussures toutes neuves.
3. Le nouvel hôtel se trouve près des jardins municipaux.
4. Sa fortune personnelle est estimée à 30 millions.
5. Les élèves doivent porter une jupe et un pullover marron.
6. L'opinion publique n'a guère changé.
7. Tournez à droite, puis continuez tout droit jusqu'à l'église.
8. La marine grecque et l'armée turque s'entraînent.
9. J'ai un vieil oncle qui habite à Toulouse.
10. Tes vêtements sont tout mouillés.
11. Les pays orientaux sont la destination préférée des jeunes cette année.
12. Nous ne vendons pas de demi-bouteilles.
13. Je cherche une veste vert clair.
14. Veux-tu laisser les fenêtres grandes ouvertes?

166B

survenus, sociales, engagées, prônées, communaux, locales, quels, politique, banalisée, mis, publiques, sociales, française, sociales, persistante, sociales, urbaine, musicales, effective, centres, premiers, grands, situés, spatiale

167A

1. A votre avis, est-ce que de Gaulle a été un grand homme d'état?
2. Les vignobles sont restés dans la même famille jusqu'à la quinzième génération.
3. Nous avons eu un hiver exceptionnellement froid et sec.

4. Cette brève rencontre à Bruges, c'est la dernière fois qu'ils se sont vus.
5. Il portait une cravate marron et un pantalon blanc.
6. Dans un petit placard sale nous avons trouvé de vrais trésors.
7. Le pauvre chien se cache sous le lit quand il y a un orage.
8. C'est un jardin vraiment énorme.
9. Il s'agit de la sécurité publique.
10. Dans le Quartier Latin il y a beaucoup de restaurants italiens et grecs.
11. Ça fait une promenade trop longue pour les enfants.
12. Les Tourettes est un si bel endroit.
13. Dans une grande avenue bordée de peupliers se dressait une statue de Napoléon.
14. C'est un roman bien écrit et passionnant.

167B

le luxe suprême, Le petit bourg, sa célèbre rade / sa rade célèbre, de sublimes yachts / des yachts sublimes, les maisons victoriennes, l'esbroufe tropézienne, la frime cannoise, ses pinèdes centenaires, des épaisses haies, des parcs gorgés, fleurs rares, leurs prestigieuses demeures / leurs demeures prestigieuses, d'une végétation luxuriante, de la légère brume, les systèmes d'arrosage automatiques

168A

1. Cette affiche est pire que l'autre.
2. Elle est aussi distraite que son frère.
3. Est-ce que tu as vu les plus grandes villas?
4. Je ne peux pas accepter ce devis. Il est encore pire!
5. Le climat à Nice est tellement plus doux qu'à Paris.
6. C'est l'autoroute la plus mauvaise que je connaisse.
7. Est-ce que la banlieue est aussi bruyante que la ville?
8. C'est la meilleure pianiste que j'aie jamais entendue.
9. Le jeune lapin est plus petit que le cochon d'Inde.
10. Ce film n'est pas si amusant / drôle que le dernier.
11. Il abandonnera le projet si le moindre obstacle se présente.
12. Les prix de l'immobilier sur la côte d'Azur sont les plus chers de France.
13. Le chiffre d'affaires est meilleur que celui de l'année dernière.
14. Ces exemples de l'art de la Renaissance sont d'une moindre importance.

168B

les plus pervers, les plus désaltérantes, les plus symboliques, au pire / au plus mauvais, les moindres règles, du plus nouveau, le plus fort, les plus insomniaques, le goût le plus détestable, le meilleur thé

169A

1. Ces couteaux et ces cuillères appartenaient à ma grand-mère.
2. Qui est son avocat?
3. Cet appareil ménager ne consomme pas beaucoup d'électricité.

4. Ils ont laissé leur voiture et leurs vélos chez nous.
5. Ce hibou habite ici depuis deux ans.
6. Tu t'es blessé à la main? / Tu t'es fait mal à la main?
7. Cette loi ne s'applique qu'à ceux qui résident en France.
8. Je me suis tordu la cheville.
9. Cet hélicoptère-là est sur le point d'atterrir.
10. C'est son sac à lui? Non, c'est à elle.
11. Ce train-ci s'arrête à Orléans, mais celui-là est direct.
12. Il collectionne les timbres, alors il en connaît la valeur.
13. Donnez-moi vos noms et votre adresse.
14. Ma tante et mon oncle sont en Grèce.
15. Son attitude positive m'a aidé.

169B
sa, sa, son, ces, ces, ses, sa, sa, ses

170A
1. Ils n'ont pas encore nommé son successeur.
2. Je ne suis pas suffisamment au courant de ce projet.
3. La décision sera prise indépendamment.
4. Sinon, tu pourrais annuler la réservation.
5. J'essayerai de vous expliquer brièvement le système.
6. Paradoxalement, il regrette son départ maintenant.
7. Peut-être que vous feriez mieux de nous rappeler demain?
8. Nous étions profondément choqués par votre comportement.
9. Nous avons cherché la lettre partout.
10. Il s'est mal préparé.
11. Heureusement que mon père était à la maison.
12. Ils se sont amusés énormément.
13. Il écoutait l'histoire patiemment.

170B
régulièrement espacées, Coupez finement, Disposez soigneusement, finalement arrosez, faites cuire le bar doucement, pas directement

171A
1. Vous feriez mieux de prendre un vol régulier.
2. Plus on apprend, plus on oublie.
3. Quand est-ce que vous avez commencé à vous sentir plus mal?
4. Les étudiants travaillent beaucoup plus dur avant les examens.
5. Je ne gagne pas autant que l'année dernière.
6. Plus tu feras du ski, plus tu seras en forme.
7. Il n'a pas maîtrisé le système aussi bien que toi.
8. Ils ont réparé le mur aussi bien que possible / du mieux qu'ils pouvaient.
9. Tu sauras mieux que lui.
10. Si tu veux faire des progrès tu devras réviser davantage.

11. Moins j'y pense, moins ça m'embête.
12. Je n'ai pas l'occasion de les voir aussi souvent que je le voudrais.
13. Tant pis si tu as une autre réunion.
14. Venez nous voir le plus souvent possible.

171B
1. davantage
2. aussi, que
3. mieux
4. Plus, plus
5. aussi / si, que
6. Plus, plus

172A
1. Je dois le faire. Je le lui ai promis.
2. Pourquoi est-ce que vous leur avez envoyé une carte?
3. Tu aimes les meubles? Ils sont nouveaux.
4. Ne prends pas cette valise. C'est trop lourde / Elle est trop lourde.
5. Je voudrais leur en parler.
6. Tu sais qu'elle possède des meubles anciens. Elle nous les a montrés.
7. On va construire des immeubles. Ce seront des HLM.
8. Où sont les clés? Elles sont dans la voiture.
9. Qu'est-ce qui se passe si un inspecteur vous arrête?
10. Laisse-la tranquille. Elle est fatiguée.
11. Nous passons quatre nuits à St Paul. C'est un village médiéval.
12. Ils ont suggéré un pique-nique. Qu'est-ce que tu en penses?
13. On m'envoie à Genève. Tu y es allé? / Tu connais?
14. On se perd dans le centre-ville.
15. Je fais des pommes de terre. Combien est-ce que tu en mangeras?
16. Va-t'en! / Allez-vous-en!
17. Ne t'en fais pas. Je m'occuperai de toi.
18. Il trouvait bizarre que nous ayons changé de banque.
19. Je vais me faire couper les cheveux.
20. Ne les mets pas dans la poubelle.

172B
je l'ai très bien connue, de le mettre noir sur blanc, elle n'y a jamais fait allusion, elle y était allée, elle ne les aimait guère, l'ont probablement mal accueillie, doit en venir, s'en occuper, il y avait vécu, les fit se rencontrer, lui plut, en fut séduit, l'y rencontrer, et à se la partager

173A
1. Comme toi / vous, je préfère envoyer un fax si c'est urgent.
2. Je pensais à vous deux hier.
3. Toi et moi, nous avons les mêmes goûts.
4. 'Chacun pour soi', c'est la société de nos jours / la société actuelle.

5. Claire et Véronique ont tapissé le salon elles-mêmes / C'est Claire et Véronique qui ont tapissé le salon.
6. C'étaient eux qui se sont trompés / ont fait l'erreur la première fois.
7. Moi, je serais parti, mais je sais que lui, il serait resté.
8. Nous préférons voir les clients nous-mêmes.
9. Tu sauras expliquer mieux que lui.
10. Qui peut aller à pied? Elle et moi.
11. Est-ce que les stagiaires peuvent partir, ou vous aurez besoin d'eux plus tard?
12. Eux, ils ne disent même pas bonjour.
13. Tout le monde devrait avoir un crayon sur soi.
14. Toi et ton voisin, vous vous entendez bien?
15. Alain et Huguette ont beaucoup d'expérience. Vous pouvez compter sur eux.
16. Si Emilie est absente, je devrai faire appel à toi.
17. Personne ne peut tout faire soi-même / tout seul.
18. C'est toi qui as appelé ce soir?
19. Le vélo est à qui, à toi ou à elle?
20. Lui et ma soeur se connaissent depuis des années.

173B
(i) Vitardo, lui; Moi, je; Nous, on; Louis, lui; La voiture, elle; Vous, vous; Moi, j'espère; Vous, vous; nous, nous; Vitardo, lui; Martine et lui, eux
(ii) le, s'il, lui, le, il, le, lui, lui, lui, le, lui, le, le, lui, Il, il, lui, l'

174A
1. Est-ce que vous empruntez la remorque de vos voisins? Non, la leur est trop petite, c'est la nôtre.
2. Ceci me semble la question la plus importante.
3. Le bois a pourri. C'est à cause de l'humidité.
4. Nous ne ferons pas un mailing. Ça / Cela ne vaut pas la peine.
5. Est-ce que c'est ton sac? Non, c'est le sien / c'est à elle.
6. Il est difficile de donner une réponse exacte.
7. Je passerai plus tard si ça / cela t'arrange mieux.
8. C'est l'année dernière qu'ils ont fait faillite.
9. Je ne peux pas venir. C'est impossible.
10. Ce sont tes frères dans la photo?
11. Ma machine à laver ne marche pas. Je pourrais utiliser la tienne?
12. Il est neuf heures moins le quart.
13. J'aime tous ses films, surtout ceux des années cinquante.
14. Ce qui m'étonne, ce n'est pas son attitude.
15. Ce ne fut pas / Ce n'est pas sans émotion qu'ils se quittèrent / qu'ils se sont séparés.
16. Nous avons interviewé vingt hôtesses de l'air. Celles qui travaillaient à temps partiel gagnaient moins.

17. Tu vois ce balcon? C'est mon appartement.
18. Nous ne savons pas qui va prendre la préretraite. C'est toujours à décider.
19. C'est demain que l'agent immobilier doit inspecter la maison?
20. Il est regrettable qu'il ne nous ait pas contactés plus tôt.

174B

il, celui, C', elle, celles, c', c', ceux, c', celui, celle, Il

175A

1. Est-ce que tu connais la femme dont il t'a donné l'adresse?
2. Ce que tu disais hier m'a fait changer d'avis.
3. Les questions que j'ai posées ont semblé / semblaient la surprendre.
4. Un matin qu'il faisait beau nous sommes partis de bonne heure.
5. On passe le film dont nous parlions.
6. La voiture à côté de laquelle il s'est garé avait un pneu crevé.
7. Je veux savoir ce que vous faites tous.
8. Voici la pièce de rechange dont j'avais besoin.
9. Les chiffres qu'il a utilisés étaient très récents.
10. La personne à qui vous avez parlé s'est trompée.
11. Les valises que nous avons perdues étaient vieilles en tout cas / de toute façon.
12. J'étais sur le point de sortir / partir au moment où la lettre est arrivée.
13. Le bâtiment vers lequel ils se dirigeaient était un ancien prieuré.
14. C'est la femme dont nous avons vu la photo dans le journal.
15. Ce qui m'inquiète, c'est qu'elle ne sait pas nager.
16. Les papiers qui sont sur la table sont confidentiels.
17. La carte est valable pour six mois seulement, ce que je n'ai jamais compris.
18. C'est la raison pour laquelle nous ne nous servons pas de la cave.
19. Les amis avec qui je fais du yoga viennent dîner ce soir.
20. Ils seront six, ce qui complique les choses.

175B

(i) qui, qu', que, que, qui, que, que, qui, qui, que, dont
(ii) que, que, que, ce qui, lequel, ce qui, qui, ce qu'

176A

1. Plusieurs parmi les nouveaux employés ont déjà reçu une prime.
2. Qu'est-ce que les enfants font à midi? Quelques-uns mangent à la cantine, d'autres rentrent chez eux.
3. Les deux frères ont très peu de contact l'un avec l'autre / se voient très peu.
4. Quelque chose de merveilleux est arrivé!
5. Elle a trois filles et chacune a eu des problèmes de santé.

6. Le chantier est interdit à quiconque ne porte pas / tous ceux qui ne portent pas de casque de sécurité.
7. Divers employés sont mécontents. J'en ai interviewé quelques-uns hier.
8. Mon collègue est quelqu'un de très timide.
9. Certains automobilistes prennent l'autoroute, d'autres préfèrent la route touristique.
10. Non, ceci ne passe pas / ça ne va pas. Tu auras besoin d'autre chose.
11. Tu veux des chaises pliantes? Nous en avons plusieurs dans le grenier.
12. Peut-être que quelqu'un d'autre a utilisé la photocopieuse.
13. Il est généreux, il est toujours prêt à aider autrui.
14. Le professeur n'a pas dit grand-chose.

176B
1. Quiconque
2. d'autres
3. Chacun
4. autrui
5. certaines / plusieurs
6. Quelqu'un
7. grand-chose
8. les uns, les autres / certains, d'autres

177A
1. Il existait plusieurs espèces de ce reptile.
2. Il se trouvait que nous avions besoin d'une nouvelle voiture.
3. Dans la pièce il s'agit d'une jeune fille qui arrive à New York.
4. Il y a eu deux accidents cette semaine.
5. Pour changer le numéro d'immatriculation d'une voiture, il faut contacter la préfecture.
6. Dans le passé il arrivait souvent que les fils étaient apprentis / mis en apprentissage dès l'âge de 14 ans.
7. Il a gelé hier soir / pendant la nuit.
8. De quoi s'agit-il?
9. Il fait un temps d'automne aujourd'hui.
10. Il se peut que nous ayons un changement de personnel.
11. Il en résulte / Il en découle / Il s'ensuit que nous ne pourrons plus financer cette opération.
12. Il vaudrait mieux répondre par écrit.

177B
1. Les étudiants doivent fermer à clé . . .
2. Nous vous rappelons qu'aucun prélèvement sur bourse n'est affectué.
3. On ne doit pas fumer dans la zone non-fumeur.
4. Nous vous conseillons de . . .
5. On ne doit pas marcher sur la pelouse.

178A

1. Leili et moi, nous nous marions au mois d'août.
2. Il y avait plusieurs groupes, dont chacun portait un drapeau.
3. Un assez grand nombre des stagiaires avaient travaillé pour une chaîne de télévision.
4. Seuls les employés et leurs enfants seront admis. / L'entrée est réservée aux employés et à leurs enfants.
5. La PDG ou sa secrétaire vous contactera.
6. La société a ouvert une succursale à Rouen.
7. La plupart des maisons ont été détruites pendant la guerre.
8. Toi et ton frère, qu'est-ce que vous faites?
9. 'Le Casino' et 'le Manoir' sont tous les deux des hôtels de luxe.
10. La plupart / Le plus grand nombre / La majorité des visiteurs d'EuroDisney étaient des étrangers.
11. La plupart des postes laissés vacants seront supprimés.

178B

(i) est, rejette, obligent, consomme, ont produit, est, envahit, représentent, provoque, proviennent
(ii) dorment, dépensent, consacrent, passent, a vu, vont, logent, traversent, ont, dénombrait

179A

1. Le rôle d'Hamlet a été interprété / était interprété par Michel Sourdin.
2. La maison avait été détruite par un incendie en 1756.
3. Les lettres seront publiées dans le journal de demain.
4. Nous avons été dérangés par le même bruit.
5. La lettre aurait été envoyée à votre adresse à Paris.
6. L'enfant a été retrouvé un peu avant minuit.
7. On nous a demandé d'assister à la réception.
8. Le nouveau stagiaire s'est fait renvoyer au bout de deux jours.
9. Ce produit se vend dans tous les hypermarchés Rallye.
10. Il est interdit de fumer dans le bâtiment.
11. Ça ne se fait pas en France.
12. On vous enverra un contrat la semaine prochaine.

179B

(i) sera mis en place, ont été prévus, seront informés, seront mobilisés
(ii) ont été inculpés, ont été prononcées, soient remis, a été suspendu
(iii) on a arrêté Serge Badinter, s'est fait inculper, s'est laissé ligoter et dévaliser, on a retrouvé les chèques

180A

1. Nous agaçons la personne là-bas.
2. Pourquoi est-ce que tu cours / vous courez?
3. Si tu rouvres la porte, je rangerai les dossiers.

4. Ils enlèvent les chaises.

5. Ce que vous dites est incroyable!

6. Quand nous lançons la balle, le chien nous la ramène.

7. Quand tu t'assois / assieds, le chat va venir sur tes genoux.

8. Qu'est ce que vous achetez pour demain?

9. Ça s'appelle comment? / Comment est-ce que cela s'appelle?

10. Lequel est-ce que vous préférez tous les deux?

11. Dis-moi s'il te rend le livre.

12. Les Normands boivent du cidre aux repas.

13. Je reçois une prime deux fois par an.

14. Tu crois qu'il exagère?

15. Tu te sens mieux aujourd'hui, David?

16. Les bijoux valent plus que les tableaux.

17. Vous prenez combien de sucres, Madame Meunier?

18. La jeune fille au pair nettoie la cuisine le vendredi.

180B

(i) rentrons, préfère, se sent, nous tenons, marche, jette, dépassent, décident, balancent, rient, font, déteste, dit, sait, détestent, prend, crie, accroît

(ii) est, règle, demande, attend, est, procurent, doit, vois, mets, donne, devient, ouvre, bascule, s'installe, tend, dit

181A

1. Tu t'es lavé les cheveux, Sophie?

2. Les gens à qui j'ai parlé nous ont dit de tourner à droite.

3. Les cygnes se sont envolés.

4. Les numéros que vous avez demandés sont occupés.

5. Où sont les clés? Tu les as oubliées dans la voiture?

6. L'avion a atterri à huit heures.

7. Quelle robe avez-vous choisie?

8. Nous nous sommes perdus à Angers.

9. Ma secrétaire leur a envoyé un fax hier.

10. Les sculptures que nous avons vues étaient exposées dans le jardin public.

11. Tu as toujours les jumelles? Non, je les ai rendues à François.

12. Martine s'est cassé la jambe en faisant du ski.

13. Tu sais qu'il y a eu une explosion? Oui, on en a parlé ce matin à la radio.

14. Le cheval est tombé dans un fossé.

15. Est-ce que vous avez sorti les géraniums?

16. Les échantillons que vous avez fournis sont trop petits.

17. Mon grand-père a beaucoup vieilli cette année.

18. Elle a monté l'escalier toute seule.

19. Quels vins est-ce que vous avez goûtés à Saint-Emilion?

20. Ils sont entrés par la porte de la cuisine.

181B

(i) j'ai fait, a tiré, m'a présenté, a giclé, a coulé, a recouvertes, a vacillé, a charrié, m'a semblé, s'est tendu, j'ai crispé, a cédé, j'ai touché, a commencé

(ii) a inventé, a consacré, a salué, a promené, a découvert, a lancé, a pénétré, s'est amarré, a fait, ont séjourné, se sont installés, est descendue, a commencé, s'est baignée, est tombée, s'est installée, a stigmatisé, s'est fâchée, l'a doté

182A

1. Elle rentra de la gare à pied.
2. Nous nous écrivîmes deux fois.
3. Les cousins rougirent.
4. Ils firent réparer la voiture.
5. Nous nous arrêtâmes devant la mairie.
6. Je vendis la ferme à la fin de la guerre.
7. Elle ouvrit les yeux, étonnée.
8. Il répondit, distrait
9. Je fermai la porte doucement.
10. Elle rendit le journal à son voisin.
11. Ils s'assirent à côté de la fenêtre.
12. Il repeignit le garage.
13. Nous revînmes au début de mai.
14. Ils jetèrent un regard / regardèrent par la fenêtre.
15. Il lui tint la main.
16. Nous ouvrîmes un petit magasin à Bordeaux.
17. Je choisis le premier livre.
18. Ils descendirent par le sentier étroit.
19. Elle mourut à Biarritz.
20. Ils finirent de parler en même temps.

182B

(i) se produisit, grossit, absorbèrent, furent, vit, fit, baissèrent, cessa, passèrent

(ii) exigea, dit, courut, fit, prit, fis, suivis, hâta, sentit, cravacha, lança, me mis, fit, laissa, mit

183A

1. La ville a été / fut détruite en 1942.
2. Comme je commençais à écrire, le téléphone a sonné / sonna.
3. Le jeune Proust lisait pendant des heures.
4. Le champ était entouré d'un fossé.
5. Nous déjeunions ensemble chaque jeudi.
6. Comme il se levait il remarqua / a remarqué le trou.
7. L'après-midi il faisait même plus chaud.
8. Quand nous étions étudiants, nous allions régulièrement au théâtre.

9. Ils chargeaient la voiture avant de partir.
10. Les cambrioleurs ont été / furent arrêtés par la police.
11. Pendant que les soldats assiégeaient le château, les habitants se sont réfugiés / se réfugièrent dans les caves.
12. Elle a été / fut blessée au cours du match.

183B

(i) j'avais, voulais, étaient, fallait, j'allais, venait, j'étais, bossais, j'ai eu, j'ai plaqué
(ii) rencontrai, fut, prenais, passait, fallait, était, chantonnait, j'eus, vis, me jetai, sourit

184A

1. Après que les visiteurs furent partis / Après le départ des visiteurs, le comte se versa un grand whisky.
2. Le dentiste a demandé un autre exemplaire de la brochure que vous lui aviez envoyée.
3. Ils s'étaient décidés à se plaindre auprès du garage.
4. Nous nous installâmes à Marseille quelques mois après que j'eus fermé le bureau à Paris.
5. La galerie exposait les nouveaux tableaux qu'elle avait achetés.
6. Dès qu'elle se fut rendue compte du danger, elle rentra téléphoner à la police.
7. Je voulais vérifier que je ne m'étais pas trompé.
8. A peine la vieille dame fut-elle morte que ses neveux vendirent la ferme.
9. Nous nous rappelâmes que nous avions oublié d'éteindre les lumières.
10. Dès qu'elle eut payé la facture, elle commença à s'inquiéter.
11. Je n'avais pas regardé mon courrier lorsque tu m'as téléphoné.
12. A peine se furent-ils endormis qu'une voiture démarra.

184B

(i) descendit, s'arrêta, avait apporté / apportait, avait paru, avaient été, étaient parties, était, voyageait, saisit, procura, oublia, se tint, se souvint, y avait / il y avait eu, avait été, avait fallu
(ii) avait paralysé, avaient été installés, avait parié, s'étaient effilochés, était intervenu, n'avait pas employé

185A

1. Quand vous serez au Mexique, nous ferons suivre votre courrier?
2. Dans cinq ans les investissements vaudront un million.
3. Quand vous arriverez à l'aéroport, vous irez / allez au sous-sol, et ma secrétaire vous donnera les clés.
4. Je saurai si j'ai le poste lundi.
5. Quelqu'un a pris la voiture. Ce sera Thierry.
6. Ce weekend il pleuvra presque tout le temps.

7. Une fois que vous aurez essayé le logiciel, nous parlerons des nouvelles bases de données.

8. On sonne à la porte. Ce sera le facteur.

9. Quand les enfants partiront / seront partis en vacances, nous ferons de la planche à voile.

10. Les plantes mourront si la sécheresse continue.

11. Le chien courra au bout du champ.

12. Vous m'enverrez automatiquement un devis?

13. Venez nous voir la semaine prochaine quand vous aurez le temps.

14. J'hériterai des actions de mon oncle.

185B(i)

Cancer: échapperez, serez, pimenterez, accuseront, aurez
Poissons: irez, imposeront, vous sentirez, arriverez

185B(ii)

1. seront, se produiront, faiblira

2. fera, se formeront, dissipera, se détacheront, sera

3. sera, pleuvra, fera

186A

1. Je préfère conduire une voiture automatique.

2. Après avoir lu l'article, il a téléphoné à son avocat.

3. Lancer un nouveau produit est difficile pendant une récession.

4. A dire vrai, David nous fait des soucis.

5. Pour louer une voiture, vous avez besoin de votre permis.

6. Oui, mais où trouver une nouvelle voiture au même prix?

7. J'ai envie de prendre un jour de congé.

8. Protéger le littoral, c'est la priorité de la région.

9. A lire la presse locale, on dirait que tous les propriétaires sont malhonnêtes.

10. Après avoir terminé ses études, elle est allée travailler aux Etats-Unis.

11. En supprimant cette allocation, le gouverment fera des économies.

12. Il a élevé les enfants seul tout en travaillant.

13. Avant de quitter l'Italie, pourquoi pas acheter une paire de chaussures en cuir?

14. Je le regardais garer la voiture.

15. Ils quittèrent l'autoroute, prenant la direction de Soissons.

16. Pourquoi vendre / se débarrasser de ce bâtiment?

17. Le surveillant de plage / de piscine, voyant un enfant en difficulté, entra dans l'eau.

18. Après s'être longuement regardés, les chiens se reniflèrent.

19. Leur demander un service? Jamais!

20. J'ai fait changer la date.

186B(i)

Bénéficier, perdant, venus, avoir appelé, déclinant, de s'adapter, promettant, Pour épauler / épaulant, multipliant, nommé

186B(ii)

1. traversant le parc national de la Vanoise
2. avoir interdit l'intérieur de la zone centrale du parc
3. en remettant au magistrat
4. Distribuer
5. A utiliser / En utilisant

187A

1. Bien qu'il fût / ait été un auteur célèbre, il ne fut pas enterré au Panthéon.
2. Nous avions demandé que vous soyez remboursé.
3. Les passagers ont attendu / attendirent que les deux trains partent.
4. Le seule pièce qu'on eût jouée / ait jouée dans ce théâtre avant *L'Avare* était *Le Cid*.
5. Il fallait que le roi parlât / parle aux nobles.
6. Le porte-parole a nié / nia que des manifestants aient menacé des riverains.
7. Pour pauvre que je fusse / j'aie été, je n'avais jamais mendié.
8. Quoi qu'il arrive, je préférerais que vous restiez ici.
9. Avant que la comtesse ne partît / parte / Avant le départ de la comtesse, on annonça les fiançailles de sa fille.
10. Il était peu probable qu'ils aient terminé la moisson.
11. Il voulait que ses enfants viennent le voir une dernière fois.
12. La veuve refusa de voir qui que ce fût / soit.

187B

(i) fût / soit, prononçât / prononce
(ii) eusse goûté / aie goûté, susse / aie su, dusse / aie dû
(iii) eût fait / aurait fait, fût / serait

188A

1. C'est le meilleur candidat, bien qu'il / quoiqu'il soit si jeune.
2. Vous devrez remplir la fiche pour que nous puissions vérifier le numéro de votre compte.
3. Nous avons déménagé de sorte que nous sommes plus près du centre-ville.
4. Nous pourrons vous offrir deux places gratuites pourvu que vous veniez chercher / vous preniez les billets avant six heures.
5. Le Lavandou est une station balnéaire bien connue. Non pas qu'il y ait autant de touristes qu'à Cannes.
6. Tu ferais mieux d'enlever la tache avant qu'elle ne s'en aperçoive.
7. Nous avons emprunté un autre ordinateur pendant que je travaille à la maison.
8. Je m'en chargerai à moins que vous ne préfériez aller à la mairie vous-mêmes.
9. A supposer que la grève soit déclarée demain.

10. N'oublie pas d'éteindre l'électricité avant de partir.
11. Le service est interrompu jusqu'à ce que les ascenseurs soient réparés.
12. Après avoir attendu une demi-heure elle décida de leur téléphoner.
13. Il a fait le plein sans que son père le lui demande / le lui ait demandé.
14. Elle ferma la porte sans réveiller le chien.

188B
ait augmenté, ait diminué, constituent, font, s'inscrive, sont, puissent

189A
1. Je regrette que nous n'acceptions les chèques qu'à partir de 100 francs.
2. Tu as peur de rater ton permis?
3. Mes parents voudraient que nous nous arrêtions chez eux.
4. Le moniteur de ski a insisté pour que nos restions en groupe.
5. Ça m'étonne / Je suis étonné que tu n'aies pas revu Marianne.
6. Est-ce que vous désirez changer de table, Madame?
7. Nous avons peur que le voyage ne fatigue mon grand-père.
8. Les habitants de la ville s'attendaient à ce que le conseil municipal réagisse.
9. Le gouvernement espère que le nombre de chômeurs commencera à baisser.
10. Nous attendrons que la route soit dégagée avant de partir.
11. Je comprends bien que tu sois déçu.
12. La police a exigé que le témoin soit interrogé de nouveau.
13. Elle était ravie que nous ayons pensé à elle.

189B(i)
fasse, gardes, regarde, te marieras, réponds, interromps, te souviennes

189B(ii)
1. réservent / aient réservé leurs places avant tout le monde
2. leur propose / ait proposé un job pour l'été
3. fassent moins de bruit une fois le rideau tombé
4. les laissent dormir comme d'habitude
5. soient fatigués et exaspérés

190A
1. Il est probable que le résultat paraîtra dans le journal demain.
2. Nous pensons que vous devrez peut-être attendre une semaine.
3. Il faut que vous fermiez / Vous devez fermer la porte à clef.
4. Pardon, pensez-vous que ce billet soit toujours valable?
5. Le chef de bureau doutait que nous puissions fournir tous les matériaux tout de suite.
6. Le gardien de prison a nié que deux prisonniers l'aient fait chanter.
7. Il est normal que vous soyez choqué par son comportement.
8. Il se peut que / Il est possible que nous louions une maison dans le Var.

9. Je ne doute pas que / Je ne me fais aucun doute que le nouveau centre commercial aura un grand succès.
10. Il est totalement inadmissible qu'il revienne.
11. Il est peu probable qu'on puisse réparer cette voiture.
12. Je ne prétends pas que ce soit un exemple parfait.

190B

y ait, est, est, est, passent, sont, donne, soit, puissent

191A

1. La première fois que nous sommes allés à Lyon, nous avons mangé chez Bocuse.
2. Notre département de marketing préférerait trouver quelqu'un qui connaisse déjà ce secteur.
3. C'est le plus beau village que nous ayons visité dans la région.
4. Elle se plaint toujours quoi qu'on fasse.
5. Est-ce que ce sont les seuls tableaux que le musée ait gardés?
6. Où que vous cachiez l'os notre chien ne manquera pas de le retrouver.
7. Je cherche une couleur qui ne soit pas salissante.
8. Quels que soient ses motifs, je ne comprends pas qu'il ait vendu ses actions.
9. C'est le meilleur forfait-vacances que nous puissions vous proposer.
10. Que les partis politiques ne soient pas d'accord, c'est évident.
11. Quelle que soit l'agence que vous choisissiez, / Quelque agence que vous choisissiez, on vous demandera de verser une caution.
12. Il n'y a rien qui vaille la visite dans cette région-là.
13. Voici une photo que nous avons prise le mois dernier.
14. Que la chasse à la baleine soit interdite maintenant, c'est un pas dans le bon sens.

191B(i)

1. soyez / alliez
2. Quelle que soit
3. qui que ce soit
4. accueille

191B(ii)

1. Quelles que soient
2. préfériez / pratiquiez
3. fassiez
4. Quelles que soient

191B(iii)

1. Quel que soit
2. soit
3. désiriez / souhaitiez
4. ait

192A

1. Si nous avions su qu'il y avait des travaux nous aurions évité la rocade.
2. Tu aurais besoin de moi cet après-midi?
3. Le journaliste a demandé / demandait si tu lui donnerais une interview.
4. Si la réunion se terminait avant quatre heures, tu pourrais prendre l'avion de six heures.
5. Moi, je ferais une chose pareille!
6. S'il avait démissionné, elle l'aurait remplacé.
7. Quand nous habitions en Provence, nous prenions le petit déjeuner sur la terrasse.
8. Elle, elle resterait dans un hôtel une étoile!
9. Est-ce que ça coûterait trop cher si nous louions une voiture?
10. Tu aurais dû renouveler ta carte Visa.
11. Je ne savais pas si tous les invités viendraient en voiture.
12. Nous devrions rendre visite à ta tante la semaine prochaine.
13. Madame Beauchamp n'a pas encore répondu. Elle serait en vacances?
14. Quand les enfants étaient plus jeunes, nous demandions à Anne de nous les garder.

192B(i)

It is rumoured that the lawyer might be paying certain journalists . . .
There is even a rumour about a large sum he is said to have received from a client . . .

192B(ii)

as though it were she who were at fault. What would have amazed Séryeuse not least in this scene would have been the attitude of his mother.

192C

pouvez, possédait, n'étaient pas piégés, permettrait, prolifèrent

193A

1. Si vous mangez dans une crêperie bretonne, commandez du cidre bouché.
2. Si Mitterand a été élu deux fois, c'est parce que les électeurs ne faisaient pas confiance aux autres candidats.
3. Si tu t'entraînais tous les jours tu serais un bon athlète.
4. Ils se seraient mariés en 1939 si la guerre n'avait pas commencé.
5. Si la mer est agitée la plupart des voyageurs préfèrent avoir une cabine.
6. Les habitants / riverains porteraient plainte si le niveau de pollution augmentait.
7. S'il était arrêté et qu'il soit inculpé, est-ce qu'il serait envoyé en prison?
8. Elle aurait fait fortune si elle s'était installée aux Etats-Unis.
9. Si les squatteurs ont refusé de partir c'est parce qu'ils savaient que la maison n'était pas occupée.
10. Si les écologistes sont élus, le site sera protégé.
11. Si vous achetez ce produit et que par la suite vous ayez des problèmes, n'hésitez pas à vous adresser à notre service après-vente.

12. L'usine aurait licencié 500 ouvriers si Méga ne l'avait pas rachetée.
13. Si j'avais un fils je l'enverrais travailler pendant un an dans les pays en voie de développement.
14. Si la Révolution Française ne commença qu'en 1789, certains écrivains l'avaient déjà prévue.

193B
(i) s'il a moins d'un an.
(ii) vous devez éviter la plage de 11 à 15h.
(iii) je le protégerais avec un écran total et je renouvellerais l'application toutes les deux heures.
(iv) s'il se baignait / s'était baigné
(v) on lui aurait réhydraté la peau avec un après-solaire et on aurait évité de l'exposer durant quelques jours.

194A
1. Partons tout de suite.
2. Ne remplis / remplissez pas la boîte.
3. Assieds-toi un instant, Solange.
4. Va-t-en, Jacques.
5. Ecrivez vos noms ici.
6. Dépêchez-vous, vous deux!
7. Prenons un café.
8. Sois / soyez prudent!
9. Jeanne, explique-moi ce que ceci veut dire.
10. Ne vous inquiétez pas, Madame Rigaud.
11. Appelez-moi si vous avez / Appelle-moi si tu as besoin de moi.
12. Ne te lève pas, Caroline.

194B
(i) Armez-vous d'opiniâtreté et de persévérance
Présentez-vous à l'université
Emportez avec vous
Remplissez le dossier et renvoyez-le
Ne misez pas tout sur une seule inscription
Ne vous inscrivez pas dans deux universités différentes
Renseignez-vous
(ii) découpe, vide, réserve, lave et équeute, découpe-la, fais fondre, verse, laisse cuire, verse, fais cuire, ajoute, poivre, remplis, sers

195A
1. Tu as vu Martine dans l'épicerie? / chez l'épicier?
2. Elle a un rendez-vous chez le dentiste.
3. Il y avait de la corruption à tous les niveaux.
4. J'ai mal au genou.
5. Est-ce qu'on peut acheter un billet dans le train?

6. Nous sommes invités chez les Guillaume.
7. Il a dû payer l'amende sur-le-champ.
8. Arrête! ça me fait mal au pied!
9. Fabrice s'est marié – c'est dans le journal.
10. Chez Stendhal les personnages sont plus importants que l'intrigue.
11. Au 6e étage il y a un balcon qui offre une vue panoramique sur Paris.
12. Dans le sud les gens mangent / on mange dehors beaucoup plus souvent.
13. J'ai cloué l'affiche au mur.
14. Chez elle, les femmes ne peuvent pas sortir seules.

195B
à, chez, dans, sur, dans, au, sur, au, à, au, à, sur, au, dans, à, A, dans, dans

196A
1. Les enfants font un château de sable.
2. A la pharmacie j'ai acheté un rouge à lèvres.
3. Le cadre était tout en or.
4. Veux-tu me donner un sac en plastique?
5. La maison au grand balcon appartient au maire.
6. Il y a un petit magasin qui vend des fauteuils en osier.
7. Quand il fait chaud je dois porter une chemise / un chemisier de / en coton.
8. Les monuments de granit résistent aux intempéries.
9. Pour le rôle de Cyrano il nous faut un acteur au nez très long!
10. Après la mort de son mari elle s'habillait en gris ou en noir.
11. Il m'a offert un très beau sac en cuir.
12. Tu ne peux pas servir le café dans des tasses à thé!

196B
(i) à, en, à, à, en, A, de, en, de
(ii) Aux, en, à, à, de, de, de

197A
1. Elle a fait le voyage de Bruxelles à Genève en car.
2. Mon grand-père a toujours voyagé / voyageait toujours en première classe.
3. Quand la voiture est tombée en panne j'ai dû rentrer à pied.
4. Ils vont arriver par le train de nuit.
5. Sa soeur a refusé de monter à cheval.
6. En été il aime faire des promenades à bicyclette / en vélo.
7. En avion il ne faut que deux heures.
8. Les enfants adorent les voyages en bateau.
9. A ce moment-là j'ai été pris de panique.
10. Il monta l'escalier à grandes enjambées.

11. Elle parlait à voix douce / doucement.
12. Leur représentant a répondu d'un ton brusque.
13. Elle courait à toute vitesse.
14. Elle se déguisa en Castillane.
15. Le propriétaire les regarda d'un air menaçant.
16. Le fermier lui donna un panier rempli de fruits.
17. Tous nos vêtements sont faits à la main / faits main.
18. Le paysage change d'une façon alarmante.

197B
(i) aux, à, à
(ii) aux, à, de, à, à, par
(iii) à, de, par, à, en, aux, du, par

198A
1. Plus de la moitié des candidats ne se sont pas présentés à l'examen.
2. Sur le moment je ne savais pas quoi dire.
3. Le prix du stage de reconversion est de 560 francs.
4. Vous devriez travailler au moins huit heures par jour.
5. Ton frère a mangé deux fois plus que toi.
6. Deux agriculteurs sur trois se disaient mécontents.
7. Moins de 25% des malades suivaient ce régime.
8. La prime est de 1000 francs.
9. L'infirmière passera vous voir deux fois par semaine.
10. La meilleure note était 12 sur 20.
11. Il a moins plu que l'année dernière.
12. Le taux de participation aux élections était de 72%.

198B
(i) de
(ii) de, de, à
(iii) de, à, par
(iv) de, par, par, de
(v) de, de, en, de

199A
1. Vous attendez depuis longtemps?
2. Depuis leur mariage, ils habitent chez ses parents.
3. Nous étions perdus depuis des heures.
4. Il n'avait pas conduit / il ne conduisait plus depuis son accident.
5. Depuis combien de temps est-ce que tu étudies l'astronomie?
6. Vous connaissiez la victime depuis longtemps?
7. Je n'ai pas revu ma tante depuis dix ans.
8. Les techniciens faisaient la grève depuis trois jours.
9. Tu n'es pas rentré en France depuis quand / combien de temps?
10. Depuis l'année dernière elle est devenue végétarienne.

11. Je cherche ce livre depuis longtemps.
12. Depuis la naissance de la civilisation l'homme a découvert des plantes médicinales.

199B
1. Depuis quand est-ce que les entreprises éditrices des titres de province se lancent dans l'aventure industrielle?
2. Depuis quand est-ce que leurs homologues parisiens s'y étaient déjà engagés?
3. Depuis quand l'essor de la presse française aurait-il pu avoir lieu?
4. Depuis quand y a-t-il eu une révolution dans le monde de la communication et de l'information?
5. Depuis quand constate-t-on la fin de l'ère du média unique?
6. Depuis quand est-ce que la France compte plus de 5 millions de postes-récepteurs?

200A
1. La flèche se dressait parmi les maisons modestes.
2. Entre nous, c'était un film très ennuyeux.
3. C'est un exemple parmi beaucoup d'autres.
4. Combien d'entre eux sont déjà allés en Inde?
5. Ils coururent vers la vieille ferme.
6. Comment est-ce que vous avez choisi entre les deux candidats?
7. Vers trois heures il sortit par la porte de derrière.
8. C'est une décision qui touche plusieurs parmi / d'entre nous.
9. Parmi ces auteurs modernes, lesquels seront toujours lus d'ici cent ans?
10. Vers quelle heure est-ce que vous avez entendu les coups de feu?

200B
(i) Parmi, parmi, entre, entre
(ii) d'entre, vers, vers, parmi, parmi

201A
1. Elle a habité Marseille de 1979 à 1990.
2. Il sera de retour dans / d'ici deux semaines.
3. J'ai annulé tous mes rendez-vous pour la semaine prochaine.
4. La nouvelle loi entre en vigueur dès aujourd'hui.
5. Ils ont vu toute l'exposition en moins d'une heure.
6. À partir de la semaine prochaine les bus ne circuleront plus après 22 heures.
7. Elle essaya de cacher son inquiétude mais au bout de quelques minutes elle fondit en larmes.
8. Le champ était inondé pendant plusieurs semaines.
9. Nous contacterons tous nos clients dès le retour de notre P.D.-G.
10. Si vous voulez louer une jeep, il y a un prix forfaitaire / un tarif réduit du jeudi au dimanche.

11. Elle a souffert pendant des années entières.
12. D'ici cinq ans, il y aura deux fois plus de voitures particulières.
13. Vous travaillez pour la même agence depuis quatre ans.
14. L'équipe norvégienne a fait le voyage en cinq jours.
15. À partir de l'année prochaine la gare aura des consignes automatiques.
16. Nous devons être de retour dans une demi-heure.

201B

(i) en, en, Dès
(ii) en, dès, A partir de, De, à, en
(iii) en, en, pendant, au bout de, Dès

202A

1. Nous venons de passer un mois en Suisse et au Luxembourg.
2. Les habitants du Sussex s'inquiétaient pour leurs plages.
3. Deux prisonniers se sont évadés à Caen.
4. Il y aura des orages en Corse et en Provence.
5. N'oublie pas de leur téléphoner quand tu seras à Bruxelles.
6. Ce produit se vend bien au Japon et aux États-Unis.
7. Les manuscrits sont conservés en Israël.
8. Ils vont faire du camping soit en Bourgogne soit dans le Limousin.
9. J'ai été nommé au Danemark.
10. Mes parents ont passé la nuit au Lavandou.
11. Le train s'arrêtera à Douvres et à Londres.
12. La plupart des touristes qui viennent au Royaume-Uni restent moins de deux semaines.
13. Chaque an il y a un festival à Sarlat.
14. La brochure propose des maisons de vacances dans le Lot.

202B

(i) en, à, en
(ii) au, dans, en, à / vers, en
(iii) à, en, en, au, en, au
(iv) à, en, en, à

203A

1. La prime est calculée en fonction de la somme investie.
2. Cette voiture est plus performante en comparaison avec les / auprès des / à côté des / par rapport aux autres.
3. Il a commencé à fumer à l'insu de ses parents.
4. J'ai dû acheter des abricots au lieu des cerises.
5. L'hôpital est fermé à cause du / en raison du tremblement de terre.
6. La frontière entre la France et l'Italie a changé à travers les / au cours des siècles.
7. Selon / D'après leur porte-parole, les vols ont un retard de six heures.
8. Comme Charles se sentait malade, ils se sont arrêtés au bord de la route.

9. Quant à Louis XIV, la France n'a guère connu la paix pendant / durant / lors de son règne.
10. La nouvelle boutique a fermé faute de clients.
11. Les vacataires / intérimaires sont payés à raison de 50 francs de l'heure.
12. Le musée a peu de tableaux du 20e siècle sauf / en dehors de / à l'exception de celui de Picasso.
13. L'eau montait jusqu'au premier étage.
14. Grâce à votre présence, la soirée a été très réussie.
15. À partir du 1er janvier vous devrez montrer votre carte d'adhérent.
16. Le couple qui habite au-dessus de notre appartement est très bruyant.
17. Nous avons pris une maison en face du jardin public.
18. Au sujet de / À propos de / En ce qui concerne votre proposition, veuillez remplir la fiche ci-jointe.
19. La municipalité va planter des palmiers le long de la promenade.
20. Je ne savais pas comment réagir face à son refus.

203B
(i) du fait de / à cause de / en raison de, à partir du, d'après, par rapport à, à l'exception de / en dehors de
(ii) En matière de / Quant à la, jusqu'à, auprès des, en cours de / lors des

204A
1. Quand est-ce que vous espérez voir votre éditeur?
2. Au lieu de leur dire la vérité, Robert leur fit croire que son père était malade.
3. Il a gagné l'élection en promettant de ne pas dévaluer le franc.
4. Le concierge viendra changer l'ampoule.
5. J'hésite à vous demander ce service.
6. Est-ce que cette chaumière est à louer?
7. Hier nous avons passé trois heures à poser la moquette.
8. Vous les avez entendus arriver?
9. 'Pizzas à emporter'.
10. Ils ont fini par demander à sa belle-soeur de leur prêter l'argent.
11. M. Dassault regrette de ne pas pouvoir accepter votre invitation.
12. Les gangsters sont partis sans rien emporter.
13. Après avoir lu la lettre, elle la déchira.
14. La direction lui a interdit / défendu de parler aux reporters.
15. Sa mère a failli s'évanouir en apprenant la nouvelle.
16. Je leur ai promis de répondre demain.
17. Après s'être regardés pendant plusieurs minutes, les chiens se mirent à aboyer.
18. Nous les avons aidés à déménager.
19. Je dois retirer de l'argent avant d'aller chercher la voiture.
20. En général, les adolescents préfèrent / aiment mieux partir en vacances avec leurs amis.

204B

de, à, à, de, de, ×, à, à, à, à, à, de, ×

205A

1. Le magasin ferme à quelle heure? / À quelle heure est-ce que le magasin ferme? / À quelle heure le magasin ferme-t-il?
2. Vous avez contacté qui? / Qui est-ce que vous avez contacté? / Qui avez-vous contacté?
3. La mairie est ouverte? / Est-ce que la mairie est ouverte? / La mairie est-elle ouverte?
4. Pourquoi vous êtes resté si longtemps? / Pourquoi est-ce que vous êtes resté si longtemps? / Pourquoi êtes-vous resté si longtemps?
5. Votre mari préfère quelle marque? / Quelle marque est-ce que votre mari préfère? / Quelle marque votre mari préfère-t-il?
6. Je peux me servir de salade? / Est-ce que je peux me servir de salade? / Puis-je me servir de salade?
7. Vous lui offrez quoi pour son anniversaire? / Qu'est-ce que vous lui offrez pour son anniversaire? / Que lui offrez-vous pour son anniversaire?
8. Les soldes commencent quand? / Quand est-ce que les soldes commencent? / Quand les soldes commencent-elles?
9. On fait la mayonnaise comment? / Comment est-ce qu'on fait la mayonnaise? / Comment fait-on la mayonnaise?
10. Elle aura déjà reçu la lettre? / Est-ce qu'elle aura déjà reçu la lettre? / Aura-t-elle déjà reçu la lettre?

205B

1. Orso s'était retiré où? / Où est-ce que Orso s'était retiré? / Où Orso s'était-il retiré?
2. Colomba envoya coucher qui? / Qui est-ce que Colomba envoya coucher? / Qui Colomba envoya-t-elle coucher?
3. Colomba paraissait attendre quoi? / Qu'est-ce que Colomba paraissait attendre? / Que Colomba paraissait-elle attendre?
4. Elle s'assura de quoi? / De quoi est-ce qu'elle s'assura? / De quoi s'assura-t-elle?
5. Elle siffla comment? / Comment est-ce qu'elle siffla? / Comment siffla-t-elle?
6. Elle saisit quel cheval par la crinière? / Quel cheval est-ce qu'elle saisit par la crinière? / Quel cheval saisit-elle par la crinière?
7. Pourquoi le cheval s'enfuit? / Pourquoi est-ce que le cheval s'enfuit? / Pourquoi le cheval s'enfuit-il?
8. Colomba rentrait dans le jardin? / Est-ce que Colomba rentrait dans le jardin? / Colomba rentrait-elle dans le jardin?

206A

1. Peut-être qu'il vaudrait mieux / Peut-être vaudrait-il mieux ne rien dire.
2. Les déchets nucléaires sont plus dangereux que ne l'admettent les responsables / que les responsables ne l'admettent.
3. 'Je crois', reprit / continua Corine, 'que le vol sera découvert bientôt.'
4. Je retourne à l'exemple qu'a cité mon collègue, le maire de Lille / que mon collègue, le maire de Lille, a cité.
5. Sans doute voudrez-vous y réfléchir.
6. Toujours est-il que les sans-abris font un cas à part.
7. Ainsi faut-il / il faut en conclure qu'il s'agit d'un phénomène passager.
8. L'avion a perdu contact, paraît-il / à ce qu'il paraît, avec la tour de contrôle.
9. En vain avons-nous / nous avons sollicité leur aide.
10. Nous avons acheté un appartement plus près du bureau. Et encore me faut-il / il me faut 20 minutes pour y arriver le matin.
11. Elle n'a pas bien compris, semble-t-il, ce qu'on lui avait demandé de faire.
12. A peine l'orage eut-il éclaté que / A peine l'orage eut éclaté que le toit s'effondra.

206B

peut-être l'invasion napoléonienne ouvre-t-elle / peut-être que l'invasion napoléonienne ouvre . . .
Sans doute la mort du Caudillo, en 1975, . . ., est-elle à l'origine . . .
les Espagnols n'admettent pas, semble-t-il, / à ce qu-il semble . . .
que manifestera rapidement Paris.
En vain les Espagnols reprochent-ils . . .,
regrette-t-on de l'autre côté des Pyrénées, . . .

207A

1. Personne ne se souvient d'un bruit inattendu.
2. Vous devriez consulter non / non pas le médecin mais un kinésithérapeute.
3. Il avait peur / craignait que je ne sois fâché.
4. Ils préfèrent ne pas se coucher trop tard.
5. Ça fait trois ans que je ne l'ai entendu jouer.
6. Rien n'est pire pour le dos qu'un mode de vie sédentaire.
7. Il a une moto, pas une voiture.
8. L'inspecteur ne doutait pas que le témoin n'ait menti.
9. Il ne reste que six invités.
10. Je n'osais pas / Je n'osais les critiquer.
11. Jamais récession n'a duré si longtemps.
12. Il y a plus de verres qu'il ne nous faut.
13. Vous n'avez remarqué aucun changement?
14. Les enfants ne sont admis à moins que leurs parents ne les accompagnent.

15. Elle lit mieux qu'elle n'écrit.
16. Nous avons décidé de ne montrer les photos à personne.

207B
non / ni, ni, jamais, ne, pas, n', pas / plus, n', qu', n', rien, Rien, n', n', que, personne, ne, n', pas / plus

Appendix
The conjugation of verbs

The sections below summarize the conjugation of regular and the most common irregular verbs. You will find the tenses and forms which are used as the basis for forming other tenses and moods. For an explanation of the full system of moods and tenses, see sections 34 to 47.

(a) The conjugation of regular verbs

-er verbs

PRESENT INDICATIVE

je donne I give

tu donnes you give

il donne he gives

nous donnons we give

vous donnez you give

ils donnent they give

FUTURE INDICATIVE

je donnerai I shall give

tu donneras you will give

il donnera he will give

nous donnerons we shall give

vous donnerez you will give

ils donneront they will give

PAST HISTORIC (INDICATIVE)

je donnai I gave

(tu donnas you gave)

il donna he gave

nous donnâmes we gave

(vous donnâtes you gave)

ils donnèrent they gave

PERFECT INDICATIVE

j'ai donné I gave / have given (etc.)

PRESENT SUBJUNCTIVE

je donne

tu donnes

il donne

nous donnions

vous donniez

ils donnent

IMPERATIVE

Donne! Give!

Donnons! Let's give!

Donnez! Give!

PRESENT PARTICIPLE

donnant giving

There are several groups of -*er* verbs which are conjugated quite regularly (on the model of *donner*) except that in some persons and / or tenses there is a minor change in spelling to reflect pronunciation:

(i) Verbs in -*cer* (e.g. *annoncer* to announce)

The *c* takes a cedilla (*ç*) before endings in *a* or *o*, e.g.

nous annonçons we announce (present indicative)

(ii) Verbs in -*ger* (e.g. *manger* to eat)

The *g* is followed by an *e* before endings in *a* or *o*, e.g.

je mangeais I was eating (imperfect indicative)

(iii) Verbs in -*emer* / -*ener* / -*ever* (e.g. *semer* to sow, *mener* to lead, *lever* to lift) and **some** verbs in -*eler* (*celer* to conceal, *geler* to freeze, *modeler* to model, *peler* to peel) and -*eter* (*acheter* to buy, *étiqueter* to label).

The final vowel changes from *e* to *è* in all persons of the future and present conditional, and in the *je* / *tu* / *il* / *ils* parts of the present indicative and present subjunctive, e.g.:

je mène I lead   *nous lèverons* we shall lift

(iv) Verbs in -*érer* (e.g. *préférer* to prefer)

The penultimate vowel changes from *é* to *è* in the *je* / *tu* / *il* / *ils* parts of the present indicative and present subjunctive, e.g.:

je préfère I prefer

(v) Most verbs in -*eler* / -*eter* (e.g. *appeler* to call, *jeter* to throw)

The consonants *l* or *t* are doubled (*ll* / *tt*) in all persons of the future and present conditional, and in the *je* / *tu* / *il* / *ils* parts of the present indicative and present subjunctive, e.g.:

tu appelles you call   *nous jetterons* we shall throw

(vi) Verbs in -*oyer* / -*uyer* (e.g. *aboyer* to bark, *essuyer* to wipe)

The *oy* / *uy* changes to *oi* / *ui* in all persons of the future and present conditional, and in the *je* / *tu* / *il* / *ils* parts of the present indicative and subjunctive, e.g.:

il aboie he barks, *ils essuieront* they will wipe

Note that verbs in -*ayer* (e.g. *payer* to pay) may change the *ay* to *ai* in the same way, but this change is optional, e.g. *nous paierons / nous payerons*, 'we shall pay'.

-*ir* verbs

PRESENT INDICATIVE
je finis I finish	*nous finissons* we finish
tu finis you finish	*vous finissez* you finish
il finit he finishes	*ils finissent* they finish

FUTURE INDICATIVE
je finirai I shall finish (etc.)

PAST HISTORIC
je finis I finished	*nous finîmes* we finished
(tu finis you finished)	*(vous finîtes* you finished)
il finit he finished	*ils finirent* they finished

PERFECT INDICATIVE
j'ai fini I finished / have finished (etc.)

PRESENT SUBJUNCTIVE
je finisse	*nous finissions* (etc.)

IMPERATIVE
Finis! Finish!	*Finissez!* Finish!
Finissons! Let's finish!	

PRESENT PARTICIPLE
finissant finishing

-*dre* verbs

PRESENT INDICATIVE
je vends I sell	*nous vendons* we sell
tu vends you sell	*vous vendez* you sell
il vend he sells	*ils vendent* they sell

FUTURE INDICATIVE
je vendrai I shall sell (etc.)

PAST HISTORIC
je vendis I sold	*nous vendîmes* we sold
(tu vendis you sold)	*(vous vendîtes* you sold)
il vendit he sold	*ils vendirent* they sold

PERFECT INDICATIVE
j'ai vendu I sold / have sold (etc.)

PRESENT SUBJUNCTIVE
je vende   *nous vendions* (etc.)

IMPERATIVE
Vends! Sell!   *Vendez!* Sell!
Vendons! Let's sell!

PRESENT PARTICIPLE
vendant selling

(b) Common irregular verbs

acquérir to acquire

PRESENT INDICATIVE
j'acquiers I acquire   *nous acquérons* we acquire
tu acquiers you acquire   *vous acquérez* you acquire
il acquiert he acquires   *ils acquièrent* they acquire

FUTURE INDICATIVE
j'acquerrai I shall acquire (etc.)

PAST HISTORIC
j'acquis I acquired (etc.)

PERFECT INDICATIVE
j'ai acquis I acquired / have
                acquired (etc.)

PRESENT SUBJUNCTIVE
j'acquière   *nous acquérions* (etc.)

aller to go

PRESENT INDICATIVE
je vais I go   *nous allons* we go
tu vas you go   *vous allez* you go
il va he goes   *ils vont* they go

FUTURE INDICATIVE
j'irai I shall go (etc.)

PAST HISTORIC
j'allai I went (etc.)

PERFECT INDICATIVE
je suis allé(e) I went / have gone (etc.)

PRESENT SUBJUNCTIVE
j'aille   *nous allions* (etc.)

IMPERATIVE
Va! Go! (but: *Vas-y* Go on!)
Allez! Go!
Allons! Let's go!

s'asseoir to sit down

PRESENT INDICATIVE
je m'assieds / je m'assois   *nous nous asseyons* we sit down
  I sit down   *vous vous asseyez* you sit down
tu t'assieds / tu t'assois   *ils s'assoient / ils s'asseyent*
  you sit down   they sit down
il s'assied / il s'assoit he sits down

FUTURE INDICATIVE
je m'assiérai I shall sit down (etc.)

PAST HISTORIC
je m'assis I sat down (etc.)

PERFECT INDICATIVE
je me suis assis(e) I sat down /
  have sat down (etc.)

PRESENT SUBJUNCTIVE
je m'asseye   *nous nous asseyions* (etc.)

avoir to have

PRESENT INDICATIVE
j'ai I have   *nous avons* we have
tu as you have   *vous avez* you have
il a he has   *ils ont* they have

FUTURE INDICATIVE
j'aurai I shall have (etc.)

PAST HISTORIC
j'eus I had (etc.)

Appendix

PERFECT INDICATIVE
j'ai eu I had / have had (etc.)

PRESENT SUBJUNCTIVE
j'aie	*nous ayons*
tu aies	*vous ayez*
il ait	*ils aient*

IMPERATIVE
| *Aie!* Have! | *Ayez!* Have! |
| *Ayons!* Let's have! | |

PRESENT PARTICIPLE
ayant having

boire to drink

PRESENT INDICATIVE
je bois I drink	*nous buvons* we drink
tu bois you drink	*vous buvez* you drink
il boit he drinks	*ils boivent* they drink

FUTURE INDICATIVE
je boirai I shall drink (etc.)

PAST HISTORIC
je bus I drank (etc.)

PERFECT INDICATIVE
j'ai bu I drank / have drunk (etc.)

PRESENT SUBJUNCTIVE
| *je boive* | *nous buvions* (etc.) |

conduire to drive

PRESENT INDICATIVE
je conduis I drive	*nous conduisons* we drive
tu conduis you drive	*vous conduisez* you drive
il conduit he drives	*ils conduisent* they drive

FUTURE INDICATIVE
je conduirai I shall drive (etc.)

PAST HISTORIC
je conduisis I drove (etc.)

506

PERFECT INDICATIVE
j'ai conduit I drove / have driven
  (etc.)

PRESENT SUBJUNCTIVE
je conduise   *nous conduisions* (etc.)

connaître to know

PRESENT INDICATIVE
je connais I know   *nous connaissons* we know
tu connais you know   *vous connaissez* we know
il connaît he knows   *ils connaissent* they know

FUTURE INDICATIVE
je connaîtrai I shall know (etc.)

PAST HISTORIC
je connus I knew (etc.)

PERFECT INDICATIVE
j'ai connu I knew / have known
  (etc.)

PRESENT SUBJUNCTIVE
je connaisse   *nous connaissions* (etc.)

courir to run

PRESENT INDICATIVE
je cours I run   *nous courons* we run
tu cours you run   *vous courez* you run
il court he runs   *ils courent* they run

FUTURE INDICATIVE
je courrai I shall run (etc.)

PAST HISTORIC
je courus I ran (etc.)

PERFECT INDICATIVE
j'ai couru I ran / have run (etc.)

PRESENT SUBJUNCTIVE
je coure   *nous courions* (etc.)

croire to believe / think

PRESENT INDICATIVE
je crois I believe   *nous croyons* we believe
tu crois you believe   *vous croyez* you believe
il croit he believes   *ils croient* they believe

FUTURE INDICATIVE
je croirai I shall believe (etc.)

PAST HISTORIC
je crus I believed (etc.)

PERFECT INDICATIVE
j'ai cru I believed / have believed (etc.)

PRESENT SUBJUNCTIVE
je croie   *nous croyions* (etc.)

devoir to have to / must / owe

PRESENT INDICATIVE
je dois I must   *nous devons* we must
tu dois you must   *vous devez* you must
il doit he must   *ils doivent* they must

FUTURE INDICATIVE
je devrai I shall have to (etc.)

PAST HISTORIC
je dus I had to (etc.)

PERFECT INDICATIVE
j'ai dû I had to / have had to (etc.)

PRESENT SUBJUNCTIVE
je doive   *nous devions* (etc.)

dire to say

PRESENT INDICATIVE
je dis I say   *nous disons* we say
tu dis you say   *vous dites* you say
il dit he says   *ils disent* they say

FUTURE INDICATIVE
je dirai I shall say (etc.)

PAST HISTORIC
je dis I said (etc.)

PERFECT INDICATIVE
j'ai dit I said / have said (etc.)

PRESENT SUBJUNCTIVE
je dise   *nous disions* (etc.)

dormir to sleep

PRESENT INDICATIVE
je dors I sleep   *nous dormons* we sleep
tu dors you sleep   *vous dormez* you sleep
il dort he sleeps   *ils dorment* they sleep

FUTURE INDICATIVE
je dormirai I shall sleep (etc.)

PAST HISTORIC
je dormis I slept (etc.)

PERFECT INDICATIVE
j'ai dormi I slept / have slept (etc.)

PRESENT SUBJUNCTIVE
je dorme   *nous dormions* (etc.)

écrire to write

PRESENT INDICATIVE
j'écris I write   *nous écrivons* we write
tu écris you write   *vous écrivez* you write
il écrit he writes   *ils écrivent* they write

FUTURE INDICATIVE
j'écrirai I shall write (etc.)

PAST HISTORIC
j'écrivis I wrote (etc.)

PERFECT INDICATIVE
j'ai écrit I wrote / have written (etc.)

PRESENT SUBJUNCTIVE
j'écrive   *nous écrivions* (etc.)

envoyer to send

PRESENT INDICATIVE

j'envoie I send   *nous envoyons* we send
tu envoies you send   *vous envoyez* you send
il envoie he sends   *ils envoient* they send

FUTURE INDICATIVE
j'enverrai I shall send (etc.)

PAST HISTORIC
j'envoyai I sent (etc.)

PERFECT INDICATIVE
j'ai envoyé I sent / have sent (etc.)

PRESENT SUBJUNCTIVE
j'envoie   *nous envoyions* (etc.)

être to be

PRESENT INDICATIVE

je suis I am   *nous sommes* we are
tu es you are   *vous êtes* you are
il est he is   *ils sont* they are

FUTURE INDICATIVE
je serai I shall be (etc.)

PAST HISTORIC
je fus I was (etc.)

IMPERFECT
j'étais I was (etc.)

PERFECT INDICATIVE
j'ai été I was / have been (etc.)

PRESENT SUBJUNCTIVE

je sois   *nous soyons*
tu sois   *vous soyez*
il soit   *ils soient*

IMPERATIVE
Sois! Be!   *Soyez!* Be!
Soyons! Let's be!

PRESENT PARTICIPLE
étant being

510

faire to do / to make

PRESENT INDICATIVE

je fais I do	*nous faisons* we do
tu fais you do	*vous faites* you do
il fait he does	*ils font* they do

FUTURE INDICATIVE
je ferai I shall do (etc.)

PAST HISTORIC
je fis I did (etc.)

PERFECT INDICATIVE
j'ai fait I did / have done (etc.)

PRESENT SUBJUNCTIVE

je fasse	*nous fassions* (etc.)

falloir to be necessary
(used only with impersonal subject *il* – see section 34)

PRESENT INDICATIVE
il faut it is necessary

FUTURE INDICATIVE
il faudra it will be necessary

PAST HISTORIC
il fallut it was necessary

PERFECT INDICATIVE
il a fallu it was / has been necessary

PRESENT SUBJUNCTIVE
il faille

lire to read

PRESENT INDICATIVE

je lis I read	*nous lisons* we read
tu lis you read	*vous lisez* you read
il lit he reads	*ils lisent* they read

FUTURE INDICATIVE
je lirai I shall read (etc.)

PAST HISTORIC
je lus I read (etc.)

511

PERFECT INDICATIVE
j'ai lu I read / have read (etc.)

PRESENT SUBJUNCTIVE
je lise   *nous lisions* (etc.)

mettre to put

PRESENT INDICATIVE
je mets I put   *nous mettons* we put
tu mets you put   *vous mettez* you put
il met he puts   *ils mettent* they put

FUTURE INDICATIVE
je mettrai I shall put (etc.)

PAST HISTORIC
je mis I put (etc.)

PERFECT INDICATIVE
j'ai mis I put / have put (etc.)

PRESENT SUBJUNCTIVE
je mette   *nous mettions* (etc.)

mourir to die

PRESENT INDICATIVE
je meurs I die   *nous mourons* we die
tu meurs you die   *vous mourez* you die
il meurt he dies   *ils meurent* they die

FUTURE INDICATIVE
je mourrai I shall die (etc.)

PAST HISTORIC
je mourus I died (etc.)

PERFECT INDICATIVE
je suis mort(e) I died / have died (etc.)

PRESENT SUBJUNCTIVE
je meure   *nous mourions* (etc.)

naître to be born

PRESENT INDICATIVE
je nais I am born
tu nais you are born
il naît he is born

nous naissons we are born
vous naissez you are born
ils naissent they are born

FUTURE INDICATIVE
je naîtrai I shall be born (etc.)

PAST HISTORIC
je naquis I was born (etc.)

PERFECT INDICATIVE
je suis né(e) I was born / have been
            born (etc.)

PRESENT SUBJUNCTIVE
je naisse

nous naissions (etc.)

ouvrir to open

PRESENT INDICATIVE
j'ouvre I open
tu ouvres you open
il ouvre he opens

nous ouvrons we open
vous ouvrez you open
ils ouvrent they open

FUTURE INDICATIVE
j'ouvrirai I shall open (etc.)

PAST HISTORIC
j'ouvris I opened (etc.)

PERFECT INDICATIVE
j'ai ouvert I opened / have opened
    (etc.)

PRESENT SUBJUNCTIVE
j'ouvre

nous ouvrions (etc.)

partir to leave / depart

PRESENT INDICATIVE
je pars I leave
tu pars you leave
il part he leaves

nous partons we leave
vous partez you leave
ils partent they leave

FUTURE INDICATIVE
je partirai I shall leave (etc.)

PAST HISTORIC
je partis I left (etc.)

PERFECT INDICATIVE
je suis parti(e) I left / have left (etc.)

PRESENT SUBJUNCTIVE
je parte   *nous partions* (etc.)

plaire to please

PRESENT INDICATIVE
je plais I please   *nous plaisons* we please
tu plais you please   *vous plaisez* you please
il plaît he pleases   *ils plaisent* they please

FUTURE INDICATIVE
je plairai I shall please (etc.)

PAST HISTORIC \
je plus I pleased (etc.)

PERFECT INDICATIVE
j'ai plu I pleased / have pleased
  (etc.)

PRESENT SUBJUNCTIVE
je plaise   *nous plaisions* (etc.)

pleuvoir to rain
(used only with the impersonal subject *il* – see section 34)

PRESENT INDICATIVE
il pleut it rains

FUTURE INDICATIVE
il pleuvra it will rain

PAST HISTORIC
il plut it rained

PERFECT INDICATIVE
il a plu it rained / has rained

PRESENT SUBJUNCTIVE
il pleuve

pouvoir to be able / can

PRESENT INDICATIVE

je peux I can (*Puis-je?* Can I?)
tu peux you can
il peut he can

nous pouvons we can
vous pouvez you can
ils peuvent they can

FUTURE INDICATIVE
je pourrai I shall be able (etc.)

PAST HISTORIC
je pus I could / was able (etc.)

PERFECT INDICATIVE
j'ai pu I could / have been able (etc.)

PRESENT SUBJUNCTIVE
je puisse

nous puissions (etc.)

prendre to take

PRESENT INDICATIVE

je prends I take
tu prends you take
il prend he takes

nous prenons we take
vous prenez you take
ils prennent they take

FUTURE INDICATIVE
je prendrai I shall take (etc.)

PAST HISTORIC
je pris I took (etc.)

PERFECT INDICATIVE
j'ai pris I took / have taken (etc.)

PRESENT SUBJUNCTIVE
je prenne

nous prenions (etc.)

recevoir to receive / get

PRESENT INDICATIVE

je reçois I receive
tu reçois you receive
il reçoit he receives

nous recevons we receive
vous recevez you receive
ils reçoivent they receive

FUTURE INDICATIVE
je recevrai I shall receive (etc.)

PAST HISTORIC
je reçus I received (etc.)

PERFECT INDICATIVE
j'ai reçu I received / have received (etc.)

PRESENT SUBJUNCTIVE
je reçoive   *nous recevions* (etc.)

savoir to know

PRESENT INDICATIVE
je sais I know   *nous savons* we know
tu sais you know   *vous savez* you know
il sait he knows   *ils savent* they know

FUTURE INDICATIVE
je saurai I shall know (etc.)

PAST HISTORIC
je sus I knew (etc.)

PERFECT INDICATIVE
j'ai su I knew / have known (etc.)

PRESENT SUBJUNCTIVE
je sache   *nous sachions* (etc.)

IMPERATIVE
Sache! Know! / Remember!   *Sachez!* Know! / Remember!
Sachons! Let's know!

PRESENT PARTICIPLE
sachant knowing

sentir to feel

PRESENT INDICATIVE
je sens I feel   *nous sentons* we feel
tu sens you feel   *vous sentez* you feel
il sent he feels   *ils sentent* they feel

FUTURE INDICATIVE
je sentirai I shall feel (etc.)

PAST HISTORIC
je sentis I felt (etc.)

PERFECT INDICATIVE
j'ai senti I felt / have felt (etc.)

PRESENT SUBJUNCTIVE
je sente   *nous sentions* (etc.)

sortir to go out

PRESENT INDICATIVE
je sors I go out   *nous sortons* we go out
tu sors you go out   *vous sortez* you go out
il sort he goes out   *ils sortent* they go out

FUTURE INDICATIVE
je sortirai I shall go out (etc.)

PAST HISTORIC
je sortis I went out (etc.)

PERFECT INDICATIVE
je suis sorti(e) I went out / have
                   gone out (etc.)

PRESENT SUBJUNCTIVE
je sorte   *nous sortions* (etc.)

suivre to follow

PRESENT INDICATIVE
je suis I follow   *nous suivons* we follow
tu suis you follow   *vous suivez* you follow
il suit he follows   *ils suivent* they follow

FUTURE INDICATIVE
je suivrai I shall follow (etc.)

PAST HISTORIC
je suivis I followed (etc.)

PERFECT INDICATIVE
j'ai suivi I followed / have followed (etc.)

PRESENT SUBJUNCTIVE
je suive   *nous suivions* (etc.)

valoir to be worth

PRESENT INDICATIVE
je vaux I am worth   *nous valons* we are worth
tu vaux you are worth   *vous valez* you are worth
il vaut he is worth   *ils valent* they are worth

FUTURE INDICATIVE
je vaudrai I shall be worth (etc.)

PAST HISTORIC
je valus I was worth (etc.)

PERFECT INDICATIVE
j'ai valu I was / have been worth
  (etc.)

PRESENT SUBJUNCTIVE
je vaille   *nous valions* (etc.)

venir to come

PRESENT INDICATIVE
je viens I come   *nous venons* we come
tu viens you come   *vous venez* you come
il vient he comes   *ils viennent* they come

FUTURE INDICATIVE
je viendrai I shall come (etc.)

PAST HISTORIC
je vins I came (etc.)

PERFECT INDICATIVE
je suis venu(e) I came / have come (etc.)

PRESENT SUBJUNCTIVE
je vienne   *nous venions* (etc.)

voir to see

PRESENT INDICATIVE
je vois I see   *nous voyons* we see
tu vois you see   *vous voyez* you see
il voit he sees   *ils voient* they see

FUTURE INDICATIVE
je verrai I shall see (etc.)

PAST HISTORIC
je vis I saw (etc.)

PERFECT INDICATIVE
j'ai vu I saw / have seen (etc.)

PRESENT SUBJUNCTIVE
je voie   *nous voyions* (etc.)

vouloir to want

PRESENT INDICATIVE
je veux I want   *nous voulons* we want
tu veux you want   *vous voulez* you want
il veut he wants   *ils veulent* they want

FUTURE INDICATIVE
je voudrai I shall want (etc.)

PAST HISTORIC
je voulus I wanted (etc.)

PERFECT INDICATIVE
j'ai voulu I wanted / have wanted
  (etc.)

PRESENT SUBJUNCTIVE
je veuille   *nous voulions* (etc.)

IMPERATIVE
Veuillez < formal >   Would you . . . / Please . . .

Suggestions for further reading

If you wish to follow up some of the areas covered in this book you may like to consult the reference works listed below.

(1) Dictionaries

Cassell's French–English, English–French Dictionary, Cassell, London, twenty-first impression (1987)

Collins Robert French–English English–French Dictionary, The, Collins, Glasgow, second edition (1987)

Le Petit Robert 1, Dictionnaire alphabétique et analogique de la langue française, Le Robert, Paris, revised edition (1990)

(2) Reference grammars

Byrne, L. S. R. and E. L. Churchill, (revised by E. Price), *A Comprehensive French Grammar*, Basil Blackwell, Oxford, third edition (1986)

Chevalier, J.C., B. Benveniste, M. Arrivé, and J. Peytard, *Larousse grammaire du français contemporain*, Larousse, Paris (1990)

Ferrar, H., *A French Reference Grammar*, Oxford University Press, London, second edition (1964, reprinted 1990)

Grevisse, M., *Le Bon Usage. Grammaire française avec des remarques sur la langue française d'aujourd'hui*, Editions J. Duculot, twelfth edition (1986)

Judge, A., and F. G. Healey, *A Reference Grammar of Modern French*, Edward Arnold, London (1985, reprinted 1987)

Wagner, R.-L. and J. Pinchon, *Grammaire du français classique et moderne*, Hachette-Classiques, Paris (1973)

(3) Contemporary usage and word power

Caradec, F., *N'ayons pas peur des mots. Dictionnaire du français argotique et populaire*, Larousse, Paris (1988)

Levieux, M. and E. Levieux, *Cassell Colloquial Handbooks: French*, Cassell, London (1992)

Murray, T., *Cassell's French Wordlist*, Cassell, London (1989)

Rey-Debove, J. and G. Gagnon, *Dictionnaire des anglicismes*, Le Robert, Paris (1981)

Index